Unbecoming British

Unbecoming British

HOW REVOLUTIONARY AMERICA
BECAME A POSTCOLONIAL NATION

KARIANN AKEMI YOKOTA

OXFORD
UNIVERSITY PRESS

OXFORD
UNIVERSITY PRESS

Oxford University Press is a department of the University of Oxford.
It furthers the University's objective of excellence in research, scholarship,
and education by publishing worldwide.

Oxford   New York
Auckland   Cape Town   Dar es Salaam   Hong Kong   Karachi
Kuala Lumpur   Madrid   Melbourne   Mexico City   Nairobi
New Delhi   Shanghai   Taipei   Toronto

With offices in
Argentina   Austria   Brazil   Chile   Czech Republic   France   Greece
Guatemala   Hungary   Italy   Japan   Poland   Portugal   Singapore
South Korea   Switzerland   Thailand   Turkey   Ukraine   Vietnam

Oxford is a registered trade mark of Oxford University Press
in the UK and certain other countries.

Published in the United States of America by
Oxford University Press
198 Madison Avenue, New York, NY 10016

© Oxford University Press 2011

First issued as an Oxford University Press paperback, 2014.

Library of Congress Cataloging-in-Publication Data
Yokota, Kariann Akemi.
Unbecoming British : how revolutionary America became a
postcolonial nation / Kariann Akemi Yokota.
p.   cm.
Includes bibliographical references and index.
ISBN 978-0-19-539342-2 (hardcover); 978-0-19-021787-7 (paperback)
1. National characteristics, American—History.   2. United States—
Civilization—1783–1865.   3. United States—Civilization—To 1783.   I. Title.
E164.Y65 2010
973.3'39—dc22   2009045749

1 3 5 7 9 8 6 4 2

Printed in the United States of America
on acid-free paper

Dedicated to the memory of my father, Takao Yokota, my mother, Keiko Yokota, and my sister, Audrey Yokota, who stood by me in years past; and to my children, Livia and Dereck, who are my hope for the future.

Contents

Acknowledgments

Readers of *Unbecoming British* will encounter a wide variety of people—merchants, missionaries, and medical doctors—who are not commonly found together within the pages of the same monograph. It was my desire as a historian to assemble a cast of characters that were captivated by disparate passions in order to discern whether they were similarly affected by America's transition from colony to nation. In a similar way, the years I spent researching and writing this book allowed me the great privilege of being part of a diverse community of friends and scholars. Each of them possesses a generosity of spirit that has enriched this work—and my life—immeasurably and has played an important role in this book's "becoming."

I derive great pleasure from bringing together areas of inquiry that are not usually studied together. Having been trained in very different academic fields, my intellectual path has been unconventional, a fact that has been the most rewarding aspect of my career. I began researching nationalism, transnational relations, identity formation, and postcolonial perspectives while a graduate student of interethnic relations at UCLA's Asian American Studies Center. Hoping to broaden my knowledge of American history, I continued to pursue these topics while earning a Ph.D. in early American history. My work in ethnic studies has amplified my sensitivity to the complexity of identity formation for people involved in transnational networks. My thanks to Joyce Appleby, Ruth Bloch, Shirley Hune, Yuji Ichioka, Valerie Matsumoto, Glenn Omatsu, Herman Ooms, Michael Salman, and Henry Yu for their contributions to my scholarship. A special note of gratitude goes to the Center's longtime director, Don Nakanishi, for serving on both of my graduate committees.

Although the story of American history is commonly told as a tale of westward movement, my research took me in the opposite direction. I wish to express my gratitude to several institutions for providing the financial assistance that allowed this Los Angeles native to spend several years traveling east to various archives. For years, I have wanted to publicly thank the scholars who served anonymously on the committees that chose to fund my work; their belief in my project made it possible for me to write this book. I also wish to thank the many individuals who extended invitations for me to present my work at seminars and conferences. I received generous financial support from the Massachusetts Historical Society, the American Philosophical Society, the Library Company of Philadelphia, the American Antiquarian Society, the Albert J. Beveridge Research Grant, American Historical Association, the Winterthur Museum, Garden, and Library, the Center for the Humanities, Wesleyan University, the Pew Program in Religion and American History, Yale University, and the McNeil Center for Early American Studies. My gratitude goes to the knowledgeable staff and fellows, too numerous to mention individually, who made the experience enriching and enjoyable. Special thanks are due to Georgia Barnhill, Rob Cox, Richard Dunn, Chris Grasso, Jim Green, Margaret Hunt, Karen Halttunen, Helen Lefkowitz Horowitz, Dan Horowitz, Margrit Kaye, Daniel Richter, Abraham Parrish, Sarah Pearsall, John Smolenski, Caroline Sloat, Jeanne Solensky, Len Travers, Margaret Welsh, Conrad Wright, Mike Zukerman, and fellow members of the McNeil Center Seminar.

As this book is about the importance early Americans placed on transatlantic journeys, it is fitting that in the course of writing it, I was able to make many of my own. Bestowing his faith in a young graduate student, Allan Macinnes provided me with the opportunity to continue my eastward journey to Scotland as a visiting lecturer at the University of Aberdeen. While there, I was introduced to life on the other side of the Atlantic by many wonderful colleagues including John Gash, Alexia Grosjean, Douglass Hamilton, Andrew Mackillop, Steve Murdoch, and Micheál Ó Siochrú. The Keogh-Notre Dame Centre funded two trips to Dublin, Ireland in order for me to participate in its summer Irish Seminar. Seamus Deane, Luke Gibbons, Kevin Whelen, and other members of the program proved the perfect guides to Irish history and culture. Whenever I returned home to Southern California, Roy Ritchie and the Huntington Library provided a welcoming and enriching intellectual environment. The Huntington Library has graciously awarded me short and long term research grants that are very much appreciated.

Faculty grants and research leaves from the departments of American Studies and History at Yale University provided the time needed to write this book. They include the Morse Faculty Fellowship and grants from the Ethnicity, Race and Migration Program, the Institute for the Advanced Study of Religion, the John and Yvonne McCredie Fellowship in Instructional

Technology, and the Electronic Library Initiatives Grant, American Digital Imaging Project. The Hilles Grant awarded by the Whitney Humanities Center at Yale contributed substantially to the production of this book.

I am delighted to have the opportunity to express my appreciation to the many colleagues and friends from both east and west who have enriched my scholarship and my life at various points in the process of writing this book. I am only sorry space does not allow me to list every person by name. My thanks to Jean-Christophe Agnew, Kenna Barrett, Tim Barringer, Alicia Schmidt Camacho, Fabian Drixler, Brian Edwards, Amerigo Fabbri, Ann Fabian, Dilip Gaonkar, Harvey Goldblatt, Sandy Isenstadt, Bob Lee, Mary Lui, Sanda Lwin, Gary Okihiro, Ken Panko, Jacqueline Robinson, Mridu Rai, Ryan Rhoades, Jean-Frédéric Schaub, Michael Sletcher, Jack Tchen, Michele Kaneshiro, Steve Pitti, Mark Quigley, Tim Snyder, Henriette van Notten, Laura Wexler, and Scott Wong.

I was fortunate to have worked with many supportive people who have helped me turn my manuscript into a book. Luke Freeman and Bobby Smiley served as my research assistants during the final stages of preparing my manuscript for publication. Their insightful queries and enthusiasm for the project increased my own excitement about the work. I am delighted to have had the opportunity to publish this book with Oxford University Press. I wish to thank everyone at the Press who has worked on my book. Reviewers and delegates of the Press offered thoughtful comments and constructive advice in their reports; their support of this project is greatly appreciated. Robert St. George deserves a special mention for his brilliant comments on the manuscript. His scholarship has inspired me and I appreciate his generosity in sharing his insights with me. I owe a very great debt to Susan Ferber, my editor at OUP who has believed in this project from its inception and has seen it through to the end. She has worked to improve this book in every way possible. Her professional dedication and personal investment in her authors are truly admirable.

I am especially grateful to a group of loyal colleagues and friends who I met in various locales in the course of my travels. Each of them gave the greatest gift any scholar could hope for when they agreed to set aside their own work in order to lend their support. John Demos offered his wisdom and infectious enthusiasm over lunches in New Haven and, most memorably, in his garden in Tyringham, Massachusetts. Everyone should be so lucky as to have Matthew Jacobson as a Chair; I am grateful to him for his continued support of this project and of my career. From the beginning Edmund and Marie Morgan have welcomed me into their New Haven home; some of my fondest memories have been made around their dinner table. From the beginning Marie took me under her wing like an academic godmother; and in the end she volunteered to lend her brilliant eye to the proofs. Alice Prochaska, Elizabeth Prochaska, and Frank Prochaska have provided years of friendship, astute intellectual guidance, and hospitality in both New Haven and London.

I am fortunate to have met fellow Angeleno Matthew Garcia at the Huntington because he has become a trusted friend and confidante. David Lloyd, who I first met in Dublin, has always understood why I embarked upon this project, and he read and improved early versions of the manuscript. I am grateful to David Igler and Peter Blodgett for sharing their expansive knowledge of western history and the Pacific and supporting me in every way possible. My grammar school classmate Tommy Babayan lent his poet's eye to my manuscript and could always be counted on for a kind word. For over a decade now Mae Ngai has offered sage advice and friendship shared over meals in Brussels, Chicago, NYC, and D.C.

Wherever I am in this world, I can count on David Waldstreicher, who has been pulling for me at every stage of my career. He has my profound gratitude for his countless contributions to my scholarship in general and this book specifically. He has always shared his expansive knowledge of the field with so many fellow scholars and I am honored to call him my mentor and friend. Very special thanks are reserved for the multi-talented Minh A. Luong who has been the most steadfast friend anyone could have. I am grateful to him for his unwavering support on countless occasions.

Regardless of where my work took me, I have always been fortunate to have had a solid base where I could return. Many people in my personal life have lived with this book over the years. including the extended members of the Yokota, Ichiho, Kato, Houben, and Tomei families. Hiddo Houben has carried drafts of the book and its accoutrements across numerous continents on more summer holidays than either of us care to remember. On occasion he has even been persuaded to put down his beloved newspapers to read said drafts, and for that I am appreciative.

By far my deepest debt of gratitude goes to my family, to whom this book is lovingly dedicated. My parents, Takao and Keiko Yokota, and my sister, Audrey Yokota, have supported me in every way imaginable. Words cannot begin to describe how grateful I am to them. My travels were enjoyable because they were always there to welcome me back. My children, Livia and Dereck, arrived on the scene as this book was in its final stages. Each born on a different side of the Atlantic, they have brought me unimaginable joy and I am grateful for their presence in my life. When I look at the two of them, I know I am home at last.

Unbecoming British

Introduction

UNBECOMING BRITISH

How Revolutionary America Became a Postcolonial Nation

> If there is any period one would desire to be born in, is it not the age of
> Revolution; when the old and the new stand side by side, and admit of
> being compared; when the energies of all men are searched by fear and by
> hope; when the historic glories of the old, can be compensated by the rich
> possibilities of the new era? This time, like all times, is a very good one,
> if we but know what to do with it.
>
> —Ralph Waldo Emerson, "The American Scholar" (1837)

A Study in Contradictions: Thomas Jefferson's American Tableaux

Stepping over the threshold of Monticello, visitors to Thomas Jefferson's home
encountered a vast array of objects that collectively may serve as a metaphor
for the emerging nation (see figure I.1). European sculptures stood alongside
mastodon bones; local and global maps hung next to plant and animal specimens and a variety of Native American artifacts.[1] Staring down like a sentry
into the two-story entrance hall was Jefferson's Great Clock, painstakingly
assembled over several years from both foreign and domestic parts.[2] The
unusual timepiece had two faces, one visible to residents inside of the house,
and another to those outside of its walls. Its interior face had a minute hand,
accurately recording the passing of time (see figure I.2a). By contrast, the
clock's exterior face was deliberately fitted with only an hour hand, since the
people working in the fields—slaves imported from Africa and the
Caribbean—needed only an approximate idea of time (see figure I.2b).
Although they could not see the clock from the peripheries of Jefferson's

Figure I.1 Entrance hall (southeast wall), Monticello. Jefferson's entrance hall served as an informal museum, presenting visitors with a mixture of natural curiosities from the New World and refined goods from the Old World. *(Monticello/Photograph by Charles Shoffner)*

estate, they could hear the resonant brass gong, imported from China, that marked the passing of each hour.

The manufactured goods, imported artwork, scientific equipment, and natural objects Jefferson assembled at Monticello were intended to demonstrate his erudition and to serve as a forum for inquiry into the natural order of the world and a site for patriotic display. He brought years of learning to the service of his nation. As a boy, he had accompanied his father on surveying expeditions for the British; later in life, he transformed his knowledge of "nature" into valuable commodities, in the form of his Indian lexicons, maps, measurements of weather, records of the growth rates of New World plants, and even birdsongs. In *Notes on the State of Virginia* (1781), Jefferson challenged the prevailing European theory that nature and animals would inevitably degenerate in the New World. To refute their claims, he sponsored an excavation at Big Bone Lick, Kentucky, and was rewarded with huge fossils that were hailed as objects of national pride (see figure I.3).

Figure I.2a Jefferson's Great Clock, interior face. Jefferson's two-faced timepiece was assembled over the course of several years from imported and domestic parts. The clock's interior face had minute and hour hands that kept exact time for Monticello's residents. *(Monticello/Photograph by Carol Highsmith)*

Nestled high atop a hill near Charlottesville, Virginia, Monticello represented an oasis of Enlightenment learning amid untamed, natural splendor (see figure I.4). Jefferson gave a great deal of thought to the construction of his residence; the architectural styles he mixed together on this "little mountain" linked this spot on the margins of the civilized world to distant European centers of refinement.[3] Elements of classical design appeared

Figure I.2b Jefferson's Great Clock, exterior face. The clock loomed over guests as they approached Monticello's entryway. The exterior face was outfitted with only an hour hand. This meant that it provided the approximate time to those outside of Jefferson's residence. *(Monticello/Photograph by William L. Beiswanger)*

throughout the building, including a frieze decorated with griffins that encircled the entrance hall. While Jefferson had never traveled to Greece or Rome, he had pored over imported books on Palladian design.[4] These embellishments to his home marked him as a learned man, but they also identified him as a provincial: as with many other cultural trends, he and his compatriots embraced the classical idiom just as it was losing popularity in Europe.

While the entry hall of Monticello represented a uniquely American blend of Old and New World elements, the parlor paid tribute to European intellectual and cultural life (see figure I.5). Among other things, it featured portraits of Francis Bacon, Isaac Newton, and John Locke, the men whose ideas had influenced Jefferson most profoundly. The art collection was meant to enlighten those who made the long journey to visit him. These objects were not merely for private enjoyment; he wanted to influence his fellow citizens with his cosmopolitan taste and at the same time prove to European visitors that Americans were capable of civility. "I am an enthusiast on the subject of the arts," he wrote to James Madison. "But it is an enthusiasm of which I am not ashamed, as its object is to improve the taste

Figure I.3 Mastadon fossils, displayed in an arrangement with other objects, entrance hall, Monticello.
Jefferson proudly displayed specimens from the excavation he sponsored at Big Bone Lick, Kentucky,
such as the mastadon fossils atop the table. Here they are pictured in an arrangement with objects such
as maps and mounted antlers, which represent the vastness and bounty of America. *(Monticello/
Photograph by Charles Shoffner)*

of my countrymen, to increase their reputation, to reconcile to them the
respect of the world and to procure them its praise."[5] Jefferson's self-
conscious words belie his need to defend his love of high culture to his fellow citizens by noting that it would help the nation to make a positive
impression on foreigners.

There was another side to Monticello, unlikely to win approbation from
the outside world. From its foundations to its furnishings to its fields, the
plantation was built and tended by enslaved African Americans.[6] In contrast to the material abundance of Jefferson's residence, the slave quarters
that stood just south of the main house consisted of a row of tiny, roughly
constructed dwellings that contained few personal belongings other than

Figure I.4 Aerial view of Monticello. Jefferson described himself only partly in jest as a "savage of the mountains of America" when he entered the "vaunted scene of Europe" as ambassador of the United States to France. Like American citizens' postrevolutionary identity, Jefferson's home was a complex amalgamation of nature and civilization. It featured natural "wonders"—Indian artifacts, fossils, and antlers—and refined goods imported from Europe—scientific instruments, wine, and art. These refined goods were all housed amid an isolated natural setting. *(Monticello/Photograph by Leonard Phillips)*

crude mattresses and cooking utensils. While most slaves (Jefferson preferred the term "servants") lived their lives in obscurity, one man, James Hemings, was a notable exception. In fact, he was among the most rare of the many refined "possessions" Jefferson kept at Monticello.[7]

While in France, Jefferson went to great lengths to provide his slave with several years of training in the culinary arts. When consuming Hemings's sophisticated European dishes such as Snow Eggs, foreign guests recognized Old World refinement, while Americans were treated to tastes they had never before experienced.[8] In spite of many years of faithful service, Jefferson denied his chef's petition for freedom in 1793.[9] As the bearer of such specialized knowledge, Hemings was too valuable to lose. His talents were integral to Jefferson's efforts to live the life of a cultured European gentleman in the woods of Virginia.

This book explores the tensions and contradictions embodied in Jefferson's possessions (both objects and people) and the rationales he and his fellow Americans had for collecting them. Like people of other nations emerging from colonialism, American elites placed a premium on adopting

Figure I.5 Jefferson's parlor (southwest wall)—a tribute to European culture and styles. *(Monticello/ Photograph by Robert Lautman)*

elements of European culture as a way of establishing their own legitimacy. The importation of material culture, ideas, and experts from the mother country was an integral part of a provincial people's attempt to construct a "civilized" nation on the periphery of the transatlantic world.[10] These transplanted Europeans and their descendants accrued cultural capital from their association with Europe while celebrating their freedom from Old World corruption and authority.[11] At the same time, the extent of their borrowing fueled insecurities about the derivative nature of what was ostensibly an independent society. Americans feared being seen by the rest of the world, not least the British, as still mired in colonial dependence; they grappled over what constituted the proper balance between innovation and emulation for a free people.

The project of nation building and developing national identity in the young United States was as much about its people's struggles in "unbecoming" what had made them British subjects before independence as it was about "becoming" citizens of a new country.[12] During the seventeenth and eighteenth centuries, settlers from Great Britain could view North America as an extension of their homeland. These men and women thought of themselves as expatriates—whether temporarily residing in the New World or permanently relocated—who believed they shared an identity with fellow subjects in Great Britain.[13] While the culturally porous society of North America certainly evinced influences from other European countries as well as indigenous and African populations, colonials took their cultural and intellectual cues from the mother country. From the perspective of Britons remaining at home, American settlers were a different people precisely because they were so distant from Europe and surrounded by "savage" people in an unfamiliar terrain.[14] By adjusting to their new environs British subjects in North America were (in the scholar Robert St. George's description) "becoming colonials": with one foot on each side of the Atlantic, they inhabited a liminal place in both societies without having a comfortable place in either.[15] Having the privilege, the education, and the finances to attempt to emulate the British elite, New World sons and daughters were born both *of* and *outside* the dominant culture. In the judgment of English contemporaries, North America's distant, displaced Britons had not only become colonial but also recognizably "American," an opprobrious term connoting marginality and inferiority and suggesting that they had become something other than British.[16]

The process of "becoming American," though it eventually brought rebelling colonists under a unified political designation, did not necessarily entail a categorical rejection of British culture.[17] Suspended between the *ancien régime* and the emerging modern capitalist culture, Americans' (particularly Anglo-American elites') sense of nationhood remained inchoate throughout the early national period.[18] Achieving nationhood, as distinct from statehood, proved a vexing task for the country's citizenry.[19] The political independence they won from the British Empire during the Revolutionary War emboldened the former colonials; the democratic republic they formed would underscore the differences between the new American state and Great Britain. But the problem of how to form a nation with clear, well-established internal ties of ethnicity, geography, and consanguinity presented numerous imponderables for these newly minted Americans.[20]

The postrevolutionary generation thus faced the difficult task of establishing both equality with and separation from Great Britain. Creating an American national identity—unbecoming British—was a tricky business. It entailed construing differences in the face of undeniable similarities (language, religion, Anglo-Saxon heritage) and attempting to diminish important differences (economic structures, geographic distance, cultural development) to establish parity. The process of self-understanding entailed wrestling with the legacy of their colonial identity, which was unbecoming British. These colonials-turned-citizens had to create an interstitial space between their former identity as British subjects and the new political and cultural context in which they now found themselves.

Americans waged their struggle to "unbecome" British without a cohesive sense of what they would become afterward. Leading figures debated about what constituted the American character hoping to find commonalities that could knit together the disparate constituencies that made up the new nation. What aspects of American life would remain the same? Did colonial hierarchies of cultural authority remain after political ties to the empire were formally broken? What cultural challenges did Americans face as they made the transition from colony to nation? These were the questions individuals grappled with as they struggled to articulate what exactly defined the American national character. While rapid political changes profoundly influenced Americans in the years following independence, the cultural bequest of British colonialism remained a strong presence in people's lives.[21]

The political and social leadership of the new country, particularly its "founders," were educated enough in the rules of British culture to know when they were viewed by foreign observers as falling short of the mark. And as middlemen between their British contacts and their fellow Americans, they could not help but see themselves through the eyes of what was still the dominant group within the transatlantic world of fashion and commerce. Owing to their birth, wealth, gender, and race, the American founders recoiled at their outsider status—whether during colonial rule or the early years of the republic. That inequities characterizing the colonial relationship continued to endure throughout the early national period, deeply affected men born to privilege. For them, the revolutionary victory was the first, rather than the last step in gaining freedom from the mother country.[22] Lingering colonial dependence—and a corresponding sense of inferiority—shaped the budding nation.[23] In the minds of American ruling elites, already removed from the prevailing intellectual trends of Europe as colonials and now even more distant as citizens of a free country, everyday life had to catch up with the meteoric political changes generated by independence.

Analyzing the process of unbecoming British necessitates adopting a periodization that is somewhat unusual for a historical study. Nation-building has commonly been presented as a process that unfolded in a linear progression, as citizens moved away from "Britishness" toward a separate American identity. However, political change outpaced shifts in culture. When one considers cultural rather than political independence, it is difficult to point to a single moment when Americans stopped looking abroad for guidance. While the analysis of unbecoming that this book covers changes over time, it is not a chronological study of nation formation.

Like periodization, examining American efforts to unbecome British requires looking at the United States as a postcolonial country in a different manner. To include it without qualification in the traditionally defined "family" of postcolonial nations would be a mistake given the geographical, historical, and temporal differences between the United States and commonly recognized postcolonial societies in Africa, Latin America, and Asia.[24] In the United States the boundary between colonizer and colonized is ambiguous; revolutionaries fighting against the British Empire also oppressed the "internal colonies" within their borders."[25] Scholarship on "settler societies" such as Australia, South Africa, and Canada provide a closer analog.[26] In 1950, an Australian scholar named A. A. Phillips coined the evocative phrase "cultural cringe" to refer to his compatriots' deep feelings of inferiority, most pronounced in their negative judgment of domestic cultural productions in art, music, and drama.[27] Postcolonial Australian artists and intellectuals, like ambitious early Americans, went abroad for education, while those at home mimicked European fashions.

N

*R*everend Timothy Dwight wrote in February 1787 that "Candour obliges us to confess" that Americans such as the artist John Trumbull and political leaders such as Thomas Jefferson "could not have attained the wealth and fame which now lie in prospect before them, had they been confined to their native country."[28] Yet in the same editorial, "An Essay on American Genius" (published anonymously), Dwight, a prominent Connecticut clergyman, a grandson of American theologian Jonathan Edwards, and a future Yale College president, also averred that "Genius is the growth of every country....There can be no doubt that America may boast an equal proportion with the Old World."[29] The process of creating a separate society out of a people who so recently thought of themselves as British in outlook and tradition was fraught with hypocrisy and confusion. Americans vacillated between celebrating their future as a sovereign nation and struggling to overcome the cultural insecurity born of their colonial past. Originally printed in the *New Haven Gazette and Connecticut Magazine*, Dwight's meditation on American "genius" is itself an object lesson in unbecoming.

Although the Treaty of Paris (1784) formally ended fighting between Great Britain and the United States, Anglo-American commercial transactions resumed, for much of the prerevolutionary commercial infrastructure remained intact. Goods still flowed along old shipping routes and through the same ports and the same merchants' establishments.[30] Americans' process of identity formation in the late eighteenth century was visible in their production and consumption of these goods; was expressed by the social relationships these economic and intellectual exchanges fostered; and was embodied culturally in the objects traveling across the Atlantic.[31]

Richard Bushman and other historians have shown how "goods are converted into distinctive signs," carrying significant social meanings for class, national, and gender formation.[32] While people hope their possessions will be interpreted as indicators of distinction or refinement, there is always a chance they will be perceived as evidence of vulgarity. This possibility can cause moments of acquisition and exchange to be fraught with anxiety. Postrevolutionary Americans who were trying to prove and improve themselves through their material acquisitions often expressed insecurity about their choices. They performed for a British audience and craved validation from them, while at the same time hoping to forge a separate American identity using imported goods.[33]

The value assigned to specific objects and bodies changed as they moved from one point in the transatlantic world to another, creating economies of relative location. If an object is transported to a place where it is rare and its qualities are in demand, its value will increase exponentially. Plants that grew in abundance in the New World, when sent across the Atlantic, were transformed into exotic specimens that became treasured additions to Old World herbaria. Borrowed from geography, the term "relative location" can be distinguished from an absolute location; the former is concerned with the relationship between distinct landmarks, whereas the latter defines location based on a fixed coordinate system of latitude and longitude. The fact that Philadelphia was 3,548 miles from London meant more to the postcolonial elite than that it could be found at latitude 39 degrees 57 minutes north, longitude 75 degrees 10 minutes west. Like people, objects have social lives and acquire different meanings depending on their movement from locations of low to high relative value. The concept of the geography of value reflects the disparity between the value people placed on a particular object in the mother country and the value it was given in the new nation.

Well aware of their continuing need for support from Britain, Americans worked hard to maintain the asymmetrical colonizer–subject (or more generally, patron–client) relationships they had previously enjoyed. They remained closer to the British than was comfortable for a free people and farther away from European centers of civility than they cared to concede. At the same time, their physical proximity to peoples whom many feared and despised—Native Americans and Africans—made the construction and exaggeration of cultural distance all the more urgent. The incongruity between where the settler Americans actually were located geographically and culturally and where they chose to imagine themselves to be created tension in their sense of identity and their efforts to unbecome British.

The Transatlantic Travels of Objects and People

This study of unbecoming charts Americans' identity formation by following the lives of people engaged in missionary, scientific, and commercial pursuits as well as objects as varied as maps, imported and domestic decorative artworks, and botanical prints.[34] These particular items blur the distinctions between the tangible and the physical, the abstract and the intellectual. Ultimately, information and knowledge can be analyzed as commodities traded in the global marketplace. Enlightened knowledge, markers of civility, and even racial attributes emerge in this study as possessions that help illustrate the efforts to create (or assert) a national version of Dwight's "American genius"—one whose formation first required unbecoming British.[35]

For Dwight, "illustrious personages" who "signalized themselves, during the revolution," in the areas of "policy, legislation, and war," had been justly lauded by the new country's citizens. But he is quick to remind readers of "rapid, though, to careless observers, imperceptible progress, that is made in cultivating the fine arts."[36] That Americans generally acclaimed political and economic change but did not acknowledge cultural achievement highlights one of the ways Dwight and his peers in the post-revolutionary period saw the process of unbecoming. For the gerund or verbal noun form "unbecoming," the *Oxford English Dictionary* (note that this British source is still regarded as the highest linguistic authority in the Anglophone world) offers an abbreviated definition: "not coming to be, or not passing into a new state of being."[37] American society found itself cast in the long shadow of the empire, the deeply embedded British cultural and intellectual life inspired the desire to keep up with European trends and placed American provincials at the mercy of foreign taste-makers. As Dwight himself acknowledged, "The age of ultimate refinement in America is yet to arrive."[38]

Working from London, Liverpool, and Manchester, British merchants and intellectuals offered self-conscious Americans everyday household objects—from porcelain and tea to maps and textbooks—that would supposedly bring civility, scientific rigor, and cultural capital to their schools and homes. European mapmakers, paradoxically dependent on Americans to provide the information incorporated in their maps, entreated explorers and government officials to supply sketches and notes, which subsequently returned to America in the form of a sanctioned science of geography. Even after Americans began to publish their own texts on geography, they continued to rely on imported books and reprints of British studies, which were still considered superior. Jedidiah Morse, the father of American geography, conceded in 1784: "our young people know more about Europe than they do about America."[39]

At the same time, George Washington fretted over how his reputation suffered every time British merchants sent him outdated, second-rate goods, underscoring the great cultural distances between his homeland and that of his ancestors. Mary Shippen's elaborate domestic rituals for taking tea evinced a national desire to participate in polite culture, leaving Americans vulnerable to the negative judgments of British visitors, who noted their foibles with amusement. In his editorial, Dwight urged Americans who were looking to accrue cultural capital to turn away from imported civilized products and hoary institutions. At the same time he wished to "lead the taste of a nation" away from "the vulgar enjoyments of cock-fighting, gambling, and tavern-haunting," and toward "pleasures of a more refined and innocent nature." Dwight invoked eminent Americans whose work had "appealed to be a bar of critical taste"—artists such as John Singleton Copley and Benjamin West.[40] But to claim these men as American cultural exemplars, the Connecticut minister had also to overlook Copley's public devotion to the Tory cause during the Revolution. Somewhat more disingenuously, Dwight failed to mention West's celebrated position in *British* artistic life, having succeeded Sir Joshua Reynolds as the second president of the Royal Academy of Artists in London—an appointment he secured as the favorite painter of King George III.[41] In this sense of unbecoming British, Americans might have embraced the politics of democracy, but they could not relinquish their cultural attachments to the refined objects and courtly trappings of the British monarchy.

Dwight complained that the "idea has become prevalent among the naturalists in Europe who have written on American subjects...that almost every species of animal and vegetable life has degenerated by being transported across the Atlantic." Mirroring the sentiments expressed by Jefferson in his *Notes on Virginia*, the New Englander proudly explained that the American patriot deftly refuted "this *humbug*" from dismissive European intellectuals with "the urbanity of a gentleman," cogently advancing his counterclaims with "accuracy" and "the sound reasoning of a philosopher." "The time is come," he concluded, "to explode the European creed that we are infantine in our acquisitions, and savage in our manners." That Dwight opened his ruminations on "American genius" with a testy rebuttal of European critics points toward national defensiveness, another unbecoming characteristic of late eighteenth-century Americans.

As an adjective, "unbecoming" is defined as "not in keeping with accepted standards of what is right or proper in polite society."[42] In this context, Americans' unflattering defensiveness and repeated national boasting was a consequence of their inferior position vis-à-vis the British, and suggested an underlying fear of committing social faux pas. Competition with the British in overseas trade often served to highlight this definition of unbe-coming. In 1784, the *Empress of China* departed New York harbor for Canton—the opening gambit in the young country's effort to challenge British imperial and commercial dominance. But trade between the United States and China developed slowly, with unanticipated obstacles, such as the indifference of Chinese traders to distinctions between British and American clients. Furthermore, American products, with the exception of items procured by various indigenous peoples, proved to be of little interest on the sophisticated Chinese market. American merchants' ignorance about what was expected of foreign traders in China caused their reputations to suffer and threatened their success. Despite their fervent efforts to follow European standards of decorum, the behavior of even the most cosmopol-itan Americans often struck foreign observers as extremely unbecoming.

"Not befitting," another definition of "unbecoming," evokes the way Americans' servile behavior and quick deference to European authorities in science and medicine betrayed an anxiety and self-consciousness that was inappropriate for a proud and free people.[43] In the late eighteenth and early nineteenth centuries, North America was viewed as a cornucopia for European academics (albeit for some a rapidly degenerating one): Anglo-American scientists gathered plants, flowers, and seeds and sent them over-seas for classification. In exchange, they received intellectual validation from European scholars who provided Latinate nomenclature and botanical the-ories that promised to transform the wilderness at the Americans' doorsteps into a taxonomic array of enlightened knowledge. Scientific theory, as it appeared in the publications of the Royal Society in London, emerged as a conduit for this variety of unbecoming: the raw materials of the New World, having passed through European universities, were eagerly received in the United States as a refined, intellectually credible form of scientific knowledge. American physicians who sought to strengthen the new nation by developing a domestic medical culture felt compelled to leave their homeland to study in Scotland. With patriotic fervor, practitioners such as Benjamin Rush and Samuel Stanhope Smith sought to heal not just individuals but the entire body politic, and contrived ways of importing medical knowledge into the United States. They also reaffirmed established hierarchies of intellectual achievement, implicitly acknowledging that the New World could not yet support the pursuit of the civilized arts and sciences. Inversely, American universities recruited prominent British scientists and scholars such as John Maclean to increase their prestige. Informed by a geography of value and the economies of relative location, this obsequious form of unbecoming defined the intellectual and cultural life of early postrevolutionary Americans.

"We are inhabitants of a new world," Dwight declared, "lately occupied by a race of savages." For Dwight and many of his contemporaries, "American genius" could be clearly demarcated between North Americans with western European ancestry and those who were either indigenous to the continent or imported from Africa as enslaved labor. In his reference to "savages," Dwight's encomium to national "genius" accents the final definition of unbecoming: the adjective that refers to "dishonest acts, displays of indecency, dealing unfairly, indecorum, injustice, or acts of cruelty." While such actions might not necessarily be a legal transgression, the term "conduct unbecoming" in military usage nevertheless includes behavior that reflects adversely on one's entire nation.[44]

In 1748, Scottish philosopher David Hume argued that light-skinned Europeans were superior to "all the other species of men," on the basis of their material advancement. In his essay "Of National Characters," he noted: "There never was a civilized nation of any other complexion than white. . . . No ingenious manufactures [exist] amongst them [nonwhite societies], no arts, no sciences."[45] Early U.S. thinkers adopted Hume's emphasis on "whiteness," despite their society's lack of advancement in the realms of culture, manufacturing, and knowledge. In 1782, several decades after the publication of Hume's essay, a founding member of the American Philosophical Society, Thomas Bond, addressed the notion of white supremacy. In the Society's Anniversary Oration, he emphasized the need for Americans to learn from European culture and to earn respect from the community of European nations through achievement in learned activities such as science. "Point out the Nation which has not Science, or that which has abandoned it," he declared, "and I will point out to you Savages or Slaves."[46]

Elite white Americans attempted to address their relative powerlessness within the transatlantic context through various strategies of internal domination.[47] Without the exploitation of labor and land, these men could not purchase the things they needed for a gentlemanly lifestyle, nor could they have the leisure time to pursue intellectual endeavors befitting Enlightenment scholars. Similarly, they blocked people of color from access to the privileges of civility. The presence of racialized others was therefore critical to the development of a national identity, fueling the need for Anglo-American elites to establish their "whiteness" (rather than identification with their European heritage) as proof of their civility. To be sure, race and ethnicity (embodied in "whiteness") did not necessarily inoculate these Americans against the experience of inferiority resulting from structural, political, and economic inequality. But it did give them protections from it that they did not extend to indigenous peoples, enslaved Africans, or women. Ultimately, whiteness became an object that conferred distinction and status on its owner, just as rare imported goods did.[48] Expanding the idea of "objecthood" and material culture, commodification of racial difference revealed the United States at its most unbecoming. Indeed, the new nation struggled to define itself economically, politically, and culturally in what could be called America's postcolonial period. Out of this confusion of hope and exploitation, insecurity and vision, a uniquely American identity emerged.

One

A NEW NATION ON THE MARGINS
OF THE GLOBAL MAP

I know most Europeans who have never cros'd the Atlantick entertain the
idea that America is nothing more than a vast forest & the inhabitants little
better than savages.

—John Pershouse (Philadelphia, 1805)

I have read that it was a saying of an ancient Greek that the first requisite
for happiness was to be born in a famous city.... To be born on...an
obscure New World transplantation, second-hand and barbarous, was to be
born to disorder. From an early age, almost from my first lesson at school
about the weight of the king's crown, I had sensed this. Now I was to
discover that disorder has its own logic and permanence.

—V. S. Naipaul, *Mimic Men* (1967)

In 1807, Philadelphia publisher Jacob Johnson issued a reprint of a popular
British geography book entitled *People of All Nations; An Useful Toy for Girl
or Boy*. In this "toy," or miniature book, each letter of the alphabet is accompanied by a picture of an inhabitant of a different nation, along with a
descriptive caption.[1] Although the book was published in Philadelphia, neither America nor the United States is mentioned in it. *A* is for Arabian, and
U is "An Urchin of Otaheite."[2] The entry for *V*, on the other hand, is the
"Virginian." Surprisingly, the illustration is not of a famous native son such
as George Washington or Thomas Jefferson but rather of a man who appears
to have both African and American Indian ancestry.[3] He has a dark complexion and is naked except for a few feathers on his head and some tied
around his waist by a string. This figure of the "Virginian" would have been
familiar to readers of the time; beginning in the mid-sixteenth century, he

Figure 1.1 *V* for "Virginian," in *The People of All Nations; An Useful Toy for Girl or Boy* (Philadelphia: Jacob Johnson, 1807). This symbol of America was common and could be found in other contexts such as the cartouches of maps. The illustrator in this case chose to highlight the fruits of the native figure's forced labor by picturing him grasping tobacco leaves tightly in his hand. *(Beinecke Rare Book & Manuscript Library, Yale University)*

was a common representation of America, appearing on maps and political cartoons (see figure 1.1).[4]

Contemporary eighteenth-century discussions about the Indians and Africans in North America emphasized the flora and fauna of their environment and the natural commodities (such as tobacco and rice) that they procured and produced.[5] In the case of the Virginian of *People of All Nations*, the fruits of his labor are highlighted by the tobacco leaves in one of his hands and a long pipe in the other. In the same book, the "Florida Indian, from North America" cultivates "rice and Indian corn on the banks of the rivers; where, in the woods, oak, pine, hickory, cedar and cypress trees abound."[6] Besides indigenous crops, the author also mentions the species of trees that were then valuable commodities. Similarly, the entry for the "Quebec Indian [who] inhabits Canada, in North America," lists the goods his people trade and says they are "very expert in [the] running and killing of wild beasts, whose skins they sell in great numbers to the English."[7]

Although European settlers had been in Virginia since the seventeenth century, they are noticeably absent from the illustrations in *The People of All Nations*. The text accompanying this copperplate engraving of the "Virginian" does, however, acknowledge the presence of Europeans and their exploitative relationship with enslaved Africans. The unnamed author, perhaps reflecting the abolitionist sentiments of his Quaker publisher, informs the book's young readers: "A Virginian is generally dressed after the manner of the English; but this is a poor African, and made a slave of to cultivate the earth for growing tobacco, rice, sugar, &c." Anglo-American settlers were awkwardly situated between the English, whose manner of dress they were able to assume by means of imported goods, and the Africans whose forced labor allowed their masters to purchase these refined items.

In the various editions of *The People of All Nations*, as well as travel narratives, maps, and geographies so popular at the time, physical locations are commonly linked with the valuable natural products their inhabitants produced and consumed.[8] Whereas New World peoples were associated with natural commodities, the "civilized" Englishman in *The People of All Nations* is marked by his consumption rather than his production. He is smiling and robust—"the man before us looks as if he was a cook"[9]—and carries a platter of steaming roast beef, the quintessential symbol of British abundance. The passage accompanying the image gives a clue to the national identity of the anonymous author, who notes: "[a]n Englishman is accused by foreigners with eating too much… *we* wish that every body may live well."[10] The basis on which the British "may live well" is not laid out explicitly; as the Anglo-American in Virginia depended on slaves' labor to make the money needed to purchase British goods, so, too, the Englishman profited from that labor in the British North American colonies (see figure 1.2).

Despite its simplicity, this diminutive nursery book expresses the Enlightenment belief in the varying levels of civility and politeness displayed by the "people of all nations." A society's commercial production and habits of consumption were thought to reflect its "character" and the level of civility it had attained. The image of Anglo-Americans carving out an existence in the middle of a wilderness inhabited by savages predominated the European imagination long after settlements on the eastern seaboard had been established.

In the late seventeenth and eighteenth centuries, a period referred to as the Great Age of Exploration, the world was dramatically opened to Europeans. Enlightenment scholars grappled with the expansion of knowledge about non-western peoples, and in doing so reformulated their views of the world.

Figure 1.2 *E* for "Englishman" in *The People of all Nations* (1807). *(Beinecke Rare Book & Manuscript Library, Yale University)*

For Scottish followers of "stadial theory," all societies evolved through four stages of development, from groups of hunter-gatherers to pastoral, agricultural, and finally commercial entities.[11] Shifts in economic organization were matched by changes in manners and morals, indicating humans' ascent from barbarism to civilization and eventually sophistication. As John Locke wrote, "in the beginning all the World was America." He reminded his civilized readers that they, too, once resembled the "wild woods and uncultivated waste of America, left to nature, without any improvement, tillage or husbandry."[12] While labeling some societies barbaric, stadial theory did hold out the possibility of their improvement through cultural, political, and economic development.[13] That societies could move from "uncultivated waste" to "tillage or husbandry" was particularly attractive to the educated classes in Scotland and British North America, which had distinctive internal populations— Highlanders and Indians—considered barbaric by Europeans.[14] Peripheral to the British Empire, both locations provided laboratories in which to observe how people who inhabited different states of nature could coexist within the same frontiers. In 1777, Dublin native Edmund Burke, who knew what it meant to be born on the periphery, proclaimed:

now the Great Map of Mankind is unroll[e]d at once; and there is no
state or Gradation of barbarism, and no mode of refinement which we
have not at the same instant under our View. The very different Civility
of Europe and of China; The barbarism of Tartary, and of Arabia. The
Savage State of North America, and of New Zealand.[15]

As Burke noted, stadial theory attempted to understand the world in its
diversity as a whole. Objects ranging from maps to children's books
addressed the desire to make sense of new and potentially frightening
knowledge of exotic people who shared the world with Europeans.

A vast symbolic space—cultural as well as physical—separated the jolly
English figure from the unclothed "Virginian." Anglo-American settlers in
late eighteenth-century America, whose identity fell somewhere between
these two figures, lacked a well-defined place on the global stage. While
cultural nationalists encouraged the domestic production of goods that
explicitly registered their recent political transformation, it was not always
reflected in their maps, geographies, and globes. Aware of the Enlightenment
image of North America as isolated and undeveloped, the new citizens of
the United States desired to change that reputation, to disassociate their
emerging nation from the centuries-old European image of their homeland
as nothing but "wild woods and uncultivated waste."[16]

The Empty Space That Was America

Especially after independence, filling in the perceived "empty spaces" of the
North American map was a way to encourage Anglo-American settlement
and the development of territories under the auspices of the newly
independent government. The preponderance of vast untamed tracts of
cartographic emptiness and the lack of civility that this implied reflected
poorly on the new nation. This was not desirable to those Americans who
wished to propel America out of its "savage" past and into a higher stage of
development.

The desire for territorial acquisition and the Enlightenment-inspired
search for comprehensive knowledge fueled efforts to gather cartographic
information about British North America.[17] In contrast to maps of Europe
that were teeming with detailed information, those of the Americas were
characterized by blank spaces sporadically punctuated by small areas of
settlement. Cartographers faced the problem of closing gaps in existing
knowledge about distant locations.[18] The more creative mapmakers filled

unexplored areas with fanciful creatures and fictitious natural landmarks.[19] Similarly, nautical mapmakers often populated their seas with illustrations of real and imaginary ships and marine life. Others included elaborate decorative motifs and descriptions and illustrations of a region's people, natural resources, and geographic features.

As residents of America, British colonists were uniquely positioned to contribute to knowledge of the New World. Colonials could participate in imperial contests for control of North America by collecting data that was incorporated into maps published in London. Moreover, these native informants, as they might be called, were effective because they could be taught the standard conventions of European mapping that were needed to survey the land around them. By the mid-eighteenth century, Anglo-American colonists had imbued the land around them with rich meaning and helped to fill in the geographic gaps of knowledge.

One important document that colonial expertise made possible was the map that resulted from the 1751 survey mission of Thomas Jefferson's father, Peter Jefferson, and the mathematician Joshua Fry.[20] First published in 1753, "A Map of the Most Inhabited part of Virginia, containing the whole province of Maryland with Part of Pensilvania [sic], New Jersey and North Carolina" was enriched by information garnered from traders who plied the Ohio River valley, such as Christopher Gist (see figure 1.3). New information was gathered and added to the Jefferson and Fry map in a number of versions, one published as late as 1800.

With Europe's increasing domination of the globe, the demand for maps as tools of conquest increased, and the charting of land and sea flourished.[21] European cartographers produced more maps of the New World in the quarter century prior to the American Revolution than they had in any period since the beginning of European expansion across the globe.[22] Yet throughout the first half of the eighteenth century, the quality and comprehensiveness of maps of North America remained poor. Not surprisingly, knowledge of the continent's interior was especially sparse, with European settlements spreading from the coastline inland, while most rivers remained uncharted and others were grossly misrepresented. Drawn on a minute scale, frequently 1:50,000,000, these maps provided only basic details such as major towns, bodies of water, forts in the backcountry, some roads and trails, and Indian hunting grounds. To boost sales, publishers often included false information about the location of silver and gold mines. In most cases, political boundaries were not based on surveys of the land but instead reflected makers' national loyalties.

European leaders recognized the power maps could wield in contests over land claims.[23] Besides their practical applications for navigation at sea

Figure 1.3 The Jefferson and Fry Map (1753). (*Library of Congress*)

and orientation on land, maps were also used by imperial powers to assert political dominance.[24] Not simply reflections of existing spheres of control, cartographic images of European nations and their New World colonies were integral weapons in battles to create and legitimize the territorial claims they purported to record objectively.[25] Modern scholars have analyzed maps as tools of power that allowed early modern colonial states to comprehend and extend their dominion, both territorial and human.[26] Producers and consumers of cartographic objects shared the Enlightenment vocabulary of spatial representation and used those conventions when depicting latitude, longitude, distance, and direction.[27] The scientific certainty represented by the natural features appearing on maps (such as a jagged coastline or a chain of mountains) gave weight to their rather more subjective claims, such as how far a nation's colonial territory extended.[28]

Throughout the eighteenth century, the British government commissioned several surveys of the Ohio River valley, a region contested by France and Britain. One of these projects was undertaken in 1754 by a twenty-one-year-old British subject named George Washington, who produced a series of maps of the Cumberland area of Maryland and Fort LeBoeuf in modern-day Waterford, Pennsylvania. As part of this project, Washington surveyed a route that would become a major highway during the Revolutionary War. Like many other ambitious young colonials, Washington began his career as a surveyor for the British Crown, at a time when surveying provided a respectable income for those without vast tracts of inherited land.[29] Washington had a natural affinity for the trade, and his eyes were trained to see the land of his birth from the vantage point of the British Empire.[30] His early training as a surveyor would prove indispensable to the task of founding an independent nation.[31]

The "Mother Map" and Her Progeny

The year after Washington surveyed the Ohio River valley, just as the French and Indian War was beginning, a map of North America by Virginian John Mitchell made its debut. Mitchell was approached by the newly appointed president of the Board of Trade and Plantations, George Montagu-Dunk, second Earl of Halifax, because of his local contacts and intimacy with the landscape of North America. Mitchell's map was printed in eight sheets and, when assembled, measured seventy-six by fifty-two inches. Only the second large-scale map Britain produced in the eighteenth century, this map enjoyed phenomenal sales and was considered by many the primary cartographic reference source, or "mother map," for close to a half a century.[32] Exceeding all expectations, it went through twenty-one editions in four languages between 1755 and 1781 (see figure 1.4).

Produced "with the approbation and at the request of the Lords Commissioners for Trade and Plantations," Mitchell's map registered Britain's various territorial disputes with the expanding Spanish and French empires. It ignored well-established Spanish territorial frontiers west of the Mississippi River and represented Britain's Iroquois allies as if they were colonial subjects.[33] To illustrate the increasing threat of French encroachment, Mitchell clearly divided North America in a way that favored Great Britain's boundary claims along the Atlantic seaboard and across the Mississippi River.[34] Despite understandable international outrage at the map's bias, Peter Collinson, a London-based merchant, enthused in a letter to Carl Linnaeus in the year of its publication that the map was "the most perfect of any published, and is universally accepted." Although its acceptance was exaggerated, Mitchell's map was an impressive accomplishment. An active member of transatlantic botanical networks, Mitchell put that work aside for five years to dedicate himself fully to the map. As Collinson noted, "Dr. Mitchell has left Botany for some time, and has wholly employed himself in making a map, or chart, of all North America."[35]

While Mitchell received credit for the map, it incorporated information from a wide range of sources on both sides of the Atlantic. In a way, the creator himself was a bricolage whose transatlantic life still muddies his biographic details.[36] Living in Britain and America, the man and the map both embodied the labor and knowledge of the colonists with whom he collaborated, in addition to European sources of information. Through his employment at the English Board of Trade and Plantations, Mitchell had free access to the world of geographic and cartographic information housed in the Public Record Office in London, including the published accounts and maps of European explorers.[37] From 1750 onward, he evaluated reports and detailed maps from colonial provincial governors for the British government, while continuing to work on his map. For empires to flourish, this information had to flow in all directions.

With the vast resources of the British government at hand, Mitchell was able to take a bird's-eye view of the continent in a way the colonials themselves could not. When he moved to London, he located himself at the command center from which the empire's organizational structures were run. Maps such as his, produced in the service of the British, imposed coherence on disparate regions such as the New England

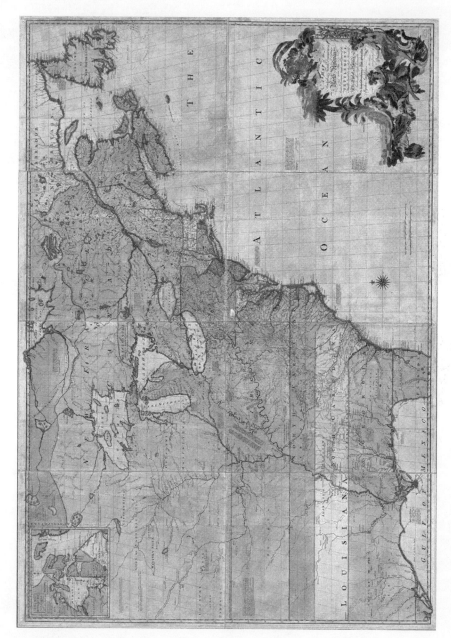

Figure 1.4 The Mitchell Map. *(Library of Congress)*

and southern colonies by visually binding individual colonies into a single geographic and political entity called British North America.[38] Pennsylvanians, New Yorkers, and Virginians were symbolically united by the authority vested in the solid black lines of the cartographer. Within those borders, British colonials in North America were drawn together, which would help to construct a shared national identity.

The British victory over the French at the end of the Seven Years' War in 1763 quelled territorial disputes in North America between the two European imperial powers; the troubles between Great Britain and her American colonies were only just beginning. Mitchell's detailed map, made possible by his dedicated labor but also through the collective efforts of the American colonists he enlisted for their firsthand knowledge of regional particularities, was shortly to be used against the British. Once they are put into circulation, objects consort with people on both sides of any political divide; their makers cannot control how they will be used or by whom.[39]

Most of the cartographic documentation of the battle sites of the American Revolution was produced in London rather than in the new United States. The first map to depict the conflict was published in London on July 29, 1775. "A Plan of the Town and Harbour of Boston," by map-maker Charles McCall, included references to the Battle of Bunker Hill, which had taken place a mere forty-three days earlier—a remarkable feature, considering that the information in the map had to be conveyed from America by ship.[40] Numerous contemporary histories, such as Charles Stedman's *History of the Origin, Progress, and Termination of the American War* (1794), mixed textual and visual geographical information, incorporating fifteen versions of previously published maps that illustrated various military campaigns.[41]

During the war, atlases gained popularity among military leaders, as well as members of the public who were eager to follow unfolding events of the war. Collections of maps were bound together with geographical illustrations, tables of useful data, and explanatory text. George Washington, as general of the Continental Army, made his own atlas by compiling forty-three foreign maps, including ones to which Americans had contributed. Organized in order from north to south, his atlas began with the territory that later became Canada and ended with New Orleans. *The American Military Atlas*, published by Robert Sayer and John Bennett in 1776, contained critical information for waging a war thousands of miles from home. Referred to as the "holster atlas" because of where British officers carried it in battle, this important reference work included six large folding maps and provided important topographical information in a convenient form.[42] The same maps were also used by American military leaders in their rebellion against the British.[43]

The British-produced *North American Atlas* was the main text that both the Americans and the British consulted to plan their strategies against one another. Published in London by cartographer and publisher William Faden in 1777, it became the most important atlas chronicling the Revolution's battles.[44] The first edition contained twenty-nine maps produced by the most renowned cartographers of the period. Along with regional maps, Faden's atlas included a series of detailed battle plans drawn by eyewitnesses.[45] Another important British atlas, Joseph Frederick Wallet Des Barres's *Atlantic Neptune*, was issued in several printings in London between 1774 and 1782.[46] This folio collection included ninety-five sea and harbor charts and views and today is considered the most impressive collection of hydrographic maps published during the period. While atlases proliferated in Great Britain during this time, no atlases were produced in America.[47] If Americans wanted to consult reference material about their own nation's emergence or plan battles against their adversaries, they had to turn to foreign sources.

At the end of the Revolutionary War, Mitchell's map was unfurled across the table during the diplomatic negotiations in Paris that secured America's independence. Widely considered the primary political treaty map in American history, it was used again to settle the many border disputes that arose between the new nation and what remained of British North America (Canada).

The shifting geopolitical borders of the British colonies in North America were reflected in maps produced by Europeans and European Americans throughout the seventeenth and eighteenth centuries. Cartographic images of the colonies brought together disparate regions such as the Northeast and the South by constructing visual unity between them as possessions of the British Empire. Conversely, black lines on a map could represent the severance of a colonial relationship that had lasted for centuries, as was the case with postrevolutionary maps that split Maine from Nova Scotia, which remained in British hands.

There was a considerable lag between the moment of political independence and the time when material objects began to reflect this new political reality, despite the haste with which people in Britain and the United States hoped to produce them. It would have been impossible to change all geographic images of the British North American colonies as soon as a stroke of a pen on a treaty transformed them into the United States of America. Therefore, former colonials had to use outdated cartographic objects that represented an authoritative geographic version of reality that did not even recognize the existence of their new nation.

While there were others who disputed his claim, London mapmaker John Wallis was commonly recognized as the first to produce a map recognizing the independence of the United States of America. Published at his "Map-Warehouse" on Ludgate Street in London on April 3, 1783, it was entitled *The United States of America laid down from the best authorities, agreeable to the Peace of 1783*. As expected, this Briton enjoyed tremendous success with this map. Wallis was only too happy to profit from commemorating America's military success against his own nation (see figure 1.5). Once again, American consumers, eager to express their patriotic pride, turned to British manufacturers to supply the objects of their desire.[48] While this object overtly celebrated the new nation, profits from its sale went to London. This is a good example of how the battle Americans fought so hard to win in the end benefited British manufactures.[49]

Figure 1.5 The John Wallis Map of 1783. *(Library of Congress)*

Figure 1.6 Cartouche of the Wallis Map. *(Library of Congress)*

The most striking feature of Wallis's new map is the decorative cartouche in its lower right corner (see figure 1.6). Here, the ubiquitous naked "savage" is replaced by elite Anglo-American heroes dressed in the manner of Englishmen.[50] Cast in a heroic pose derived from the Apollo Belvedere, George Washington strolls alongside the figure of Liberty, whose hand dramatically gestures to the word "America." On the other side of the cartouche sits Benjamin Franklin, with a quill pen poised over a blank book. He is gently guided by Minerva at his elbow, while Justice, blindfolded, stands benevolently behind him. Making one of its first appearances on a British-made map, the American flag flies triumphantly above the scene, saluted by a winged angel with a trumpet at its lips. New World plants such as tall pine trees and squat tobacco plants—the only objects that remain constant in cartouches from both the pre- and postrevolutionary periods—complete the tableau. Although the creator of this image clearly felt the need to transform the usual tawny figures representing America to white men, the same was not true of the flora.

Citizens on the Margins of the Map of Empire

Entrepreneurial Americans did attempt to compete with British mapmakers in the years following the Revolution. In 1784 Abel Buell, a resident of New

Figure 1.7 The Buell Map. *(Map Collection, Yale University Library)*

Haven, produced *A New and correct Map of the United States of North America Layd down from the latest Observations and best Authority agreeable to the Peace of 1783.*[51] In his haste to beat out overseas competitors, he made several errors of omission.[52] Although he boasted in advertisements that his map was the "*first* ever compiled, engraved and finished by one man and an American," his effort crudely incorporated the boundaries established by previous mapmakers (see figure 1.7).[53]

It would take several decades for Americans to free themselves of their dependence on foreign maps, even those depicting their own homeland.[54] Mapmaking in the United States did not develop fully on a scale comparable to that in Great Britain until the 1840s. Only then did commercial enterprises and governmental agencies begin to support large-scale, systematic mapping programs of the country. In the immediate postrevolutionary years, American mapmaking was driven by practical administrative and political purposes. During this early period in the nation's history, American cartographers focused on creating maps that would help to settle the numerous territorial disputes that occurred between individual states.[55]

Mapping was central to the expansion of the United States, as it had been to the empires of Europe. After the Revolution, Americans transplanted the idea of their new nation on top of the plan initially determined by British imperial structures, forming administrative units (states formerly known as colonies) and aggressively vying with other nations (Indian, British, French, and Spanish) for territory and influence. Given George Washington's cartographic training as well as the educational background of other American leaders in the founding generation, it is not surprising that they employed European methods of ordering, measuring, and organization as they set about establishing their own nation. The sciences of cartography and geography, the work of surveying, and travel writing became the genres for describing the physical attributes of the United States of America.

When Anglo-American settlers appropriated Indian land in North America, they thought they were "civilizing the wilderness" through the expansion of the British Empire. There was continuity between the imperial outlook articulated by Locke and the method by which the United States government continued to fill the (supposedly) empty spaces. Once it proclaimed itself free from the tyranny of the empire, the U.S. government annexed territory previously gained for the British Crown.[56] Supported by the government, white settlers unleashed from British constraint moved west into Native American homelands. Believing that settling on these lands raised their level of civilization, Anglo-American settlers sent spurious information from the New World about Indians that corroborated European presuppositions about the Native Americans' presumed savagery. And so, while European cities were saturated with meaning, knowledge of the New World remained vague.[57] For European cartographers, America's spaces did not invoke religious, historical, or cultural meaning as they did for Native Americans.

In his diary entry for September 18, 1794, Nicholas King of the Manuscript Division of the Library of Congress lamented the state of mapmaking in the United States:

> On [the ideal] map should be delineated the *Actual Courses* of the Rivers and Water Courses within its bounds.... The Map should likewise shew the Face of the Country, such as the Hills, gentle slopes, Valleys, Marsh Grounds and Morrasses. These should be so far accurate as to give a Stranger the just idea of the Country.... But such my Dear Sir are not the American Maps. Four lines of about an inch and

half in length include a thousand Acres, and a waved line through it with a pen, is to represent a River, a Brook or a Run, as you may happen to find it![58]

Producing maps that transformed empty cartographic space into measured and labeled parcels of land encouraged citizens of the new nation to establish new settlements. Published in 1798, Charles Williamson's *A Map of the middle states, shewing the situation of the Genesee Lands and their connection with the Atlantic coast,* was specifically aimed at promoting settlement. Its first edition showed only two cities—Bath, New York, and Baltimore, Maryland. An expanded edition published the following year added seventeen new villages in Ontario and Steuben counties in New York. By its 1800 publication, the subtitle *Observations on the Proposed State Road* appeared under the comprehensive title *A Map of the Middle States of North America Shewing the position of the Genesee County comprehending the Counties of Ontario & Steuben as laid off in Townships of Six Miles square Each.* In addition to more words in the title, there were now dozens of rivers and towns, as well as land grants, developments, and state lines, on the map. Spaces on maps previously undifferentiated and undefined were now demarcated throughout New York and adjacent states.[59]

Even with these additions, King's complaints about accurate mapping still applied, and the problem was exacerbated by the absence of geographical information for much of the Northern Hemisphere. Geographic and topological ignorance was reflected in the 1804 *Map of the United States, Exhibiting the Post-Roads, the situations, connexions & distances of the Post-Offices, Stage Roads, Counties, & Principal Rivers* published by Abraham Bradley, Jr.[60] Produced shortly before the Lewis and Clark expedition in 1806, this map included a large inset, entitled "Map of North America," in which the vast majority of the continent west of the Mississippi lay unmarked. This lack of geographic information, which became the impetus for Jefferson to initiate Lewis and Clark's famous expedition, also announced an American bid to rival European power and dominance.[61]

Despite long-standing competition and conflict between France and Britain, the two nations considered one another equals. When speaking of America, however, both took on an air of superiority. As one American historian explained, "Their words were sometimes those of age to youth, parent to offspring, master to apprentice, teacher to pupil."[62] It would take generations of Americans to shift this disparity—a struggle that included geographic self-representation.

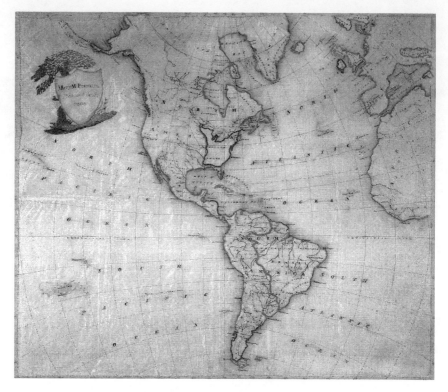

Figure 1.8 Mary Franklin's silk map. In contrast to prerevolutionary British maps of America, this hand-sewn map places the new nation at the center of the composition. Executed using silk thread and ink on a silk background, it is an expression of its maker's emerging pride in her national identity. *(Winterthur Museum & Country Estate)*

For a responsible citizenry to unbecome British, common men and women needed a basic knowledge of their country's geography, as did the schoolchildren who would lead the next generation. Juvenile geographies had to address the issue of the supposed empty spaces textually as well as visually, providing a geographical narrative alongside maps showing the placement of nations. In his popular book *A Concise Account of North America*, British major Robert Rogers offered his definition of an ideal geography of America, which brought together "such facts and circumstances as…appear to me to be most interesting." Because the genre was meant to be didactic, the author took pains to "reduce [the factual details] to an easy and familiar method, and contract them within such narrow limits that the whole may be seen, as it were, at once."[63] In these geography books, the relatively recent "discovery" of America was discussed in contrast to long-established European nations.[64]

This narrative emphasis on the comparative youth and underdevelop-
ment of the United States vis-à-vis Europe continued for decades into the
nineteenth century. Goldsmith's Connecticut reprint of a British geography
noted, "America was unknown to the inhabitants of the other continent, till
a little more than three hundred years ago, when it was discovered by
Christopher Columbus; and hence it is frequently called the New World, in
contradistinction to the eastern continent, first known, and hence called
the Old World."[65] By emphasizing the position of the United States, as Mary
M. Franklin did in her 1808 hand-stitched silk map of the Americas (see
figure 1.8), citizens were able to visually and textually reorient the world.
Requiring countless hours of labor to create, Franklin's handiwork expressed
an emerging nationalism and illustrated the way the public embraced the
logo-map as a symbol of the new nation.[66] Franklin's handmade piece,
while reflecting the widespread importance of the map to nationalism, was
unique. Nevertheless, American maps and geographies were strikingly similar to their British precursors in both content and form. As such, they represented the physical manifestations of unbecoming: the simultaneous
cultural emulation and repudiation of British precursors, and the continuing
influence of the colonial experience on Americans in the early national
period.

How Many Miles from London?

In the years of warfare between Britain and the colonies, Americans relied
on British textbooks, including geographies, that enjoyed great popularity
during the latter half of the eighteenth century.[67] In 1783, the year the Paris
Peace Treaty formally codified America's independence, the geographical
text most commonly used in American schoolrooms was *Guthrie's
Geographies*, written by a Briton, Sir William Guthrie.[68] This book, among
many others, placed England at the center of the empire and left the United
States on the peripheries of a transatlantic world centered in Europe. The
genre of the geography had particular resonance in the emerging nation;
although the location of the former British North American colonies had
not physically changed, there was a significant shift in the political orientation of its people, which geographies attempted to discuss and clarify. These
books covered the basic subjects of the field: description of the Earth's surface, its physical features, natural and political divisions, the climate, productions, and population of the various countries of the world.[69] Until
postrevolutionary patriotism inspired efforts to produce geographies

domestically, British texts were used exclusively in American schools. To some, this was not fitting for a people announcing their independence from the very structures these images and texts described.

Well into the nineteenth century, British geographies, maps, and geographical tools still represented the gold standard of the field. In 1825, publishers in New Haven reprinted a British geography entitled *A General View of the Manners, Customs and Curiosities of Nations* by the pseudonymous "Rev. J. Goldsmith."[70] An advertisement in the back of the book featured other works, including "Willet's and Adam's geographies with atlases, Keith on globes, and other books by Goldsmith on England, Rome, and Greece."[71] Richard Phillips (the real name of this geography's author) also endorsed the best geographic tools, all of which were made in Britain. American customers could purchase these items from a firm that sold imported fancy goods, books, and stationery in New Haven and Charleston, South Carolina. As late as 1829, the New York publisher of *A Peep at the Various Nations*, S. King, billed himself as the person "Of whom may be had the greatest variety of British Toy Books...in the United States."[72] In its entry for "Bohemian," the book situates Bohemia "about one thousand miles eastward from London." Similarly, China is described as being "about five thousand miles from London." Strikingly, the United States is not even included in this account of nations. These were American books, but where was America?

A "Juvenile Hasty Production": The First American Geography

The Federalist and Congregationalist minister Jedidiah Morse was among the most vocal critics of Americans' dependence on the former mother country for geographical descriptions of their own country, calling it a "disgraceful blot upon our literary and national character" (see figure 1.9).[73] In a preface to one of his books, he told his fellow citizens that it would no longer be acceptable "to receive the knowledge of the Geography and internal state of our own country, from a kingdom three thousand miles distant from us—to depend on foreigners, partial, to a proverb, to their own country, for an account...of the American States."[74] For Morse, to continue to rely on imported geographies was unsuitable for educating a new generation of freeborn American citizens.[75]

After the Revolution, Americans continued to purchase British geography texts such as Sir William Guthrie's *Geographical, Historical, and*

Figure 1.9 "Jedidiah Morse," painting by Samuel F. B. Morse (c. 1810), oil on wood panel, 72.1 x 58.1 cm. In this portrait executed by his son, Samuel, Jedidiah Morse is depicted as a scholar dressed in a fine damask morning gown. His style of dress reflects popular fashion trends in the eighteenth century among elites. This type of gown, also referred to as a banyan, was influenced by Middle Eastern styles and often paired with a soft turban that was worn in place of the formal periwig. In this portrait Morse is surrounded by the trappings of scholarly inquiry; displayed on the cases behind him are his own books, which include *Universal Geography*, *Elements of Geography*, and *American Gazetteer*. Sitting alone on the shelf above these works is a volume of his sermons. *(Yale University Art Gallery)*

Commercial Grammar and Robert Rogers's *Concise Account of America*. In 1788, Noah Webster criticized this reliance on outdated imports noting: "Another defect in our schools, which, since the revolution, is [*sic*] become inexcusable, is the want of proper books."[76] In his essay "On the Education of Youth in America," Webster observed that the "minds of youth are perpetually led to the history of Greece and Rome or to Great Britain."[77] He noted disapprovingly that American children were growing up "constantly repeating…debates upon some political question in the British Parliament" rather than "the settlement and geography of America; the history of the late revolution and of the most remarkable characters and events that distinguished it."[78]

Despite the best intentions of cultural nationalists such as Morse and Webster, residents of the infant nation found a complete break from the former mother country impossible. For Morse, the solution was complex; it mixed posturing as independent while freely borrowing information and technology when it suited him. In the preface to his 1793 *American Universal Geography,* he asserted: "To import from Europe all their literary works, and their mechanical, nautical and Geographical improvements and discoveries, is highly useful and proper."[79]

In the absence of domestic publications for schools, Morse was inspired to write "an American geography" entitled *Geography Made Easy: Being a Short, but Comprehensive System of that very Useful and Agreeable Science.*[80] This book was based upon lectures the author had written while teaching at a school for young women in New Haven. He did this while studying theology at Yale and *Geography Made Easy* was undertaken shortly after he received his degree.[81] Although Morse's goal was to help Americans break free of their dependence on British publications in the postrevolutionary period, he depended heavily on Old World sources. His book was patterned after Guthrie's popular geography text, *A New Geographical, Historical, and Commercial Grammar,* as well as Englishman Richard Turner's *New and Easy Introduction to Universal Geography,* written in 1780.[82]

Targeted at a young audience living in a young nation, Morse's book was modest in comparison to the British books he used as models. Readers of Guthrie's standard work were presented with a two-volume set of 728 pages;[83] *Geography Made Easy* totals only 212. Morse's book was composed in a straightforward manner and arranged in a simple layout. It situated the reader in shrinking concentric circles of geographic scale, starting with a brief discussion of the solar system. After providing a few principles of geography, the text discusses the physical location of the United States and devotes sixty pages to describing individual states. The balance of the book covers the rest of the world and is taken largely from the same British sources Morse wished to correct. He lifted passages directly from his rival, even when they reflected an obvious English bias. In one example, he reprinted a passage declaring that English women, "in their shapes, features and complexions, appear so graceful and lovely, that England is termed the native country of female beauty."[84]

Morse later expressed some embarrassment about *Geography Made Easy,* describing it as a "juvenile hasty production" written after he received his "first degree at Yale College, at the age of 22."[85] He attributed the work's shortcomings to (among other things) the pressure he was under to publish it as quickly as possible. The preface explained the work was "at first

intended...as a manuscript only" for the use of a school under his
"immediate instruction." However, due to "various considerations," he said,
he had been "induced to...exhibit it to public view."[86] Among these considerations, he admitted in a letter to Richard Price in London, was the "want
of fortune to defray the heavy expenses."[87] He also noted that most inhabitants of the United States could not afford to purchase the more elaborate
British imports. This was indeed a common concern with many of the
European goods that American consumers desired. Eventually, as the
American market grew, savvy manufacturers began to offer cheaper versions of such goods for American customers. Morse's estimation of his
audience proved correct; the modest volume enjoyed anything but modest
sales.[88] In a letter to his father on January 8, 1785, Morse described his
incredible success: "My Geographies sell beyond my most sanguine
expectation. I have sold between 3 & 400 within 3 weeks. The reasons why
I have not sent you more was because they could not bind them so fast as
they were wanted here."[89] Despite its commercial success, Morse recognized
the flaws in his first domestic geography and immediately began to contem-
plate more serious works. While acknowledging pecuniary, worldly concerns, he made his grand intentions clear: his geographies would attempt to
break from dependence on the former mother country and would defend
his birthplace against long-standing British condescension toward his fellow citizens.

During the early years of American nationhood, a powerful motivation
for national unification derived from British contempt, both real and imagined. This disrespect, which had brought together widely disparate colonies in a unified American revolutionary movement, continued to serve
them well after independence. If nothing else, Americans, whether from
Virginia or Massachusetts, slaveholders or abolitionists, could share in this
sense of perceived mistreatment by Great Britain. In June 1798, Dr. David
Ramsay, a historian and politician, wrote to Morse bitterly complaining
about how the British dismissed the intellectual work of even the most
gifted Americans.[90] Although Ramsay himself had "escaped pretty well"
from the sharp tongues of British critics, he was nonetheless indignant
about what "they have said of Mr. [John] Adams's, Mr. [Thomas] Jefferson's
and Mr. [Timothy] Dwight's performances." Ramsay's statement betrayed
his outrage. Loyal to his compatriots, he felt these men of intellect were not
taken seriously because they were Americans. The British, he protested,
"affect a contempt of every production that is American, and a total indifference to what is going on, on this side of the Atlantic." While Americans
felt the need to stay abreast of news from Britain, the opposite was not true,

reflecting the unequal relationship. The British critics' unmerited and severe strictures on the literary performances of Americans had the effect of making him "more of an American than ever." British books and book-sellers also monopolized the international market, which further angered him: "Even Mr. [Thomas] Jefferson's book [*Notes on the State of Virginia*] does not sell. The truth is, they do not wish to encourage literature or man-ufactures among us."[91]

During the early national period, the rate at which American textbooks in other fields of study were produced (for instance, in the natural sciences) contrasted with the prompt appearance of American geographies. Indeed, the first remotely comprehensive work in natural history, Benjamin Smith Barton's *Elements of Botany*, did not appear until 1803.[92] That domestically published geographic textbooks appeared so soon after the end of the Revolutionary War reflected the American desire to see these volumes as explicit symbols of cultural nationalism.[93] American geographies literally placed the new nation on the world map. Akin to historical studies, they hearkened to the nation's arrival in an official and scientific manner.[94] Writing in the *New Haven Gazette and Connecticut Magazine* in 1787, Morse proclaimed: "We are independent of Great Britain and are no longer to look up to her for a description of our own country."[95]

In 1789, as the new American government was being established, Morse published *The American Geography; or, A View of the Present Situation of the United States of America*. If his first attempt at an American geography had been only a mere sketch of the nation, this work was intended to be his masterpiece. In the preface he noted:

> Europeans have been the sole writers of American Geography, and have too often suffered fancy to supply the place of facts, and thus have led their readers into errors, while they professed to aim at removing their ignorance. But since the United States have become an independent nation, and have risen into Empire, it would be reproachful for them to suffer this ignorance to continue; and the rest of the world have a right now to expect authentic information.[96]

Morse promised his readers that *The American Geography* would "grow and improve as the nation advances toward maturity."[97] He presented the book to the American public as the nation's living offspring, appealing to readers' patriotism to encourage them to participate in its care. Even if the monetary gains were benefitting the author alone, American readers were also made to feel invested in the book's success. "[L]ike the Nation of which it treats, it is but an infant, and as such solicits the fostering care of the country it describes... and the Author will gratefully acknowledge ever friendly communication which will tend to make it perfect."[98]

Impressive for an American book of this period, the octavo volume of *American Geography* contains 534 pages, including folding maps and a table of distances. More than seven-eighths of the book is devoted to the geography of the United States, and according to the common standards of the genre set by the British models, it included historical, sociocultural, and political information. In contrast to the imported geographies that Americans were used to, Morse's emphasis on domestic issues placed the United States at the center of geographical inquiry. Yet for Morse's most patriotic supporters, this was not enough. They urged him to exclude discussion of all locations except the United States. Given his intention to sell the book for classroom use, he ruled against this suggestion, once again choosing profit over ideology. On April 1, 1789, four days after *American Geography* appeared, he noted that his "Geography is already introduced into Yale College as a text book." Exuberant, he was convinced that this "flattering circumstance [would] tend, more than any thing, to give the book a reputation."[99]

Profiting handsomely from the nationalist project, Morse now earned his livelihood in royalties from the book's multiple publications. Within five months of its publication, half of the first print run (consisting of three thousand copies) was sold, and within less than a year, the publisher requested a second edition. Before finishing that edition, in 1790, the Boston firm Thomas & Andrews would publish an abridged version especially for classroom use.[100] This 322-page duodecimo volume sold well enough, and several more editions of the text went to press. Morse's personal and financial success earned him approbation from the leading intellectuals in the early national period, among them Jeremy Belknap, Ezra Stiles, Eleazar Wheelock, David Ramsay, and Ebenezer Hazard.[101] The only domestic rival to Morse's book would be Nathaniel Dwight's *Short but Comprehensive System of the Geography of the World*, first published in 1795.[102]

Joseph Priestley, the famous scientist who fled to the United States to escape political persecution, wrote to Morse after reading his geography. In his August 24, 1793, letter, Priestley thanked Morse for his "excellent treatise of Geography" and confessed: "We had but a very imperfect idea of America before." Similarly, Daniel Christoph Ebeling, a noted expert on American geography who resided in Hamburg, Germany, related in his correspondence of October 1793 that he [Ebeling] had been "misled by following English authors and had imbibed from them prejudices which the perusal of your [Morse's] work has happily removed."[103] Writing again to the American, Ebeling maintained that Morse's geographical works would correct the "many imperfect and false accounts Europe has of your country."[104]

Despite the book's success, however, *The American Geography* did not contribute any original knowledge to the field.[105] While touted as the symbol of independence from servile imitation, Morse's newest work borrowed heavily from the same British authors he had vowed to upstage. Unlike geographer Lewis Evans, whose 1755 *Analysis of a Map of the Middle British Colonies in America* had actually contributed to the existing knowledge and methodology of the field, no maps or new cartographic projects were ever ascribed to Morse.[106] In a letter to Ebeling, Morse conceded that much of his book, including the layout, structure, and even content, was taken from British models: "When I adopted my plan, Guthrie's was in high repute and it was in a manner necessary to adopt his plan."[107] Morse's approach underscores a common theme in American culture during this transitional period. Citizens were caught between the urge to innovate and the need to adhere to European standards and traditions, which conferred both national and Old World legitimacy.

Morse publicly acknowledged that his motivation was stoked by his dissatisfaction with the short shrift Americans had been given by British authors. In the preface to a later edition of his work, Morse attacked the "deficiency" and "falsity" of William Guthrie's statements about the United States of America. He simply felt the British did not write enough about the country and what they did write was untrue. Morse spoke against the long-standing practice of turning to the former mother country for self-definition:

> It is not to be supposed that European Geographers should be as well acquainted with America as with their own country. Accordingly, we find that their accounts of the United States are not only very concise, but very inaccurate. To attempt to give American youth a knowledge of their own country from these imperfect and erroneous sketches, would be as fruitless as absurd; it would be to instill into the minds of Americans, British ideas of America, which are far from being favourable or just.[108]

Morse then criticized the "disproportionate" amount of space Guthrie dedicated to Great Britain in a work falsely "profess[ing] to give us a complete geographical description of the world."[109] Incidentally, Morse did not advocate for a geography that gave equal space to all nations but merely substituted an American bias for a British one, devoting the majority of the work to domestic geography. After all, Morse argued, "Americans ought to know their own country better than any other."[110]

Despite his nationalist sentiments, Morse did not hesitate to borrow from the British: "to import from Europe all their literary works, and their mechanical, nautical and Geographical improvements and discoveries, is highly useful and proper," he said.[111] And import he did. The second edition of his geography, published in 1793, added a volume devoted to the "Eastern Continent" that was compiled from Guthrie's *Geography*—the British book he hoped to displace in American classrooms. The new edition, in two octavo volumes, totaled more than sixteen hundred pages. To match its expanded size, the title was changed to *The American Universal Geography, much Enlarged with a Second Volume on the Eastern Hemisphere.*[112] Despite this grand title, the book was basically a compilation of British texts placed between new American boards.[113] Even its publisher, Thomas & Andrews, imported special type from Great Britain to produce Morse's future editions.[114] Yet Morse claimed that his book was better suited to American tastes and needs than any European book because it was compiled and published by an American citizen.[115]

To break British intellectual hegemony, Morse urged Americans to achieve cultural independence through, among other things, choosing his geography over the British alternatives. Appealing to patriotic pride, he described how before the Revolution, "Americans seldom pretended to write or to think for themselves. We humbly received from Great Britain our laws, our manners, our books, and our modes of thinking; and our youth were educated as the subjects of the British king, rather than as citizens of a free and independent republic."[116] He warned: "[the] propriety of importing any of our school books from Great Britain, unless they are previously modified and adapted to the genius of our republican government, is very questionable; as we otherwise run the hazard of having our children imbibe from them the monarchial ideas, and national prejudices of the English."[117] Morse publicly solicited information for his books from Americans across the country, asking for help from both learned public figures and common folk he had never personally met. Besides writing letters to acquaintances, in 1787 Morse circulated questionnaires to citizens living in different regions of the United States. The Philadelphia request, printed in August 1787 and addressed "To the Friends of Science," welcomed input from all who were inclined instead of limiting his inquiry to "such Gentlemen as are able and likely to furnish answers," as was initially planned.[118]

These vague questionnaires emboldened the citizens of the new nation to respond enthusiastically.[119] Morse's call for help from his fellow Americans, exhorting them to "contribute to the public good," spread far and wide as newspaper editors republished his letter.[120] As the advertisements emphasized, Americans could dispute the misinformation and stereotypes circulating about their country and fill in the blank spaces in international knowledge about their homeland. In a broadside addressed to "To the Friends of Science" that Morse published in Philadelphia on August 7, 1787, the author complained that, "Geographers of foreign countries" were not "possessed of the proper materials, and not equally interested in this part of their subject" and had "filled their accounts of these states with numerous inaccuracies." Morse roused his fellow citizens with a call to arms: "It is time these inaccuracies were corrected. We are independent of Great-Britain, and are no longer to look up to her for a description of our own country."[121]

Legislators also took part in this project. Thomas Tucker of South Carolina told his colleagues in the House of Representatives about Morse's project and secured congressional support. Governor Robert Livingston of New Jersey informed his staff to search for data they could send to Morse.[122] Having enlisted enthusiastic contributions from across the country, he billed his geography as an all-encompassing patriotic project, despite the book's private publication, sole authorship, and proprietary profits.[123]

Damaging his work's scientific accuracy, however, Morse relied on quasi-geographical works written by amateurs. In several instances, he reproduced misinformation and fables, such as an account of the so-called hissing snakes of Lake Erie. His nationalist predilections undercut his stated goals of objectivity, as the national identity of the authors, rather than their accuracy, determined their inclusion. The first edition, in particular, was littered with evidence of this practice.

Morse's book also borrowed heavily from previously published works; over half of his material about Virginia and much of his chapter on Pennsylvania were culled from Thomas Jefferson's new *Notes on the State of Virginia*, which reflected its own nationalist bias. Like Morse, Jefferson was aware of the politics of maps. For one map, he highlights the liquid "channels of communication" linking his state with the lands beyond its borders suggesting its vitality as a center for trade. Indeed, his *Notes* stretched Virginia's terrestrial domain to its outer limits until it was "a huge mass of land, larger on its own than England itself."[124] By consulting works such as Jefferson's, Morse addressed the unavailability of the latest European scholarship.[125]

Recording and discussing geopolitical boundaries, geographies were charged with meaning, especially during the postrevolutionary period when these demarcations were in flux. In his writings, Morse recognized that political change was occurring faster than material objects could register these shifts. Objects such as geographies or maps could therefore easily become obsolete even before they appeared in print. He cataloged his "misgivings" about his ability "to undertake the description of...a Country rising into importance with unexampled rapidity and to attempt, in successive editions...to keep pace with the progress of things." Whether this was evidence of humility or a rhetorical convention uttered for colleagues and readers is unclear. All the same, Morse did not hesitate to continue with his grand intellectual and cultural plans.[126]

Morse's *Geographies*, in their multiple editions, were reprinted frequently and were among the most widely read geographical books written in and about America.[127] In 1794, a Rhode Island judge hailed him as "our first American Geographer";[128] and by 1800, the reading public had recognized him as the "father" of American geographies.[129] As the copious pencil marks left by readers young and old in the extant copies of his books attest, people not only purchased Morse's volumes but read and interacted with them.

Whatever accolades Americans might have garnered from their own compatriots, recognition from the former mother country was still prized above all else. For fervent nationalists, this quest for British approbation after independence was a complicated impulse. To Americans like Morse, the desire for foreign recognition did not diminish their pride in America but helped increase the reputation of the new nation. Despite his lofty rhetoric about domestic pride, Morse wanted to establish a reputation that extended beyond the nation's borders, and he devoted a great deal of time to trying to get his book published in London. In a letter to Dr. Richard Price, Morse humbly inquired about securing the English copyright for his work: "I have undertaken & completed the work wholly at my own risque & expense & wish to avail myself of every advantage that may arise from its publication in England as well as America, as far as may be consistent with your Laws."[130] Responding to Morse on May 18, 1789, Price flatly stated "no such thing is Possible," and continued: "An edition of your book having been printed in America, every bookseller here is at liberty *without asking your leave*, to import it, or print and publish it if he pleases."[131] After years of borrowing liberally from foreign sources, Morse was pained to imagine British authors doing the same, without his receiving any monetary remuneration.

Undeterred, Morse persisted in his efforts to sell his books in Britain. He contacted London bookseller John Stockdale, hoping to convince him to publish some of his writings.[132] Morse eventually convinced him to issue a reprint of *The American Geography* in 1792.[133] From the start, their relationship was unequal, as the British bookseller defined the terms of their interactions. Because Morse had no legal recourse to stop Stockdale from reprinting his works, the American relied on the Englishman's good faith to give him a share of any profits made from his book sales. Stockdale had experienced problems with American customers in the past. When Morse asked about placing a printing order, the London publisher demanded the money in advance: "I know by woeful experience the difficulty of getting payment from America."[134] Referring if only partly in jest to the continuing instability of U.S.-British relations, Stockdale wrote: "I could execute the order in three months, but I should not like to have my debt paid by America going to war with England."[135]

In accordance with common practice of the time, Morse accepted British goods as payment, and items from Stockdale's book stock were part of their arrangement. Ironically, given his opposition to Americans' dependence on British books, Morse requested from his publisher many titles discussing America in some way: Arrowsmith's "2 maps of America," Perry's *English Dictionary*, "Missions in America," and even two copies of Morse's own *Elements of Geography.*[136]

One of the printing orders Morse hoped to hire Stockdale to complete was an order for five thousand copies of every map that appeared in Guthrie's geography text. "It is impossible to say what the expense of engraving the Maps to Guthrie would be," answered Stockdale, "but I should suppose £80 or £100. Paper, & printing of 5000 of each about £400."[137] Unfortunately, Morse's reply does not survive. That five thousand copies of Guthrie's maps would have provided the correct number of maps for a reprint of Morse's geography hints at a possible motive. The quality of Morse's maps had been publicly criticized, which was especially damning for a geography book;[138] but Morse appears to have been prepared to insert these maps into the pages of his own volume.

Despite disappointing sales of *American Geography*'s first English edition, Stockdale issued a vastly improved second edition that substituted maps by the famed English geographer Aaron Arrowsmith for Morse's inaccurate and unattractive ones. The publisher's note explained:

It was the Publisher's intention to have given a complete set of Maps on a very extensive scale; but finding that Mr. Arrowsmith had in great forwardness two large ones of America, compiled from authentic materials that he had recently received, and knowing that preference would be given to him, being universally allowed to be one of the first Geographers now living, the Publisher has presented him with the whole documents he had in his possession, and declined proceeding with the plates that he had already begun.[139]

This new text presented its readers with mixed but revealing messages. While English maps placed the prime meridian in London, Morse's text used Philadelphia as the reference point for listing longitude.

Stockdale's sales expectations for his new edition of Morse were dashed by the publication of a competing book by an English author who borrowed Morse's strategy. A Baptist preacher from Plymouth, England, William Winterbotham lifted and reprinted six hundred pages from Morse's *American Geography* for *An Historical, Geographical, Commercial and Philosophical View of the United States of America, and of the European Settlements in American and the West Indies.*[140] "I now have reason to lament my printing it in such a size," Stockdale confessed. "Winterbottom's [*sic*] has certainly hurt mine very much."[141] Although Morse could do nothing about the plagiarized publication of his work in England, the American geographer was quick to sue Londoner John Reid when he tried to publish the Englishman's book in New York.[142] Alexander Hamilton and James Kent took the case pro bono, and it became the nation's test case for American copyright law.[143] Embittered by Winterbotham's publication undercutting his own sales, Stockdale wrote Morse: "I sincerely wish you may succeed against the Pirates of your works in America."[144]

That Morse's work was published by Stockdale (as well as John Jones of Dublin, Ireland, whose edition competed successfully with Stockdale's) and then copied by Winterbotham suggests some European interest in the subject matter. In 1796, Philadelphia physician and patriot Benjamin Rush wrote to Morse and informed him that a "celebrated limner wishes to have a copy of your face to be placed in London among the pictures of American gentlemen who have attracted public attention."[145] Despite his compatriot's flattering news, Morse must have realized that the information about the United States, rather than British acceptance of him, was what motivated European readers. Charles Dilly, who issued Morse's *American Gazetteer* with Stockdale in 1799, wrote that the "demand for this Edition" was not "at all equal to my expectation," indicating that sales of Morse's books in Europe were mostly lackluster and never lived up to the expectations of British publishers.[146]

National Objects and Regional Tensions

Morse's books, meant to provide a uniform American voice to counter British misrepresentation, revealed all the unbecoming tensions within the nation. His regional identification with New England, and Connecticut specifically, was apparent. In the opinion of southern readers, this regional privileging was woefully misplaced in a work hailed as an inclusive nationalist project. For Morse, Connecticut was the yardstick by which to measure regions outside of New England, and he did not attempt to hide his admiration for his birthplace's well-ordered, pious, and politically "tranquil" society. By contrast, he was judgmental about the religious practices and manners of the southern part of the nation.

Like earlier eighteenth-century British geographers—who commonly wrote about the world without leaving their cozy studies in England— Morse's information became much more vague and subject to fancy as he moved farther from his personal point of reference. He expressed embarrassment at the provinciality of his first book and agreed with critics' charges that his "ideas scarcely extended beyond the limits of my native State, Connecticut."[147] But these shortcomings, he noted, had been "composed in the Infancy of Geographical knowledge in America."[148]

Although aware of his own regional prejudices, Morse did not attempt to correct for them in his subsequent works. He derived his information about the South from a short visit and previously published accounts, often by British visitors.[149] Nevertheless, he confidently registered his disapproval of southern life and society and proclaimed Virginia to be a cultural desert. In his section on Williamsburg, Morse criticized the manners and morals of its citizens, pronouncing: "Every thing in Williamsburg appears dull, forsaken, and melancholy—no trade, no amusements, *but the infamous one of gaming*, no industry, and *very little appearance of religion*."[150] In comparison, after the British writer Isaac Weld visited Williamsburg in the spring of 1796, he wrote that social life there was "more extensive and more genteel at the same time than what is to be met with in any other place of its size in America."[151]

Many southern readers bristled at Morse's negative description of them, just as American colonials had when faced with Europeans' dismissive, judgmental reports about the "wilds" of America. Regional cultures continued to have great importance in the early republic; for many Americans local identities were more personally meaningful than national identity.[152] In 1795, St. George Tucker published a spirited rebuttal to Morse's negative pronouncements: *A letter, to the Reverend Jedidiah Morse, A.M., author of the 'American Universal Geography'. By a citizen of Williamsburg.*[153] Tucker was offended that Morse had labeled his work with the "pompous title of the '*American Universal Geography.*'"[154] How dare this man speak on behalf of the entire country? Tucker wrote: "the name of this Geographer evinces his locality of sentiment and the place of his Birth, where I will undertake to say there is scarcely such a thing as a fellow-feeling prevailing, although we are consolidated and made One—no Philanthropy—nothing like that liberality of Sentiment which pervades and animates our Southern world."[155]

A judge on the Virginia General Court and a professor of law at the College of William and Mary, Tucker studied astronomy, conducted scientific experiments, and worked on a five-volume edition of the English jurist William Blackstone's *Commentaries* for American audiences from his plantation.[156] A prolific scholar, he also wrote *A Dissertation on Slavery: With A Proposal for the Gradual Abolition of It, in the State of Virginia* (1796) and *A Letter to a Member of the General Assembly of Virginia on the Subject of the Late Conspiracy of the Slaves; with a Proposal for their Colonization* (1801) in which he advocated the removal of America's slaves to Indian country, that "immense unsettled territory on this continent."[157] A vestryman as well, Tucker took umbrage at Morse's pronouncement about the lack of culture and religious piety in the southern United States. Tucker asserted that he had been excited by Morse's preface to his book, which promised a geography finally "divested of the false colouring of prejudice, and exhibiting truth in all its genuine simplicity and lustre."[158]

The citizens of Williamsburg, Virginia welcomed Tucker's published rebuttal to the views of the northern author who had written so disapprovingly about their city. Regional animosity had been escalating since Alexander Hamilton had introduced his fiscal policies, and Tucker's pamphlet appeared when Chief Justice John Jay's Treaty with the British in 1794 had generated controversy, exposing the tenuousness of the links between the states. Deputized by Washington and Hamilton to travel to London to ease Anglo-American trade tensions, after his return Jay faced severe criticism from some Americans who felt that he had not upheld national sovereignty. In particular, southern slaveholders believed Jay had not done enough to advocate for their claims against British textile interests, and he had opposed France, whose support had been indispensable for winning the war. This further polarized national sentiment, and the controversy, some argue, significantly contributed to the formation of the nation's political party system.[159]

In his critique of Morse, Judge Tucker also gave prescient expression to the growing instability of the Union. In the judge's view, Morse had arrogantly misrepresented the South:

> Every circumstance of human Life (both political and civil) proves how unfit the States were for such an Union as ours. How many Males and Females are there, who might live tolerably happy merely as Friends and Neighbors, who would not be happy if married together? Tempers, customs, manners, Education and a thousand things more shou'd be weighed and consider'd before an Union should take place. But God help us! we are allied too closely and strongly to be divorc'd easily, although our Husbands and Wives shou'd be ever so tyrannical.[160]

Although Morse had set out to correct the misrepresentations and falsehoods written about America by foreign authors, Tucker criticized him for doing the same to the South. Tucker, who was generally considered a mild-mannered man, ended his scathing criticism of Morse's work by pointing out that he had relied on an unreliable British account. According to him, Morse's source was a statement written by a servant of a gentleman who resided near Fredericksburg—someone, Tucker implied, not worthy to make such pronouncements.

Tucker was not alone in his displeasure with Morse's books, although the first two editions of the *American Universal Geography* sold over ten thousand copies combined. James Freeman, a minister at King's Chapel in Boston, went so far as to publish a pamphlet, *Remarks on the "American Universal Geography,"* in which he criticized Morse for his regional prejudices and use of untrustworthy sources.[161] The geography, meant to build a common national identity, exposed the fractured regional identities of the new states in the postrevolutionary period.

A "Proper Place": Savage Locations and Civilized Goods

Morse was not the only American in the postrevolutionary period who highlighted his national identity in order to sell geographies. The complex genealogy of one book in particular illustrates the newfound currency that a person's American heritage could hold and the transnational exchange of geographical knowledge in this period. The title page of the 1784 edition of *Geography epitomized; or, A tour round the world: being a short but comprehensive description of the terraqueous globe: attempted in verse, (for the sake of memory;) and principally designed for the use of schools* identified the author only as "an American." Robert Davidson, the man behind the work, subsumed his personal identity to that of his nation, deeming that to be of greater interest to potential British and American readers. One edition listed both Philadelphia and London as its place of publication, documenting the transatlantic exchange of knowledge in this period.[162]

American authors in the years following independence were torn between adhering to traditional modes of presenting information and demonstrating their willingness to publicize anything that extolled the importance of the United States. William Woodbridge's *Rudiments of Geography,* published in Hartford in 1822, placed the nation within a larger international context.[163] This book started with a detailed and explicit explanation of the order in which nations appear in the book. In the preface, Woodbridge admitted to readers that he had gone against his own beliefs to satisfy their patriotic desires. In his previous edition, he discussed Europe first, and even though "the author considered this the proper place," he has bowed to his readers' wishes and reversed the order in the new edition. Emphasizing the European origin of the citizens of the United States and their consequent link to civility, Woodbridge explained that "Europe was first in order" because it stood as "[the] portion of the world from which the present inhabitants of our own and every other civilized country first came, and from which their arts, learning and manners were derived. But he has found the habits and views of instructors so much opposed to a change, in the established custom of placing America first, that he has thought it expedient to adopt the usual order in the present edition."[164]

The considerable space Woodbridge spent on the issue of placement and order in this study indicates the meaning his American readers assigned to seemingly minor details. He attempted to reorder the geographical orientation of the transatlantic world by decentering Europe. Prior to this time, it was assumed that explorations of the globe would originate in Old World centers of civilization. But with the advent of American nationhood, this was changing. In these extremely unstable times, even the ordering of nations in geographies held profound political implications.

Domestic geographies were popular because of their patriotic messages, yet the importation of British geographical publications or the reprinting of British geographies by American publishers continued in the nineteenth century. Although postrevolutionary consumers placed great importance on the act of affixing national identities to objects, the criteria they used were neither straightforward nor consistent. For instance, though publishers were working in America, they were often foreign born or even newly arrived immigrants from Britain or Ireland. Moreover, the materials used to make the books also communicated ambiguous messages. Paper was often imported, and even if a book's paper was made in America, the type had to be shipped over from Britain.[165] Despite their different covers, books often contained the same content as their British-made counterparts.[166] Part British and part American, these objects were not straightforward in the messages they conveyed to consumers.

An important geography of the period, Richard Phillips's *General View of the manners, customs and curiosities of nations* (published under the pseudonym "the Reverend J. Goldsmith") illustrates this point. The content of his book clearly reflected the British origin of its author, despite the fact that it was an American-made object printed in the United States in 1825 by Babcock and Son of New Haven.[167] Phillips, a prolific author of a vast number of geographies and travel books, also published several geographies specifically for use in schoolrooms. His books were chosen for republication by American firms such as Johnson & Warner, which in 1810 published his work on the native inhabitants of North America and the "remarkable curiosities" in the United States.[168] This was one among many books about North America written by an English author and read by American readers. Considering Americans' fervor to develop a domestic geography, it is surprising that this book was selected for republication by an American firm, especially in view of its use of geography's visual codes to express the supremacy of the British Empire.[169] Goldsmith proclaimed exuberantly: "A hundred volumes in folio could not so clearly illustrate these objects as a single map! No power of language could describe the island of Great Britain, the boundaries of its counties, and the positions of its towns, so obviously, and so forcibly, as a map. *To become acquainted with maps, should, therefore, be the primary business of every student in geography.*"[170]

Readers in Britain as well as America who used these British books were taught a particular way of seeing and understanding the wider world. These works began their textual tour of the world "at home," assumed to be Great Britain. They then moved outward in widening concentric circles, transitioning from the English provinces, Wales, Scotland, and Ireland to other "civilized" western European nations. Readers would then travel to increasingly exotic locations, including the wilderness of North America.

Accordingly, Goldsmith's book begins its tour of the world by describing the "United Kingdom of Great Britain and Ireland" as "unequalled" in "Her wealth, the value of her manufactures, and the extent of her commerce." He goes on to praise the "intelligence and industry of her inhabitants, the excellent form of her political constitution, the just administration of her laws, and the independence arising from her insular situation," which "combine to render her an object of admiration to all other nations." In juxtaposition to the vast continent of North America, the author notes that Europe is the "smallest of the grand divisions or quarters of the world, but is inhabited by an active and intelligent race of people."[171]

The narrative presented in Goldsmith's book asserted England's centrality, and arranged other geopolitical entities in relation to the British Isles. London cast a wide shadow over the rest of the world. Boasting "upwards of a million inhabitants," London, as Goldsmith described it, was the "largest and most opulent city in Europe."[172] Both Scotland and Ireland were characterized in relation to England. Ireland was a land of mostly "catholics [*sic*] who complain much of the oppression of the English."[173] Colonial rivalries between European empires over their New World possessions were integrated into the geography's overall narrative, yet the sympathy of the author firmly resided with the British.[174]

Geographies also provided tools that trained students to locate Great Britain as their point of reference. These texts instilled such skills in young readers as how to read maps and determine the time in different locations on the globe. Using London as a point of reference served the larger purpose of encouraging readers to see the world around them from an imperial perspective.[175] Goldsmith's book featured "Plain Directions for projecting and drawing maps" and other exercises meant to characterize and categorize different national groups around the globe. Again, Great Britain was used as the point of reference in problems requiring the reader to draw the meridians and parallels for a map of the country.[176] The shared temporal and spatial orientation with Britain, used since the first English settlers came to America, carried great weight, and Americans maintained Greenwich as their prime meridian.[176] Exercises asked: "What time is it noon in Europe, compared with other parts of the world? What time is it in other parts of the world when it is noon in Europe?"[178] As late as 1827, Joseph Hart also had American students calculate time and space using British referents for his book, published in Philadelphia, of "geographical exercises for...New-York high schools, and adopted by the public school society." Although "Americans count Longitude from the meridian running through New-York, Washington, or Philadelphia" and the "French count from the meridian of Paris, and the English from that of London or Greenwich," Hart instructed his youthful American audience to "Trace the meridian—and mention the longitude either East or West from that meridian used on your map" from Iceland and New York, using the "meridian of Greenwich."[179]

Geographies published in America during the postrevolutionary period contained a multitude of conflicting national perspectives. The editors of the American reprint of Goldsmith's geography provided regular extended footnotes throughout the text, ostensibly written by a "Senior Editor" who offered an American corrective to the opinions of the British author, a running commentary that supplied a counternarrative to Goldsmith's writing. Whereas Goldsmith provided a sweeping British imperial perspective on world geography, the American editors interspersed an increasingly localized view. Their interpolations moved from America to New England, Connecticut, and finally New Haven, and commented on subjects regularly covered in geographies, such as physical location and the state of manufactures. These revisions also described New York as the "first commercial city in the United States," and Pennsylvania as "one of the greatest manufacturing states in the union," due to the "Quakers (Friends) for their still, correct method of doing business, and for their peaceful, amiable deportment."[180] The Senior Editor then discussed the state of Connecticut vis-à-vis the rest of the world:

There is no position on the globe better situated than Connecticut for manufacturing, for internal industry:—No aid is wanted but the old standing policy of France, England & c. For this we must look to our general government,—and they must not forget that our soil is frozen half the year; that our day-light then lasts but 9 or 10 hours; that it can only be lengthened by torch-light;—and if torch-light is not required at home, it will be sought for at the tavern:—There is the grand theatre for politics and *flip*;—and if the government will not keep pace with the population,—there even the democrats will call for a "*King*—and 'overturn,' and 'overturn,' until 'he whose right it is shall reign.'"[181]

He concludes by explaining the local condition of the city of New Haven:

Until recently three-fifths of the town tax of New Haven was required to sustain the poor; but her paupers and silly gossips diminish as her manufactures increase. The narrow, contracted method of doing business in Connecticut is now yielding to more liberal views—So certain as the earth continues to roll on, there will be a canal from New Haven to Massachusetts—in less than 30 years, New Haven (excepting Boston,) will be the first town in New England.[182]

To substantiate his prediction about New Haven's eventual rise, the Senior Editor cited the amount of butter and cheese Connecticut exported. The American counternarrative expressed here emphasized the importance the citizenry placed on material objects as indicators of national development. The forecast of the United States' future productivity in this other American geographies was inspired by a need to insert the new nation into world geography and help it ascend to its proper place within the international community.

Closing the Gap: Americans in a Moral Geography

In addition to commerce and politics, geographies produced in this period also addressed questions of race, placing humanity on a continuum from savage to enlightened. Civility was gauged by factors such as Christian beliefs, levels of cultural achievement, and forms of governance.[183] Goldsmith declared that for his geography he gathered "copious accounts of the manners, customs, and curiosities of nations...and they contain every remarkable and entertaining fact, authentic anecdote, and interesting trait of national character, which is to be found in the most respectable books of voyages and travels, and in the voluminous works of modern geography."[184] Similarly, William Woodbridge's *Rudiments of Geography* (1822) presented readers with a "moral geography" in the visual form of a chart, a key at the bottom of the world map presented different symbols representing various levels of civilization.[185] Nations of the transatlantic world were labeled "Enlightened," at the top of the scale. Although the term was reserved for western European nations, the United States was granted membership in this exclusive club by the book's American author.

In these discussions, the recently formed United States occupied an unusual place. Based on European Enlightenment ideas but located in the wilderness, the new nation was inhabited by both transplanted European settlers and "savages."[186] Accordingly, there were some troubling aspects about the United States in the late eighteenth and early nineteenth centuries. Unlike older European nations, the United States was proximate to heathen natives, and was distant from centers of learning, arts, and culture. Therefore, American authors highlighted other characteristics, principally the new nation's republican form of government, which allowed people to choose their own leaders.[187] A representative form of government made up for the nation's lack of cultural and material development.

Americans in the postrevolutionary period hoped to maintain connections with Great Britain. They emphasized the growing number of routes between ports in America and Britain. "The increase of Liverpool," noted Zachariah Allen, "has nearly rivalled that of New-York. Between these two cities, the communication by numerous packet ships is almost as constant and unintermitted [*sic*], as between two neighboring villages."[188] Many texts from this period grappled with theories about the cultural significance of a nation's placement on a certain parallel of latitude. Some American authors believed that the United States was located at the same latitude as ancient civilizations, which would augur well for future cultural development. Other Americans, such as Allen, stressed that the "climates of the United States are colder than those of similar parallels of latitude in Europe." Despite the climate, the future of the United States looked bright: "This seemingly untoward circumstance may probably be considered a blessing; for it contributes to preserve a people industrious and virtuous, and capable of maintaining unimpaired their rights." Again, geographic links between the United States and Britain were emphasized: "Idleness and vice, being usually found in company, are becoming almost synonymous terms … and if the United States and England had the Italian climate … Their hardy yeomanry would be found relaxed and effeminate."[189] Writing as "the practical tourist," Allen was impressed by England, for although "No portion of the population of the globe enjoys more of the comforts and common luxuries of life, diffused throughout all ranks, than the inhabitants of New-England," the "stranger in England within a few hours of travel … is remarkably impressed with the spectacle of the wealth and resources of this little island."[190]

American authors attempted to close the gap between the new nation and Europe by emphasizing a shared Christianity. Their faith would both tie them to Britain and distance them from Asians, Africans, and other New World peoples. Woodbridge's "Definition of principal religions professed by mankind" described Christianity as the "true and holy religion professed by Europeans, and by most civilized nations in other quarters of world."[191] Christianity was linked with civility and enlightenment and contrasted with religious systems such as "Mahometanism." Believers "in the impostures of Mahomet," who "contrived to propagate religion by fire and sword" were said to make up a "considerable portion of [the] nations" of Asia and Africa.[192] At the extreme of the religious spectrum was "paganism or polytheism," in which "many savage nations to the present day" practiced the "most absurd superstitions, and worship idols and images of various kinds, as is fully described in many parts of this work."[193]

Whereas Americans and British, though physically distant, remained culturally tied to one another, Anglo-Americans and American Indians were physically close and culturally disparate. Manufacturing and the possession of polished material objects were important to the civilizing process. John Pershouse, for instance, notes: "The post road from Philadel[phi]a to Boston has the appearance of being as well clear'd & as thickly inhabited as most counties in England."[194] Manmade structures and manufactures distanced Anglo-Americans from the empty wilderness, the savages, and the savagery in their midst. Yet they feared, along with their fear of savagery, that overdevelopment and overcommercialization would lead to corruption and poverty. The belief that if a society became too civilized, its love of luxury would lead to eventual decay and decline. Pershouse wrote: "we are not constantly distress'd with the sight of groupes of poor emaciated ragged objects craving charity—the working people all appear to be well cloth'd & fed—it is very rare to see a battle or riot of any kind in the streets."[195] His comments are representative of the attitude that the nation could strike a balance between the two extremes: though it didn't have grand architecture and monuments, it was also free of poverty and class warfare—though this was not in fact true.[196]

Buying the Earth, but Not the Stars

On December 26, 1796, the president of the College of New Jersey, Samuel Stanhope Smith, sat down at his desk in Princeton, New Jersey, and composed a letter to Samuel Bayard in London regarding the purchase of twelve-inch globes for his students' use. Scholars of the day considered globes necessary for the instruction of even "the youngest student." With these models, they would be "enabled to comprehend the several real and apparent motions of the heavenly bodies, which, to persons unacquainted with these subjects either pass unnoticed, or are involved in inexplicable difficulties."[197] According to the prolific English author Benjamin Martin, objects such as globes and orreries (mechanical models of the solar system) were integral for instruction in chronology, astronomy, geography, and navigation, knowledge of which was considered primary "among those Qualities requisite for forming the Scholar and the Gentleman."[198]

Globes were sold in sets that included both terrestrial and celestial models representing the "earth and heavens...in a natural and striking manner."[199] The received wisdom was that the science of geography and astronomy were "so intimately connected" that, according to one British author, it would be "in vain to expect to acquire a complete knowledge of one without the other."[200] As he wrote this on a winter day in 1796, however, Smith could not afford both models. He implored Bayard to convince his merchant to split a set of globes to save on the expense: "if you can get six or eight terrestrial globes, without the accompaniment of the celestial, it will be much more useful and agreeable to us."[201] Smith's students would have to be content with sharing the one communal celestial globe already owned by the college. Smith justified his unusual request by writing that "as they are for students to *practice* [on] our large celestial globe in the college will be sufficient." Acknowledging that he was pushing the limits of acceptability, he conceded to Bayard, "if that is not practicable, let the four *pair* be sent."[202] Because the college was in need of so many other objects from London, Smith had to overcome his embarrassment. Although the school could afford to buy the Earth, they could not have the stars.

At the time Smith was writing to London, it was impossible to procure globes domestically; the first commercial American model did not appear until fourteen years later, when the farmer and blacksmith James Wilson, a resident of Londonderry, Vermont, offered his "New Terrestrial Globe" for sale to the public.[203] Living in a remote town far from the nearest American center of knowledge, much less European ones, Wilson had gleaned everything he knew about geography, cartography, engraving, and astronomy from the *Encyclopaedia Britannica*.

The first president of the United States of America was an ambitious colonial who lived on the margins of the British Empire and got his start in life as a surveyor contributing to the project of expanding the New World territory on behalf of the mother country. It is no surprise that Americans adopted such imperial forms of control as the charting and claiming of "uninhabited" territory in their attempts to bestow legitimacy on their ever-expanding nation. Mapmaking during the interstitial years between the colonial and postrevolutionary period was fraught with contradictions, as Americans tried to link themselves to the Old World while simultaneously constructing their nation as an independent entity.

Decades after their independence was won, Americans were disquieted by the fact that Europeans still thought of them as inhabiting a mysterious and uncivilized land. Americans expressed indignation about the old prejudices, stereotypes, and cartographic errors contained in British maps and geographies about North America. Cultural nationalists—the most famous being Jedidiah Morse—made efforts to solicit common people's (often erroneous) contributions in order to glean new information that he then integrated into the first published U.S. geographies.

These new narratives—subversive of the old order and attempting to establish a new one—were inserted into what were essentially reprints of British works. Geographies produced in the early republic are examples of unbecoming British in a rather sly and populist fashion. Another interesting aspect of the subversive American geographical narrative is that it immediately found other, less civilized groups around which to orient its assertion of civility, the South being one important example. Time and again, Americans' efforts to "unbecome" British simply replicated colonial hierarchies.

Well into the nineteenth century, Americans' lack of the technology and finances to make their own maps on a large scale prolonged their dependence on the British scholarly infrastructure to geographically define their nation. This dependence, particularly in something as freighted with symbolic meaning as a national geography, seemed unbecoming of a free people. Inspired to create a narrative of American national identity, citizens did so in many different ways and for many different audiences: from private consumption in the case of Mary M. Franklin's hand-sewn map to the widely publicized campaigns for geographic independence staged by Jedidiah Morse, and finally the national project of the Lewis and Clark expedition—a product of Thomas Jefferson's patriotism.[204] These Americans' creation of their "imagined community" (to use Benedict Anderson's term) served to feed a new form of patriotic consumerism—and is a clear example of their (sometimes unsuccessful) efforts at unbecoming British.

Patriotic consumerism would emerge as a central issue in the process of unbecoming British.[205] Geographic objects were among a dazzling array of items sent from Europe to North America. The eighteenth century was a time of both consumer and political revolutions, so it is no wonder that these sweeping movements influenced one another. Objects served as conduits for people's expression of political messages (homespun, tea), and political messages inspired new forms of objects to be created (textiles and ceramic decorated with maps and political prints). Material culture would be integral to the discussions and debates over the formation of new identities in the transatlantic world.

Two

A CULTURE OF INSECURITY

Americans in a Transatlantic World of Goods

> We must endeavor to forget our former Love for them [the British] and to
> hold them, as we hold the rest of Mankind, enemies in war, in Peace Friends.
>
> —Thomas Jefferson, "fragment of the composition draft of the Declaration
> of Independence (1776)

> It is not from a love of the English but a love of myself that I sometimes
> find myself obliged to buy their manufactures.
>
> —Thomas Jefferson, letter to Marquis de Lafayette (1786)

What's Love Got to Do With It? Postrevolutionary Americans' Desire for British Goods

In 1786 Thomas Jefferson, then minister plenipotentiary to France, wrote to
President John Adams's secretary in London asking for a favor. Jefferson
wanted William Smith to find him "a pair of chariot harness...plated, not
foppish but genteel, handsome without being tawdry." At the time, Jefferson
needed a special dispensation to bring these foreign goods into France.[1]
When the Marquis de Lafayette learned of this request, he wrote to Jefferson
and questioned his purchase of contraband items from England. Rather
than disregard the comment, or respond with humor, Jefferson became
defensive. He felt the need to explain his purchase and offered a painfully
earnest explanation, stressing his "reason" was "a very obvious one": the
French did not make plated harnesses "as far as I have learnt."[2] He then
made a weak jab at France's restrictions, noting that their diplomats in
America were allowed to purchase items from any country they pleased.

On his return from Europe, Jefferson entered the United States bearing eighty-six crates of goods and large debts. The spending habits of the founding fathers are not simply a matter of antiquarian interest.[3] The fact that this was a popular topic of discussion among Jefferson's contemporaries is indicative of the more profound political meanings people ascribed to an individual's purchasing habits. Jefferson's comments to the marquis reveal the links he made between purchases, national loyalty, and international alliances. "It is not from a love of the English but a love of myself that I sometimes find myself obliged to buy their manufactures," Jefferson wrote, in the same letter to Lafayette. His remarks highlight the cultural dilemma for Americans like him: consumers simultaneously coveted and repudiated British goods. To be sure, the same quandary can also be generally discerned in the new nation's relationship with its British identity. Jefferson's defensive reaction regarding his consumer choices betrayed an unbecoming insecurity and guilt about his deep desire to possess British goods.

To consume or not to consume British imports was the question on many Americans' minds, and the answer carried political meaning.[4] Cultural and material exchanges between the postrevolutionary United States and Great Britain were asymmetrical just as they had been in the colonial period. American elites continued to look to the Old World not only for refined goods but also for direction on how to use them.[5] And so while cultural and economic autonomy from the British was an ideal to which Americans aspired in the years following the Revolution, old templates of dependence remained in place long after the war ended.[6]

Traditionally, political histories of the United States have focused on the establishment of a new political system of governance; cultural shifts have been depicted as more gradual, subtle processes than the transition from monarchy to democracy. In this quest to document American life, the enduring aspects of America's colonial culture have been overlooked. For members of colonial settler societies like America, rebelling against the mother country required new citizens to repudiate membership in a club into which many of them had been fighting to gain admission.

For these colonial subjects, their geographic locations were powerfully linked—both economically and culturally—with the products they produced. The connection between America's unrefined, raw materials and the technologically advanced manufactures of a recently industrializing Britain further reinforced the perceived differences. There was a continuity in the trade patterns and types of objects being exchanged between North America and Britain both before and after the Revolution. One of the mechanisms powering the apparent contradiction between political proclamations of independence and the former colonials' unbecoming self-consciousness was the transatlantic exchange of objects. People on both sides of the Atlantic took advantage of relative differences in scarcity and abundance of goods as they moved objects from one location to another. Americans supplied raw materials to Britain that were converted there into manufactured goods the colonists later purchased (for instance, cotton grown in the southern American colonies was shipped to textile mills in Britain and returned to North America as finished cloth for colonial consumption).

When Anglo-American trade resumed after independence, the United States continued to export natural products to Great Britain as they had been doing for generations. What changed was their increased anxiety regarding their reliance on British manufactures. Despite the eagerness of leaders such as Alexander Hamilton to develop home manufactures in the 1780s and 1790s, Americans failed to produce competitive goods. As in the revolutionary conflict, trade restrictions leading up to the War of 1812 encouraged the growth of American industries. However, in the peace that followed the end of the war, British manufactured goods flooded the American market, and U.S. production was overwhelmed by the mother country's economic domination.

Exchanging Nature for Civility

> Why should that petty Island, which compar'd to America is but like a
> stepping Stone in a Brook, scarce enough of it above Water to keep one's
> Shoes dry; why, I say, should that little Island, enjoy in almost every
> Neighborhood, more sensible, virtuous and elegant Minds, than we can
> collect in ranging 100 Leagues of our vast Forests.
>
> —Benjamin Franklin (1763)

> [The colonists] ransack the seas and the wilds of America...to make
> payment for [British goods], and the improved lands are cultivated chiefly
> for the same purpose.
>
> —*The Power and Grandeur of Great-Britain* (1768)

Benjamin Franklin describes the land of his birth as a place with a dearth of refinement that is endowed with a plethora of natural resources. Others like him who possessed a cosmopolitan outlook were both self-conscious about America's roughness and proud of their local identity. Continuous immigration from the mother country further complicated the process of forming an American identity. Transplanted Englishman William Eddis expressed a viewpoint similar to Franklin's. Applying a positive gloss to the current state of American society, he conceded: "Though we are yet far behind the mother country with respect to cultivation and improvements," the Chesapeake, for instance, "affords a surprising variety of excellent fish.... Poultry and wild fowl abound [as well as] beef, mutton, pork and other provisions." If his environs were lacking in civility, at least his stomach was full.[7]

North Americans were enthusiastic participants in the quest for profits in which they traded foodstuffs and raw materials for the manufactured goods they desired. The 1768 pamphlet *The Power and Grandeur of Great-Britain* describes the nature of the rapidly expanding transatlantic trade.[8] As the quote in the epigraph notes, Americans raided the natural resources surrounding them in order to buy British goods.[9] Eddis, who had come to America in 1769, echoed this point when he observed: "To settle and to cultivate lands must be their [Americans'] first great object; and the produce of these exertions they must barter in exchange for European manufactures."[10] Extractive industries such as fishing, fur trapping, and forestry preceded agriculture as America's trade mainstay and remained important throughout the colonial period.[11]

London's monopoly of the East India trade secured its role as the center of the entrepôt (import and reexport) trade and thus ensured Britain's economic dominance. A myriad of export goods produced in locations scattered throughout Great Britain and the rest of its far-flung empire sat in huge warehouses before being shipped to distant locations within their vast trading network.[12] In North America, however, factory prices, market size, and more profitable alternatives to manufacturing inhibited the growth of American industries throughout the eighteenth century.[13] Surveying the situation in 1774, William Knox observed that colonists found it more profitable to "cultivate their lands and attend the fisheries than to manufacture."[14] American farmers boosted their productivity significantly by applying agricultural advancements developed in England and other parts of Europe.[15] Their surplus agricultural products were then sent to worldwide markets via the mother country in exchange for the purchase of more British goods.

The ideal colony did double duty in its contributions to the economic strength of the mother country by serving as suppliers of the raw materials and consumers of the goods made from them.[16] The production of manufactures increased throughout the eighteenth century, and they found a "readier market" in the colonies of North America and the East and West Indies than in other European nations.[17] Americans purchased "merchandize of an almost infinite variety, numberless useful and useless articles [that] are now yearly furnished to three millions of people." Thus as America's population increased, so would the power of Great Britain. In this way, as an observer noted, the "neglected outcast, has been the agrandizement [*sic*] of its parent; for with their increase, the British trade keeps pace."[18]

Commentators on both sides of the Atlantic noticed how the "quickening of the consumer market" pulled ordinary people into transatlantic networks of exchange and, by extension, a perspective that oriented them around British society. In the years leading up to the Revolution, increasing numbers of ordinary Americans were able to purchase imported goods formerly reserved for the wealthy, such as tea and chinaware.[19] The increase in consumer demand was accompanied by (some would say a result of) the growing array of goods on the market.[20] Americans—rich and poor, Anglophile and Anglophobe—relied on imported goods to conduct their daily lives. Merchants' advertisements of goods newly arrived from Britain dominated colonial newspapers from Boston to Charleston.[21]

While proponents of domestic manufactures made the argument that the items purchased from Britain consisted primarily of easily forsaken, superfluous trifles and gewgaws, this was not the case. British merchants supplied necessities such as woolens, cottons, cutlery, tools, and pottery in a quantity and quality that was unmatched in the domestic market.[22] In a 1769 appeal for home manufactures, Benjamin Rush argued that North America's ample resources alone could challenge British economic dominance: "There is scarce a necessary article or even a luxury of life but what might be raised and brought to perfection in some of our provinces.... Mulberry trees are so plenty among us that we might raise silkworms in a few years to supply us with all the silks we want, as oak leaves (when those of the mulberry are not to be had) have been found in China to afford a food to the worms."[23] Despite Rush's boasts, the iconic eighteenth-century American yeoman farmer most likely wore clothes cut from imported textiles and drank Chinese tea from an imported cup before taking up British tools and using updated agricultural methods developed in Europe.

For large-scale manufacturing to succeed in America, many things were required, including technological expertise, large amounts of capital, and cheap labor, all of which were lacking in the eighteenth and early to mid-nineteenth centuries.[24] As Eddis observed in 1773, "[a]t present, it is evident that almost every article of use or ornament is to be obtained on much more reasonable terms from the mother country than from artisans settled on this side of the Atlantic."[25] To produce commercially even a simple piece of porcelain required expertise as well as a large outlay of capital to build and equip the pottery factory. Because of these restraints, Americans would not be able to compete successfully in the large-scale manufacture of refined tableware until the twentieth century.

A few entrepreneurs attempted to start pottery manufactories in reaction to the restrictive measures passed in Britain. On September 5, 1771, a piece in the *Pennsylvania Gazette* announced Gousse Bonnin and George Anthony Morris's plans to open a "China Manufactory." Offering "both Wholesale and Retail" trade, the factory would sell a "general Assortment of AMERICAN CHINA."[26] A month earlier, an anonymous "Pennsylvania Planter" (in fact, Bonnin himself) had published a broadside stressing the need for domestic manufacturers. Addressed "To the Public," it linked the opening of the manufactory to the health of the body politic. Like other early American ventures, this private commercial enterprise would be presented as a public contribution to the "Honour of Pennsylvania" worthy of support by the "Friends of Liberty." The author listed numerous accomplishments of his compatriots, including those in the "liberal Arts and Sciences" that "would have done credit to any State in Europe." These achievements were all the more impressive, the author argued, as Pennsylvania was "an infant Colony, scarcely risen One Hundred Years from the rude Vestiges of Nature."[27]

The Pennsylvania Planter hails Bonnin and Morris's American China Manufactory—founded after the abrogation of the Townshend Acts of 1767, which asserted Parliament's right to tax the colonies for a variety of imported goods—as a patriotic enterprise. It will counter "our Mother Country['s]" conviction that "she has a Right to manufacture every Article we consume...our very Drink is to come through her Hands, or pay to her Support." The Pennsylvania Planter connects the "salutary Influence of our Laws, and the perfect liberty which we enjoy" to the material development of the nation, for "Liberty, in every Region is the genuine Parent of Industry and Learning." Domestic manufactures were considered crucial to a society greatly in need of "saving Cash...else we shall soon be a ruined People [whose] Property will be transferred to the other side of the Atlantic."[28]

Citizens of the United States celebrated the American China Manufactory's creations as proof of the nation's growing independence from Great Britain (see figure 2.1). Yet despite their production in Philadelphia, Bonnin and Morris's pieces revealed mixed cultural and artistic parentage: they depended on the recruitment of European artisans, many of whom were loathe to relocate to the colonies. To convince these skilled artisans to come to America, the owners paid for their passage and promised them lucrative wages.[29]

America's dependence on foreigners was a result of its taste for imported luxury items. Registering mild disapproval but also resignation, the Pennsylvania Planter declared in his broadside:

Figure 2.1 Soft-paste porcelain basket (6.4 x 9.4 cm) manufactured by the American China Manufactory, formerly known as Bonnin and Morris (Philadelphia, Pennsylvania, c. 1770–1772). This is one of the earliest examples of American-made porcelain. Producing fine earthenware was very costly and entailed complicated technological processes. Throughout the colonial period and for the first half of the nineteenth century, American consumers who desired porcelain had to rely on imports from Europe and Asia. This piece is made to resemble those produced in England that in turn were imitative of the styles of Chinese export porcelain. Like other fledgling American manufacturers the American China Manufactory enjoyed a boost from the anti-importation movement. However, they were ultimately unable to compete with more well-established European ceramics manufacturers. The doors of the factory closed for good in 1773 after two years of operation. *(Yale University Art Gallery)*

I would not have it supposed, that Happiness is naturally connected with China Ware, or even with Tea, its general Attendant; I sincerely wish they were both, with all their concomitant Plagues, in the Bottom of the Red sea; but we must consider Matters as they are, and try to make the best of them, rather than hope for a perfect Revolution. The Use of China is introduced, and well established; Custom has rendered it some how necessary; we must and will have it, whatever be the Consequence.[30]

When it opened, Bonnin and Morris's manufactory won the attention of prominent Philadelphians, including Benjamin Rush, Thomas Wharton, and John Cadwalader. Local scientific organizations such as the American Philosophical Society and the Library Company of Philadelphia took interest in the project as well. Deborah Franklin sent her husband samples from the factory, which stood out as the only manufactured good amongst a quintessential offering of American foodstuffs, including "Buckwheat & Indian Meal," which arrived "safe & good;" "dry'd Peaches," and apples that he described as "the best I ever had."[31] Franklin thanked her for them in his January 28, 1772, letter from London, in which he indicated that he was "pleased to find so good a Progress made in the China Manufactory" and wished it "Success most heartily."[32] Despite his and other Americans' enthusiasm, by November 1773 he was writing about the factory's demise.

Several factors contributed to Bonnin and Morris's failure, prominent among them their inability to compete with European imports. The American China Manufactory's potential for success required large numbers of patriotic customers, who would be expected to override their interests as consumers for the greater good of American manufacturing. As Bonnin's broadside asserted: "if we do not encourage imperfect Works, we shall never get perfect Ones." It also criticized the author's neighbor, an émigré to America, "rocked in the very Cradle of Despotism," for his lukewarm patriotism. Although he purported to "prefer Home Manufactures to Foreign," this neighbor would nevertheless buy American products only if they were "were equal in Quality and Price; until that Time, he counts it his Duty to buy at the cheapest Shop." Admitting that the quality of the domestic products had not yet reached the level of its British rivals, Bonnin warned that "by purchasing pretty and cheap foreign Manufactures, we shall, in a little Time, have nothing left wherewith to buy Goods of any Kind."[33] This sentiment was echoed by Joseph Shippen, Jr., the secretary of the Provincial Council, after a visit to Bonnin and Morris's Southwark Street factory:

> This china is in general esteemed preferable to that made in England, as to its fineness, or quality; but as yet it has rather too yellowish a cast, owing to the want of a particular ingredient used in the composition for glazing; which could not hitherto be imported from England on account of the Non-Importation agreement; but the owners of the factory expect a quantity of that article in the first spring vessels; and then they are in hopes of making a great improvement in that particular.[34]

The repeal of the Townshend Acts before the American China Manufactory opened had removed the financial incentive for American consumers to buy domestic goods. Difficulties luring foreign workers to America also contributed to the eventual failure of the enterprise; British law prohibited the immigration of skilled workers. Speaking to an audience of Staffordshire potters after the Revolutionary War, English pottery manufacturer Josiah Wedgwood expressed pleasure in the fact that his New World rivals had failed. He informed his listeners that Bonnin and Morris had closed down, having "had no chance of succeeding" in the first place.[35] The public sale of the "whole of the buildings" was announced on May 5,

1773, in the pages of the same newspaper that had trumpeted the opening of the American China Manufactory just two years earlier.[36]

Americans did have a long-standing tradition of producing simple red earthenware. A craftsman, working perhaps with an assistant, used the same traditional techniques—unchanged during the colonial and early national period—to produce this type of everyday object. Small-scale local production was possible because locally sourced red clay was used. Unlike more durable (and fashionable) types of pottery, redware did not require expensive firing equipment.[37] But this ware, while functional and widely used, was neither as refined nor as durable as imported pieces (see figures 2.2 and 2.3).

Figure 2.2

Figures 2.2 and 2.3 The majority of pottery produced in America consisted of simple earthenware crockery made from locally available materials such as this piece of redware. The British Parliament allowed colonials to make such items because it was not profitable enough for their manufacturers to make these types of goods for export. American potters were usually amateurs who made items for their own use. For example, farmers would make pottery for use in their own households during seasons that were less busy. Although both of these pieces commemorate Lafayette's second visit to the United States in 1824, the level of technological sophistication they reflect vary widely. The simpler redware plate was handmade in America, while the blue and white transferware pieces were imported from Britain. By this date, the turnaround time for a piece of commemorative porcelain was very quick, so consumers were able to buy these pieces shortly after the event occurred. *(Winterthur Museum & Country Estate)*

In a similar way, the fledgling American textile industry catered to down market goods such as a rough material commonly known as "slave cloth," which, as its name indicates, was used to clothe slaves in the American South and the plantations of the West Indies. Despite what he described as Americans' access to "infinite" natural resources, Eddis doubted that they would ever be able to produce textiles "of a superior quality." He did concede that they "may probably be enabled to manufacture" the "coarse cloths for the wear of servants and negroes."[38] Similarly, American producers also made other utilitarian items such as vessels for use in the chamber, kitchen, and pantry that were not worth the cost of importing from Britain.

Fabrics in a wide array of types and quality constituted half of all British imports to America and an even higher percentage of the goods sent from colonial port cities to the countryside for retail.[39] Cloth purchased from British merchants was more readily available than domestically produced textiles throughout the eighteenth and early nineteenth centuries.[40] Contrary to the romantic notion of American women at their spinning wheels, most were not producing their own wool and flax or making their own cloth at this time.[41] The figures for American consumption of imported linen, the "utility fabric of the period," are illuminating: almost six and a half million yards of plain linens were exported from Great Britain and Ireland between 1769 and January 1772.[42] The variety of linen ranged from coarse, unbleached osnaburg, which covered the backs of laborers, to fine, bleached fabric decorated with mother-of-pearl buttons and silk cross-stitching that required reapplication after each wash.[43] British woolens, which were well-protected commodities, arrived in America in great quantities and a wide variety of qualities. The objects made from them ranged from fine worsted damask for ball gowns to rough fabrics used for slave blankets and winter clothing.[44]

Material dependence on imported British goods fostered a larger, pan-regional culture; the residents of distant colonies looked alike because they all purchased fabric from Britain. Whether toiling in Maryland, the Carolinas, or, later, in Mississippi and Georgia, slaves were clothed in the same inexpensive Welsh woolens.[45] The wealthy were drawn together by a common thread, as dresses made of the same imported damask silk were worn by women in New York and Delaware.[46] Silk manufactured thousands of miles away drew Americans together along class lines in a way that cloth made from their own hands could not. In a world of expanding consumer choices, the fabrics people wore and the beverages they drank played an increasingly important role in establishing their identities. Shopkeepers carried an extensive array of fabrics including "broad-cloths, serges, camlets, ozenbrigs, cotton checks, damasks, calicoes, cambricks, sattins, taffeties, [and] highland plads [sic]."[47] As the eighteenth century progressed, colonials could buy the same textiles as English consumers soon after they were produced. Yet they did not control their own consumer destinies. Regardless of the vast array of objects available on the market, they could only legally obtain the goods that the British navigation acts permitted.

Britain's economic strategies, guided by mercantile principles, encouraged colonial dependence on imported goods and worked in tandem with American consumers' preferences for imports. If price and availability were key factors influencing Americans' buying habits, another was the social meaning ascribed to both domestic and imported goods. As in other satellite societies, the "allure of the foreign" drew customers, serving as an indicator of civility and refinement. While this shared consumer culture encouraged the development of a common transatlantic identity, it also reinforced an asymmetrical relationship between Great Britain and the United States.[48] When visiting Europeans saw a familiar British object being used by an American consumer, it sparked recognition but also produced a feeling that the dainty porcelain cup or gilt mirror was somehow "out of context" in a frontier home—much in the same way

North American colonial elites viewed European objects in Indian settlements. Did this perspective in either case help bring disparate people together or did the seeming incongruity separate them further, opening the door for ridicule?

Benjamin Franklin's Paradox

When I read the advertisements in our papers of imported goods for Sale—I think of the Speech of a philosopher upon walking thro' a fair "how happy am I that I want none of these things."

—Benjamin Rush, quoting Benjamin Franklin (1788)

Being Call'd one Morning to Breakfast, I found it in a China Bowl with a Spoon of Silver. They had been bought for me … by my Wife, and had cost her the enormous sum … she had no other Excuse or Apology to make, but that she thought *her* Husband deserv'd a Silver Spoon & China Bowl as well as any of his Neighbors.

—Benjamin Franklin, *Autobiography* (1793)

A public proponent of simple living and abstemious habits, Benjamin Franklin spoke out against his fellow colonists' insatiable desire for foreign imports, noting disapprovingly that the "greatest part of the trade of the world was carried on for Luxuries most of which were really injurious to health or Society—such as <u>tea tobacco</u>—<u>Rum</u>—<u>Sugar</u>—and <u>negro Slavaes</u> [*sic*]."[49] Yet he also found himself taken in by temptation. While advocating abstemiousness and vegetarianism, Franklin partook heartily in the joys of rich continental cooking while traveling abroad.[50] Even as he linked habits of consumption to independence, Franklin, like other Americans, was aware of the nation's contradictory behavior, unable to remove himself from a transatlantic cultural system that he both critiqued and inhabited.[51]

And so it was that silver and china ended up on Benjamin Franklin's breakfast table, despite his negative views of these fine objects and his public disapproval of their effects on American society. In his *Autobiography*, first published in 1793, he warned readers to "mark how Luxury will enter Families, and make a Progress, in *Spite of Principle*."[52] This statement acknowledged the impossibility of preventing the march of such items into the inner sanctum of the home. Franklin provided a detailed description of his family's belongings prior to the intrusion of luxury, noting how his "Table was plain & simple," his " Furniture the cheapest," and his "Breakfast was a long time bread & Milk (no Tea,) and I ate it out of a twopenny earthen Porringer with a Pewter Spoon." Yet over time, these simple items were replaced by Deborah. The acquisition of pricey imported objects was coupled with an increase in socioeconomic standing, and the amount of possessions one acquired grew with one's success. The china bowl was "the first Appearance of Plate & China in our House, which afterward in a Course of Years as our Wealth encreas'd, augmented gradually to several Hundred Pounds in Value."[53] Nevertheless, it was Deborah, not Benjamin, who had purchased the first commercially available domestic porcelains, a sauceboat from the short-lived firm of Bonnin and Morris.[54] But on a larger scale, the accumulation of fine goods could be seen as proof of a society's progress along the scale of refinement and civility.

*A*lthough Franklin blamed his wife for purchasing the luxury imports, he, too, purchased expensive British wares for his Philadelphia home.[55] During a 1758 trip to London, Franklin sent Deborah various and sundry items, including fabrics for gowns, tablecloths, curtain fabrics, candle snuffers, coffee cups, table china, and silver cutlery.[56] Expressing his conflicted attitude to such goods, Franklin declared the four silver salt ladles he bought to be of the "newest, but ugliest fashion."[57] His flippant comment nonetheless reveals how he and other American consumers often made choices based on the mandates of European fashion rather than on their personal taste.

Once he had given in to these luxury items, Franklin registered concern about his wife's ability to use and display them correctly. Ignorance often led Americans to commit many a faux pas; inadvertently going against the dictates of fashion was a common pitfall for provincial consumers and was often pointed out by European observers.[58] To avoid this indignity, Franklin included detailed directions to his wife explaining, for instance, the exact procedure for attaching borders to the British carpets he had sent. He stressed that care should be taken to "make the figures meet exactly."[59] Deborah also received instructions about the correct use of an imported candlesnuffer that Franklin noted was "a new contrivance" made exclusively for spermaceti candles. His elaborate explanations indicate that these goods were not yet common in America.

The tension in Franklin's correspondence illustrates the competing desires to exhibit both gentility and simplicity through possessions. At odds with the critique of luxury that also existed in American society, the "rise of the genteel" influenced the development of the new nation's culture into the nineteenth century.[60]

What motivated American men and women to live their lives in a quest for, as Samuel Adams carped to one correspondent, the "baubles of Britain"?[61] For Adam Smith, when people went about "bettering" their condition, their actions went beyond the physical comforts or economic value provided by these items: "It is the vanity, not the ease, or the pleasure which interests us."[62] American consumers, cognizant of the vast distances separating them from European arbiters of taste, hoped that high culture could be conveniently packaged for transport across the Atlantic in the form of refined objects. As such, imported objects such as teacups, mahogany tables, punch bowls, and looking glasses, as well as the social rituals built around their proper use embodied cultural and social value. These objects drew North America closer to the mother country.[63] Each acquisition of an imported painting and each staging of a European play indicated the progress not merely of the individual purchaser of these commodities but of American society as a whole.[64]

Progress thus was linked to consumption. Early Americans could derive comfort from the widely held faith in the western migration of civilization. This widespread belief in the migration of the arts and high culture was expressed in the Renaissance concept of what was called *translatio studii*, or the "theory of translation."[65] Beginning in Eden, the march of civility supposedly matched the movement of the sun across the sky: to Jerusalem and Babylon and thence to Athens, Rome, Paris, Amsterdam, and London. This idea was losing popularity in Europe, but like the out-of-date goods the colonists purchased from abroad, it retained popularity in America.[66] "[T]raveling from east to west," as Jedidiah Morse elucidated in the 1793 edition of his *American Universal Geography*, the imperial march of occidental culture's "last and broadest seat will be America. Here the sciences and the arts of civilized life are to receive their highest improvements."[67] For men like Franklin, too, this glory was destined for America: "'tis said, the Arts delight to travel Westward. You [Great Britain] have effectually [*sic*] defended us in this glorious [French and Indian] War, and in time you will improve us."[68] Or as John Adams explained to Benjamin Rush: "There is nothing…more ancient in my memory than the observation that arts, sciences, and empire had travelled westward; and in conversation it was always added since I was a child, that their next leap would be over the Atlantic into America."[69] The tutelage of England was a necessary component to the plan. This hope for a transatlantic migration of arts and culture begins to explain why many Americans placed a premium on the ownership of refined objects. Beyond their use and trade value, these goods fulfilled the promise of civility and the development of high culture in the distant colonies. Indeed, even the Englishman Eddis attributed the sharp rise in consumer demand for British goods to the project of civilizing the frontiers.[70] More and more goods were imported from Britain in order to "supply the real and imaginary necessities" of Americans, who were engaged in transforming "uncultivated tracts" into "flourishing establishments."[71] (See figures 2.4 and 2.5.)

Far from an abstract theory, this belief in the westward migration of civilization imbued even the most prosaic objects and events—the widening of a town's lane, an additional wharf erected on the shore, or an American publication of Cicero's *Cato Major*—with an optimistic message that cele-

Figure 2.4 "Liberty Displaying the Arts and Sciences," painting by Samuel Jennings (1792). Like many of the people and objects discussed in this book, this painting has transatlantic origins. The artist, a native of Philadelphia, was living in London when he painted it for the Library Company of Philadelphia. It is believed to be the first antislavery painting by an American artist. Many of the Company's directors were Quakers who were involved in the Abolition Society. They requested that broken chains be placed under Liberty's feet. The painting also illustrates the notion of *translatio studii,* or the inevitable westward movement of learning and civilization. Americans hoped they would be the next society to enjoy the supposed dawning of learning. The scene includes symbols representing painting, architecture, mechanics, and astronomy. The books Liberty is placing on the pedestal in front of her refer to, among other things, agriculture, commerce, and philosophy. *(Library Company of Philadelphia)*

brated the progress of American civilization.[72] Franklin called the appearance of Cicero's work a "happy Omen, that Philadelphia shall become the Seat of the American Muses."[73] When newspapers and transatlantic letter writers reported that the "light of Athens" or the "advent 'rous [*sic*] Muse" had reached colonial Philadelphia or Charleston, they were referring to everyday happenings such as the opening of a hospital or the publication in Britain of a fellow colonial's poems. Foreign critics often commented on Americans' tendency toward hyperbole and boastfulness.[74]

The availability of a wide variety of British goods inspired optimism about the prospects of America's cultural improvement, and ships carrying the latest news and goods were welcome sights. As one observer noted: "Already ... it is really possible to obtain all the things one can get in Europe in Pennsylvania, since so many merchant ships arrive there every year."[75] Yet ignorance of the latest fashions, paired with material and social dependence on British goods, exposed American insecurity. Americans' anxiety was often revealed in the exhaustive level of detail in their letters to English contacts. The partners of the transatlantic firm of Wallace, Davidson & Johnson, for instance, fretted over the risks of trying to sell high-priced silks, fancy cottons, and woolens to ignorant American customers. Johnson expressed concern whether "what was 'fashionable' in London would be recognized as such in M[aryland]D."[76] He went to great pains to communicate his business acumen to his doubting partners back home in America, writing in another letter: "I have sent all the books ordered by Miss Bordley, Miss Turner and Mr. Love. They are packed special and marked on them. I am in hopes our millinery will please; many of the things are very cheap and very fashionable."[77] He conceded in one letter that the firm's competitors for the Annapolis trade would in all likelihood beat him in delivering "more quantities of supplies" earlier in the year. He counted on his taste to make up for what he lacked in speed: "I trust that we shall have one advantage, our goods being better in quality, more fashionable and better chosen they must [be], from my having time and seeing them myself, whereas those shipped by the merchants are never seen by them but hurried up as quick as may be."[78]

Transatlantic merchants served as middlemen who translated the needs and desires of their American customers into material form whenever they chose an object for their clients. Well into the nineteenth century, Americans relied on English contacts to provide expert guidance to procure fashionable goods. It was common for American printers and booksellers who sold imported prints to rely on British dealers to decide what was sent across to them. The English publisher Robert Sayers supplied eager customers in Boston, New York, Williamsburg, Philadelphia, and Charleston. For the most part, the images that found their way to America were the reflection not of colonial tastes but of what London dealers chose to send to them. The most popular prints depicted various aspects of life in Britain rather than local scenes. Landscapes of England and Scotland, "heads" of English celebrities such as Laurence Sterne and David Garrick, and engravings of the English royal family adorned American walls.[79] Shared tastes in print and material culture created an imagined community that drew provincials into the larger circle of cosmopolitan tastes.[80]

Like merchants, skilled artisans and artists were in the business of converting abstract desires into concrete objects. Another way American consumers strengthened their links to their mother country and, by implication, strengthened their own claims to civility was to commission local

Figure 2.5 "Liberty In the form of the Goddess of Youth, giving Support to the Bald Eagle," stipple engraving printed in colors by Edward Savage (1796). In this image, the American artist Edward Savage (1761–1817) depicted the classical figure of Columbia in the guise of Liberty. Since the beginning of the eighteenth century, Columbia was used to represent the British North American colonies; during the Revolutionary conflict, this image was adopted by American patriots as a symbol for the emerging nation. In this composition Columbia is surrounded by an array of national symbols including an American flag, the bald eagle, and a liberty cap. She tramples the symbols of monarchical tyranny—a medal and garter of a royal order, shackles, and the key to the Bastille—under her feet. Lending a sense of historical context to the picture, Savage places the figure in front of Boston Harbor during the evacuation of the British fleet. This image was reproduced in prints, needlework compositions, and reverse glass paintings by American, English, and Chinese artists. *(Yale University Art Gallery)*

artisans to create items that emulated British fashions. In John Singleton Copley's 1768 painting of silversmith Paul Revere, the future American patriot sits behind a polished mahogany table wearing a crisp white linen shirt and blue waistcoat of wool or matte silk adorned with two gold buttons of the type made in his own shop—the idealized colonial gentleman at work.[81] Scattered in front of the successful artisan are burins and a needle, tools used by silversmiths to decorate finished pieces (see figure 2.6).[82]

With chin resting contemplatively in hand, Revere cradles a gleaming, globular teapot about to be embellished with a wealthy colonial patron's coat of arms.[83] This teapot, made in the British tradition but crafted by the

Figure 2.6 "Portrait of Paul Revere," painting by John Singleton Copley (c. 1768–1770), oil on canvas, 89 x 72 cm. Paul Revere celebrated his identity as a silversmith rather than a member of the colonial elite. John Singleton Copley's painting of Paul Revere seems to capture his political identity by portraying him in shirtsleeves surrounded by the tools of his trade. Yet the visual message conveyed by *Revere* is not as straightforward as it would seem. Revere's shirt is made of high-quality linen cloth and is adorned with ruffled sleeves. Furthermore, the very act of having one's portrait executed separated him from the common man. *(Museum of Fine Arts, Boston)*

Bostonian's skilled hands, rests at the center of the composition, signaling the importance of European culture in America. The portrait is the only completed one by Copley to depict an artisan dressed in a casual (yet still refined) manner with the tools of his trade.[84] Both the teapot and the portrait, and indeed American identity itself, proudly bore the mark of British influence, while expressing a distinctive local character.

Portraiture exhibited people's self-conscious construction of their identities.[85] That Revere was captured holding a teapot he was preparing to decorate with a heraldic motif may strike a discordant note. After all, due in part to Revere's role in the revolutionary protests, tea became a symbol of British oppression. Indeed, the event that later became known as the Boston Tea Party forged a strong connection between tea and unrest in popular memory. This foundational moment in American history, played out on the stage of a rapidly expanding consumer society, would touch the lives of both the artist and his subject in very different ways: Revere was one of the organizers of the protest, while Copley's father-in-law, Richard Clarke, owned the tea that protesting colonists dumped into Boston Harbor.[86]

Although they found themselves on opposite sides of the political divide, Copley and Revere shared commonalities linking them to material life in the colonies. Born of humble origins as sons of immigrants, both improved their social standing by creating valuable objects for customers intent on emulating the trends of the mother country.[87] Before the loyalist beliefs of Copley's in-laws forced him to leave for Britain in 1774, he made his living painting colonial clients amid imported fashionable possessions such as books, calico, chintz, damask, ribbons, lace, and buckles.[88] His extensive oeuvre may be read as a richly illustrated catalog of the imported goods that were an integral part of elite colonial society.[89] These fashionable objects were invaluable to those living on the periphery of the transatlantic world. For them, these imported possessions marked their prosperity amid the rough environs of America.

During the period of conflict that began in the mid-eighteenth century, protest organizers politicized the consumption of British goods—everything from textiles to china vases and tea—by linking unfair trade practices and dependence on British goods with the suppression of liberty. The decade prior to the Revolutionary War reflected the increasing politicization of everyday objects, as evinced by the strategies the colonists employed, including nonimportation movements, embargoes, and domestic anti-consumption campaigns.[90] While Americans boycotted many British items such as paint, paper, and lead, the commodity that is most heavily laden with political significance is most certainly tea. During the eighteenth century,

Americans consumed the same if not more tea per capita than their British brethren. In fact, it was their continuing fondness for tea that made the decision to forsake it such a powerful political statement. An article appearing in a Boston paper in 1768 dramatically described it as dangerous "bait" meant to "allure us [American colonists] to their snare." The author proclaimed, "TEA! [H]ow I shudder at thy fatal-Stream!" and warned his compatriots not to risk even a single "Right of a British Subject" for the "evil weed."[91]

Tempest in a Teapot: Politics and Material Culture during the Revolution

> Long did I endeavour with unfeigned and unwearied Zeal, to preserve from breaking, that fine and noble China Vase the British Empire: for I knew that being once broken, the separate Parts could not retain even their Share of the Strength or Value that existed in the Whole, and that a perfect Re-Union of those Parts could scarce even be hoped for.
>
> —Benjamin Franklin to Lord Howe (July 20, 1776)

For at least a decade, trouble had been brewing between American colonists and the British Empire.[92] On the evening of December 16, 1773, Samuel Adams convened a meeting at the Old South Church, where he informed the five thousand people present of Governor Thomas Hutchinson's insistence on landing the British East India Company's ship *Dartmouth* in their midst.[93] The ship was the first to arrive in Boston Harbor after the institution of new regulations. According to the provisions of the Tea Tax passed that same year, duties would be levied on the ship's cargo of tea within twenty days; if unpaid, the ship's freight would be seized from the captain, claimed by the Company's agents, and forcibly placed on sale. Leaders such as Samuel Adams and John Hancock had tried to persuade customs officers to send the ship back without unloading the tea, but their pleas had been met with Governor Hutchinson's refusal. Adams dramatically proclaimed, "This meeting can do no more to save the country." The same evening, fifty young men from prominent local families disguised themselves as Indians, let out a few war whoops, and headed for Griffin's wharf, followed by a growing crowd.[94] They heaved forty-five tons of tea contained in 342 chests, worth 10,000 pounds sterling, into the cold waters of the Atlantic. Thousands lined the waterfront to witness the rebels breaking open the wooden chests of imported tea leaves (see figure 2.7).[95]

The incident in Boston Harbor illustrates the politicization of consumer goods during the revolutionary crisis and in the years following independence.[96] Americans were taken aback by Britain's series of new taxes and stricter regulatory practices. These represented a radical departure from previous times, in which British officials for the most part had turned

Figure 2.7 Engraving originally captioned "Die Einwohner von Boston werfen den englisch-
ostindischen Thee ins Meer am 18 December 1773." [The inhabitants of Boston throw the English-East
Indian tea into the sea on 18 December 1773.] The illustration was published in M. C. [Matthias
Christian] Sprengel (1746–1803), *Allgemeines historisches Taschenbuch, oder, Abriss der merkwürdigsten
neuen Welt-Begebenheiten: enthaltend für 1784 die Geschichte der Revolution von Nord-America*
[A general history, or, Survey of the most curious New World events: containing for 1784 the history of
the revolution of North America.] (Berlin: Haude und Spener, [1783]). Sprengel was a professor of
history at Halle University when he wrote this book. *(From a copy in Beinecke Rare Book & Manuscript
Library, Yale University Library)*

a blind eye to their infractions.[97] The decision to dump the precious cargo
overboard revealed the symbolic weight the consumption (and destruction) of British goods then carried. Despite the rhetoric espoused by the
patriots claiming that they despised the "pernicious weed," the gesture
would have been hollow had tea not been a vital part of their culture. By

the mid-eighteenth century, after British merchants had secured a steady supply of tea (which lowered its price), the habit of tea drinking was adopted by the lower classes (see figure 2.8).[98] The "lesser sort" drank less costly tea out of the inexpensive blue and white porcelain that was sent to America as ballast in the ship's hold. On transatlantic voyages, light tea and heavy porcelain literally counterbalanced one another.

At the time of the protest, Americans were said to consume more than a million pounds of tea each year, yet only one-quarter of that amount was purchased legally from the British East India Company. To a large extent, Americans were drinking tea smuggled from other locations such as the Netherlands. Owing to its importance to the British economy, Parliament attempted to bail the Company out of its financial woes by passing the Tea

Figure 2.8 "The Quilting Frolic" (1813), painting by John Lewis Krimmel (American, born in Germany, 1786–1821), oil on canvas, 42.5 x 56.5 cm. Trained in Stuttgart and London, the artist immigrated in 1809 to Philadelphia, where he was active until his death in 1821. This painting illustrates the expansion of the transatlantic world of goods. Imported objects such as the tea set seen here (being carried by an African-American girl) were not restricted to the elite in American society. This image of frontier life also shows how objects infiltrated the remote regions of the nation. Archeological digs have also unearthed the fact that Native Americans used objects such as imported tea cups. (*Winterthur Museum & Country Estate*)

Act. The legislation lowered the price of tea sold to America and eliminated all taxes on tea save for a minimal tariff of 3 pence called the
Townshend tax. British lawmakers assumed that Americans' economic
self-interest and fondness for tea would prevail. Economist Adam Smith
reasoned the taxes would not be "very hurtful to the colonies," because
"land is still so cheap, and consequently, labour so dear among them that
they can import from the mother country, almost all the more refined or
more advanced manufactures cheaper than they could make them for
themselves."[99] But to the Americans who joined the protest movement and
formed the intercolonial Committees of Correspondence, the Tea Act
threatened the very foundation of representative government. Americans
faced a dilemma: in order to satisfy their craving for imported luxuries,
they would have to accept the right of the British Parliament to levy direct
taxes on them.[100] Given the colonists' "passion" for the "evil weed," the
events at Boston Harbor and earlier resolutions to "discard from our houses
that most pernicious article of Luxury, Tea," rendered the political protest
even more powerful.[101] As Benjamin Rush exhorted: "As for bohea and
green tea, let them be banished forever from our tables and buffets: a bowl
of sage and baum tea is worth an ocean of both of them."[102] The revolutionary break from Britain occurred as the material world of colonial
Americans was at the height of its Anglicization.[103]

A lawyer by training, John Adams creatively interpreted the nonconsumption agreement when he asked a woman whether as "a weary traveler," he
would be allowed to "refresh himself with a dish of tea, provided it has been
honestly smuggled, or paid no duties?" According to Adams, the woman, who
possessed a much stricter interpretation of the principle of eschewing British
goods, answered: "No, sir ... we have renounced all tea in this place, but I'll make
you coffee." When recounting the story to his wife in a letter, Adams admitted
he was contrite: "Accordingly I have drank coffee every afternoon since, and
have borne it very well. Tea must be universally renounced, and I must be
weaned, and the sooner the better."[104] The effort by American patriots to "wean"
themselves of their dependence on British goods was not easy.

Although tea became a symbol of America's oppression (see figure 2.9),
it remained a coveted commodity for patriots and loyalists alike. Four years
after the events at Boston harbor, a hidden cache of tea, probably belonging
to "a great Villian Fled to New York," was discovered in Paramus, New Jersey,
by American troops in the midst of battle. Their commanding officer,
General Nathaniel Heard, said that "the party who found it ... seems to think
they are intitled [sic] to the benifit [sic] of it," but Heard forbade "their making use of any of it." After mulling the matter over for ten days, he decided

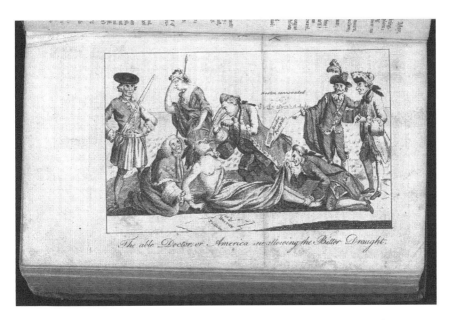

Figure 2.9 "The able Doctor or America Swallowing the Bitter Draught" (1774). This satirical print created by an anonymous artist illustrates in a literal manner the politics of consumption in the revolutionary conflict. Here a scantily clad Native American woman, who represents the British North American colonies, is forced by the British to swallow a scalding pot of tea, while other Europeans look on and Liberty averts her gaze. The British figures include John Montagu, 4th Earl of Sandwich, William Murray, 1st Earl of Mansfield, Frederick North, 2nd Earl of Guilford, and John Stuart, 3rd Earl of Bute. Pictured witnessing this violent event are Charles III, King of Spain and Louis XV, King of France. The print was published by the *London Magazine* 43 (May 1774): 184 and later reprinted in the *Royal American Magazine* [Boston: Printed by and for I. Thomas], vol. 1, no. 10 (June 1774). *(© Trustees of the British Museum)*

to consult his commander-in-chief about the tea.[105] Apologetic for having to "trouble your Excellency with these Little affairs," Heard nonetheless felt the matter warranted contacting Washington directly. His commander-in-chief must have also deemed the matter of importance, for he penned a handwritten note in response ordering the coveted leaves "To be sent to the Quarter Master General for the use of the Army."[106]

Washington's wartime correspondence reveals that these "Little affairs" were considered vital to establishing the legitimacy of the struggling patriots in the eyes of the watching world. This was not the only time during the war Washington wrote a letter about tea. Two years later, while stationed at West Point, he allotted the precious commodity with great attention to military rank: "Fifty pounds of the best quality for future disposal: one pound of the best kind to each General Officer; half a pound of the same to each field officer and head of a staff department and a quarter of a pound p[e]r. man of the remainder to any other officer of the army who shall apply."[107] Washington's careful instructions suggest the symbolic importance of refined goods in the establishment of a social hierarchy. The general's actions reinforced the military power structure through the careful and deliberate distribution of supplies and luxuries during a time of wartime scarcity.[108] But even in battle, Washington recognized the importance of refined goods such as tea and porcelain, commodities that would later come to play a role in the establishment of the nation.

To Properly "Fix the Taste of the Nation"

The repudiation of British governance did not bring about a repudiation of its goods. Looking into the homes of the Founding Fathers would quickly dispel any notion that only a Loyalist would harbor a penchant for luxury imports.[109] Having purchased British goods for his entire life, Washington was expected for political reasons to curb his habit when as a representative from Virginia to the First Continental Congress in 1774 he pledged his allegiance to nonimportation and nonconsumption agreements. Yet as the leader of the emerging nation, he believed it was his responsibility to purchase tasteful goods that would properly "fix the taste of the nation" and reflect a civilized culture. Even the most ardent patriots made compromises, often justifying their transgressions as being in the service of the nation's reputation.

On the evening of July 9, 1776, as Washington planned for the defense of New York City against approaching British troops, he made time to arrange the purchase of elegant British and Chinese goods for his home. Dealing with loyalist merchants Frederick and Philip Rhinelander, the rebel commander outlined exactly which imported British creamware dishes, sauceboats, plates, and fluted bowls he wanted to buy; the most costly items in his request were three china bowls. From another import merchant, he ordered china cups, saucers, and other tea service items.[110]

When Washington and other colonial elites pledged to change their lifelong purchasing habits by signing nonimportation and nonconsumption agreements, they did not agree to abandon European standards of gentility. To the contrary, their dramatic bid for independence intensified their desire to project a sense of propriety to the rest of the world. Americans fought to win the respect of Europeans and recorded their pleasure when they were treated as equals. Continental Army officers, often hailing from humble beginnings, took it as a great compliment when their British counterparts invited them to socialize between skirmishes. They often attributed this social success to the fact that they presented themselves in attire befitting an officer and a gentleman (see figure 2.10).

While in the field, Washington purchased items for use in the tent he had set up for his receiving of foreign representatives, both friend and foe. He seems to have achieved a measure of success in his attempt at establishing a somewhat refined atmosphere. The Marquis de Chastellux recorded the restorative powers of Washington's hospitality, noting that he was made to "drink three or four of his silver camp cups of excellent Madeira" before continuing on his journey.[111]

While the general was able to purchase with relative ease silver pieces such as these camp cups from local artisans in towns near his encampments,

Figure 2.10 "Washington as Colonel of the Virginia Regiment," painting by Charles Willson Peale (1772), oil on canvas, 50 1/2 x 41 1/2 in. Washington fought with the Virginia Regiment as a subject of Great Britain during the French and Indian War. He very consciously followed British protocol and fashion in order to appear to be a gentleman worthy of respect and honor. This painting was the only one done of Washington prior to the Revolutionary War. *(Washington-Custis-Lee Collection, Washington and Lee University, Lexington, VA)*

porcelain was difficult to buy domestically. This proved a problem in 1779 as Washington prepared a dinner for French allies to celebrate the first anniversary of their alliance. He wrote to his deputy quartermaster, John Mitchell, about the problem: "My plates and Dishes, once of Tin, now little better than rusty iron, are rather too much worn for delicate stomachs in fixed and peaceable quarters." In such situations, political compromises had to be made, and the general was prepared to make them. He wrote: "I thereby desire that you send me a sett [*sic*] of Queens China to be had."[112] Washington's compromises are about more than setting a smart table; they reflected the importance he placed on the respectability of the nation.

Throughout Washington's adult life, his extant records show, he purchased chinaware from abroad. His correspondence reveals his careful deliberations about the various objects that would help transform him into a cultured gentleman (see figure 2.11). He placed his first order in his twenties and his last in 1798, the penultimate year of his life.[113]

In his first transaction, Washington traded three hogsheads of tobacco for "fine oblong china dishes," a clear example of the transatlantic movement of natural goods for refined objects. Wedgwood's imported Queensware replaced salt-glazed stoneware at Mt. Vernon shortly after the Staffordshire

Figure 2.11 Set of dinnerware owned by George Washington. If the emerging nation was to earn legitimacy in the eyes of the world, its leader would have to live in a manner befitting a gentleman, and that meant displaying a wealth of imported goods. *(Winterthur Museum & Country Estate)*

potter initiated his marketing campaign in 1767.[114] Washington's purchase gave meaning to Wedgwood's boast that the "demand for this s[ai].d *Creamcolour,* Alias, *Queen's Ware,* Alias, *Ivory,* still increases. It is really amazing how rapidly the use of it has spread almost over the whole Globe, & how universally it is liked."[115] Throughout the eighteenth and nineteenth centuries, men like Washington set their tables in the "old English or covered-table plan."[116]

Men of the Virginia Tidewater gentry to which Washington belonged considered architecture, interior design, and outfitting the dining table appropriate pursuits in their desire to master the art of "genteel" living.[117] They did their shopping, which entailed a great deal of detailed transatlantic correspondence, through merchants. This reliance was fraught with tension. American customers often suspected they were being taken advantage of when they purchased imported goods. When objects arrived damaged, as they often did, customers could never be sure whether they had been broken en route (as the supplier would argue) or inferior goods had been sent from the start. Dependence on imported goods made Americans vulnerable to abuse. Transatlantic correspondence in which American consumers articulate to British merchants their deep displeasure about shoddy goods and inflated prices display a depth of emotion indicating that much more was at stake in these exchanges than mere commercial concerns. At the most basic level, desirable imported objects reflected status and the ability to order and recognize superior products from abroad. Conversely, the arrival of a substandard piece was not merely a disappointing economic exchange; it further implied the recipient was not "worthy" of the merchant's "regard." As such, it served as an informal index of the respect and influence a person commanded.

Decades of experience had trained Washington to respond to problems encountered in commercial exchanges. Even as his troops were fighting the British, the commander-in-chief wrote humble letters to his London buying agent, "chinaman" Richard Washington, to complain about receiving second-rate or out-of-date china. Introduced to the London merchant by a fellow planter, the general had never met the man but had to trust him to choose a set of goods "agreeable to the present taste" and "good of their kind."[118] As Washington confessed, "I should be glad to cultivate the most intimate correspondence with you, not only of names-sake but as a friend, and shall endeavour in all things to approve myself worthy of your Regard."[119] This keen interest in British luxury items during wartime would be puzzling without an understanding of the social and cultural importance of these objects.[120] Washington recognized that his attention to refined consumption, far from being a trivial concern, was necessary to establish position and authority, both among his own men and with his enemies.[121]

Washington's attention to refined consumption and authority was demonstrated in his correspondence with the British firm Robert Cary & Company. In a letter dated September 28, 1760, the Virginian alludes to his previous directives, which have been ignored, and peevishly notes that he has been sent outdated goods:

> It is needless for me to particularise the sorts, quality, or taste I woud choose to have them in unless it is observd; and you may believe me when I tell you that instead of getting things good and fashionable in their several kinds we often have Articles sent Us that could only have been used by our Forefathers in the days of yore. 'Tis a custom, I have some Reason to believe, with many Shop keepers, and Tradesmen in London when they know Goods are bespoke for Exportation to palm sometimes old, and sometimes very slight and indifferent Goods upon Us taking care at the same time to advance 10, 15 or perhaps 20 pr. Ct. upon them.[122]

Despite his displeasure, he nevertheless placed several more orders for "such Goods as are wanting," including at least one for Martha Washington. This particular request also illustrates the recirculation of goods between Great Britain and America. Washington explained that his wife "sends home a Green Sack to get cleand, or fresh dyed of the same colour; made up into a handsome Sack again woud be her choice, but if the Cloth wont afford that, then to be thrown into a genteel Night Gown." Interestingly, for a man who had never traveled to England, he referred to it as "home" here. Because the "Pyramid you sent me last year got hurt," Washington sent the broken pieces back, beseeching his correspondent that his replacement "be securely Packd."[123]

Clearly the situation was unchanged a decade later for attorney Peter Lyons, whose correspondence with the British firm John Norton and Sons mirrored that of his fellow Virginian. In July 1771, Lyons voiced his displeasure at the firm's suppliers, whom he asserted were "extremely negligent or deceitful, for they send us Goods at the highest prices that are coarse and bad, so that they are scarce fit for use." But he offered, trying to foster goodwill, "Mrs. Lyons could have returned her Cambrick & Handkerchiefs, but she did not choose to trouble you with them."[124]

Convinced his foreign correspondents were sending him shoddy goods because of their indifference to Americans, Lyons wrote two months later complaining once again about the quality of the textiles sent. This time, he explicitly asserted his compatriots' equality with their England counterparts: "I know they [British merchants] think anything good enough for Virginia," he wrote, "but they should be informed better, and be made to know that the people in Virginia have a good taste and know when they are imposed on, as well if not better than most of their Gentry of Quality in England." If that would not convince the manufacturer of the "impositions of your Tradesmen and the badness of their Goods," he attached a "piece of Handkercheifs [*sic*] that were sent the year before," writing "I beg you will deliver them & try to shame them for their behavior." After all, he maintained, when Americans "send to London it is to get the best of Goods in their kind not so much regarding price as quality." Conceding his British correspondent must be "tired of hearing" about this matter, Lyons acknowledged that this was a common experience for Americans.[125]

The function of imported, refined objects as agents of civilization was crucial to understanding America's continuing dependence on Great Britain in the postrevolutionary period.[126] Purchase of imported goods was facilitated by the people who were producing, marketing, selling, buying, and conveying those items to a particular destination. The object Washington desired reflected his education, refinement, and authority, for it took a great deal of influence to procure this sort of item during such a chaotic time.

Imported luxury goods were politicized during this highly charged period, and their use—what one drank and out of what type of vessel—reflected one's political and national identity, as well as one's class (or class aspirations). Americans wanted to distinguish themselves from the British yet also wanted to adapt aspects of monarchical culture in order to add gravitas and legitimacy to their new nation.[127] American major general William Alexander, for instance, had his coat of arms emblazoned on a set of imported china ordered during the Revolution. An oxymoron of the era, Alexander was a patriot who insisted on his right to the British aristocratic title of Lord Stirling. While he was able to persuade his American friends and colleagues to address him thus, he failed to persuade the House of Lords to acknowledge his claim to the title and the right to use the coat of arms. Living thousands of miles away, Alexander insisted on his aristocratic status and went into debt in order to outfit his home in the manner befitting a British lord.[128] He was not alone in his embrace of these status symbols; George Washington put his family crest of a winged griffin seated on a coronet on many a commissioned piece both before and after the Revolution (see figures 2.12 and 2.13).[129]

For former colonials, adapting aspects of monarchical culture to their society's own needs played an important part in the complex process of moving toward independence.[130] Although Americans prevailed in the war, the hard work of cultural redefinition, the elusive goal of the "completion of independence," had yet to be achieved.[131]

The volume of imports in the early national period surpassed prewar levels.[132] The short duration of nonconsumption practices highlighted the links Americans made between imported goods and the civilized refinement to which they aspired. While these tensions were manifest in the years leading up to the Revolution, after 1783 the importation of British products (like tea) not only resumed but increased.[133] Paul Revere himself cashed in on his fellow citizens' postrevolutionary desires for the cachet that accompanied these items; in addition to emulating European styles in his work, he

Figure 2.12 Embroidered coat of arms. In both the pre- and post-Revolutionary periods, Americans proudly displayed their family coat of arms. They commissioned artisans to incorporate them into various household items and also made decorative items themselves. This embroidered piece was stitched in Massachusetts by an unknown person. The maker's family coat of arms was wrought with metallic threads on a background of black silk. It measures 71.755 x 71.755 cm. *(Yale University Art Gallery)*

Figure 2.13 Silver cruet stand, caster, and bottles featuring the Washington coat of arms. George Washington's family had been presented with their coat of arms in England; he often used it to decorate his possessions. *(Mount Vernon Ladies' Association)*

sold imported English textiles, as well as other goods. Political disentanglement was in many respects more straightforward than abandoning the material practices Americans had always considered their own. In effect, rebelling against the mother country required supporters to reject a part of themselves.

In the years following the Revolution, Americans teetered between the promise of a glorious future as an independent nation and a sense of cultural insecurity resulting from their colonial past. The lack of parity in transatlantic exchanges meant the relationship between the two nations was not reciprocal—despite the Paris Peace Treaty's declaration of mutual equality.[134] A lack of financial capital and technological expertise greatly added to America's dependence on Europe following the Revolution. However, the dependence did not end there. The desire to stay connected to the mother country through the importation of fashions, ideas, and goods kept them within the orbit of British control. Not only did Americans import refined goods; they adopted dictates on how exactly to use them.[135]

Common practices such as drinking imported tea in a parlor from imported porcelain cups had meanings that kept evolving. The same imported tea service that in 1766 would have reinforced elite status through emulation of British standards had by 1776 become an affront to the patriot cause. By 1786, the accessibility of mass-produced imported pottery to less affluent segments of American society was seen as proof of the spread of democracy in the nation. Within this hierarchy, objects made by Americans that imitated European goods (such as Revere's fine silver teapot) straddled the boundary between imported and domestic goods.

The mixed messages communicated by these objects reflected the conflicts arising from the colonists' former dependence on the empire. In the first years after independence, the United States hovered between the bright future of a sovereign nation and the difficult present reality of a culturally insecure society beset with a colonial history. Although Americans were proud of their independence, the process of creating a new social order out of a people so recently considered British in both outlook and tradition was fraught with hypocrisy and dislocation. Despite major changes in the two countries' political relationship, in other respects the United States remained locked in a system of reliance on Great Britain. Key aspects of the colonial commercial structure were largely unaffected by the political transition, yet the significance of this dependence and the meanings placed on the objects and commodities themselves changed dramatically.[136] Just as new citizens tried to locate their young society on the map of the transatlantic world as an act of self-definition, they also contemplated if and how their newfound independence would alter their relationship to the material world of imported and domestic products.

Indeed, those living on the periphery of the transatlantic world in the early national period took great pride in any small success at manufacturing imitations of British goods.[137] Arguably, the highest compliment one could give of an American product was that it resembled a European object or even approximated its quality. Fashioned from American-made woolen fabric, George Washington's inaugural suit met with approval because it was "so handsomely finished, that it was universally mistaken for a foreign manufactured superfine cloth."[138] As one of the most historically significant outfits of the age, its specifications were debated by politicians and the public alike.[139] A badly cut, roughly made homespun suit would reek of embarrassing provincial rusticity, while fancy British cloth cut in the latest style would project a sense of servile emulation unbefitting the new president of a free people. A suit of American cloth made to resemble an English one as closely as possible seemed the best compromise. Like early American identity itself, objects such as Revere's portrait and Washington's suit were fraught with contradictions, reflecting both the new nation's British past and its American future.

Yet, as Americans made the transition from subjects to citizens, this continuing reliance on the mother country became increasingly troubling to many. If not unacceptable, the situation was at least in need of self-justification and explanation to the rest of the world. Much of the energy of the founding generation was expended doing just that. Cultural emulation and material dependence may have been acceptable for a provincial subject of the British Empire, but it was behavior that was unbecoming for a citizen. Americans addressed the problem in different ways, each of them understandable but yet not fully satisfactory. Each approach grappled with the attempt to separate objects from politics, an impossible task.

Consuming Problems and Some American Responses

> Though emancipated from foreign political domination, the people seemed yet chained in complete dependence upon the workshops of Europe—from which, notwithstanding our marvelous progress, they are not entirely liberated.
>
> —J. Leander Bishop, A *History of American Manufactures* (1866)

American observers were still lamenting their dependence on Britain well into the nineteenth century, as author Leander Bishop did in his massive three-volume history of early American manufactures.[140] Before the Revolution, Benjamin Rush had been among the most vociferous advocates for domestic manufactures and was implacably opposed to importing more British goods. Writing from London in January 1769, he entreated colonists to "save our sinking country…by encouraging American manufactures. Unless we do this, we shall be undone forever."[141] In 1775 as president of the United Company of Philadelphia for Promoting American Manufactures, he famously asserted: "A people who are entirely dependent upon foreigners for food or clothes must always be subject to them."[142] Yet, even long after the war, his personal correspondence reflects a different attitude toward Britain and its goods.[143] In 1810 Rush urged his son James who was studying medicine abroad to buy large quantities of "cloathes [*sic*], instruments &

medicines in London" that were not available in America. To become a "scholar" and "gentleman," James had appear "cultivated," and ownership of the proper goods provided an effective way to do so. He finished by saying that the "great City" of London was the "epitome of the whole world...Nine months spent in it will teach you more by your 'eyes and ears,' than a life spent in your native country."[144]

By constantly imbuing objects with national meaning, citizens of the United States aspired to standards of gentility that drew on a European, aristocratic past while also embracing the democratic, liberal, and capitalist values that would come to define the nation. In a society where social relations were extremely fluid, those who could use refined objects to demonstrate civility would benefit socially.[145] Adherence to standards of gentility could be used as a prerequisite for trust in the rapidly burgeoning and increasingly fluid society of the early republic.[146]

Genteel activities such as taking a "sociable dish of tea" with one's equals (or better yet, one's betters) had a great deal of significance in eighteenth-century America.[147] From its initial introduction into British culture, tea consumption connoted gentility, civility, and wealth. To partake in the formal rituals of tea, one needed a great deal of two things: leisure time (tea parties took up several hours in the middle of the day) and money (spare time, proper surroundings, and possession of the proper accoutrements). Because of its aura of aristocratic refinement, tea became the ideal object around which to organize political protests during the periods of heated tension between America and Britain.[148] As noted, the consumption and enjoyment of tea did not end when Americans renounced hereditary privilege; it was merely suspended for specific political purposes and quickly embraced once again when the crisis was over.

For the elite classes, tea drinking was a performance meant to be appreciated by one's peers. Tea drinking became inextricably linked to the ceremony it accompanied. Material objects changed and disciplined human action, and the popularity of tea drinking transformed the home as westerners set aside special places where tea was to be enjoyed.[149]

It was a point of pride for Americans to display the same fashionable objects that made up a well-appointed European tea table (see 2.14).

Taking tea required much more than the leaves that were brewed; one needed a vast array of goods, such as tea tables, porcelain pots, and wooden stands, that facilitated the consumption of this unassuming leaf. European fashions dictated what style of teapots, trays, tablecloths, utensils, cream and sugar containers, sugar tongs, glassware, cups, and saucers were appropriate.[150] Seen in this light, Revere's teapot made to the standards set in

Figure 2.14 "The Samels Family," painting by Johann Eckstein (1788). Long after the Revolution was over, Americans continued to look to Britain for their fashion cues. The interior of this American home is decorated in the English style. Note the imported Chinese figures that adorn the mantlepiece. *(Museum of Fine Arts, Boston)*

England can be better appreciated. These items were made from the best woods, metals, and ceramics by artisans and skilled workers from both sides of the Atlantic. They were enjoyed within the elite home in specially demarcated wood-paneled rooms, while seated on comfortable chairs and surrounded with sumptuous drapery and handsome chests. The ritual of tea drinking functioned as a way to define social groups, and a great deal of pressure was involved in keeping up with the latest changes in teapot decoration, the newest fad in sugar tong design, and the varying ways one should hold a teacup. Chinaware represented the status and taste of a family, and therefore elegantly equipped tea and dinner tables became the focal point in the refined home. French and English cookbooks at this the time used the term "the art of the table" to describe the placing of dishes in elaborate, symmetrical compositions that resembled plans for formal gardens.[151]

Complex rules of etiquette had to be followed if one wanted to drink tea in the proper manner. One had to know how to hold a cup, where exactly to sit, and how to signal silently when no more tea was desired. Despite their earnest attempts to emulate Europeans, Americans invariably developed idiosyncratic ways of drinking tea that bewildered foreign guests. Their hospitality was "hot-water torture" to a European visitor unaware of the local manner used to refuse a cup of tea: placing a spoon atop an upside-down cup. Because it was considered poor manners to refuse a cup when offered, the bloated guest "decided after emptying it to put it into his pocket until the replenishments had been concluded."[152] Tea taking separated social classes, and revealed those who were comfortable and familiar with the highly ritu-alized norms and those who were not. Tea drinking rituals allowed peers to judge a person's character on the basis or his or her deportment.

In contrast to the common practice surrounding the consumption of alcoholic drinks, women played a central role in taking tea.[153] Usually the host's eldest daughter or the youngest married woman in the group was expected to orchestrate the performance.[154] The presence of both men and women allowed for gossiping, discussing business, courting, and celebrating life events such as marriages and engagements. In Philadelphia, Nancy Shippen's "tea hour" was known to extend from afternoon until eleven o'clock in the evening, with both male and female guests singing, conversing, dancing, and playing cards and chess. Prominent political figures such as George Washington, Thomas Jefferson, and Alexander Hamilton were counted as visitors to the Shippen residence, where they "drank a sociable dish of Tea."[155]

As Americans began to separate politically from Great Britain, the more self-conscious among them began to ponder whether they would be able to continue to enjoy the imported goods they were so fond of within this new political context climate. People devised several imperfect solutions to address the complex problems in their world of goods. One response was simply to continue to buy British goods. This was easy to do, for as Leander Bishop reports, "Immense cargoes of foreign manufactures were already crowding the portals of the nation before peace had thrown open the gates of commerce."[156] British manufacturers wasted no time in eagerly wel-coming their American customers (or rather their money) back into the fold. In 1784, London silversmiths Joy & Hopkins wrote in a letter respect-fully addressed to "His Excellency Gen. Washington" that they were "eager to recapture the American market interrupted so inconveniently by war."[157] They need not have worried, for Washington resumed purchasing British items immediately after the war, albeit with a certain sense of discomfort he had not felt as a colonial subject. He looked to Europe for fashion advice and to new technology in the latest tablewares for tea. Writing to his nephew

Bushrod Washington in New York, the statesman inquired about whether the newly invented silver-plated ware was indeed "fashionable and much used in genteel houses in France and England...and whether among them, there are Tea urns, Coffee pots, Tea pots, and other equipage for a tea table, with a tea board, Candlesticks and waiters large and small, with the prices of each." Tellingly, he asked that his nephew not reveal his identity: "These enquiries you may make in behalf of a friend, without bringing my name forward, 'till occasion (if a purchase shou'd happen) may require it."[158]

Washington was by no means the only American to return to Europe for refined goods. Indeed, the American consumption of a dazzling array of British goods grew so much that by the end of the eighteenth century, the new nation became the most significant consumer of British exports in the world.[159] Between 1796 and 1800, the British reaped an annual average of nearly 7,000,000 pounds sterling from exports to the United States.[160] The remarkable growth of American trade was underscored by the American goods the British were importing: wrought iron, lead and shot, white salt, tanned leather, beaver hats, and textiles such as flannel, men's worsted stockings, and fustians, a coarse, sturdy cloth made of cotton and flax that was largely used for working men's clothing.[161] British manufacturers were even willing to absorb substantial losses on their initial postwar shipments, and sent large consignments of goods for auction on generous credit terms.[162] According to a member of Parliament, "it was even worth [our] while to incur a loss upon the first exportations, in order by the glut to stifle in the cradle these rising manufactures in the United Sates, which the war had forced into existence, contrary to the natural course of things."[163] Their efforts were successful because American consumers eagerly purchased the British goods, to the detriment and most often the demise of fledgling domestic manufactures.

Catalogs, pattern books, and fashion journals contributed to the increase in Americans' postrevolutionary appetite for the latest in British fashion. Each of these publications exposed consumers to the ever-expanding world of goods awaiting export to them (see figure 2.15).[164]

More than a generic list of items for sale, fashion journals such as *The Repository of Arts, Literature, Commerce, Manufactures, Fashions and Politics* provided readers with a voyeuristic window onto Rudolph Ackermann's shop on the Strand in London through a series of plates. As its editor explained: "It will afford the opportunity of entering into a partial detail of the different manufactures that are exposed in them for sale."[165] Not only could distant American readers of Ackermann's *Repository* learn about the newest trends in British furniture and clothing, they also could touch

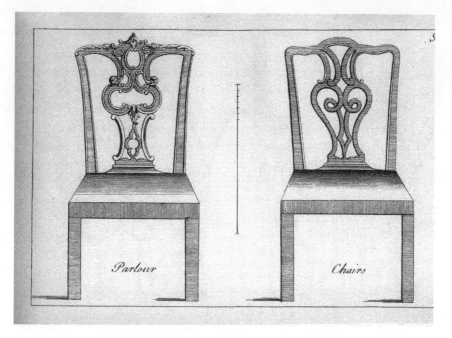

Figure 2.15 Chair design, illustration in *The Cabinet and Chair-Maker's Real Friend and Companion*
(London: Henry Webley, 1765), by Robert Manwaring (British, active 1760–70), etching and engraving,
12.9 x 19.5 cm., engraved by Robert Pranker (British, active 1750–1774) (plate 9). Pattern books
illustrating furniture and architectural designs became extremely popular in the eighteenth century,
encouraging the emulation of English design patterns throughout the transatlantic world. They supplied
provincial artisans with patterns that they could draw upon. When political tensions arose between
America and the mother country, the need for domestic products emulating popular English fashions
increased, and European craftsmen were encouraged to come to America. *(From a copy in the collection
of Sterling Memorial Library, Yale University)*

swatches of the newest textiles sent by manufacturers.[166] The most novel
feature of this periodical was a regularly published plate entitled "Allegorical
Wood-Cut, with Patterns of British Manufacture" (figure 2.16).
"Manufacturers, Factors and Wholesale Dealers in Fancy Goods" were
"requested to send Patterns of such new Articles" as met the "requisites of
Novelty, Fashion, and Elegance."[167] One volume featured an "imperial green
shawl print" that was "expected to rank high on the list of winter fashion."
Ackermann asserted, "We doubt not that this fabric will be purchased with
avidity by females of taste." "Considerable quantities" were "preparing at the
different manufactories" of England, and potential buyers were directed to
Messrs. Waithman and Everington, No. 104, Fleet-street, to purchase the
fabric at 4 shilings per yard.[168] While Americans depended on the British to
dictate their styles, Britons looked to France for inspiration. Ackermann,

Figure 2.16 "Allegorical Wood-Cut, with Patterns of British Manufacture." From Rudolph Ackermann, ed., *The Repository of Arts, Literature, Commerce, Manufactures, Fashions and Politics*, 1st ser., London, no. 11 [November 1809], unnumbered plate following p. 344. *(From a copy in the Henry Huntington Library Collection)*

who lived in Paris for a time, based his publication on Pierre de la Mésangère's journal *Meubles et Objets de Goût.*[169]

In addition to fabrics, the newly developed type of British pottery, also known as transferware or Queensware, was popular in the decades following the Revolution. For early entrepreneurs in the pottery industry, technological advances coincided in a fortuitous manner with the political upheavals that were taking place in the Atlantic world. During the war, artisans were developing a technique for producing decorated, affordable pottery for the growing middle classes both at home and abroad. Pioneer

Josiah Wedgwood was famous for his embrace of innovative methods of mass production and industrial planning associated with the Industrial Revolution. In the early 1760s, he developed a new type of cream-colored ceramic that he described as "a species of earthenware...quite new in its appearance, covered with a rich and brilliant glaze, bearing sudden alterations of heat and cold, manufactured with ease and expedition, and consequently cheap."[170] In addition, he adopted a new technique in which prints engraved onto copperplates could be transferred onto huge quantities of this pottery much more cheaply than hand-painted decoration.[171]

While improvements in manufacturing techniques increased the amount of pottery being exported to America, they did not necessarily enhance its quality or the timeliness of the designs being sent over. America went from a minor outlet for outdated goods to the most important trading destination for English pottery.[172] Yet European observers familiar with life on both sides of the Atlantic noted that despite their importance as customers, Americans still did not receive the prime pieces coming out of Britain. These comments delivered an extra sting for Americans, who were famously sensitive to criticism from foreign observers. Never noted for her tact, Margaret Hall published observations about the foibles and failures of the developing society that caused quite a stir. She wrote about overhearing "some American ladies remarking...that they thought the American glass quite as prettily cut as the English." At first she thought it a "great stretch of national prejudice," until she remembered "how inferior a quality of goods of every description is sent to this country. You cannot really form an idea," Hall wrote, "of the trash that is to be found in the best shops."[173] During his trip to America from Europe in the last years of the 1810s, Axel Klinkowstrom, a native of Sweden, remarked that English imports "are of such quality as not to allow close scrutiny."[174] Even so, U.S. citizens were willing to go into debt to buy these products. Noting the "exaggerated consumption of English goods" in America, Klinkowstrom predicted that despite "all the geographical and natural advantages this country possesses," America would find itself "in debt and unable to pay her obligations to England."[175] In other words, American consumer habits would keep the nation in an unequal relationship with its former mother country.

After the end of the war for American independence, British manufacturers in major industries such as textiles and pottery promptly began custom designing their wares so as to tug on Americans' patriotic heartstrings, in order to persuade them to open their purse strings. Entrepreneurs produced items that encouraged the former colonials to express their nationalism in material form. As soon as their country lost the war, British manufacturers sought images meant to evoke the victors' national pride to transfer onto pottery. Rousing scenes of the defeat of the mighty empire soon adorned jugs, plates, and mugs. No time was lost in packing the holds of ships to America with these items.[176] With a few passes of an engraving tool, printed textile manufacturers scratched out all references to Britain, and a redcoat was instantly transformed into George Washington (see figure 2.17).[177]

Figure 2.17 "Apotheosis of Benjamin Franklin and George Washington," bed curtain (Britain, c. 1785), plate-printed linen-cotton. In this heroic image of the founding fathers, Washington is driving a chariot while Franklin, in his signature fur cap, stands next to Liberty. Note also the cherubs holding a map of the eastern coast of the United States. *(Collections of Colonial Williamsburg)*

With these minor changes, the same piece of fabric took on greatly altered political meanings. A jug produced in England for the American market portrays a rebel soldier, probably George Washington, standing on the head of the British lion. In case the image was not enough, English makers also included the inscription "By virtue and valour we have free'd our country, extended our commerce, and laid the foundation of a great empire" (see figure 2.18).[178]

A series of cream-colored transferware pieces depicted revolutionary battles in which the rebels emerged victorious.[179] English suppliers such as Enoch Wood, Wedgwood, and Neale and Company did not merely cater to

Figure 2.18 Jug produced in England for the American market, decorated with a rebel soldier, probably George Washington, standing on the head of the British lion. In case the visual image was not enough, English makers also included the inscription "By virtue and valour we have free'd our country, extended our commerce, and laid the foundation of a great empire." *(Winterthur Museum & Country Estate)*

a desire for patriotic commercial goods in America; they played an active role in creating it.

Objects like transferware pottery decorated to appeal to the American market simultaneously communicated an anti-British message while reinforcing the centrality of the empire in the transatlantic material world. The complex industrial processes needed for successful competition with British manufactures of tableware were not established in the United States until the early years of the twentieth century. While a single silver teapot could be produced by a local craftsman like Revere, making an entire tea or table service consisting of between forty-five to three hundred pieces required a highly specialized division of labor, which Americans did not have.[180] In an ironic turn of events, Americans' pride in their wartime victory fueled the economic revitalization of the English pottery industry.[181]

Americans' desire for these refined imports supported a network that spanned the Atlantic of people—potters, engravers, printers, modelers, packers, and dealers—who were involved in producing and delivering the coveted objects. In the late 1790s, for instance, affluent Philadelphians called on William H. Richards when they wanted to purchase English pottery wrought in the newest styles. As the only official American agent of the Herculaneum Pottery of Liverpool, Richards served as a critical link between British pottery manufacturers and their targeted customers across the Atlantic.

Conflicting meanings were embedded in products imported into America at this time (see figure 2.19). Some scholars have expressed skepticism that British manufacturers would be capable of producing objects that carried negative portrayals of their nation.[182] But many entrepreneurs separated politics from business, while others did not support the war against the American colonies and therefore would have had no qualms about producing such goods.

As they circulated, imported objects acquired layers of meaning for provincials trying to find their place within the expanding world of goods. As noted, for a people who had repudiated aristocracy, American consumers embraced Queensware and myriad other refined goods and practices with remarkable enthusiasm, as is apparent from the archeological digs at American settlements between 1790 and 1830.[183] Each site contained fragments of countless pieces of fine imported tableware once cherished by its owners. To be sure, British entrepreneurs were primarily motivated by profit rather than ideology or politics, but their marketing strategies also influenced the way Americans expressed their political identities during the early years of the republic.

Figure 2.19 Statue of Benjamin Franklin mislabeled "Washington," produced by a British manufacturer in the early nineteenth century. *(Winterthur Museum & Country Estate)*

One Response: London Calling a Massachusetts Innocent Abroad and the Asymmetries of Exchange

The American merchant Henry Bromfield, Jr., was a popular guest in the homes of his acquaintances in London in the 1780s and 1790s, especially when he brought them preserved quinces from his family home in Massachusetts. Reputedly, he returned the "great kindness and hospitality" of his esteemed and influential contacts with natural delicacies from America. The simple gift of fruit preserves was valued because "[s]uch were never seen in England." It was said "all who taste them declare they are the finest Preserve ever imported into this Country."[184] In a letter home, Henry reported that those who had "heretofore partook of your Quinces that were sent here spoke of them as the most delicate sweetmeat they ever tasted." Asking for more, he insisted "a few therefore will gratify me an opportunity of such a return for many Instances of Civility I am often receiving.[185]

A member of a Boston merchant family, Henry Jr. had moved to London to expand his family's commercial interests.[186] The Bromfields traded raw materials such as potash, logwood, rum, and furs from the New World for the manufactured goods of Britain, such as woolens, silks, and a variety of fancy articles. With each arrival in London of an American ship, the young merchant would make social calls to his London connections. The peppers, cranberries, and quinces his family grew in Harvard, Massachusetts, were considered exotic New World crops. After explaining to his father how successful the quinces had been in gaining favor among the English, he suggested that "––a bar[rel]…of Cranberries will also afford a like opportunity."[187] And so it did. In another letter, he reported that the shipment "reached me safe" and "have afforded opportunity for gratifying several of my Friends."[188]

This traffic of New World goods and British manufactures was carefully orchestrated through a series of detailed letters that spanned two continents and as many decades. These letters were a mixture of business and personal correspondence, including precise instructions regarding goods sent as presents, which complicated the boundary between market transaction and private gift. While they were ostensibly given as tokens of friendship, these objects also had important business implications, for they helped Henry Jr. to build prosperous social relations. The instructions he gave to his family back home about what types of objects they should procure were always specific and were informed by his merchant's eye for market needs and customer desires. Bromfield took advantage of the relationship between scarcity and high demand in one location and the abundance of supply in another.

Using American hams as gifts was a bit more complicated.[189] Ever the sharp businessman, Henry Jr. noted to his father that he was "uncertain" whether "it will be worth while to receive them from America" because they "pay a very considerable Duty on Importation." After giving it a bit more thought, he declared "it will be worth while to buy them" because they "are much superior in flavor to those commonly sold here."

Once the shipments arrived in England, Henry allocated these exotic gifts carefully, devoting the same close attention to the supply of home-grown gifts he gave to his stock in trade. Making sure he did not run out, the respectful son politely alerted his father to the need for another shipment noting that the: "Quinces you sent before [are] not quite gone... [and] remain delicious."[190] Before asking his father for more gifts from their New England farm, Henry precisely accounted for the way prior shipments had been distributed: "with some of them [the quinces] I gratified the old Lady of Fetherstone and some I presented at Islington—all join in praising them—."[191]

The rank and influence of the recipients held interest for Bromfields on both sides of the Atlantic, and this information was updated and detailed in Henry Jr.'s letters. One of the people to whom Henry "presented" the fruit was a Mrs. Crampton, a "Lady extremely pleasing and amiable," he related, but perhaps more important, the wife of a "Gentleman of the first Influence and Fortune in this Place." Thanks to the precious gifts, Henry was "rec'd [*sic*] with great kindness and hospitality" at their house.[192]

Sending objects back and forth was also a way to remain connected to family back home. Although married with a family in England, Henry described a mental geography that closed the distance between London and Boston:

> We should rejoice to join them [the family] and was Harvard within the same Distance of London as it is of Boston we should frequently leave the Den of Business for the more pleasing Engagements of rural Life, and exchange the smoaky [*sic*] atmosphere of the city for the purer air of the Country, but my Lot is here... [and to] be contented with it is a Duty—the affection however I am ever with you and to pray for your Happiness I am never unmindful.[193]

The gifts from London most appreciated by Henry's family back home in America were books, magazines, and fancy manufactures.[194] In the same letter, he itemized what he had sent in the care of a Boston merchant, including several books: a volume of White's *Sermons*, four volumes of "elegant extracts," two volumes of the "beauties of History," two volumes of Knox's *Essays*, two volumes of *Youth's Friend*, and a "ladies humor book for 1790." These titles were designated for members of the household and close friends.[195] Throughout the years, Henry Jr. sent his father issues of British periodicals, which he hoped would "administer some amusement in your retirement." He would send them by different vessels in care of Mr. Cabot, who "after reading them" forwarded the books to Henry's father.[196] Four years later, Henry was "glad to perceive the Books sent you have proved so acceptable."[197] He went on to ask his father to give more details as to what titles to choose:

as you do not give any Intimation what Subject you wish...whether of Religion, History, Travels, Biography, Philos[sophy], and c., and the Diversity is so great, and my own Reading so small, that I am utterly at a Loss what Books to choose—instead of those which I did send I had purchased Robertson's History of South America and afterwards exchanged it—if there is any particular Book you wish for I shall be glad to know it.[198]

Americans depended on their foreign contacts for access to information on the latest trends and styles. Henry noted to his family: "I am myself [a] Subscriber to a nice Edition of Doctor Dodridge's *Works* in 10 volumes which are now nearly finished." He added that a friend had "purchased five of the volumes and carried them out with him and I am sure will be very ready to lend them to you if desired. . . . He has also another Book which he lent me, and which I now return him, entitled Scott's Essays—they are upon the essential Points of Christianity and written in a very perspicuous and easy manner—I was so pleased with [them] as to procure them for myself and have requested him to favor you with Perusal of them."[199]

Besides books, Henry also sent a variety of manufactured goods to his family in Massachusetts. These included a "velvet cap," "cotton hose," "a dress," a "cotton waistcoat pattern," "a child's box," "super fine cloth for garters," "three pairs of mixed silk hose," and a "sword sent to Mr. Brewster." For his father, Henry sent a special gift of a new cane, for he recalled that when last "at Harvard your Canes were either very antique or broken." He continued, "I request your Acceptance and hope it will prove a good one." Gifts sometimes went astray on the long journey, as did a "the Bundle with the Fishing lines and materials" sent from London. Indeed, the younger Bromfield was "exceedingly Sorry...as they were a compleat [*sic*] set and valuable."[200]

The flow of natural and manufactured objects between the Bromfields followed the same pattern as the general trade: natural commodities originated from New World locations and were traded for the manufactured goods of the Old. The Bromfields' personal exchanges—both gift and business—mirrored the macroeconomic trends of the eighteenth century that were predicated on the principles of the mercantile system, whose laws were designed to subsume colonial interests within those of the mother country. After independence, in both large- and small-scale interactions, this exchange of objects between Britain and the United States was invariably colored by the asymmetrical economic and cultural relationship between these erstwhile compatriots and former adversaries.

Another Response: People in Glasshouses or the Struggles of Domestic Manufactures

> Shall domestic manufactures be encouraged and in what degree, by restrictions on foreign manufactures? The apportionment of taxes on the various descriptions of property is an act which seems to require the most exact impartiality; yet there is, perhaps, no legislative act in which greater opportunity and temptation are given to a predominant party, to trample on the rules of justice.
>
> —*Federalist* (no. 10)

Americans earned the reputation of constantly bragging about their national "firsts," even those that seemed insignificant—from inventions like the banjo clock to minor milestones such as the production of lead pencils using domestic graphite.[201] It seemed to many foreign observers that the boasting was disproportionate to the accomplishments. Needless to say, neither of these events made the news in London.

Although the British public was not interested in the latest manufactured products from the United States, Americans, as noted, continued to rely on imported goods from the mother country in the years following the Revolutionary War. This relationship of unequal exchange had political implications. Alexander Hamilton believed that economic and political freedom were inseparable, and therefore set out to challenge British dominance of the American market. In his opinion, the "best way to rid the young nation of its dependence on British imports" was to develop domestic manufacturing.[202]

Ironically, those who set American economic and material independence as a priority looked to Mother England for guidance in doing so.[203] For Hamilton, Great Britain offered a useful model for Americans as they set about establishing domestic industries. He proposed that the government "orchestrate the transfer of technology across the Atlantic by smuggling restrictive goods and advanced machinery and encouraging the migration of experienced workers" despite the fact that it was illegal under British law. His detractors questioned the wisdom of his approach not on ethical grounds, but because they believed that Great Britain was a corrupt, materialistic society and feared that by emulating its economic practices, the United States would develop in a similar fashion.[204]

Despite these concerns, during the early national period, many entrepreneurial Americans were willing to beg, borrow, and steal in order to compete with the British. Indeed, it is fitting that "Yankee" is a derivative of a Dutch slang term for pirate or smuggler.[205] Although these Americans were engaged in a form of industrial espionage, they evinced no guilt about their efforts to increase their commercial and technical knowledge.[206] On the contrary, notable public figures from Benjamin Rush to Mathew Carey praised efforts to steal information and equipment because of the benefits this brought to the struggling new nation. Hoping to learn of the latest in European scientific developments, Rush advised his son James to "be all eye, all ear" while the young man was overseas studying medicine.[207] This sentiment was proudly shared by many Americans; local newspapers openly flouted British law by publishing information about British machinery in their pages.[208]

Other Americans journeyed to Europe specifically in order to gather insights into the "useful arts" of manufacturing. As late as the 1830s, they were still engaged in what might most aptly be termed tourist espionage. Zachariah Allen even wrote a book entitled the *Practical Tourist,* that documented his efforts. In it he declared that his "principal design" in crossing the Atlantic in 1825 to visit England was to learn about the "effects of the important improvements in machinery upon the state of [British] society at the present day."[209] In contrast to the trips Europeans took to the United States to see the natural wonders or gentlemen taking the Grand Tour of Europe for pleasure and personal refinement, the "practical tourist" visited factories to collect useful information.[210] Picturesque vistas and world class museums were not of interest to this man. Instead, Allen visited factories filled with the "smoke of furnaces" and "resounding with the deafening noise of machinery" and conversed with "men devoted to the common handicraft labors of life."[211]

Allen's itinerary targeted industrial centers that produced the things Americans purchased most often. One of his stops was in Staffordshire which was the heart of the British pottery industry. While there he went to a porcelain showroom where he saw "a collection of the most splendid China vases, and other productions from oriental potteries" as well as a "frail collection of earthenware" on shelves like an exhibition, and "a strange collection of old[?] teapots of high and low degree; tea cups of the size of a nut shell and bowls of stately swelling dimensions, that might have accommodated the 'three wise men of Gotham.'"[212] Allen noted to his readers back home that Staffordshire boasted "finest clay suitable for the supply of the immense potteries, which furnish whole nations with ware for their tables."[213]

Goods imported from Great Britain dominated the American market as a result of the strength of its industries. During the colonial period, the establishment of manufactories had been prohibited by Parliamentary laws and American manufacturers struggled to survive. Producing fine porcelain and glassware on a large scale entailed detailed knowledge, skilled workers, and large amounts of capital. As a result these factors, these industries struggled in the United States until well into the nineteenth century. Consumer preference for imported goods also played an important role in the continued popularity of British products.

Faced with these challenges, American entrepreneurs adopted various schemes in order to gain a foothold in the industry. In some respects, their former colonial status worked to their advantage after the Revolution: they enjoyed a long-standing familiarity with the British system, a shared language, and friends and relatives overseas who possessed technical knowledge. Skilled British craftsmen became the foundations upon which American shops and mills were built.[214] The recruitment of foreign artisans to America was not limited to Britons or to the postrevolutionary period. In 1764, Americans persuaded a German craftsman named Henry William Stiegel to set up a glassworks in Manheim, Pennsylvania. Recognizing Americans' penchant for British designs, Stiegel abandoned his own German styles and hired English artisans, glasscutters, and engravers to produce his high-quality lead glass pieces. Using English glassware as a reference point for his customers, he paid for the following advertisement: "FLINT GLASS, viz. decanters, wine glasses, tumblers, Etc.... equal in beauty and quality to the generality of Flint Glass imported from England."[215]

After the Revolution, Americans increased their efforts to convince skilled Europeans to journey to United States. In August 1784, a glassmaker from Bremen, Germany, named John Frederick Amelung immigrated with sixty-eight other artisans to Frederick County, Maryland, to open a glass manufactory there. He seemed well positioned to succeed with several letters of introduction from Benjamin Franklin, John Adams, and other leading public figures.[216] When it was completed, the New Bremen Glass Manufactory boasted a community of almost 500 residents and produced the most refined glassware in the country. Although Amelung met with initial success, he was disappointed by the lack of reliable private and formal government support for his business. In 1787 Amelung wrote a pamphlet entitled *Remarks on Manufactures, Principally on the New Established Glass-House, near Frederick-Town, in the State of Maryland,* which called upon American patriotism in an attempt to increase the sales of his glassware. He closed his remarks by recommending "this Manufactory to the kind patronage of every true friend of this Country, and to the Public in general," noting that his personal business success would be "advantageous to this and the neighbouring States."[217]

Americans' resistance to purchasing domestically produced goods created problems for Amelung's business. Like Stiegel, he was compelled to adopt English styles of glassmaking more popular with the majority of

American customers. Even with these aesthetic changes, consumers continued to exhibit what the German glassmaker perceived as a servile preference for imported wares. He urged potential customers to "be above the common prejudices [held by Americans] that the foreign goods are better than the home manufactured, and...using them [domestic goods], through their good example, persuade others to follow them." Amelung tried to convince people that his glassware was "cheaper, and of a better quality, than a great deal of what was imported." Yet he also admitted that his "manufactory had not arrived to the greatest perfection."[218] Faced with these various difficulties, he was forced to close his doors in 1795.[219] The artisan's attempt to produce quality glassware in the United States was thwarted by the practical challenges of manufacturing refined goods at competitive prices as well as the widespread American preference for imported goods.[220]

Due to these challenges, the survival of American glasshouses was largely dependent upon the state of Anglo-American relations at any given moment. The nonimportation movements that were taken up during the Revolutionary crisis created a shortage of British goods and provided the impetus for the establishment of American manufactures. Their success was temporary; many businesses failed when imported goods once again became available to American consumers at the end of the war. The British were aware of the disadvantages their rivals faced. In a report dated November 10, 1789, Phineas Bond, the British Consul at Philadelphia noted that "America must for a long time my Lord be under the necessity of purchasing and importing vast quantities of British or other European manufactures...Manufactures wh[ich] require art, labor, and expence [*sic*] to any great extent of either, may be attempted but they will often fail for want of capital."[221]

In the same way, the postrevolutionary conflicts between the United States and Great Britain in the early nineteenth century created opportunities for the establishment of American manufactures. Between 1807 and 1814, the Embargo Act of 1807, the Napoleonic War, and the War of 1812 created the impetus for the further development of American manufactures. During this period, forty-four glasshouses opened in America. However, just as in the late eighteenth century, domestic manufactures struggled to survive when trade with Britain resumed after the war.[222]

It would take generations for domestic manufacturing to match Great Britain's industrial sophistication and productivity. Importing technological knowledge and recruiting knowledgeable people from Europe continued into the second half of the nineteenth century.[223] While elite Americans' preferences for foreign goods were influenced by factors such as superior craftsmanship and lower prices, their infatuation was also fueled by the desire to achieve refinement through the possession and proper use of the latest fashionable items from abroad.

To make matters worse, as a legacy of the restrictive legislation of the colonial period, American consumers became dependent on British suppliers for goods imported from other parts of the globe. Chinese imports were in particular demand in the early national period. While Americans had relied on British imports of goods from Asia, with the newly won rights of an independent nation, one attempt they made to gain an advantage over the British was to send ships directly to China.

Three

A REVOLUTION REVIVED

American and British Encounters in Canton, China

With clearance from BELLONA won
She spread her wings to meet the Sun,
Those golden regions to explore
Where George forbade to sail before.

—Philip Freneau, "On the First American Ship That Explored the Route
to China and the East-Indies, after the Revolution" (1797)

On the frigid morning of February 22, 1784, excited crowds braved the winds blowing across New York harbor to witness the inaugural voyage of the *Empress of China*, the first vessel to travel to Canton under the American flag. On the very day the *Empress* set sail, the *Edward*, a ship bound for London, departed from the same harbor to deliver the Congressional ratification of the Articles of Peace between the United States and Great Britain.[1]

The timing of these two launches could not have been more auspicious for they took place on George Washington's fifty-first birthday. The *Empress*'s historic undertaking inspired the hopes of many citizens for the new nation's potential during a period of uncertainty. While financial gain was doubtless on the minds of investors and onlookers alike, this initial journey to China was more than an ordinary commercial venture.

For many Americans, such as poet Philip Freneau, the *Empress*'s journey to Canton symbolized both America's independence and future promise. In his poem "On the First American Ship that Explored the Route to China and the East-Indies, After the Revolution," whose first stanza is quoted in the epigraph to this chapter, the author describes the *Empress*'s journey:

> To countries plac'd in burning climes
> And islands of remotest times
> She [the *Empress*] now her eager course explores,
> And soon shall greet Chinesian shores,
>
> From thence their fragrant TEAS to bring
> Without the leave of Britain's king;
> And PORCELAIN WARE, enchas'd in gold,
> The product of that finer mold.
>
> Thus commerce to our world conveys
> All that the varying taste can please:
> For us, the Indian looms are free,
> And JAVA strips her spicy TREE.[2]

Freneau's poem captured the excitement and spirit of the moment. Aware of the profit-making opportunities in the Far East, colonial Americans had longed to explore what Freneau described as those "golden regions," "Where [King] George [III] forbade [us] to sail before." Freneau's poem announced that his compatriots were "To that old track no more confin'd, / By Britain's jealous court assign'd." This journey to China would prove that the "bird of Jove," which symbolized the American eagle, would be free to soar. Having won "clearance from Bellona," the goddess of war, Americans were unfettered by their former colonial masters.

While for Americans the freedom to send a ship to Canton may have represented the severing of ties to Great Britain, the rest of the world had yet to be convinced. Chinese officials did not recognize the Americans who traded in Canton as a separate political entity from the British for almost four months after Captain John Green of Philadelphia guided his vessel into Whampoa Reach on August 28, 1784.[3] Apart from merchant and custom receipts, the new nation went entirely unmentioned in the Qing Dynasty's official records until 1787.

This initial American foray into Chinese waters revealed a nation striving for cultural self-definition and struggling to establish diplomatic and economic relations with other nations. The objects that crossed the Atlantic (and later the Pacific) illustrate how relations between nations were articulated through the language of goods and trade, specifically in the vocabulary of material independence. For proud postrevolutionary Americans material prosperity represented independence; they no longer wanted to remain beholden to British suppliers. Writing to Lafayette just after the signing of the Treaty of Paris, George Washington expressed his disinclination to "send to England (from whence formerly I had all my goods) for any thing I can get upon tolerable terms elsewhere."[4] The nation's entrance into the lucrative Asian trade marked the initial effort of a former colonial client state trying to transform itself into a player in a global capitalist economy.

Under the British Navigation Acts of 1660, 1663, and 1696, American colonists had been barred from directly accessing foreign ports.[5] These parliamentary measures were inspired by mercantilist economic principles and intended to benefit the imperial center in London. The Acts restricted commercial carriage in the empire to British ships and effectively prevented colonies from freely trading with nations other than the United Kingdom. Advocates of mercantilism, for example the Earl of Shaftsbury, perceived that colonies, made to supply the mother country with raw materials for domestic consumption and production, could also guarantee proprietary markets for British manufactured exports—often made from the colonists' own raw materials.

Prior to independence, British merchants enjoyed the exclusive right to legally supply American subjects with goods from Asia. Under British law, crown-chartered companies such as the British East India Company, were granted exclusive access to lucrative foreign markets. By 1715, the British East India Company had developed a highly organized system of trade in Canton, which served to quench the British and American thirst for tea. For the new citizens of the postrevolutionary era, to be able to purchase goods directly from China was a sign of their newly won national autonomy. An entry in the *Salem Gazette* dated August 21, 1783, registered the possibilities of direct trade with China:

> A deep interest is felt here at the prospect of extending our foreign trade. In reference to preparations for a voyage to China in the fall from Boston, our Gazette has the ensuing passage. "We have, at an earlier period than the most sanguine whig could have expected or even hoped, or than the most inveterate tory feared, every pleasing prospect of a very extensive commerce with the most distant parts of the globe."[6]

Freed from imperial mercantile restrictions, Americans now had access to a world of exotic goods. The China trade was one part of a much larger East Asian trade that encompassed several locations throughout the Pacific world. The most prominent port within this larger system was Canton, where postrevolutionary American merchants focused their attention.

Despite their optimism, Americans soon discovered that success in China would be more elusive than they had anticipated. Buoyed by independence, Americans initially ignored the economic depression that resulted from their split from the British Empire. While America's political separation from Britain opened up markets such as China, it barred them from formerly lucrative commercial outlets in the British Empire, most significantly the West Indies. Moreover, Americans no longer enjoyed the protection of the British Royal Navy, which left them vulnerable to piracy on the high seas. And although formal trade barriers were lifted at the end of the war, other obstacles remained to secure the China trade.

"Becoming Decency" and the Launching of the "Empress of China"

The Americans' arrival in Canton can be seen as part of a larger, centuries-long story about untold wealth awaiting Europeans in Cathay. Of course, European explorers had stumbled on lands they would eventually name America while searching for a route to the riches of the East. Newly independent Americans also tried to find an eastern route. President Jefferson intended Lewis and Clark's expedition not only to chart the recently acquired territory from France, but also to map new trade routes to China. Like that quest to expand national boundaries in North America, it was hoped that the *Empress*'s voyage would help identify new areas where the nation could expand the scope of its influence.[7]

Along with the potential for economic gain, the foray into the Chinese market strengthened national confidence and pride.[8] In 1783, Boston shipbuilders constructed the *Empress* (originally named the *Angelica*), a 368-ton vessel specifically designed for ocean trade. A year later, Philadelphians outfitted the *Empress* with most of its funding and crew. Finally, on May 11, 1785, New York's dockworkers and citizens, who had seen the *Empress* off, celebrated her safe return to the Hudson River. Reflecting on the ship's passage to China, the *New York Packet* proclaimed: "All hearts seemed glad, contemplating the new source of riches that may arise to this city, from a trade to the East-Indies; and all joined their wishes for the success of the *Empress of China*, with thanks to those concerned who thus early and nobly stood forth the friends of commerce and their country."[9] In this expression of economic patriotism, friends of commerce were, by definition, friends of their country. Investment in the voyage expressed confidence in the infant nation.

Boston merchant families, who had dominated trade during the colonial period, were not the first to enter America's race to China's shores. Rather than trying to capture new market opportunities, they hoped to reestablish trade routes they had used prior to 1776. Thus, most of the first commercial vessels that sailed to China after the Revolution were owned by investors in other port cities such as Philadelphia, New York, and Salem, Massachusetts. The number of extant porcelain pieces with the coat of arms of New York and Pennsylvania suggests the importance of these states' involvement in the China Trade.[10] Nevertheless, America's China gambit was seen as a national project. Just six days after the *Empress* sailed from New York harbor, Philadelphia's *Independent Gazetteer; or the Chronicle of Freedom* published an account: "Captain and crew, with several young American adventurers, were all happy and cheerful, in good health and high spirits; and with a becoming decency, elated on being considered the first instruments, in the hands of Providence, who have undertaken to extend the commerce of the United States of America, to that distant, and to us, unexplored, country."[11] The nation's future economic prosperity would be blessed by God himself.

The article's reference to "becoming decency" reveals the desire of these postcolonial Americans to prove their capacity for decorous conduct to the rest of the world. Such remarks are common in reports of the time; the respectability ascribed to American mariners underscored the expectation that they serve as virtuous national representatives, rather than merely commercial adventurers. Writing on behalf of himself and the other owners of the ship, Daniel Parker, in a letter dated New York, January 25, 1784, told *Empress* captain John Green "on board as on Shore to cultivate the good will & friendship of all those with whom you have dealing or Connections." In Parker's estimation, this "good will & friendship" was of national importance because "You will probably be the first who shall display the American Flag in those distant Regions, and a regard to your own personal honor will induce You to render it respectable by integrity and benevolence in all your Conduct and dealings; taking the proper precautions at the same time not to be yourself imposed on." In many cases, the same ships and crews that had served during the Revolutionary War were now engaged in the China Trade—another quest for international recognition and glory. The list of men who led the earliest voyages to Canton reads like a roll call of prominent revolutionary veterans: John Green, Samuel Shaw, John Barry, Thomas Truxton.[12] Many of the key figures involved in the first voyage of the *Empress of China* were also connected through membership in the elite Society of the Cincinnati, an organization reserved exclusively for officers who had served under General Washington. When peace had arrived, many of the leaders of the revolutionary army, including Shaw, had found himself "destined to enter upon civil life, in debt, without property, and with no other foundation of hope than the character he had attained and the general confidence which his talents and integrity had inspired" (see figures 3.1 and 3.2).[13] The China trade offered them much-needed employment.[14]

The *Empress*'s journey to Canton provided a testing ground for negotiating diplomatic relations and foreign trade. The break from Great Britain was so recent that the ship's owners were unsure if the rest of the world would recognize their independence or in fact if they had even heard about it. Their doubts were well founded. Swift reported in a letter to his father that "the Chinese had never heard of us [Americans], but we introduced ourselves as a new Nation."[15] In anticipation of this problem, the *Empress*'s owners and their supporters persuaded Congress to form a committee to draft a sea letter, or passport, to accompany the ship to China. The influential New Yorker Gouverneur Morris wrote to Charles Thomson, the Secretary of Congress, asking him to write a document that would be "couched in such ample Terms as may procure a respectful Notice of the Bearer."[16] The Congressional authors were happy to oblige: the overly florid prose of the sea letter they produced reflected the new government's uncertainty about the appropriate manner in which one nation should address

Figure 3.1 Dinnerware plate. American orders for porcelain dinnerware from China were decorated with patriotic emblems, such as eagles, the arms of states, and the badge of the Society of the Cincinnati, shown here. George Washington, the president of the Society, is thought to have owned this particular piece. *(Winterthur Museum & Country Estate)*

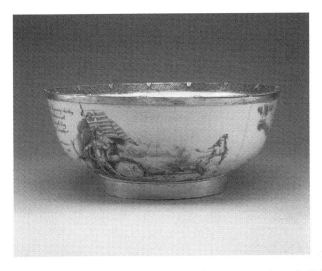

Figure 3.2 Punch bowl. This bowl was custom made in China between 1786 and 1790 for New Yorker Ebenezer Stevens. The Chinese artisan made an exact copy of a written certificate of the Society of the Cincinnati, dated December 1785, onto the surface of the bowl. Chinese artisans in search of possible designs for the export market often copied images from documents they found, including the Great Seal of the United States, coins, insurance papers, and shipping documents. *(Winterthur Museum & Country Estate)*

another. The formal salutation with which the committee opened the letter took the request for employing "ample terms" quite literally: "Most Serene, Serene, most puissant, puissant, high, illustrious, noble, honourable, venerable, wise and prudent Emperors, Kings, Republicks [*sic*], Princes, Dukes, Earls, Barons, Lords, Burgomasters, Councillors, as also Judges, Officers, Justiciaries [*sic*] & Regents of all the good Cities and places whether ecclesiastical or secular who shall see these patents or hear them read."[17] The letter was inscribed, in a careful copperplate hand, on a large piece of parchment festooned with a pale green ribbon and emblazoned with the official (yet crudely fashioned) seal of the United States, which ran the length of the document.[18]

In addition to the sea letter, the *Empress*'s owners asked Congress to give Captain Green a bundle of official documents (including the Declaration of Independence) to confirm America's legitimate emancipation from the British. In his correspondence with the Captain, Daniel Parker emphasized: "I have delivered to you herewith not only the declaration of Independence, but Copies of the several treaties made with the different European powers, and also a Sea Letter from this State signed by the Governor thereof. You will show these things as Occasion may require and avoiding all Insult to others you will consult your own Honor and that of the Country whose

Commission you bear; if any are Offered to you."[19] Both Congress's sea letter and Parker's counsel to Green indicate that the *Empress's* crew was seen to represent the nation as a whole. As it turned out, Chinese officials were unimpressed by the gestures of the inexperienced Americans. The seal of the United States that was affixed to the sea letter did nevertheless come in handy for Chinese artisans, who, recognizing the Americans' delight in this design, hand-copied it onto countless pieces of export porcelain in order to increase sales.[20]

As during the Revolution, Americans relied on European allies to help them blaze the path to independence. Old World nations provided safe harbors throughout the arduous journey to China, as Freneau would not have admitted: "No foreign tars here allow'd / To mingle with her chosen crowd. / Who, when return'd, might, boasting, say / They show'd our native oak the way." His words embodied the contradiction between the desire for independence and America's continuing dependence on other countries in the postcolonial period.

Those directly involved in the voyage to China were more realistic in their preparations. The ship owners assured Captain Green: "Letters both from the French and Dutch Ministers here" (in the United States) would "secure you a friendly reception in the ports of their Respective Nations" that dotted the route to Canton.[21] Indeed, the official documents came in handy in the course of the voyage. On meeting Europeans in Macao, the Americans gave the "gentlemen copies of the treaties between America and the European powers in amity with her" and were provided with meals and lodging.[22]

The French in particular offered assistance during the course of the *Empress's* inaugural journey. Five months after leaving New York, the *Empress* arrived unprotected in the waters of the Sunda Straits off the coast of Borneo, an area swimming with Malay and Chinese pirates. By a stroke of good fortune, the Americans met with two French ships whose officers were shocked to hear that the newcomers planned to pass through the straits without protection. As a gesture of goodwill, the French sailors vetted the sea charts of the inexperienced Americans and offered to accompany them for the rest of the journey to Canton. Writing of Captain Green's decision to accept the French offer of assistance, Samuel Shaw, the ship's supercargo (the person on board responsible for purchases), observed that Captain d'Ordelin who commanded the French ship *Triton* "expressed a wish to render us every service in his power" and that the Americans "concluded to go in company with him to Canton," as he had "been there eleven times, and is perfectly acquainted with the navigation in these seas."[23] Coincidentally, d'Ordelin had fought alongside the Americans during the

Revolution. Reminiscing about the war, the French ship captain recalled to Shaw that "the day before he left Paris, the Marquis de Lafayette received the order of the American Society of the Cincinnati, and that the king had granted permission to such officers as were entitled to it to accept and be invested with it." Shaw reported that "the French are much pleased with the honor done to their nation by the institution."[24]

The *Empress*'s crew also encountered British representatives in Macao who were unexpectedly gracious: "They allowed it to have been a great mistake on the part of their nation—were happy it was over—glad to see us in this part of the world—hoped all prejudices would be laid aside—and added, that, let England and America be united, they might bid defiance to all the world."[25] Diplomatic niceties aside, the records of the British East India Company indicate that the British were perhaps not as "glad" about American competition and the loss of the colonial market as they insisted. But they couldn't prevent the former colonials' arrival in China, and a few years later were courageously supported by the Americans in a standoff with the Chinese.

"A Great People" Enter Quietly onto the World Stage

The wave of enthusiasm that began with the launching of the *Empress of China* continued long after the voyage was complete. On the ship's return in 1787, the highly regarded periodical *American Museum* published the correspondence between Samuel Shaw and John Jay, the nation's minister for foreign affairs.[26] As soon as she heard the news of the ship's return, New York resident Rebecca Rawle Shoemaker was compelled to report it to her son Edward, then living in England. In a letter dated May 12, 1785, she wrote that the ship had "just arrived at New York from Canton in the East Indies—with a full cargo. She sailed from New York in February 1784 and Capt. Bell may be expected from the same place in a few weeks. Thee finds we are become a great people."[27]

American citizens hoped that the arrival of their compatriots in China would make a loud noise on the world stage. Those who stayed at home had the luxury of holding onto those dreams, while those directly on the scene would soon realize that their entrance would be a quiet affair. Compared to the British East India Company's ships, the *Empress of China* was so diminutive that many people in the harbor of Canton thought that the American craft was simply hailing the arrival of a British vessel. At the time, the average British ship carried more than five hundred tons, while American vessels generally held between two and four hundred tons. John White Swift, a sailor on the *Empress of China*, commenting on mistakes made during the maiden voyage, advised that future American sailors should request a ship "at least 700 or 800 Ton" as "our's is much too small."[28]

In the years after the *Empress* sailed, inexperienced and ambitious American entrepreneurs embraced this advice, thinking larger ships would necessarily yield larger profits for their owners. The plan backfired, inasmuch as the American market soon became saturated with imported goods, forcing prices down dramatically. In Salem, Elias Haskett Derby had the *Grand Turk* built to carry 560 tons. Samuel Shaw and Thomas Randall's *Massachusetts* could stow eight hundred tons, but was so beset by structural problems (owing to its construction from green wood) that it arrived in Asia with "blue mould an inch thick" in its hold. In the case of the former U.S. naval frigate *Alliance,* purchased in the summer of 1785 by Philadelphia financier Robert Morris and launched in 1787 under Captain John Barry, the ship's size—nine hundred tons—proved ill suited for the China trade.[29] The vessel was abandoned on Petty's Island in the Delaware River, north of Philadelphia.[30] These miscalculations of demand, sparked by ardor for expanding the potentially profitable China trade but tempered by lack of experience, left the United States with a declining balance of trade in 1789 and 1790.

If size mattered to the Chinese viewers, so did visual symmetries. The red, white, and blue standard, which was the symbol of America's freedom was strikingly similar to the pennant that graced the flagstaffs of the familiar and powerful British East India Company ships.[31] To add to the confusion, the men the Chinese encountered on deck looked the same as the British and they spoke the same language. Indeed, Americans and Britons even shared the same fore- and surnames, and both nations' customers ordered similar family coats of arms painted on delicate porcelain pieces. Once the purchasing patterns of Americans became established, it was apparent also that London fashions dictated American tastes. In fact, four months after the *Empress*'s arrival, official Chinese trade records were still listing American ships as British vessels. Perhaps it was some consolation to the former colonials that as long as they were considered British, they could avoid paying the customary tributary "gifts" that new commercial partners had to pay to the Chinese government in order to be permitted to enter into the coveted trade with them. Eventually, American merchants earned Chinese recognition, and received nationally distinct monikers, including "flowery-flagged devils" (referring to the stars on the American flag) or simply "the New People" (see figures 3.3 and 3.4). All the same, to many

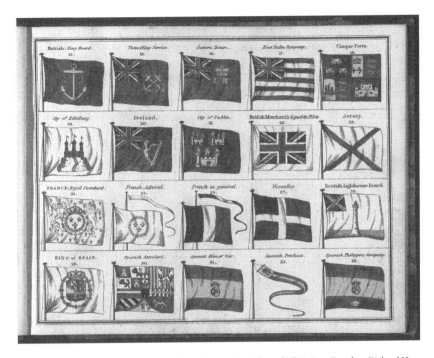

Figure 3.3 "East India Company," flag 17 from *The Maritime Flags of All Nations* (London: Richard H. Laurie, 1832), hand colored engraving. (Flag 17 is second from the right in the top row of this illustration.) One of several flags flown by the British East India Company; this one was current in 1784. There are notable similarities between this design and the one adopted by the United States of America. *(Yale Center for British Art, Paul Mellon Collection)*

confused Chinese merchants, these Americans simply were "second chop [pass required in order to trade in Canton] Englishmen."[32]

The Chinese and the Barbarians

American merchants were not alone in asserting their uniqueness to Chinese officials, who were generally unconcerned with the finer distinctions between the peoples of the various nations trading in Canton. The Chinese lumped westerners together as *fan guei* (foreign devils).[33] Before the first Opium War (1839–1842), the Chinese court dictated all terms of trade, and were disgusted by what they considered the European expatriates' unruly and lawless behavior. The decision to exercise extremely tight control over foreign traders was a result of China's earlier dealings with the British, Portuguese, and Spanish. In 1757, the Chinese court decided to

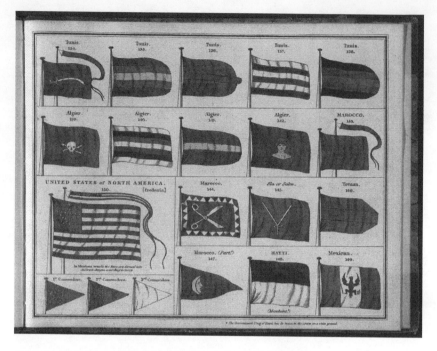

Figure 3.4 "United States of North America," flag 150 from *The Maritime Flags of All Nations* (London: Richard H. Laurie, 1832), hand colored engraving. This illustration of the flag of the United States of North America (bottom left, enlarged) appeared in a book published in London. *(Yale Center for British Art, Paul Mellon Collection)*

restrict to Canton all foreign seaborne trade and deputized local officials to treat all foreign traders as tribute-bearing representatives of vassal nations.[34] Shaw described the strictly demarcated areas of Canton (which western women were not allowed to enter): "On the whole, the situation of the Europeans is not enviable; and, considering the length of time they reside in this country, the restrictions to which they must submit, the great distance they are from their connections, the want of society, and of almost every amusement, it must be allowed that they dearly earn their money."[35] William Hunter, who spent time in Canton, reported that non-Chinese had to keep "within a space approximately 300 feet from the banks of the Pearl River and 10 miles from Whampoa Reach. In breadth from east to west, there was an area of about 1000 feet." Contrary to the common assumption of Chinese backwardness and powerlessness at this time, Europeans continued to acquiesce to Chinese demands through the end of the eighteenth century.[36] Accordingly, the already complicated Anglo-American relationship became

Figure 3.5 "Hong bowl," detail of American flag over American "factory." Modern scientific dating suggests that the American flag was painted in at a later date than the rest of the bowl's decoration. Hoping to sell this bowl to American customers, the Chinese artisan most likely painted the American flag over that of another country. (*Winterthur Museum & Country Estate*)

triangulated with their Chinese hosts, while the French presence stoked long-standing enmities between the two large European powers.

Even Britain, the most established foreign nation in Canton, felt its position in the port city was tenuous; its representatives were not spared Chinese disdain for foreign traders. The few exclusive privileges granted to the British by the Chinese court, which included a dispensation that allowed them to use the Chinese language in their transactions, were jealously guarded. In 1793, the British government sponsored a mission to China, led by Lord George Macartney (see figure 3.6), to address their dissatisfaction with the "disadvantages under which European countries trade," convinced that Great Britain had "felt" them "in a peculiar manner."[37] As English author William Winterbotham explained in his 1796 book *An Historical, Geographical, and Philosophical View of the Chinese Empire... To which is added, A Copious Account of Lord Macartney's Embassy, Compiled from Original Communications*, Canton's triangulated dynamic— with the United States, Britain, and China vying for control—influenced London's decision to send the English aristocrat to Peking. "As the existence of the government of Great Britain depends on its commerce, and as from the rising importance of the United States of America, and the progress of

civil and religious liberty in Europe, many of the old channels must be in a
manner shut with respect to British manufactures, the English government
acted with the strictest view to its own interest, in planning the embassy to
China for that purpose."[38] The importance of the mission for the British
was indicated by the "Great expenses" that "were incurred, and many exertions made to render this embassy worthy of the country from which it
was sent."[39] Macartney, however, found the Chinese emperor unmoved by
British concerns, and the potentate rather condescendingly declared that
he would not

> sacrifice the interest of his own people to any for connections, and
> would only continue his avowed partiality for the English while he
> found it for the advantage of his own subjects, and [if] they [the
> English] conducted themselves in their common intercourse in such
> a manner as to deserve it.[40]

As members of Macartney's mission would also realize, even common
Chinese subjects were decidedly unimpressed with them. One member of
the mission recorded his humiliation at Chinese derision: "To our morti-
fication we here observed, that our appearance excited rather more ridicule than respect; and bursts of laughter accompanied every transient
sight of us from our contemptible vehicle."[41] It certainly could not have
helped that a sign reading "Tribute from the Red Barbarians" had been
affixed to Macartney's own boat as he and his retinue made the journey to
Peking.

The British were outraged by the treatment afforded them by the
Chinese. Indeed, as Winterbotham reported, the British "were long distinguished, only, by the contemptuous appellation of *Hong-mow-zhin*, which,
as nearly as can be translated, may answer to that of *carotty-pated race*."[42]
The British were scandalized, for example, by their forced confinement in
quarters, as evidenced by one man who noted that they "find it very insult-
ing" to be treated more like "prisoners of the state" than dignitaries.[43] The
Chinese court's policy not to recognize any treaties with foreign nations
meant that they regarded the mission not as a diplomatic one between dignitaries of equal rank but rather as a tributary visit. This view was particularly difficult for the aristocrats who were used to being treated with
deference. In Winterbotham's summary of the Macartney mission, he
emphasized the uniqueness of the Chinese situation insofar as the British
were continuously reminded of their inequality vis-à-vis the Chinese
Empire. The Chinese were unlike other "others" that Britons had come

Figure 3.6 "The Right Honorable Lord Macartney," mezzotint print on paper (London: Thomas Simpson, 1790). Portrait of Lord Macartney, head of the first official British effort to create a formal treaty relationship with China in 1793. He suffered a humiliating defeat when the emperor refused to grant him his requests. *(Courtesy of Trustees of the British Museum)*

across in their profit-seeking ventures around the globe. The cultural, artistic, scientific, and agricultural accomplishments of China were not easily dismissed (and the Chinese would not easily allow them to be forgotten) even by those most inclined to do so. What was surprising and therefore worthy of note to Winterbotham, as well as other Britons and Europeans, was the "disdainful indifference, shewn by the Chinese" to what was considered to be the marvels of European technological achievement. Through western eyes, the Chinese people's apparent smugness or self-satisfaction meant that their culture had stagnated for centuries. For example, Winterbotham noted that even after decades of regular contact with European sailing vessels, the Chinese did not "turn their thoughts to changing or improving their own."[44] As in the case of the voyage of the *Empress of China*, there was a great disparity between exalted expectations at home and the reality met with in China.

Thus, within Canton's triangulated relations, the Americans might have been following the British lead, but the British discovered that they were taking their cues from what Macartney described as China's "displayed grandeur and elegance," which "filled the eye with delight." His mission had "quitted England with a view of prepossessing the Chinese with exalted sentiments of the grandeur and opulence of the British nation, and for the purpose of obtaining those political distinctions and commercial privileges which no other European nation could boast."[45] Recounting an audience with the emperor, the British nobleman remarked, "The commanding feature of the ceremony was that of calm dignity, that sober pomp of Asiatic greatness, which European refinements have not yet attained."[46] He continued his gushing description: "Thus I have seen 'King Solomon in all his glory'...I use this expression, as the scene recalled perfectly to my memory a puppet show of the name" seen as a child "which made so strong an impression on my mind that I then thought it a true representation of the highest pitch of human greatness and felicity."[47]

Despite this acknowledgment of Chinese accomplishments, some Britons, particularly those lacking firsthand experience, underestimated them, perhaps a result of the arrogance born of colonial success in other locations around the globe. Macartney did not have the luxury of ignorance or for that matter arrogance. In a journal entry on January 15, 1794, he wrote: "Nothing could be more fallacious than to judge China by any European standard."[48] Winterbotham observed that Macartney's haughty approach toward the court in Peking was "better calculated to succeed with a nation of Indians, or with a petty African Prince, than with the government of China; for if the court of Pekin was to be swayed by splendor, much more ought to have been done to have accomplished it than was done."[49] Most likely, it would have been a losing battle. The emperor did mark the occasion by writing a verse about how the "king of the red-haired English" had sent an envoy to his ancient kingdom:

Formerly Portugal presented tribute;
Now England is paying homage....
My Ancestors' merits and virtues must have reached their distant
    shores.
Though their tribute is commonplace, my heart approves sincerely.

Curios and the boasted ingenuity of their devices I prize not.
Tho what they bring is meager, yet,
In my kindness to men from afar I make generous return,
Wanting to preserve my good health and power.[50]

Chinese records show that China's officials were unimpressed by westerners and their standards of culture and refinement. For several years, British merchants tried unsuccessfully to convince the Chinese that their woolens were worthy of wearing.[51]

To be sure, for nearly a decade after the *Empress of China* arrived in Canton, the British continued to find it necessary to press the issue of differentiating themselves from the Americans. Recording the American presence in Canton, Macartney remained altogether unimpressed by the size of their ships and the quality and quantity of the purchases they made. In his journal entry for December 29, 1793, he patronizingly wrote that these "'second chop' Englishmen" gauchely brought teas ("which are the principal articles they take"), and ones "of a very inferior kind...chiefly paid for in dollars."[52]

In an official request to the Chinese court, the Crown's representatives requested "that the English be not confounded with other persons who trade at Canton and speak the same Language, but [are] a different nation and inhabit a very different part of the world called America."[53] This British request inadvertently highlights the constructed and relative nature of national differences. In Macartney's postscript to his "First Report to the East India Company" of December 1793, he reassures his readers: "I have taken care to put the Viceroy sufficiently upon his guard against confounding with British Subjects to those of the United States of America, whom the People of Canton have already learned to distinguish under the name of Yankees."[54]

*I*n the postrevolutionary period, the obvious markers of language and race could not be employed by the British and Americans in China; thus, flags and maps were employed to make the point. To advance his didactic objective, Macartney resorted to providing visual tokens of his country: "I have supplied the Viceroy with the appropriate flags of the respective Nations."[55] Americans used similar methods and materials to emphasize that they were a separate people from the British. Shaw tried to change Chinese perceptions about his people's insignificance by using maps to illustrate the vastness of his homeland: "when by a map we conveyed to them an idea of the extent of our country, with its present and increasing population, they were not a little pleased at the prospect of so considerable a market for the production of their own empire."[56] Shaw was sure to point out the size of the North American continent rather than the current political boundaries of the nation, in an attempt to persuade the Chinese of the importance of the United States.

Lingering American insecurities, British condescension, and mutual suspicion marked Anglo-American interactions in China. Representatives of the British East India Company took a proprietary attitude toward the newcomers and freely dispensed advice in a manner reserved for familiars of lesser standing. For their part, Americans involved in the China trade resisted entering into relations of inequality with their more seasoned British counterparts by cultivating their relations with the French in the hopes that the two European rivals would compete to serve as their patrons.[57] As in the Revolutionary War, Americans were the beneficiaries of long-standing disputes between Great Britain and France.[58] Shaw observed: "it was not difficult to discover their [the British] jealousy of the French; nor could they conceal their dislike of the good understanding we kept up with them [the French], which would sometime appear, in spite of their [British] breeding."[59] The newcomers artfully made it a habit to be seen by the British in the company of their Gallic friends. During their first visit to the British in Canton, Shaw and his retinue arrived at a dinner hosted by the British East India Company "in company with the [uninvited] French gentlemen."[60] This disrespectful gesture was not lost on France's principal rival. As Shaw recounted, after the rest of the "company had risen from table," that night, the British representative, who "wished to set us right," pointed out the Americans' faux pas: "We were...not a little disappointed at your coming together [with the French], and you may remember we then told you there had been a mistake on your part, for which we were exceedingly sorry; for, 'trust me gentlemen,' added he, with a smile, 'that *we* would not designedly have put you in such company.' "[61]

Despite their attempts to assert their independence in Canton, Americans of the *Empress* did not rebuff British attention. It was quite flattering to imagine their former colonial masters (with this term being loosely used) and wartime enemies (with this term being literally used) formally receiving them as equals in a place from which they hitherto would have been excluded. Many Americans were eager to reestablish—without the inequality of the colonial relationship—the close ties they had so recently shared with Britain. The bonds shared by Britons and Americans were even more keenly felt in such an unfamiliar location. Shaw reported that the "gentlemen of the [British] factory," including "many of their captains[,]visited us, gave invitations, and accepted ours in return."[62] Social calls such as these had obvious political ramifications and were seen as important markers of respect. If there was no longer any way to prevent American merchants from entering Canton, then the British were not averse to establishing a civil relationship with them. According to Shaw, on the arrival of the *Empress*, the chief at the British East India Company expressed the hope that "our nation and theirs would ever maintain a friendly correspondence."[63]

Americans preferred French to British assistance and documented the aid former revolutionary war allies gave to them en route to Canton as well as upon arrival in the Chinese port city.[64] In his November 30, 1784, correspondence with the French consul, Shaw complained that Chinese officials continued to mistake his American colleagues for English. He begged the French consul to impress on the Chinese "that we are the subjects of a free, independent and sovereign power."[65]

Even as Westerners competed fiercely with one another for the best prices and goods, they nevertheless had occasions to cooperate, since the Chinese authorities often dealt with the *fan guei* as a single group.[66] A newcomer to the scene, Shaw recorded his general impression of the community: "Europeans at Canton do not associate together so freely as might be expected—the gentlemen of the respective factories keeping much by themselves, and, excepting in a few instances, observing a very ceremonious and reserved behaviour."[67] The Danish provided the "only occasion when there appears to be any thing like a general intercourse" by hosting a "concert of instrumental music," performed "by gentlemen of the several nations, which every body who pleases may attend."[68]

Eager to prove themselves equal to Europeans, Americans in Canton expressed pride at any indication of acceptance and acknowledgment shown them by members of the various foreign trading houses. "The attention paid to us at all times by the Europeans, both in a national and a personal respect, has been highly flattering," Shaw wrote.[69] Thomas Randall, joint supercargo of the *Empress*, recorded that "our reception from all the European nations who had factories there, viz the English, Dutch, French, Danes, Swedes, and imperialists, was friendly and polite."[70] Shaw also kept careful records of their reception and the "civilities" shown to them, noting the order in which representatives called on them and listing invitations they received to attend national dinners and suppers. His careful record of details that did not directly relate to trade indicated that the mission was more than just a commercial endeavor.

Americans relied on Europeans for practical advice that was crucial for their success. To do business in China, one had to be versed in an elaborate and exacting system of etiquette, bribery, hierarchy, and deference—precisely the sorts of things Americans thought they had escaped after breaking free of British rule. They were at a distinct disadvantage because of their ignorance of the proper protocol deemed necessary for foreigners there. Randall noted that he and his colleagues "endeavored to obtain all the information we could respecting the Chinese, and the mode of transacting business with them" from the Europeans.[71] As "new Adventurers in this commerce," the supercargoes of the *Empress* were unsure how to obtain the best price for their goods from the Chinese merchants. Fearing they were being taken advantage of, "anxious for the interests of our employers, and our minds agitated with doubts," they "advised with an European friend" who helped them navigate the tricky waters of commerce.[72] Whenever possible, Americans avoided asking Britons for assistance in person; they did not hesitate, however, to consult written sources. After all, the similarities in language and tastes made British sources helpful and convenient. Randall sent "extracts from the English companies['] directions to their supercargoes" to Hamilton.[73] This information was perused and passed among eager Americans seeking to learn more about the trade. One handwritten and handbound British manual is littered with marginalia in the handwriting of an American seafarer. The comments direct the purchaser to do everything that the British do, though on a more modest scale. This document serves as a metaphor for the Americans' initial position in Canton, with the newcomers literally placed in the margins of British blueprints.[74]

Despite their attempts to learn from the Europeans, Americans still made numerous errors of judgment during these early years; their frequent gaffes affected their success. Shaw recounted in his logbook the humiliation he suffered because he neglected to bring the customary "sing-songs" (clockworks or other mechanical gadgets) as a gift for the "hoppo," as the highest ranking customs official was called, and his legions of subordinates. Traditionally, when they entered Canton foreigners presented these gifts, referred to as "cumshaws," as a symbol of their appreciation for the honor of trading with the great Chinese Empire.[75]

It was crucial for foreign traders to adhere to form, because as far as the Chinese were concerned, trading with the Celestial Empire was a privilege that was granted as a form of largess and could be taken away at whim. As one English author explained, the Chinese did not even place great value on the precious specie they demanded from outsiders.[76]

With respect to commerce, the Chinese entertain an opinion that it is useful only so far as it eases them of their superfluities, and procures them necessaries: on this account, they consider even that which they carry on at Canton as prejudicial to the interests of empire. "They take from us," say they, "our silks, our teas, and our porcelain: the price of these articles is raised through all the provinces; such a trade, therefore, cannot be beneficial. The money brought us by Europeans, and the high-priced baubles which accompany it, are mere superfluities to such a state as ours. We have no occasion for more bullion than what may be necessary to answer the exigencies of government, and to supply the relative wants of individuals."[77]

Emperor Ch'ien Lung dictated a mandate to King George III in 1795: "Though you assert that your reverence for our Celestial dynasty fills you with a desire to acquire our civilization, our ceremonies and code of laws differ so completely from your own that…you could not possibly transplant our manners and customs to your alien soil."[78] In this statement the Chinese emperor asserts that acquiring an object represents more than just completing a business transaction; ownership of a refined good symbolizes the possession of civility and culture of the society that produced it and by implication, that society's superiority to the buyer hoping to acquire it. This is similar to Americans' desire to obtain the products of Britain's manufactories as a way to establish their own civility. Furthermore, the doubt expressed by the emperor mirrors that of the British, who looked down on American attempts to attain status by possessing the proper goods.

One of the main concerns of the emperor was to prevent foreign influences from (as he saw it) infecting and defiling Chinese society. This was the main reason why European traders were physically segregated and forced to reside in the demarcated area of Canton in which, recalled William Hunter, "There were thirteen buildings total, and therefore the area was called Thirteen Factory Street." In Chinese, the terms "hong" and "factory" are interchangeable, if not identical, because factories included dwellings and offices. Hongs were strictly places of business, according to Hunter, who explained that the word "factory" was in this context synonymous with "agency" rather than "manufactory" (see figures 3.7, 3.8, and 3.9).[79]

To keep tight control over foreign trade, the imperial court authorized a group of thirteen Chinese merchants, collectively referred to as the "co-hong," to oversee the purchase and sale of all goods. Every ship was required to have a member of the co-hong "sponsor" it. The Chinese merchants were responsible for the behavior of the foreign traders with whom they did business. Acting as a security merchant was a lucrative position and the men who were appointed paid for the privilege of serving in this capacity.

One crucial piece of information that Americans gleaned from their more seasoned counterparts was that their success depended to a large extent on which co-hong merchant sponsored their vessel. It also became clear that it would be the Chinese representative who chose *them* rather than the other way around. "We experienced that this body of Hong merchants possessed more power than we were aware of," Randall observed with surprise. From a businessman's perspective, the most significant manifestation of this power was the ability to set prices on goods. Describing him as "a mandarine [*sic*], as well as a merchant of great opulence," Randall noted that their ship's security merchant "had an influence over all the rest of the Hong Merchants" and therefore had "monopolized the business of purchasing" their cargo. Because of this, they were forced to accept "a price we thought far inferior to what we could get, if we could obtain a freedom in our trade."[80]

Figure 3.7 This hong bowl visually narrates the arrival of foreign traders in Canton. For years prior to Americans' arrival in China, foreign traders had been purchasing such objects as souvenirs. Elaborate, more durable versions of modern picture postcards, these objects depicted the exact site in a foreign land where visitors had spent time; China traders could show them to family and friends back home. As the design shows, each nation maintained its own building, identified most prominently by its flag. (*Winterthur Museum & Country Estate*)

Figure 3.8 Detail of hong bowl showing American flag over American "factory" in Canton. *(Winterthur Museum & Country Estate)*

Americans' lack of funds, social standing, and political power proved a great obstacle to them as they tried to win the respect of both Chinese and European colleagues. Due to the relative insignificance of the monetary value of their cargo, Americans often faced difficulties finding a member of the co-hong who was willing to take them on as clients. American traders complained to their compatriots about the fact that no co-hong merchant in Canton was willing to take on the burden of a nonprofitable ship. Shaw noted, "When it happens that a ship has but a small cargo, an individual of the co-hoang [*sic*] is unwilling to be its fiador [guarantor], as perhaps his profits will not pay the duties."[81]

Figure 3.9 Detail of hong bowl showing British "factory" or headquarters in Canton. The British East India Company's dwellings were the most opulent of all the foreign factories. Americans were intimidated by the material splendor and cultural polish of their British counterparts. *(Winterthur Museum & Country Estate)*

As Chinese merchants gained prestige and influence, they became less willing to deal with insignificant clients. The most powerful members of the co-hong chose to deal exclusively with the British East India Company. Over the years, the co-hong merchant Puankequa, who initially sponsored the *Empress*, gained greater stature within the community in Canton. He was described by one source as possessing "immense property, great influence, and a high, independent spirit." In order to thwart their competitors, the British East India Company's representatives guarded their ties with him zealously. They were especially keen to prevent their American competitors from having access to his services. An unnamed source, instructing a supercargo, wrote of Puankequa: "He is devoted to the English, who endeavor to engross his whole attention and influence. He will not [any longer] undertake to Secure American Ships, either because it might not be agreeable to the English, or because their Concerns are not of consequence enough to merit his attention; and, having the choice of the business at Canton, he confines himself to the English and Spaniards." Forced to look elsewhere for a sponsor, an unnamed American supercargo was instructed to seek out Kingean, a Chinese textile merchant respected for his vast knowledge of the trade, "who is a rich old Man and of a well established House, but whose acting partner is rather slippery and tricky, though a Man so well instructed in the business of Canton, that it will be well to deal a little with him, to have the benefit of his instruction and information."[82]

American traders inserted themselves uneasily into the complex relations between Chinese authorities and European traders in this distant, unfamiliar land. Upon their arrival in Canton, Americans struggled to establish an identity that was separate from that of their British counterparts. Their modest success was reflected in the eventual appearance of the American flag on "hong bowls," which recognized in a tangible manner the arrival of traders from the United States of America. These decorative items created for the western export market featured scenic depictions of each of the foreign headquarters in Canton. Recognizing the potential to make a profit from American buyers, Chinese manufacturers instructed their artisans paint over another nation's flag with the colors of the United States of America (see figure 3.5).[83]

Trading Commodities and Identities

The American taste for Chinese goods had been shaped by British suppliers throughout the colonial period, so it stands to reason that consumers in both nations had similar tastes. Items such as "hand-painted wallpaper, bamboo silk-mounted window blinds, a dressing box with a glass, and lacquered fans" were acquired to adorn their homes and their persons.[84] The paradoxical desire to emulate aspects of British culture while simultaneously defining freedom as the repudiation of things British is reflected materially in the objects from the China Trade that survive today.[85]

At the time of the *Empress*'s journey to China, objects such as "PORCELAIN WARE, enchas'd in gold," had transformed from symbols of British imperial dominion into objects of freedom, highlighting the American ability to acquire goods from distant lands.[86] Again, Freneau captured the spirit of this transformation and the politicization of consumption of foreign items when he declared how the "fragrant TEAS" from China were all the more tasty because they were procured "Without the leave of Britain's king."[87] The most profitable goods from the China Trade were teas,[88] silks, nankeens (a durable cotton cloth that commonly came in an unbleached yellow color),[89] and porcelain,[90] so a great deal of attention was paid to discerning the quality of these items.

Although he claimed to have simple tastes befitting his republican beliefs, in fact he had a proclivity for fashionably furnished interiors that were "agreeable to the present taste."[91] And he had an obligation—not unlike the "decent" mariners whose conduct was expected to reflect well on their homeland—to present himself, and by extension the new nation, in a dignified and respectable manner. This aspiration toward gentility was facilitated by his contacts with the members of the mercantile elite of Philadelphia and New York and of the American expatriate community who were closely involved in selecting his tableware and ornaments. These men exerted inordinate influence in setting the purchasing trends in America, because they were the first to have knowledge of and access to unique new objects. Turning to alternative foreign suppliers such as China and France for fancy goods was a gesture toward a postrevolutionary effort to break the English monopoly of Americans' access to refined goods.

Wealthy American ship owners called on their supercargoes to survey what was on offer in China and bring back "anything you think curious and worth while." Robert Morris, the owner of the *Alliance,* which left Philadelphia for Canton in June 1787, requested items for personal use from his supercargo George Harrison, including "an assortment of Garden Seeds, some Gold and Silver Fish, Birds."[92] However, buying trinkets was not Harrison's primary purchasing responsibility. His official duty was to follow Morris's instructions for procuring teas, textiles, and porcelain. Morris explained: "I have not been able to command again so much silver as I wished. I am therefore very desireous [*sic*] that you should obtain the Black Teas for the return Cargo or as many of them as possible, either for Bills on Paris, Amsterdam or London, or on Credit and that the value of the Silver should be invested in Porcelain, fine Teas, Nankeens and Silks in such proportions as shall be mentioned by and by."[93] Porcelain was highly prized by American traders because it was in high demand in the United States and could be used as ballast to counter the lightness of the textiles and teas. The inventory of the *Empress* recorded that it brought back over fifty tons of "Chinaware" to the United States on its initial voyage.[94]

The surge of interest in Chinese goods was not limited to the American elite. After independence, a significant increase in middle-class ownership of Chinese goods was documented in Plymouth, Massachusetts, Providence, Rhode Island, and Chester County, Pennsylvania.[95] One study of ceramics from Plymouth, Massachusetts, between 1621 and 1800 demonstrates that prior to the 1770s, Chinese porcelain was owned mostly by merchants and by mariners of all income ranges, including common sailors. By the beginning of the nineteenth century, the occupations of those who owned these objects had broadened considerably to include schoolmasters, yeomen, widows, and a sailmaker. Apparently, common people not directly involved in the trade had the means to own china cups, plates, teapots, and mugs.[96]

Like British customers, Americans eagerly sought pieces of porcelain decorated with family coats of arms and patents of nobility.[97] European commentators could not resist remarking on how impressed the supposedly antiaristocratic patriots were with such objects. American consumers had no qualms about undermining European rules of etiquette. For instance, an American family would invent a coat of arms if one had not been conferred on them, a practice that was frowned on by the College of Heralds in England. Artisans placed advertisements in newspapers offering customers such a service. Even as Americans claimed distaste for British customs, they also coveted objects that would confer rank and status on their postcolonial owners in the traditional manner.

Americans' attempts to purchase such custom-made objects often met with disappointing results, owing to their inexperience in communicating with Chinese suppliers. There are examples in which artisans embellished pieces of porcelain with the phrases "Copy these arms exactly" and "This is the drawing to copy," obviously meant as instructions to the artist. While the results of these errors of transmission may seem comical to observers today, they reflect Americans' failures at emulating their experienced British counterparts—and were undoubtedly disappointing to customers at the time.[98]

Like the British, the Chinese reserved the "best" quality goods emerging from their workshops for their own use and produced goods specially made for the export market (see figures 3.10 and 3.11). This was true of all three of the most important trade items of the period: tea, porcelain, and textiles. The objects of the China trade symbolize the intersection of fantasy and

Figures 3.10 and 3.11. Hard-paste-covered tureen and jug. Americans arrived in China ready to enter into trading relations at the same time that China's trade with Britain was lagging due to the growth of the British porcelain industry. Items like these were custom decorated with patriotic symbols in order to appeal to American consumers. *(Winterthur Museum & Country Estate)*

reality: the fantasy being the ideas each culture had about the other and the reality being the undeniable physical presence of the object.

In order to succeed, China traders had to possess the ability to inspire the fancies of their customers at home as well as a deep understanding of the rules and vagaries of the Chinese market. Goods there were plentiful and varied in quality; lack of experience made Americans easy targets for fraud.[99] Ultimately, the success of each costly trading venture to Canton depended on the prowess of the supercargo. Even though ship owners attempted to provide as many detailed instructions regarding purchases as they possibly could, in the end, supercargoes had to be able to make spontaneous decisions on the ground about what they should purchase.

Survival in this market also entailed knowing what *not* to buy. Those with more experience in Canton knew of the danger of purchasing adulterated goods. One British author warned: "We must not confound with real tea every thing that the Chinese call *tcha*." For instance, it was said that in the province of Chang-tong, "what is sold as tea is but a kind of moss" that grew on rocks and in some of the northern provinces; "although the merchants vend[ed] it under the name *tcha-ye* [tea-leaves] that which was sold as tea was in fact not composed of real leaves." The British author warned his readers that : "If this commodity is adulterated even in China, can we flatter ourselves, that the tea we have in Europe is pure, and without mixture!"[100] An unidentified set of purchasing instructions from the 1798–99 season warned that a variety of tea called *anchoy souchong* was often "passed on the Americans & others, who are not skilled in Teas.... It resembles Souchong.... It has a high, fresh fragrant smell, and is a very excellent Tea for present use, but soon loses its virtue, and will be of little value after 12 Months, especially after a Sea Voyage."[101]

Unscrupulous Chinese traders were not the only ones to defile the purity of the tea supply. In later years, Americans excited the ire of British merchants by cutting tea with inferior leaves and selling the result to eager buyers under the names of superior varieties. The absence of legal standardization and supervision by the U.S. government allowed merchants from the United States to engage in this sort of questionable practice to a greater extent than their European counterparts. For all their disadvantages, the newcomers were good at making a virtue (or rather a profit) out of the setbacks they encountered.

The late eighteenth century arrival in China of merchandise-hungry Americans coincided with important technological and economic changes in both China and Britain. In the late seventeenth century, the Chinese responded to soaring European demands for porcelain by restoring ancient kilns; by 1719, about one million Chinese were earning their livings producing goods primarily for the export market. To increase production, artisans standardized forms and split the decoration process into two stages. They applied basic embellishments at the site of production; later, customized details were added in Canton to the customer's specifications. These changes to traditional practices of porcelain making, geared to market needs, contributed to a decline in the overall quality of the objects. At the same time, British manufacturers enjoyed success in their efforts to compete with Chinese makers of pottery, with the help of Parliament, which levied a protective duty of 150 percent on imported goods. Owing to these changes, the desires of American customers for Chinese goods kept the struggling Chinese pottery industry afloat for the next several decades.[102]

Americans and the Ginseng Trade

While American merchants were intimately acquainted with their customers' desires, those of the Chinese were less clear. The ships that left American docks in the late eighteenth century were loaded with American natural products such as tar, pitch, and cordwood—none of which would prove of interest to the Chinese. Ship owners incorrectly assumed that the Chinese would desire the same raw materials as the British. Other American goods—including turpentine, planks, tin, cordage, wire, broadcloth, and lead ballast—would prove equally difficult to sell to the Chinese. Years later, Americans still did not seem to grasp the market in China, for the 1786 cargo manifest of the *Grand Turk* from Salem, Massachusetts, listed the same items, as well as tobacco, flour, butter, bar iron, oil, sugar, chocolate, spirits, ham, candles, soap, cheese, and fish—none of which appealed to Chinese tastes. As the emperor haughtily declared in his poem, the Chinese had no need for the rum, salted fish, barrel staves, lumber, or flour. If, in the world of trade, power was expressed through who wanted more from whom, the Chinese were definitely in the best position and the Americans at this time in the worst.

Eventually, Americans would learn that their most valuable asset for carrying on trade with the Chinese was their ability to procure natural products: namely, the ginseng root and pelts they could obtain from Native Americans. Merchants from the United States embarked on a quest for refined goods that would ensure that their nation, located on the periphery of the "civilized" world, would be accepted among the ranks of the western

European nations. Ironically, while this journey beckoned them to cross the globe in search of refined goods to adorn their natural habitat, when they got there, it was the very goods of nature that would buy them what they desired.

To the delight of American China traders, ginseng grew wild in the mountainous backcountry of the northeastern United States. In a letter to Hamilton, Randall described ginseng as "the only article of much consequence in our cargo."[103] Legendary for its medical properties, the best quality American ginseng could fetch its weight in gold on the Canton market. Unbeknownst to European settlers, for generations Native American tribes had known of the curative powers of this elusive plant, which favored secluded spots in the shady hardwood forests of North America.[104] Prior to America's entrance into the China trade, no one would have predicted that their economic prosperity would be hitched to this ungainly root. Yet in 1790, Samuel Shaw published "Remarks on the Commerce of America with China," an essay in *American Museum* celebrating the potential significance of the ginseng trade to the prosperity of the new nation (see figure 3.12).[105]

The only ginseng previously available to the Chinese grew in eastern Tartary, in North Central Asia, where it provided the "principal riches" of the region.[106] Due to its scarcity and value, the emperor enjoyed the sole right of ownership of all that was procured, some of which he sold to his subjects at a hefty profit. The small root was believed to help every ailment from indigestion to impotence. According to Chinese belief, it was also valuable because of its humanoid form, and one particularly rare specimen was lauded for the size of its fifth appendage. Winterbotham described "Gin-Seng" as the "most esteemed of all the plants of China" in the 1796 edition of his *Historical, Geographical, and Philosophical View of the Chinese Empire*. "Chinese physicians speak of it with a kind of enthusiasm, and enumerate, without end, the wonderful properties which they ascribe to it."[107] Adding to the mystique surrounding the plant was the impossibility of growing it from seed, "rendering sowing them useless and thus increasing its scarcity and price."[108] The plant would not grow in "too open places" and "delights in shade and shelter from sun."[109] Ginseng was so coveted that each year the emperor "sent 10,000 soldiers into the region for six months to collect it." Mandarins were also dispatched who "oversaw the entire production" and in the end conducted a "systematic searching" of the common men to make sure "no one" (or more likely no ginseng) had "been lost."[110]

This market seemed a natural entrée for American China traders who could procure and ship large quantities of ginseng to Canton. According to another article in *American Museum,* "upwards of four hundred and forty

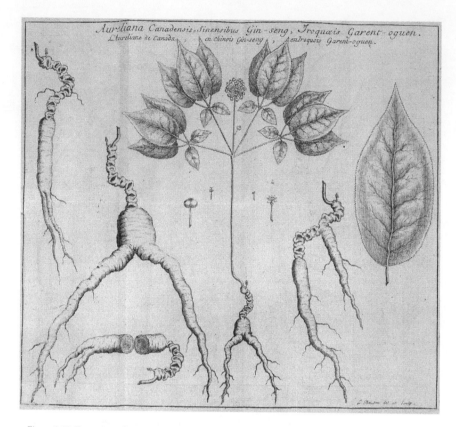

Figure 3.12 Engraving of ginseng entitled: "Aureliana canadensis, sinensibus Gin-seng, Iroquoeis, Garent-oguen," published in Joseph-Francois Lafitau (1681–1746), *Memoire Presente a Son Altesse Royale Monseigneur le duc d'Orleans, Regent du Royaume de France: Concernant la Precieuse Plante du Gin-seng de Tartarie, Decouverte en Canada* (Paris: Joseph Monge, 1718). This humble root was one of the few North America trade objects desired by the Chinese. Anglo-Americans depended on Native Americans to gather ginseng that grew wild deep in the interior. In later years, animal pelts, another natural product procured by Native Americans, proved to be another valuable North American commodity on the Chinese market. *(Beinecke Rare Book & Manuscript Library, Yale University Library)*

peculs [58,665 pounds] were carried thither by the first American ship in 1784."[111] The Americans' inexperience led to mistakes in gauging the market. A member of the crew of the *Empress* wrote from Canton on December 3, 1784: "We brought too much Ginsang [*sic*], a little of the best kind will yield an immense profit but all the European Nations trading here bring this Article, & unfortunately this Year ten times as much arrived as ever did before."[112] Two years later, according to the same source, "more than one thousand eight hundred peculs [about 240,000 pounds] were sold there, one half of which was carried in American vessels." The observer predicted that despite the glut, the root would hold its value: "Notwithstanding this increased quantity, the sales were not materially affected: and it is probable there will always be a sufficient demand for this article, to make it equally valuable."[113]

Due to this surge in demand, provincial Americans suddenly found themselves linked to the transnational networks wherein raw materials were being exchanged for exotic refined goods from Asia. Theologian Jonathan Edwards complained that Native Americans were neglecting other concerns to roam the woods in search of the root, encouraged by the rewards from European American entrepreneurs.[114] In January 1802, Amos Porter, a resident of Bennington, Vermont, was busy getting ready for the long journey to Canton.[115] A speculator at heart, after learning of the profits to be made in China, this thirty-eight-year-old bachelor spent two and a half months traversing New England in search of ginseng to trade for porcelain, tea, and silk. As he traveled, this astute businessman collected the root from Native Americans and orders for Chinese tea sets from the eager Anglo-American "ladeys" he met along the way. When he reached Boston, he boarded the *Amethyst* and headed for China.[116]

In Porter's journal, his musings on the business aspects of the trip are interspersed with his enthusiastically patriotic sentiments about the venture that for Americans was still new and experimental. At sea on July 4, 1802, the passengers celebrated the "27th Anniversary of American Independence."[117] The day did not begin auspiciously, for as Porter related, they "did not hear the discharge of Cannon" or the "sweet sound of Musick" that he "was used to" at home.[118] Still, as "true Americans," the group "forgot not the land where freedom dwels [sic]" and accordingly had a good stiff drink in the name of patriotism. The men then returned to their cabins, "received refreshment suitable," and "like the Aborigines of our Country related the most interesting events which produced the many advantages we enjoy!"[119]

Porter's journal provides a firsthand account of everyday life in Canton and specifically the trade in ginseng. The business of buying and selling the cargo immediately commenced with the arrival of the *Amethyst* in Canton on August 30, 1802. Already by September 1, Porter had made preliminary arrangements to sell his load of ginseng. He brought samples of his crop to various merchants over the course of the next several days and finalized his sale with "Mr. Exing [he later took the name Loqua] the new Security Merchant" on September 7 and 8, with the final weighing of the goods taking place over the following days.[120]

The trade in ginseng became very important to American China merchants who pinned their hopes on this lucrative trade. But they would soon find they could not corner the market on it, due to competition from

British merchants. To the American China traders' dismay, they discovered that their British competitors were selling ginseng that had been originally procured from the United States. In 1784, when Americans first entered the Chinese market, most of the ginseng in Canton was "brought from Europe...the greater part of which must have been previously sent thither by citizens of the United States."[121] This root had been the only American product imported into China by the British East India Company during the colonial period. It had been sold to British merchants by Anglo-Americans who acted as middlemen between the British and the Native American tribes. After the war, American suppliers continued to sell ginseng to the British. While the ginseng trade preceded the development of an independent American nation, it would became a key factor in establishing the new nation within the global economic community.

This is an example of how, in some cases at least, profit won out over nationalism, for Americans did not hesitate to sell their natural goods to the British traders who were competing against their compatriots for profits in the China trade. The first U.S. ship to leave the nation's shores for China in 1783 never made it to Canton, because its cargo of ginseng was sold to the British along the way. The Massachusetts sloop *Harriet* encountered several officers of the British East India Company at the Cape of Good Hope. Alarmed by the possibility of American competition, the Britons shrewdly offered to purchase the ship's load of ginseng for double its value in Hyson tea, so as to discourage American competition in China.[122] Eager to make a profit, and well aware of the market for tea, the Americans happily turned around and headed for home.

Besides the problem of competition, Americans failed to process and control the quality of their ginseng as carefully as the British. According to one account "genseng shipped from England, though originally from this country, is in higher repute on this account, for they more carefully cull it."[123] Chinese connoisseurs knew that, as with all goods on the market, not all ginseng was created equal: "It is also to be observed that bad genseng pays a duty the same as good, and the bad being mixed with the good, it is a work of time to separate it, therefore every pecul of bad genseng adds to the cost of the good."[124]

It was difficult for patriotically (and fiscally) minded Americans to accept that the Chinese preferred to buy American ginseng from British merchants. Ever the conscientious advisor to his country, Thomas explained the problem and suggested solutions to America's reputation for dealing in second-rate ginseng in his report to Hamilton: "this country produces two species of genseng, *one of* them nearly of equal quality to the Tartary genseng provided proper pain was taken to gather it in due season, and care taken in properly drying it."[125] Thomas doubted that this crucial change in business practices would take place, largely because the United States lacked an established government-supported trading company that could compete with the British East India Company. In his opinion, to prepare ginseng properly for market required "Too much capital for a single merchant to risque [*sic*], and when a [American] company is formed, it is made up in such a hasty manner, that they are obliged to purchase such genseng as is at market, and have never carefully attended to have it well garbled."[126] Thomas expressed a common complaint made by businessmen, scientists, and diplomats in the early republic: they needed more government support to compete with the British and other Europeans.[127] When this was not forthcoming, and emulation of British practices was not successful, Americans looked to new ways to prove themselves and to succeed in forming their own identity in the global community.

A New Route to China: The Northwest Fur Trade

The first American ship to Canton crossed the Atlantic and followed the Europeans' sea route around the Cape of Good Hope. Americans commonly followed the paths of exploitation that more experienced Europeans forged as they expanded their influence across the globe. Yet, as in other sectors of early American life, after an initial period of failed attempts to emulate European practices, they began to cast about for innovations that would allow them to succeed on their own terms.

Over the years, Americans experimented with alternative routes to China that included stops in places such as the Isle de France, Batavia, Borneo, Calcutta, Bombay, and ports throughout Southeast Asia. From these far-flung locations, they collected natural items that, like ginseng, they knew little or nothing about, such as sandalwood in Hawaii (then known as the Sandwich Islands) and birds' nests (for soup) in Borneo. Most significant, however, Americans developed a new route to China, sailing around Cape Horn and traversing the northwest coast of North America to Nootka Sound (located west of modern-day Vancouver) before crossing the Pacific.[128] This time it was not ginseng the Americans were after, but another natural product: fur, or "soft gold," as it came to be known. Like ginseng, pelts were procured with the assistance of Native American tribes. Americans and Europeans on trading voyages brought firearms, axes, pots, blankets, beads, cloth, and "trinkets" to the Pacific Northwest in exchange for the valuable pelts. These were later sold to the Chinese nobility, who used the fur to line their silk clothing during the cold winter months.[129]

The idea for America's postrevolutionary northwest route to Canton was hatched while Connecticut native John Ledyard was serving as a crew member of the British ship *Discovery* on Captain James Cook's final voyage.[130] The four-year journey through the still-uncharted waters of the Pacific occurred at a crucial moment of flux in Anglo-American relations. Unbeknownst to the crew, the Declaration of Independence had been signed days before they left the dock in England on July 12, 1776. Just prior to independence, Franklin had been helping the British to strategize how to use Cook's earlier findings to expand into new territories. It is not surprising, then, that he and other early Americans recognized the importance of the region to the growth of the United States.

Ledyard's responses to what he observed on his trip reflected the growing separation between the American colonists and their mother country; although still a subject of Great Britain, he used the trip to scout out economic opportunities for his native land. He was struck by the exquisite beauty of sea otter pelts shown to the crew by Northwest Indian tribes; he was even more impressed, later in the voyage, when he learned of the profits that could be made in Canton from fur. The first American on record to sail the Pacific, Ledyard encouraged his compatriots to enter the lucrative China trade by exchanging furs from the Pacific Northwest for highly coveted products such as tea and silk. In the spring of 1783, he began to try to drum up support for his trading idea, both in person and by publishing an account of his journey. Known as the "American Marco Polo," he spent his life unsuccessfully seeking financial backing for his plan in the hope that America would achieve economic dominance in the Pacific. Although his scheme was premature, it proved prophetic.

In 1787, the *Columbia* set off for the Northwest Coast to follow the route Ledyard had imagined. Other ships were to follow this route. In 1796, the aptly named man-of-war *Otter* landed in California; its crew, captained by Ebenezer Dorr, had traveled thousands of miles in search of the luxuriously thick, black, shiny pelt of the otter, with its breathtaking silvery gleam, and measuring five feet long and more than two feet wide. The *Otter* helped open up this trade to other American ships, which eagerly combed the area from the Aleutian Islands to Baja California in search of these valuable pelts that could garner up to $300 apiece in Canton.

As this trade in North American pelts began in earnest, Americans participated in clandestine exchanges with local native tribes against the prohibitions of the Spanish, who at the time laid claim to trading rights in the region. Competition by British, Russian, Spanish, and French traders for dominance in these waters and the adjoining land of the Pacific world were already long-standing. Americans came to dominate this trade, but only after 1812.

Seal pelts also garnered a profit in the Chinese market. After returning from his voyages, Dorr sponsored further expeditions in this fur trade. On September 11, 1799, he and his relations instructed Captain Samuel B. Edes to travel from the "Falkland Islands, Georgia, Isles of Amsterdam, St. Paul's in the southern ocean to the islands of Maasfurero and Juan Fernandez in the South Pacific Ocean" in search of hides; "set your people to work killing seal and preserving their hides," either by drying or pickling, "as weather permits well dried is our wish in Preference."[131] The ship was outfitted with provisions for three years, with the men on board supplementing their supplies with the "flesh of fish birds and seal." Dorr estimated that Edes's crew would be able to procure "50–60000 prime seal skins in one season." Edes was then ordered to take the bounty to China to sell. He was to receive 7 percent of the profits after cost and his men $30 each. In addition, he was entitled to five tons of space in the hold of the ship.

While the ships' ledgers tallied profits and losses, they did not record the trail of blood left in the wake of these expeditions. Entire animal populations were decimated in the waters frequented by these fur hunters. The human damage was devastating as well. The social structures of the Native American tribes that supplied these furs were ultimately destroyed by the pressures of the trade.[132] Thus it was through a variety of strategies, including the destruction of flora and fauna, that Americans gained dominance in the China market in the late nineteenth century. Although not the first to trawl the rich waters of the cold Pacific for fur-bearing mammals, Americans would dominate the trade after their British competitors were expelled after the Americans won the War of 1812.

Americans Compete in Canton

The merchants of the new United States entered international trade with more ambition than expertise, and suffered some painful rebuffs in their attempts to take advantage of the patterns of trade and cultural relationships already established by their British competitors. Americans responded to the demand for raw commodities from the remote corners of North America and gave up trying to sell manufactures the Chinese considered crude and undesirable. It was only after the British victory over China in the

Opium War of 1842 that American merchants really began to overcome their Old World competitors in the China trade. That year, a British comic journal published the following lines:

> With this nation so deluded
> Peace is happily concluded:
> Let us now no longer teaze
> The unfortunate Chinese.
> We are happy to befriend them;
> Cotton night-gowns we will send them;
> For their use we will import
> Articles of every sort.[133]

The British were not the only beneficiaries of this military victory; American traders, now equipped with fast, oceangoing clipper ships and large quantities of competitively priced goods, followed close behind them. Emulation had given way to innovation. By the mid-nineteenth century, American traders would rival and even outstrip the British companies whose competition had seemed so daunting in the postrevolutionary era. The American traders accomplished this by responding faster to the growing Chinese market and by buying Chinese goods of lesser quality than the British. In this new situation, as in so many others before, the movement and exchange of goods became a new arena for the formation of national identity and for the negotiation of America's place in the world.

If British luxury imports had been politicized and seen as a symbol of oppression and dependence before and during the Revolutionary War, then Chinese imports procured directly by American merchants in the postrevolutionary era became for Americans an important symbol of their nation's independence and freedom to expand into and exploit the lands and seas beyond the confines of their former colonial world. The Americans' development and eventual domination of the trans-Pacific trade promised that they could propel their nation's status upward by taking advantage of their geographical position between Europe and the Far East.[134]

Four

SOWING THE SEEDS OF POSTCOLONIAL DISCONTENT

The Transatlantic Exchange of American Nature and British Patronage

"No one in Europe can. . . appreciate correctly the difficulty of the task [producing a comprehensive scientific study of the flora of South Carolina] in which I have engaged. The want of books, the want of opportunities for examining living collections or good herbaria, the want of coadjutors, have all served to render my task arduous, and to multiply its imperfections."

—Stephen Elliott, President of the Literary and Philosophical Society of South Carolina (c. 1825)

The Unfortunate Incident of the Florida Sandhill Crane

For several years, a sketch of the Florida sandhill crane made by Pennsylvanian William Bartram was the only proof that British naturalists had of the bird's existence (see figure 4.1).[1] This was because Bartram's own men had shot, roasted, and eaten the rare specimen while on a collecting excursion through the American Southeast sponsored by their English patron, John Fothergill. Fortunately the artist had executed a drawing before supper commenced. The incident was explained by naturalist George Edwards: "This specimen was shot by Bartram's hunter companions." To the dismay of British naturalists, Bartram's sketch was the "nearest approach to a type specimen" in existence, "the original having been eaten."[2] Time and again, exasperated British naturalists discovered that despite painstakingly detailed instructions, their provincial American contacts in the field mishandled—or in this case ate—their specimens. When organizing their transatlantic exchanges, well-known men such as Sir Joseph Banks experienced the same frustrations as common Americans did when the delicate British manufactures they had ordered arrived broken at their destination.[3]

Frustration and disappointment abounded on both sides of the Atlantic. In 1777, Bartram returned to his home in Pennsylvania, after four long

Figure 4.1 Black ink and watercolor print entitled "Wattoola Great Savanah Crane [Florida Sandhill Crane] [*Grus canadensis pratensis*]", drawing by William Bartram [1774], 270 x 220 mm. This drawing from the collections of the British Museum was the closest thing to a type specimen for European and American natural scientists. (*British Museum*)

years and twenty-four hundred arduous miles, not to accolades and invitations to lectureships in London and Edinburgh but to silence. Much had changed in the transatlantic world while Bartram was traipsing through the backwoods. He had set off on his journey as a loyal subject of the British Crown; when he returned, America was fighting for independence. Although his compatriots had succeeded in gaining their freedom, Bartram would find that inequality defined the exchange between America and Britain.

While on his travels, Bartram had sent hundreds of rare finds representing "New Genera or Species" to London. Still in the dark about the fate of his life's work in 1788, Bartram took up his pen and wrote to a British contact, Robert Barclay, noting that he had "never learn'd what became of the [his] specimens." Despite being shown such disrespect for so many years, he assumed the humble stance of someone speaking to a superior.

In a tone that stood in stark contrast to the haughty attitude Banks often took with his American contacts, Bartram noted he would "cheerfully offer for the inspection and amusement of the curious" duplicates he had in his possession. He assured his English correspondent that he would be not be "expecting or desiring no other gratuity than the bare mention of my being the discoverer, a reward due for traveling several thousand miles mostly amongs't Indian Nations which is not only difficult but dangerous, besides suffering sickness, cold & hunger. But with a perfect Sense of gratitude I with pleasure acknowledge that Noble Fothergill [for] liberally supporting me whilst in his employ with ample pecuniary assistance."[4] The material evidence of Bartram's efforts can be found today in the British Museum of Natural History, where thirty-eight of the specimens he sent to Barclay in 1788 are still housed.[5]

The Nature of Exchange and the Exchange of Nature in the Transatlantic World

Americans went deep into the wilderness that was their own backyard and came out with nature newly packaged in a range of salable and transportable forms, including dried plants and animal bodies, cuttings for propagation in Great Britain, and detailed field notes and sketches for botanical classification. This chapter examines how colonial and postrevolutionary Anglo-Americans transformed nature into a commodity to be exchanged for British patronage during the eighteenth and early nineteenth centuries, and Americans' attendant anxieties related to their role as native informants rather than fellow philosophers, churchmen, and botanists. Aspiring Anglo-Americans commodified their access to the exotic plants and people of the New World in order to gain recognition and support from powerful individuals in the metropolis.[6] While this unequal relationship of exchange had its roots in the colonial period, Americans' distaste for their subordination became more acute after independence.[7]

Most colonial naturalists toiled in obscurity, while the information they produced formed the basis of European botanic knowledge of their regions.[8] Their sketches, like the dried specimens they gathered, were considered raw material from which botanical art was made rather than that art itself. As draftsmen, Americans lacked the sophistication of those classically trained in the conventions of the western European aesthetic tradition. The "lack of perspective and in drawing the microscopic details" were seen as "the points in which native artists are mainly deficient," as the British naturalist Sir Joseph Hooker put it.[9] Bartram's career was defined by his failure to garner widespread public recognition of his artistic talent and field research.

Natural products commonly found in North America became valuable commodities when they were transported to European centers of study. The creation of the cultural value of these New World objects of nature was related to a change in their location from a place of abundance to one of scarcity, much as the mercantile system shifted and revalued other types of goods. British naturalists, whose prestige and expertise were founded on the breadth of their exotic collections, coveted plants that most Anglo-Americans thought worthless.[10] Foliage that was trampled under the feet of Americans each day could provide a valuable addition to an Old World garden or herbarium. As the wealthy English merchant and plant enthusiast Peter Collinson complained, "What was common with them but rare with us they did not think worth sending."[11]

As noted, the early Americans had little more than natural products to offer in exchange for the refined manufactured products of China, Britain, and Europe. Indeed, European opinions of what was most valuable about America were dominated by notions of the primitive and exotic, including commodities such as tobacco, cotton, and sugar, as well as knowledge about native tribes and African Americans. Enlightenment thinkers such as Adam Smith were at the center of the refined production of knowledge but far removed from the sources of the raw data on the basis of which they made their scientific claims.[12]

Transforming Nature and "Natives" into Commodities

In 1786, twenty-year-old Benjamin Smith Barton left Philadelphia and set off for medical training in Edinburgh. On his arrival in the Scottish capital, Barton went about trying to gain access to the city's intellectual circles. He and other American naturalists and physicians benefited from the long-standing European interest in knowledge about the "wild environs" of the New World. Barton astutely commodified his knowledge of American "nature" by publishing widely and speaking on the subject, seeing it as the surest path to distinction in Europe for an American man of science. He found enthusiastic audiences for his presentations on the "natives" of North America—both plants and people—at learned societies in Britain, as when he presented his lecture "Natural History of the American Savages" at the Speculative Society.[13]

Barton also capitalized on British interest in American themes through publishing. Edinburgh intellectuals eagerly anticipated Barton's *Observations on Some Parts of Natural History*, a monograph on the ancient Indian mounds of North America in which he discussed such mounds in western Pennsylvania and suggested that the builders might have been the Toltecs of Mexican antiquity.[14] Barton based this work on observations he had made two years earlier while assisting his uncle, David Rittenhouse, with a boundary survey expedition in western Pennsylvania. He also circulated two unpublished essays on the occurrence of albinism in the African American population and the origins of the North American Indian.[15]

Barton was soon honored with memberships in several professional societies in Edinburgh, including the Speculative Society, the Royal Medical Society, the Edinburgh Natural History Society, and the Society of Antiquaries of Scotland.[16] These honors distinguished him from the majority of Americans studying abroad and revealed a shrewd ability to make the most of his exotic New World background. Before leaving Britain, Barton laid the groundwork for continuing his work, promising several prominent naturalists that he would supply them with objects from the wilds of his native Pennsylvania. Like other Americans, he would exchange Indian and African American skulls, animal parts, plant cuttings, and seed specimens for access to publishers and the latest in European scientific knowledge.

Throughout the colonial period, Americans with scientific and artistic aspirations relied on the support of influential British patrons to include them in transatlantic cultural exchanges. The correspondence between men of science in North America and the Royal Society attests to Americans' continued dependence on Britain decades after the Revolutionary War. While president of the Society, Sir Joseph Banks received numerous requests from the United States: scientific queries, publishing proposals, and other professional matters.[17] Barton established his usefulness to Banks by promising to procure for him botanical prints, seeds, and dried specimens. On May 26, 1793, Barton wrote to Banks that although extremely busy with "the duties of my academical [*sic*] station," he had found time to send "a few specimens," including one from the Blue Ridge Mountains of Pennsylvania, and pledged that he would "not forget to send to you from time to time, specimens of our indigenous plants." In another attempt to draw Banks into a relationship of exchange, Barton noted that he would be "glad to have your opinion concerning them."[18]

Barton enlisted the help of anyone who could gather unusual plants and information from the outer fringes of the western frontiers of the newly formed United States.[19] He sent out numerous questionnaires to individuals on the frontier regarding Indian tribes of North America, asking them to speculate on topics such as the age at which Indian girls began to menstruate. He gathered information from European immigrants passing through Philadelphia, from fellow American botanists, from men on official business to the Native American tribes, and from the Native Americans themselves. Among Barton's most important sources of information was William Bartram.

Barton's British contacts made him an important source of European medical and scientific information that was hard to obtain in America. This privileged access to a scarce commodity enabled Barton to start the *Philadelphia Medical and Physical Journal,* one of the first American scientific and medical journals, in 1804.[20] In recognition of the value of his transatlantic connections, and in an effort to reinforce them, Barton dedicated the first volume to Banks, "one of his majesty's most honourable privy council and president of the Royal Society of London."[21] The enthusiastic dedication belied Barton's craving for acknowledgment of his countrymen's efforts to pursue refined knowledge. He wrote that he was "anxious to show you, that in the United-States there are also cultivators of this noble science." Barton also acknowledged "how great have been [Banks's] services and merits" to botanists in America and to him personally. "To you, Sir, I am, certainly, indebted for a portion of what little reputation I may have in life."[22]

Barton's effusiveness toward his patron suggests the asymmetrical relationship between European and American intellectuals at the time. Americans traded exotic specimens from a largely unexplored continent in exchange for manufactured goods and scientific training from the Old World. This traffic entailed a variety of objects: firsthand topographical observations in exchange for published maps, ginseng root for fine tea and porcelain, plant and animal specimens for abstract classificatory schemes and botanical taxonomies, information about American Indians for entrée into British scientific societies. The movement of these objects and ideas took place within a network of exchange in which America was considered less civilized than Europe.

As discussed in the previous chapter, ginseng, the odd-shaped root that grew wild in the Pennsylvania backcountry, was one of the few things American traders could procure that was of any value to the Chinese. The transnational trade in ginseng illustrates a geography of value in which commodities are transported from regions where they are plentiful to others where they are scarce. In the American West, ginseng was of some value to the Indian tribes who used it in medicine; and whereas it was of no value at all to Anglo-American settlers in Philadelphia, it had an extremely high value half a world away in China. Similarly, men of letters in Britain whose prestige and expertise was derived by the breadth of their botanical collections valued plants that Americans found worthless.

"To Equal Their European Brethren": The Exchange of Souls

American Congregationalists also relied on the dynamic between scarcity and abundance to maintain their place in the transnational exchange of culture, even going so far as to commodify the souls of the Native Americans around them. In many ways, the souls of Native Americans had a value similar to that of other "natural" objects. Try as they might, groups like the Missionary Society of Connecticut (CMS) found that they could not disentangle themselves completely from the taint of savagery.[23]

The United States of America was located on the margins of the transatlantic world, where so-called savages resided. Americans and British were physically distant, yet culturally similar to one another, whereas Anglo-Americans and Indians were physically close and culturally disparate. Unlike European missionaries who had to travel great distances to find so-called heathens to convert, Americans already lived among them. "Savages" were scarce in Britain and plentiful in America: this relationship of scarcity and plenty led to the commodification of savage souls. The value the British placed on this particular New World commodity meant that the American missionary societies who had easy access to Native Americans garnered more attention from London than they otherwise would have enjoyed.

However, within this process of commodification lay a central tension: proximity to "savage" populations disturbed Americans who were trying to demonstrate to the world that theirs was a civilized society. Anglo-Americans' self-consciousness about their rusticity existed in the colonial period; at this time many identified themselves as Englishmen who happened to live in North America. Although the Revolution broke formal political connections to the British Empire, Anglo-Americans certainly did not want to replace them by linking their identity with nearby Indian tribes. A delicate balance had to be reached by those white Americans who wished to construct a unique national identity that was neither European nor Native American.

In the years following the Revolution, American missionaries looked to London for guidance in establishing a separate national missionary organization. Although these New World men valued their ties to a worldwide missionary movement, their priorities often clashed with those of their British missionary mentors.[24] For instance, CMS members were reticent about converting local Native American tribes despite the fact that they wanted to win the approval of their colleagues in the London Missionary Society (LMS) who were pressuring them to do just that.[25]

Unfortunately for the Americans who wanted to impress their British brothers, the LMS defined success in the missionary field as work among the Indian tribes, an area the CMS wanted to avoid.[26] In its first letter to Connecticut's Committee of Missions in 1789, the LMS encouraged the Americans to work among the native population; in each of their ensuing letters, they continued to urge the Connecticut missionaries to increase their work among the Indians. In a letter dated January 31, 1801, T[homas] Howeis assured Reverend Abel Flint of Hartford that the LMS was waiting in expectation for news of the Americans' success. Howeis wrote: "Nothing will be more grateful to us than to hear your increasing progress."[27]

The LMS appealed to God to convince the American missionaries to follow their lead and make the conversion of native peoples their first priority. Speaking in his capacity as secretary of the British organization, George Burder voiced his concern about Americans' strong preference to send missionaries to work with New Englanders who were settling new frontier communities rather than to Native Americans.[28] Burder wrote: "our prayers continue to ascend with yours that He in whom hands is the residence of the Spirit, may abundantly increase their numbers, and enable your Society not only to visit the vacant churches, but to extend your Christian benevolence to the native heathen, multitudes of whom are perishing for lack of knowledge." The Londoners continually reminded the Connecticut missionary workers that Native Americans lived nearby. One LMS leader remarked how fortunate the Americans were to have "near in local situation multitudes of the Heathen." The reports sent to the CMS by the LMS told tales of the hardships involved in sending missionaries to Africa and Asia in order to find potential converts.[29]

The CMS tried to live up to the expectations of the British,[30] but its missionary efforts remained primarily focused on white settlers.[31] There were a number of other ways the LMS set the agenda for the work of the Connecticut missionaries. In a letter dated July 1803, Burder attempted to "excite and animate a Spirit of more vigorous exertion in all hands" for the promotion of "the same great object"[32] by encouraging the CMS to begin a Bible society in America like the one initiated by the LMS. "Permit us Brethren to urge you to institute a similar engaging in your vicinity, and also to try what can be done to promote the object for which such enquiries [sic] are entered upon. And we shall feel particularly pleased in submitting any communications on the Subject to the Christian Brethren who have entered with diligence and Zeal on so noble a pursuit."[33] Despite their unwillingness to change their agenda regarding Native Americans, the leadership of the CMS believed that the ideas emanating from Britain were models worthy of emulation. The Americans formed a "Book Committee" in September 1803, a few short months after the letter from London was received.[34] The CMS attributed the origins of the American Bible Society—still in existence today—to the direct urgings of their British counterparts. They traced the spread of the innovation of "distributing gratuitously the Holy Scriptures, without note or comment among the poor," first from the "establishment and exertions of the British and Foreign Bible Society, and subsequently in the formation and labors of numerous similar societies in Europe, Asia, and America." An article in the CMS's periodical proclaimed: "In imitation of the laudable example set by this PARENT Society, numerous auxiliary societies have been formed in Great Britain: and in this country 'Christians' have shown a disposition to emulate the conduct of their transatlantic brethren."[35]

The Connecticut Congregationalists' use of "Parent" to describe the British society reveals how they conceptualized their relationship to the former mother country. As the article states, American evangelicals had a "disposition to emulate" those with whom they used to share membership in the British Empire and with whom they continued to share membership in the Redeemer's Empire. But if brothers could strive for equality with each other, it was uncertain if children could surpass their elders.[36] Although the American missionaries followed the LMS's lead in forming a book committee, they modified its activities to suit their own needs. Not surprisingly, the London missionaries hoped that the CMS's Book Committee would produce translated versions of Christian writings for Indian nations. Instead, the American committee purchased books in English and published pamphlets, broadsides, and annual narratives for distribution among western white settlers. In contradiction to London's evangelical goals of converting Indians, the Americans preached to the converted, publishing works such as the "Summary of Christian Doctrine" published in 1803, which documented the basic tenets of the Congregational faith.

The grandeur of the missions the British and the American societies were able to sponsor depended on their social and material conditions. Initially, American Christian organizations could not afford to send representatives to distant locations in Asia, Africa, and the South Pacific as the LMS was doing. The newcomers hoped that they would eventually be able to undertake similar overseas projects as a way to prove their equality with their British counterparts. The American Board of Commissioners for Foreign Missions (ABCFM) was founded in 1810 and began the following year to make plans to undertake just these sorts of ambitious projects.

Despite the fact that the founding of ABCFM was supposed to represent American independence from the British, one of the organization's first acts was to send a lone emissary, Adoniram Judson, Jr., on a "special mission" to the LMS's Board of Directors to request financial assistance. The demands made by the ABCFM seemed a bit unrealistic; they hoped to receive the money without strings attached. The ABCFM had four volunteers ready to go overseas but wanted the LMS to pay their way, give them "ample and correct information relating to missionary fields," provide them the "requisite preparations for missionary services," and tell them "the most eligible methods of executing missions." Judson was instructed to find out "if circumstances should render it desirable, you and your brethren can be supported in Missionary service for any time, by the London funds, without committing yourselves wholly and finally to the direction of the London Society."[37] Not surprisingly, the LMS did not agree to the terms of the demands. Burder did offer to hire the four Americans as members of their own missionary society. However the ABCFM would have no control over the missionaries.

In letters written in July and August 1803, Burder urged the CMS to focus instead on all of the heathen souls being lost within easy reach of American missionaries.[38] In the first letter, he assured his coreligionists in Connecticut: "We doubt not the common Interest of Zion have lain sleep upon your Hearts; and that we have shared the Blessing of your prayers... we therefore address you in the confidence of fraternal regard that you may abound more and more.... We wish to animate a Spirit of more vigorous exertion in all hands to promote the same great object."[39] Although the sentiments expressed were polite and encouraging, the message was mixed. Did the LMS doubt the zeal of the American missionaries? Had their lack of action warranted a question about how much "interest" in spreading the gospel lay in their hearts? By contrast, the Connecticut missionaries did not feel the need to express similar directives to the LMS.

The CMS's halfhearted attempt at converting the natives did not bear fruit, despite the desire to live up to British expectations. From the beginning, the Board of Trustees of the CMS was skeptical about the viability of such missions and was thus hesitant to put resources into the endeavor. After receiving a scouting report from Reverend John Sergeant of New Stockbridge in 1800, the trustees noted: "The contents of the letter [from Sergeant] are such as lead us to fear the business will fail."[40]

Ironically, it seems as if Sergeant's own report regarding the feasibility of Indian conversion in part convinced the CMS to reject his later request to begin a mission. Early in 1802, Abel Flint wrote a letter denying Sergeant's proposal to conduct missionary work among the Indians on behalf of the CMS, citing "lack of funds."[41] Sending along a record of the Board's vote, Flint wrote: "The Trustees wish to do every thing in their power towards Christianizing and civilizing the Indians...but from the present state of their funds they do not conceive themselves authorized to meet your proposition as you will see by their vote."[42] In the following year, Reverend Elijah Waterman delivered a sermon that heaped scorn on this excuse for not sending missions to Indians:[43] "This objection generally comes from those whose covetousness is [i]dolatry; but no people, in proportion to their numbers, are more able to contribute to the support of Missionaries than the inhabitants of Connecticut.... God has given abundantly into our hands the means of holding out the cup of Salvation to the heathen tribes."[44] In February 1804, when the CMS sent Reverend Joseph Badger to recall Reverend David Bacon from the Michimackinia Indians to redirect him to work among white settlers in New Connecticut, the CMS revealed that funding was not at issue. In a letter to Badger, Flint wrote: "The reason why Mr. Bacon is recalled from where he now is, is that there appears no probability of his succeeding among the Indians in that vicinity."[45]

The message the CMS sent to the British regarding their efforts among the Indian tribes differed from their internal expressions of doubt and lack of enthusiasm toward the project. In 1805, the CMS apologized to the LMS for its lack of missionary work among the Indian tribes: "We regret that it is not in our power to communicate to you the pleasing intelligence that the Gospel is spreading among the Indian Tribes on our borders."[46] Although the leaders blamed their failure on several factors their main argument was that they first had to attend to the white settlers in the western territories. They also blamed traders who did not wish to "promote the civilization and Christianization of the poor, benighted Savages," wishing to keep them in "ignorance and barbarity that they may the more easily obtain an advantage over them in their trade."[47] Their failure to work with Native American tribes on a large scale represented an inability to live up to British standards.[48] The CMS strove to meet the expectations of their more powerful counterparts not out of a simple need to emulate them, but as an attempt to prove that Americans were equally capable of success.

From the very beginning, the men who ran the CMS attempted to establish the United States as an important center in the international missionary
effort. Building on the rhetoric that saving heathen natives was an international priority, the editors of *Connecticut Evangelical Magazine* claimed that
their journal would have plenty of material for its pages: "The wonderful
spirit of religious missions to heathen people, and to our new and scattered
settlements on the borders of the wilderness, which, within five years, hath
awoke in both Europe and America, furnishes much new and interesting
matter."[49]

By asserting the importance of the American West in awakening a spirit
of mission all over the world, the Connecticut missionaries defined America
as the central site of transatlantic missionary work and the inspiration for
British efforts, rather than the other way around. They were striving figuratively and literally to put themselves on another type of map, one that
represented the progress of global Christian activity. Despite the grandeur
of their claims, rhetorically shifting the center from the Old World to the
margins of America was simply not enough to erase Americans' desire to be
recognized by the British as players on a global scale.

The Hierarchy of Scientific Objects in Transatlantic Scientific Networks

Mirroring a larger movement and transformation of commodities across
the Atlantic, scientific knowledge and specimens were gathered in raw form
in the United States and then refined in European centers of knowledge
production. The processes of transformation for plants and animals involved
naming, almost invariably in Latin. These objects were refined through
inclusion in universal categories that Enlightenment thinkers were creating
in Scottish and German universities. Such scientific knowledge was then
reimported at great cost by Americans, who had to procure interesting and
exotic samples in order to trade for the scientific books they desired.
Americans, such as the father-and-son team John and William Bartram and
Benjamin Smith Barton, acted as middlemen and visual translators between
the unexplored "wilds" of the New World and Great Britain.

The networks of exchange of raw scientific information about North
America for finished scientific objects from Britain that functioned in the
postcolonial period already had a long history. People had been sending
New World seeds and dried plant specimens to centers of learning in Europe
since the later part of the sixteenth century. European authors creating
descriptive works about nature and illustrations for books consulted collec-

tions of preserved specimens from North America housed in London.[50] Seeds transported across the Atlantic were coveted by British botanists and aristocrats whose passion to add to their botanical and pleasure gardens fed the quest for New World specimens. For their part, aspiring American botanists needed access to the fruits of intellectual endeavors being produced in faraway European centers of knowledge. British botanical enthusiasts proved to be key contacts for Americans involved in all aspects of natural history.[51] This set of mutual needs and desires established long-term transatlantic relations of exchange.

London merchant Peter Collinson and his associate Dr. John Fothergill, the proprietor of one of the finest botanical gardens in London, were among the key nodes in this network.[52] They were among the most influential patrons of North American botanists during the mid- to late eighteenth century. As the British agent for the Library Company of Philadelphia, Collinson became friendly with intellectually minded Americans such as Franklin and Bartram, who could supply Collinson and his wealthy clients with rare plants from the American frontier.

If amateur American naturalists wanted to participate in metropolitan cultural networks, it was incumbent on them to be able to exchange goods that fulfilled their wealthy and cultured British patrons' desire for the exotic. British philosophers amassing natural history collections depended on reliable American contacts who knew enough about botany to be able to correctly locate the specific natural specimens they requested. Perhaps even more valuable was the American who could also identify new species, for cuttings of plants not yet seen, identified, or categorized by fellow European men of letters were highly prized.

Throughout the eighteenth century and well into the first half of the nineteenth century, prominence among American naturalists was commonly measured by the number and notoriety of their European correspondents. This relatively small circle of well-connected individuals who were the leaders of early American public life remained dependent on British approval for success within their own society. They organized learned societies and wrote letters of introduction for fellow provincials traveling across the Atlantic. The relationships between Americans like Franklin, John and William Bartram, and Barton, and Britons such as Banks, Collinson, and Fothergill, were based on a shared interest in science and botany. Franklin's famous experiments with electricity would not have been possible without the scientific apparatus from London that Collinson had sent to him at the Library Company. It was Collinson and Fothergill who recognized the scientific significance of this experiment and arranged

to have the findings published in Britain.[53] These transatlantic alliances significantly impacted the development of a fledgling American society.[54]
Franklin managed to win the powerful Englishman's patronage for the
Pennsylvania Hospital, where Fothergill's donations of British goods formed
the nucleus of the hospital's library, the first of its kind in America. To this
day, the Englishman's initial gift of William Lewis's 1761 *Experimental
History of the Materia Medica* is noted as the first volume in the institution's
collection. Fothergill sent other scientific objects back with American students studying in Britain; when William Shippen, Jr., returned to America
after graduation, he was given anatomical casts and paintings that were
critical for medical instruction.[55]

Like his close friend Franklin, John Bartram depended on British
patrons for his reputation and success. Among his other activities, he was
a founding member of the American Philosophical Society.[56] His correspondents included Collinson, who was also a benefactor of the Library
Company of Philadelphia; Sir Hans Sloane, physician to King George II
and president of the Royal Society; John Dillenius, director of the botanical
garden at Oxford University; and Philip Miller, director of the Chelsea
Physic Garden and author of the most widely distributed book on gardening
in America, *The Gardener's Dictionary* (1731).[57] The American naturalist's
steady stream of correspondents constituted a who's who of British and
European intellectuals.[58]

John and William Bartram scoured the far reaches of the mid-Atlantic
region in the service of their English patrons, such as Fothergill and
Collinson. The Bartrams possessed a great talent for hunting down discoveries that were prized in Europe. They collected numerous new specimens
on their extensive ramblings, and John's eclectic accumulation of rare and
unusual plants eventually grew into a commercial endeavor that lasted for
several decades. At the request of numerous European patrons, father and
son gathered seeds, bulbs, and live plants from his garden in Philadelphia
and sent them across the Atlantic where they were transplanted into the soil
of hundreds of British gardens.

Although John Bartram was paid in cash or gifts for his work, he profited
more from the prestige these relationships of transatlantic exchange
bestowed on him. For the benefit of his American friends and neighbors, he
proudly displayed the tokens of appreciation he received from important
people in Britain.[59] There was the copy of Philip Miller's popular *Gardener's
Dictionary* on which Bartram inscribed "A Present from ye Right Honorable
Lord Petre." In another instance, Bartram asked Collinson to take the specie
given as payment for North American plants and purchase a silver cup

inscribed with the aristocrat's name. The inscription on the cup was crafted to imply that the men were friends, rather than partners in a business deal.[60] For Bartram, a colonial subject living at the far reaches of the British Empire, these objects were the material embodiment of his importance within the larger imperial structure.

Through their relationship with powerful individuals in Britain, naturalists working in the colonies—British North America, India, the West Indies—participated in the expansion of the Empire.[61] King George III appointed John Bartram a royal botanist for North America in 1765, a few years after Britain acquired Quebec, Florida, and the land east of the Mississippi as part of its spoils of the Seven Years' War with France. The wartime acquisition of the vast new territory created the need for the British to take stock of their windfall. The appointment of Bartram was a reflection of his long-standing relationships with powerful people in Britain. Although the post paid only a modest stipend, the honor it bestowed on Bartram was priceless. It was his job to explore the newly acquired territory with an eye for extracting profits from it for the benefit of the British Empire. Wasting no time, Bartram went on a mission to complete a botanical survey, taking along William, who exhibited a talent for drawing from nature, to produce sketches of the plant life they intended to discover.

William Bartram's Trying Career

William Bartram's career as an artist and naturalist encapsulates the frustrations and subordination faced by Anglo-Americans who operated within transatlantic networks of material exchange centered in London. Like the vast majority of Americans, Bartram was not wealthy enough to pursue his love of art without the support of wealthy English patrons. During the early part of his career, Bartram sent his images of the wilds of America to Collinson, who brought them to the attention of influential and aristocratic British botanists, garden lovers, and amateur collectors such as the Duchess of Portland, who solicited drawings of American shells.[62]

The young hopeful from Pennsylvania met his first regular patron, British naturalist George Edwards, through Collinson. A botanical print entitled "Small Mud Tortoise" provides evidence of the three men's relationship, for its heading, written by Edwards, notes that it was "sent from Pensilvania by Mr. Bartram to my worthy friend Peter Collinson, Esq; F[ellow].R[oyal].S[ociety]. who on all occasion is ready and willing to

oblige me with the use of every new subject he receives from foreign countries" (see figure 4.2).[63] Eventually, Edwards procured drawings for his
book *Gleanings of Natural History* (1758) directly from Bartram.[64] This was
a perfect arrangement for Edwards, who, try as he might, never distinguished himself as a particularly gifted botanical artist.

Despite this major shortcoming, Edwards established unique credibility
as a naturalist thanks to his close ties with his American man-in-the-field.
Personal relationships with talented colonials made Englishmen like
Collinson and Edwards valuable to European elites who were interested in
learning about and collecting American natural objects and had the money

Figure 4.2 Engraved, hand-colored print entitled, "The Small Mud Tortoise, Smelling Strong of Musk,
Haveing a Sharp Horn Poynted Tayl from Pensilvania. Drawn from Nature of the Bignes of Life, by
George Edwards," engraving from a drawing by William Bartram. An etching of this drawing (Plate 287)
was published in George Edwards (1694–1773), *Gleanings of Natural History: Exhibiting Figures of
Quadrupeds, Birds, Insects, Plants*, 3 vols. (London: Printed for the author, at the Royal College of
Physicians, 1758–1764), vol. 2. *(From a copy in Beinecke Rare Book & Manuscript Library, Yale University
Library)*

Figure 4.3 Engraved, hand-colored print entitled, "The Marsh Hawk [*Circus cyaneus*], and the Reed birds, all from Pensilvania," drawing by William Bartram. Executed from life in 1758 and published in 1760, 285 x 120 mm paper size. An etching of this drawing (Plate 291) was published in George Edwards (1694–1773), *Gleanings of Natural History: Exhibiting Figures of Quadrupeds, Birds, Insects, Plants*, 3 vols. (London: Printed for the author, at the Royal College of Physicians, 1758–1764), bound in between pages 172 and 173). (*Image from a copy in Beinecke Rare Book & Manuscript Library, Yale University Library*)

and inclination to pay for the information. Edwards highlighted this triangular transatlantic relationship in his published work. For instance, his description of the print "The Marsh Hawk and the Reed Birds, all from Pensilvania [*sic*]" attributed a great deal of significance to its source: the illustration was "engraved from a drawing" that, he emphasized, had been "*done from the life* in Pensilvania [*sic*]" by Bartram, who was identified as a "native of that country."[65] (See figure 4.3.) That the information was seen as more "authentic" having come from a "native" allowed Edwards to weigh in on the scientific dialogue among Europeans.[66] On the strength of the raw materials Bartram provided, Edwards amended the work of eminent naturalists in his publications.[67] He challenged the noted naturalist Mark Catesby's *History of Carolina*. In contrast to Catesby's short foray to America to conduct research, Edwards's informant had the distinct advantage of year-round residence and was thus able to observe the migratory patterns of birds during the winter months, when European naturalists returned home.[68] Observations about birds that only a full-time resident could make figured largely in Bartram's notes because they were the most valuable assets he could offer his English client.[69] Even though Edwards had not observed the bird firsthand, he was able to speak with an authority that other Europeans working solely from shriveled specimens in collections could not.[70] In the excitement of one who has himself discovered something previously unknown, Edwards wrote: "As I do not find this Hawk described by Catesby or any other author, I am unwilling to slip the opportunity of giving its figure."[71]

Despite how integral the young American's contributions were to the whole endeavor, in the end it was Edwards who stood in judgment of Bartram's veracity: "I have great reason to think Mr. Bartram very correct in his drawing, and exact in his colouring, having compared many of his drawings with the natural subjects, and found a very good agreement between them."[72] Regardless of Edwards's willingness to vouch for Bartram's expertise, the English botanist preferred receiving actual specimens from America that he could comment upon himself.[73] Receiving Bartram's drawings alone was not as desirable because Edwards then had to trust their accuracy if he was to use them in his own published work.[74] On the print "The Little Blue-grey Fly-catchers, Cock and Hen," in *Gleanings of Natural History*, Edwards made special note that "These birds, with their nests, I received from my obliging friend Mr. William Bartram."[75] This was a particularly gratifying shipment for Edwards, who commented happily: "The subjects of this plate I take to be new, as I cannot discover any figures or descriptions agreeing with them." By "new" Edwards meant that the species had not been written about before in European published work. It did not matter if Native Americans had lived among them for years, or even that Anglo-American colonials on the frontier had seen them often. The audience he addressed in his books was the British reading public. In his description of his print of "The White-throated Sparrow, from Pensilvania [*sic*] and the Yellow Butterfly, from Carrolina [*sic*]" (see figure 4.4), he wrote: "I believe neither of the subjects of this plate have till now been known to us." The "us" he meant was apparent.

European naturalists valued Bartram not for his artistic talent or his intellect but for the firsthand information about American wildlife found in the drawings, collected specimens, textual descriptions, and field notes about migratory habits he provided. Another quality that made William

Bartram such a valuable source for British naturalists was his ability to form close relationships with Native Americans. This ability helped his artistic career greatly because plants and native peoples were considered part of the landscape of America. In his drawing "Indian Shot, Bandana of the Everglades, or Golden Canna," Bartram blended images of North American plant life and Native American artifacts, including a stone pipe bowl given to him by a Creek chief in present-day Alabama (see figure 4.5, p. 172).[76]

In order to keep their English patrons supplied with information, Americans traveled through unexplored territory, the "empty spaces" on maps of North America in search of information.[77] Looking for natural species considered previously "undiscovered," they climbed trees and

Figure 4.4 Engraved, hand-colored print entitled, "The White Throated Sparrow, from Pensilvania, and the Yellow Butterfly, from Carrolina" (British Museum), drawing by William Bartram. An etching of this drawing (Plate 304) was published in George Edwards (1694–1773), *Gleanings of Natural History: Exhibiting Figures of Quadrupeds, Birds, Insects, Plants*, 3 vols. (London: Printed for the author, at the Royal College of Physicians, 1758–1764), bound in between pages 198 and 199. *(Image from a copy in Beinecke Rare Book & Manuscript Library, Yale University Library)*

Figure 4.5 Engraved, hand-colored print entitled, "Indian Shot, Bandana of the Everglades, or Golden Canna [*Canna flaccida Salisb. (Cannaceae)*]" (British Museum), original drawing in black and brown ink by William Bartram The original was executed in 1776 on paper measuring 249 x 188 mm. An etching of this drawing was published in George Edwards (1694–1773), *Gleanings of Natural History: Exhibiting Figures of Quadrupeds, Birds, Insects, Plants*, 3 vols. (London: Printed for the author, at the Royal College of Physicians, 1758–1764), bound in between pages. In this print the artist blended Native American artifacts with North American plant life. In 1775 Bartram traveled along the Mississippi River to Georgia. Along the way he visited the Native American town of Mucclasse in present-day Alabama. The stone pipe bowl in the illustration was modeled after the pipe given to him by a blind Creek chief who he met there. *(Image from a copy in Beinecke Rare Book & Manuscript Library, Yale University Library)*

snatched nests, shot birds, skinned and cured mammals, and then shipped them across the Atlantic. Beginning in March 1773, William Bartram traveled over twenty-four hundred miles through the southeastern part of North America to collect seeds and plant specimens for Fothergill. Although Bartram had been doing this since he was a little boy accompanying his father on similar trips, Fothergill felt it necessary to supply him with detailed instructions on how to collect, preserve, ship, and draw the plants and shells he found (see figure 4.6).[78]

Figure 4.6 Engraved, hand-colored print entitled, "The little Thrush from North America drawn from life of its natural size. August the 13, 1757," drawing by William Bartram. An etching of this drawing (Plate 296) was published in George Edwards (1694–1773), *Gleanings of Natural History: Exhibiting Figures of Quadrupeds, Birds, Insects, Plants*, 3 vols. (London: Printed for the author, at the Royal College of Physicians, 1758–64), bound in between pages 182 and 183. This drawing was Bartram's feathered admission ticket to the Europeans' natural history debates about the migratory habits of this bird. *(Image from a copy in Beinecke Rare Book & Manuscript Library, Yale University Library)*

Through the years before and after the Revolution, Bartram and his father handed over several more noteworthy specimens to their European patrons, who often registered them and therefore claimed the formal credit for their discovery. Among their most celebrated findings was the *Franklinia*, a rare flowering tree that the Bartrams named in honor of fellow Pennsylvanian Benjamin Franklin (see figure 4.7, next page). This is an example of a "type specimen," on which the priority of discovery and the acceptance of a taxonomic name were based. Such official recognition of scientific findings was harder for Americans to achieve, because they lived and worked at the margins of Anglo-American networks of exchange centered in London.

Figure 4.7 Print from a watercolor entitled, "Frankliania [*Franklinia alatamaha*]," drawing by William Bartram. The drawing for this type specimen was executed in 1788 on paper 478 x 354 mm. An etching of this drawing was published in George Edwards (1694–1773), *Gleanings of Natural History: Exhibiting Figures of Quadrupeds, Birds, Insects, Plants*, 3 vols. (London: Printed for the author, at the Royal College of Physicians, 1758–64), bound in between pages. *(British Museum)*

William Bartram nurtured both the New World plants and the networks of British patronage his father had established. When John Bartram died in 1777, William took over his botanical garden, which was recognized as the best in North America.[79] During the Revolutionary War, William revisited the places he and his father had visited together in order to continue to supply his European patrons with the goods they desired. In the postrevolutionary period American naturalists maintained their transatlantic relationships in part to earn a respected place for the United States among the civilized nations of the world. They recognized that ironically the development of an independent national culture depended on a continuation of links with the British Empire.

RESIDENCE OF JOHN BARTRAM,
BUILT WITH HIS OWN HANDS, A. D. 1730.

Figure 4.8 Engraving entitled "Residence of John Bartram, built with his own hands, A.D.1730."
Bartram supplied exotic New World plants to the most opulent gardens of Europe. However, after
visiting Bartram's humble home, Massachusetts representative Manasseh Cutler pronounced that it
was, "No garden of Eden." *(American Philosophical Society)*

The "Very Badly Arranged" Garden: Nature for the New Nation

On Saturday, July 14, 1787, in the midst of their interminable disagreement
over the issue of state representation, the beleaguered members of the
Constitutional Convention took a field trip to Bartram's famed garden near
Philadelphia. Having heard so much about it and in need of a break from
their debate, the delegates set off for Kingsessing, a few miles from their
meeting place in Philadelphia. They arrived unannounced and found
William working outdoors with the plants. According to Massachusetts
representative Manasseh Cutler, it did not meet their heightened expectations.[80] They thought Bartram's garden would be a source of national pride
and glory as an emulation of the aesthetic style of grandeur found in
European botanical gardens. Cutler, who was known himself for his
botanical research, was disappointed that Bartram had the plants "very
badly arranged," for they were "neither placed ornamentally nor botani-
cally, but seem to be jumbled together in heaps" (see figure 4.8).[81]

   In contrast to the ordered, sumptuous gardens he supplied, Bartram's
was a "borderless botanical garden" designed for the sole purpose of producing wild plants for sale and exportation to the mother country (see
figures 4.9 and 4.10). It was said that all of Pennsylvania was Bartram's

Figure 4.9 Plate from Philip Miller (1691–1771), *The Gardener's Dictionary* (1735). Although the extended title of the book notes the book was intended for use in England, Americans often used the book for ideas on how to design their gardens. *(From Philip Miller,* The Abridgement of the Gardeners Dictionary, *5th ed., corrected and enlarged [London: Printed for the Author, 1763], copy in Beinecke Rare Book & Manuscript Library, Yale University Library)*

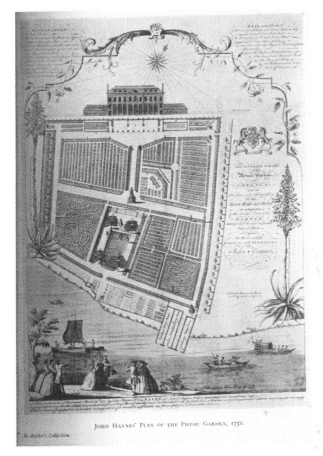

JOHN HAYNES' PLAN OF THE PHYSIC GARDEN, 1751.

Figure 4.10 "Survey of the Botanic Gardens at Chelsea, 1751," from the engraving by John Haynes. An illustration of the Chelsea Physick Garden. Well-established formal gardens like this one were among the famous sites Bartram supplied. Reprinted in Reginald Blunt, *Paradise Row* (London: Macmillan and Company, 1906), illustration facing page 38. *(Copy in British Art Center Reference Library, Yale University Library).*

garden, for if conditions were right, he would plant pricey exotics far beyond the boundaries set by the fence on his property. Bartram was not bothered by this haphazard system in which rare plants grew hidden among weeds. His plants were arranged on the basis of their natural needs for sun, water, and soil type rather than the criteria of color, size, and season of bloom used by his customers.[82]

For generations Americans with genteel aspirations exceeding those of the Bartrams attempted to emulate British formal gardens. Those with the resources to travel abroad gathered information on the latest trends in garden design and shared them with their fellow colonials back home. Samuel

Sewell enthused about the garden of New College at Oxford University in a letter bursting with details that would allow those back home to replicate its design to the best of their abilities.

Americans who were unable to go to Britain themselves could import the knowledge in the form of English books on the topic, such as *The Gardener's Dictionary* (1735), the most widely distributed book on gardening in America.[83] Americans continued to emulate British practices in gardening after the Revolution (see figure 4.9).[84]

Bartram's nursery was a far cry from the aristocratic gardens he supplied in Britain and on the Continent, which were created to inspire awe among genteel visitors.[85] Gardens can be read as texts revealing the desires, aspirations, and values of their owners and designers. What, then, would be communicated by the fact that Bartram's garden was haphazard, was not aesthetically pleasing, and existed only for the functional, economic purposes of supplying European gardens with exotic New World specimens? Americans such as Cutler wanted their new nation to be able to boast of having a world-renowned garden on a par with those in Europe, but there was no denying that Bartram's garden did not come close in comparison.

The American delegates' disappointment at the lack of European grandeur in Bartram's garden reflected a crucial aspect of the postcolonial period in American history. These elite Americans shared definitions of culture, taste, and gentility with their European counterparts and wanted, as a matter of national pride, their new nation to meet those standards, while being freed from aristocratic chains.

Unfortunately for William Bartram, the hopes and artistic ambitions of an aspiring American artist were not high among the priorities of those in the metropole, who were engaged in furthering the interests of the British Empire.[86] To his utter frustration and disappointment, many of the sketches he risked his life to obtain languished unpublished in the possession of his English patrons, who later gave them to other British botanists to use at will.[87] Bartram feared that the years he devoted to executing the polished botanic drawings were going to go to waste, yet there was not much he could do, toiling as he was in relative obscurity at the outer reaches of the transatlantic world. Bartram puzzled over the deafening silence from the other side of the world, not wanting to admit he had been forgotten.[88]

Bartram relied on the scarcity of American botanicals in British gardens as the key to earning international recognition for his work. However, both he and Jefferson, who tried to make similar use of the moose, another rare

American specimen (as will be discussed later), were unable to engender the sort of response they had wanted to achieve. They found it was not enough to rely solely on scarcity as the basis of their access to imperial venues where America's cultural potential could be exhibited.

Postrevolutionary Patronage, or a Name to Call Your Own

> I long earnestly for a Return of those peaceful Times, when I could sit down in sweet Society with my English philosophic Friends, communicating to each other new Discoveries, and proposing improvements of old ones.
>
> —Benjamin Franklin to Sir Joseph Banks (September 9, 1782)

The story behind the botanical drawing "The Alegator of St. Johns" exemplifies how tantalizingly close yet frustratingly distant William Bartram was from the metropolitan approbation and recognition he so intensely desired. While this drawing is recognized by Bartram scholars as among "the most famous and most important drawing executed" by the naturalist, it failed to earn him international recognition for naming this fierce creature.[89] While possessing artistic skills and a natural talent for observation, Bartram lacked the formal education that European naturalists possessed. He completed the drawing in 1791 while traveling up St. John's River in eastern Florida. Though he had accurately captured the animal's likeness in its natural environment and completed a full description of its habits, he failed to provide a valid scientific binomial name for it. Had he been able to do so, he could have been credited with naming the entire species.[90] In the end, the official credit for naming the creature was given to French naturalist François Marie Daudin, a decade later in 1801.[91] The Frenchman, who is credited with naming many North American reptiles, used Bartram's work, *Travels through North and South Carolina, Georgia, East and West Florida, the Cherokee country, the extensive territories of the Muscogulges or Creek confederacy, and the country of the Chactaws. Containing an account of the soil and natural productions of those regions; together with observations on the manners of the Indians*, extensively to help him describe many new North American species.

It was not only a matter of better positioned European botanists appropriating Americans' raw data for their own publications. There were jealousies and competition between Americans as well. Their newly developed sense of national identity did not simply erase individual ambitions and internal strife among them as they competed with one another for recognition from London. One particularly egregious case involved Barton's attempt to appropriate William Bartram's work and publish it in Europe. After struggling with failures and obscurity, Bartram finally completed a draft of his *Travels,* the notes for which he had taken several years earlier under the patronage of Fothergill. Shortly after he delivered the manuscript to prospective American publishers, Bartram discovered that his old friend Barton intended to steal his work. Recognizing the value of Bartram's observational skills, Barton hoped to publish the manuscript in Britain under his own name. He was personally acquainted with people at the European centers of knowledge production and thus more able than Bartram to take advantage of the system.[92] The unequal allotment of power and resources created competition among Americans as they fought for British recognition.

Seeking a different route to success, some botanical artists began to frame their scientific work in terms of national patriotism. These naturalists translated natural data into Eurocentric forms of scientific knowledge at home rather than sending it to Britain to be classified. A group of American scientists, called by one scholar "patriot improvers," saw their scientific efforts as a means of building the nation.[93] Since settling in the New World, Anglo-Americans had earned their livelihoods exporting what they foraged from the supposedly "untamed" backwoods of the Atlantic world. Now that they were an independent nation, they would process these raw materials— cotton, wool, and botanical specimens—themselves.

Natural history, botany, and medicine appealed to American students, both colonial and postrevolutionary, because of the abundance of unique plants and animals (including those humans identified as Native Americans and African Americans) that fascinated European audiences. Observational data that could only be gathered domestically was a valuable commodity, whereas American dabblings in theoretical branches of science such as mathematics were ignored.[94] Isolated Americans fared better in branches of science that had descriptive components and did not require regular contact with other scholars.[95] They reported to the world community natural events such as the eclipses of Jupiter's moons, the transits of planets across the sun, and earthquakes. For instance, the Transit of Venus in 1761 provided colonials with an opportunity to enter into transatlantic discourse. In a cruel twist of fate, scientists in Philadelphia were unable to participate in this worldwide effort because, as a contemporary explained it, the only suitable telescope in the city was temporarily unusable because its speculum was being resilvered in London.[96] If empiricism became the hallmark of early

American science, it was a method that reflected their structural marginality in the scientific community.

A good example of Americans' attempts to translate their findings into acceptable forms of scientific knowledge themselves is Humphry Marshall's eighteen-volume *Arbustrum Americanum: The American Grove, or, an Alphabetical Catalogue of Forest Trees and Shrubs, Natives of the American United States, Arranged According to the Linnaean System.*[97] Whereas most scientific publications listed the author's credentials (scholarly degrees earned, memberships in learned societies), Marshall's title page claimed as his scholarly credential the fact that his results were "compiled from actual knowledge and observation."[98] What the author lacked in formal training and professional contacts he made up for in his predawn explorations of the vast North American forests.

Learned American naturalists tried to add value to their raw observations. The impulse to classify and name new plants and animals at home in America became a nationalist project in the postrevolutionary period.[99] But first, naturalists had to process and convert their empirical observations into forms of knowledge based on European classification standards. Linnaeus's *Systema Naturae* provided everyday Americans with a universally recognized language with which they could begin to classify the natural world into distinct fields of study. For instance, the vast array of unique North American birds, when classified in this way, formed the basis of American ornithology; a scattering of fossils became paleontology; a rainbow-colored variety of fish, ichthyology.[100] Thus packaged, this knowledge could be exported for consumption by Europeans.

While the Linnaean system created new possibilities for the inclusion of provincials within a transnational scientific community, Americans were also aware of the challenges they continued to face. One major obstacle was a lack of the comprehensive specimen collections that were vital to taxonomic classification and identification of new species. The only Linnaean collection of any significance first reached America in 1794, brought back from Britain by Dr. David Hosack, a New Yorker who had developed a fondness for natural history while studying in Edinburgh.[101]

A hardworking, practical man, Hosack went to great trouble to procure scientific equipment, natural history specimens, and books he knew were unavailable in America. During his two years abroad, he collected the scientific materials he needed to continue his intellectual pursuits at home.[102] He documented his "Sacrifices for procuring ye necessary materials for prosecuting those Subjects—an extensive Library—a Chemical apparatus—an Herbarium a collection of ye most necessary objects in ye other parts of

Nat[ural] History Minerology &c."[103] The most precious commodity Hosack managed to procure was an herbarium that included some specimens from Linnaeus's original collection. He had managed to convince the owner of the collection, Sir James Edward Smith, to give him duplicates from his collection. Ironically, some of the samples had originally been collected in America.[104] Two years after his return to America, Hosack noted in a letter to his former teacher, Benjamin Rush, how happy he was that he had prepared so well. As one of the few people with any formal knowledge of natural science living in a largely unexplored country, he enjoyed a prominent place in the field in America.[105]

American botanists of the early republic knew that gaining the recognition of an important figure in British science, such as Sir James Smith, president of the Linnaean Society, was important for the success of natural science in the new United States. Smith appeared on the dedication page of Barton's 1800 study *Collections for an Essay towards a Materia Medica of the United-States*. Highlighting his patron's international connections and highlighting his affiliation with American institutions, Barton described Smith as "a foreign member of the American Philosophical Society, the President of the Linnaean Society, and member of the Royal Academies of Turin, Upsal and Lisbon."[106] The obsequious Barton humbly presented his work to Smith, expressing the "pain" he felt at the shortcomings of American natural science.[107] The Philadelphian explained that natural history was "yet an infant science" in the United States and excused the "extremely imperfect" nomenclature produced by Americans. Recognizing that American attempts to appropriate the naming process had led to a number of flawed and risible results, he apologized to his European audience on behalf of his compatriots for a lack of "acquaintance with the properties of our productions."[108]

A crucial problem with many American attempts to appropriate scientific naming and classifying processes was an inadequate facility with Latin. As a solution, some schools tried to strengthen classical language training, but on the whole the American response was to remove Latin and other classical language requirements from their educational systems, a reaction born of the recognition of their own weakness.

In an attempt to distinguish his own products from the failures of his compatriots, Barton explained that his ultimate goal in writing the tract was "convincing you [Smith] that there are some lovers and cultivators of Botany in the United States."[109] In a letter to Sir Joseph Banks, Barton agreed with Banks's criticisms of other American botanists (in this case, Humphry Marshall) and their bungling attempts to mimic the naming systems of Europeans. He wrote: "you have justly remarked, that it is not easy to 'comprehend' our American botanists; and Marshall is, undoubtedly, supreme in the obscure, and unintelligible."[110] If Barton's treatment of his fellow American colleagues was uncharitable, it reflected the vulnerability he felt in being lumped in with them and his ardent desire to be accepted by his British correspondents.

Patriotic postrevolutionary Americans were indignant that they were thought of as intellectually inferior to the British. While a medical student in Great Britain, James Rush observed in a letter back home to his father: "They would as soon believe that our trees bear golden apples, as that any thing useful in medicine should come from America."[111] He went on to describe how British professors dismissed "with a toss of indifference" the theories of even the most successful American physicians (including his own father), noting with condescension that perhaps they would "do very well for young philosophers" but were of no interest to the British. Adapting a biblical phrase, James complained to his father about "these men who strain at the gnats of innovation and swallow…whole mammoths of their own grey bearded absurdity."[112]

American students studying in Britain commonly expressed annoyance at the way Britons talked so authoritatively about America when few of them had firsthand knowledge of the country. What had once been a vulnerability—distance from the center of science—now became a strength: proximity to nature. The irony is that James wrote his letter from Great Britain, where he was studying, because an equivalent education could not be obtained in the United States. His very presence in Britain contradicted his insistence on American equality.

Desperate to "Supply the Deficiency": American Science as a Material Practice

Furnish'd as all Europe now is with Academies of Science, with nice Instruments and the Spirit of Experiment, the Progress of human Knowledge will be rapid, and discoveries made of which we have at present no Conception.

—Benjamin Franklin (July 27, 1783)

In the postrevolutionary years, American men of science lacked the institutional support and domestic funding their British counterparts enjoyed, without which even the most gifted could not pursue full-time scientific investigation. Instructors who taught natural history and natural philosophy in the American universities engaged in other activities in order to make a living. For example, Benjamin Smith Barton, Samuel Latham Mitchell, and Benjamin Waterhouse were physicians, served as medical faculty, and taught natural history as a secondary commitment. Astronomers David Rittenhouse and Andrew Ellicott worked as surveyors and clock-makers, and did other jobs in order to support their families. Henry Ernest Muhlenberg, James Madison, and Manasseh Cutler were clergymen. Barton noted with regret that "the principal cultivators of natural science, in the United States, are professional characters, who cannot, without essentially injuring their best interests, devote to these subjects that sedulous attention which they demand."[113]

In order to pursue scientific experiments, the first order of business for American natural scientists was to procure the necessary equipment, no simple task from thousands of miles away from their source. In 1790, seven years after the end of the Revolution, Samuel Stanhope Smith bemoaned the fact that the vast majority of the scientific instruments that had "formerly belonged to this Seminary were either destroyed or carried off during the war."[114] With the "funds of the institution" being "so inconsiderable," Smith planned a series of fundraising campaigns.

Desperate to "supply the deficiency" of money, Smith played to the patriotic egos and consciences of the homegrown sons of the College of New Jersey.[115] An official resolution of the Board of Trustees ordered that a circular letter be printed soliciting donations from scattered alumni and "Friends" of the college in towns across the country and abroad. This letter attested to the fact that the very "reputation of the institution" hinged on the possession of these imported goods from Europe.[116] As the minutes of this meeting of the Board noted, "a proper Apparatus is absolutely necessary for the successful cultivation of, and instruction in, several parts of natural philosophy."[117] After all, the scientific instruments made in Europe were needed to produce enlightened scholars made in America.[118] Through their determined effort, Smith, the Board of Trustees, and the friends of the struggling college were somehow able to raise enough private funds to purchase "a tolerable apparatus for chemical experiments."[119]

During the years following the Revolution, struggling American men of science carefully protected each and every piece of apparatus they owned. If a piece of equipment available only in Europe or Britain was broken, research would grind to a halt until a transatlantic source could be located, often through an intricate series of correspondence, and the object purchased, packed, and shipped to America. If the replacement item was broken in transit, as many fragile pieces of glassware were, the process would have to begin again, with more time and money lost. The exiled

Joseph Priestley learned this lesson from many abortive attempts to import equipment for his experiments from British suppliers to his new American home, located several bumpy miles outside Philadelphia. His frustration with the difficulty of procuring apparatus is palpable in his correspondence with scientifically minded friends in Britain.

The limited supply of equipment available to American colleges and the difficulty of replacing lost or broken apparatus compelled men of science to guard their professional possessions jealously. Their unwillingness to share scarce resources hindered teaching and learning in America at a time when it was most needed.[120] An agreement Professor John Gorham of Harvard made in 1816 with one of his students encapsulates this dilemma. Gorham's laboratory assistant was expected to prepare and demonstrate experiments and afterward to clean, dry, and return used equipment to their proper shelves. Although the aspiring scientist received some money from his mentor, the most valuable payment was access to the precious equipment required for his own experiments. The details of this agreement were telling; the student only had access to "such vessels, materials, and instruments as, if broken or exhausted, may be replaced [by importers of British goods] from Boston." He was forbidden to use the "more valuable apparatus, tests, etc., which can be procured only in Europe."[121]

After the Revolution, in order to ensure that transatlantic lines of assistance remained open, American correspondents emphasized to their British patrons the challenges they faced. It was particularly important to do so in light of the recent political rupture between America and Britain. A degree of dissembling took place in requests for assistance as Americans reinscribed their dependence on their British counterparts as a means to ensure they would receive the assistance required to gain their cultural independence.

American physicians and botanists struggled with a material marginality that forced them to depend on Britain decades after the formal political break. They often appealed to British sympathy for their deprivation using familial metaphors when imploring their English "elder brethren" to bestow favors on their younger, poorer, and less fortunate American siblings. In 1811 Waterhouse lamented: "Our elder brethren in Europe know not the difficulties that the first settlers in science have to encounter." This language was also used by Americans engaged in nonscientific activities as varied as missionary work and art. Similarly, in 1825 Stephen Elliott wrote: "No one in Europe can appreciate correctly the difficulty of the task in which I have engaged. The want of books, the want of opportunities for examining living collections or good herbaria, the want of coadjutors, have all served to render my task arduous, and to multiply its imperfections."[122]

Many Americans derived great pleasure from the fact that Europeans, such as the noted English naturalist Thomas Nuttall, showed a scientific interest in the United States. The European publication of scientific studies of previously unexplored American territory and the plant, animal, and human life living there put the nation on the map both literally and figuratively. For example, Nuttall's *Genera of North American Plants* (1818) and *Introduction to Systematic and Physiological Botany* (1827) gained widespread attention in Europe and renewed interest in these American subjects.[123] In search of greater opportunities, Scottish naturalist Alexander Wilson moved to the United States in 1794 to study North American bird life. In 1802 he embarked on a major project to write a definitive illustrated work on North American birds. He published the multi-volume work *American Ornithology,* in Philadelphia between 1808 and 1814.[124] The popularity of these studies worked to the advantage of fledgling American naturalists by raising and revitalizing Europeans' interest in the United States.

Americans' feeling of resentment toward their continued dependence on more powerful Europeans existed for decades. Many individuals urged their compatriots to make an effort to take ownership of scientific knowledge about their land away from the British. For instance, Reverend Henry Ernest Muhlenberg declared that new species discovered in the United States should be named only by Americans.[125] Ironically, Muhlenberg's European training at the University of Halle in Saxony allowed him to undertake the study of botany in America.[126] He depended on Europeans for help. Immediately after the end of the Revolutionary War, Muhlenberg sent American plants to Europe so they could be identified and categorized by naturalists there.[127]

Obtaining ownership of scientific knowledge while also gaining international recognition and approval was not an easy or expedient process; however for Americans who saw it as a matter of national pride, it was an ongoing battle. In the 1821 article "Botany in the United States," the *North American Review* celebrated the flourishing of botanical science under the "legitimate auspices of Americans" and to "the refutation of the prevalent European belief in the inferiority of the soil and produce of North America."[128] Americans wanted to enter into transatlantic scientific debates at a theoretical level in order to modify existing tenets of European science with their empirical observations.[129] Five years later, these issues were still pressing, indicating that science in the United States had yet to come into its own. In his *Anniversary Address Delivered before the New York Lyceum* (1826), James DeKay argued that "instead of blindly using the eyes of foreign naturalists, or bowing implicitly to the decisions of a foreign bar of criticism," American investigators should proudly announce their own findings.[130]

For Americans involved in transatlantic intellectual networks, the ultimate goal was to become intellectually equal to the Europeans. It was a difficult feat, because of the Americans' distance from the scholarly networks they so cherished. Barton and American naturalists in general struggled constantly against the ease with which Europeans could appropriate and receive all the credit for their own empirical observations.[131] Although by the 1750s the Linnaean system had been widely used to identify New World species, the act of naming a new North American "type specimen" was politicized in ways it had not been before. Like many other cultural activities, the Anglo-American networks of material exchange—in this case in scientific knowledge—continued as they had done in the colonial period, but now they were imbued with a newly national meaning for Americans.[132]

A s the Revolution wound down, Jefferson became embroiled in a mammoth effort to dispel the theory of the famous naturalist Georges-Louis Leclerc, Comte de Buffon, regarding New World flora and fauna.[133] According to Buffon, climatic influences had caused American plants and animals to degenerate from more robust European prototypes: they were smaller, weaker, and less fertile.[134] To the dismay of Jefferson and other patriots,[135] the Abbé Raynal had then applied this theory to the "race of whites, transplanted from Europe."[136] Raynal pointed to the lack of cultural achievement in the arts and sciences among citizens of the new nation: "America has not yet produced one good poet," nor could it boast "one able mathematician, one man of genius in a single art or a single science."[137]

Jefferson's *Notes on the State of Virginia*, published while he was ambassador to France, was a public response to these charges. In this work's sixth chapter, which bore the disarmingly neutral title "Productions Mineral, Vegetable and Animal," Jefferson declared that the theory of New World degeneration was "just as true as the fable of Aesop."[138] He also wanted to prove scientifically that the New World animals (and by extension humans) were not only equal but superior to those in Europe. To accomplish this, Jefferson needed to procure an animal specimen that would demonstrate the vigor of American nature. He enlisted the help of General John Sullivan, a Revolutionary War hero, to send to Paris the largest moose that Sullivan, with the help of his Indian guides, could find in the forests of New England. This would enable Jefferson to substantiate his claim that a full-grown European reindeer could walk under the belly of an American moose.

Jefferson spent three years, wrote more than thirty letters, and paid nearly 50 pounds sterling to obtain his specimen. At one point during the expedition, Sullivan reported, "every Indian near was at work to prepare the bones and cleanse them from the remaining flesh." Twenty additional men were hired to trek into the woods to carry out this "expensive and difficult" project.[139] Jefferson's detailed preserving and packing instructions were not followed, however, and Sullivan was "much mortified" with the results.[140] Not only was the carcass decomposing quickly, but this particular moose had diminutive horns. Anticipating Jefferson's disappointment, and not quite understanding the protocols of European science, Sullivan included in his shipment several large elk and deer antlers, which he said "could be fixed on." Prior to reaching France, the behemoth had a layover in London. After a series of mishaps, it landed on the doorstep of a confused John Adams, minister plenipotentiary of the United States, who nevertheless sent it on to France. It arrived at Jefferson's residence in Paris in an advanced state of decay in late September 1787.[141]

Despite its ragged appearance, Jefferson sent the moose on to Buffon, along with the horns of another moose, as well as that of "the caribou, the elk, the deer, the spike horned buck and the roebuck of America." He included a copy of his *Notes on the State of Virginia* and a humble letter saying that he was offering these New World specimens in case they would "have the merit of adding anything new to the treasures of nature, which have so fortunately come under your observation, and of which she seems to have given you the key." Jefferson hoped they would prove to be of "some gratification" to the famous man. He assured Buffon "it will always be pleasing to me to have procured" these objects for him.[142]

Jefferson hoped that the moose would be displayed in the King's Cabinet as proof of America's virility.[143] But Buffon was not convinced. He never retracted his theory of degeneration in the New World (although Americans consoled themselves with the belief that he was just about to do so when he died).[144] In fact, his theory spread, infecting other scientific studies of the Americas.[145]

The specter of degeneracy by association put Anglo-American provincials such as Jefferson in a defensive position in transatlantic society. The one advantage that they enjoyed exclusively was the ability to directly observe the "savage" New World people and places that were the source of so much European fascination. In the *Notes on the State of Virginia*, the postcolonial author established his credentials by asserting that, unlike Europeans, he could talk about Indians "from my own authority" or from people he knew personally "on whose truth and judgment I can rely." Buffon had never set foot in North America, but his opinions on the New World still trumped that of the native Virginian. By appealing to European centers of learning for acknowledgment, Jefferson had fallen back into the colonial role of the client seeking civilized patronage.[146]

Scarcity, Abundance, and the Rules of Scientific Exchange

Sending his research to noteworthy and well-connected British correspondents, Barton rightly feared that they would incorporate his findings into their own publications, take credit for the ideas, and become famous for them. Americans were so far away from the formal and informal scholarly institutions, and networks of Europe that they were constantly operating at a disadvantage. Those closer to the center of scientific knowledge production held a near monopoly on refining raw observations and specimens into scientific theory that was read and recognized by an international community. More important, Americans in the field were too useful to Europeans as gatherers of natural knowledge to be allowed to graduate from that position.[147]

In order to combat the hierarchical nature of this network, Barton resorted to dishonest behavior in his failure to uphold his end of transatlantic bargains with renowned British men of science. An example of this was his dealings with the famed London zoologist Thomas Pennant. The gestation of Pennant's *Arctic Zoology* spanned the years of America's transition from colony to nation. In the advertisement for the first edition published in 1784, the Englishman explained that he had begun his study "a great number of years past, when the empire of Great Britain was entire, and possessed the northern part of the New World with envied splendor." He then explained how the change in status of America had forced him to change the title of his study:

> Let me repeat, that this Work was designed as a sketch of the Zoology of North America. I thought I had a right to the attempt, at a time I had the honor of calling myself a fellow-subject with that respectable part of our former great empire; but when the fatal and humiliating hour arrived, which deprived Britain of power, strength, and glory, I felt the mortification which must strike every feeling individual at losing his little share in the boast of ruling over half of the New World. I could no longer support my claim of entitling myself its humble Zoologist: yet, unwilling to fling away all my labors, do now deliver them to the Public under the title of the ARCTIC ZOOLOGY.[148]

Even though Pennant changed the title of his study out of respect for the newly independent nation, the networks for specimen exchange had not changed since the colonial period, and he would continue to rely on familiar informants. In the first edition of his book, Pennant described his reliance on sources scattered throughout the British Empire. He compared his secondhand research method unfavorably with that of his role model "FRANCIS WILLUGHBY, Esq.; who died in 1672," who he noted would have undertaken "an actual inspection in the native country of the several subjects under consideration." Noting his reliance on dried specimens sent from New World to Old, Pennant wrote: "I must content myself to do, in a less perfect manner, from preserved specimens transmitted to me; and offer to the world their Natural History, taken from gentlemen or writers who have paid no small attention to their [the specimens'] manners [physical and behavioral characteristics]."[149]

Pennant made a public call for American informants to help him enrich his study in the future, noting that their input would "be gratefully received."[150] He wrote: "Whatever is wanting in the American part, I may foresee, will in time be amply supplied. The powers of literature will soon arrive, with the other strengths of the new empire, and some native Naturalist give perfection to that part of the undertaking, by observations formed on the spot, in the uses, manners, and migrations. Should, at present, no one be inclined to take the pen out of my hand, remarks from the other side of the Atlantic, from any gentleman of congenial studies, will add particular pleasure to a favorite pursuit."[151]

While preparing another edition of his book, Pennant wrote to Barton on October 17, 1790, to request his field notes. He asked Barton to give him research assistance for *Arctic Zoology* in exchange for introducing "a rising genius of the new world to the literati of the old." Flattered that Pennant had asked for his assistance and willing to fully take advantage of the relationship of exchange, Barton promised to send his notes on American animals in return for the proceedings of a European scholarly society. After receiving what he desired, however, Barton held onto his notes, putting off Pennant's string of increasingly exasperated letters.[152] When it was clearly too late for the prominent Englishman to use them in his publication, Barton finally sent the promised materials. He even had the nerve to accompany them with the request that Pennant announce in his book that Barton also intended to publish his own manuscript based on his observations.[153] The revised edition of *Arctic Zoology* was published in February of 1793, months before Barton sent his notes to England.[154]

Figure 4.11 Cartouche of *A Map of the British Empire in America, with the French and Spanish Settlements Adjacent Thereto* (1733), by Henry Popple. The link between American nature and European mercantilism is seen in this cartouche. The figure on the bottom right, representing North America, gestures toward the British merchants unloading a ship full of imported manufactures on the shores of the New World. Next to her at the lower right stands an open coffer, symbolizing the potential profits of the New World. *(Map Collection, Yale University)*

$\mathcal{S}$carcity, abundance, and the movement of objects from one location to another in order to take advantage of differentials in value—these were the driving forces behind transatlantic scientific exchange, just as they were in the trading of other commodities.[155] In such efforts, information about American Indians took on the same epistemic value as William Bartram's botanical drawings. Postrevolutionary Americans involved in science continued to exchange their knowledge of the New World "savage" environment for membership in the established scientific community of the Old World, at the same time claiming, but falling short of achieving, the status of civilized equals. This specific kind of exchange reflected the undeveloped, unrefined status of the United States vis-à-vis Europe. As Susan Scott Parrish argues, Anglo-American forays into British and European science may have resulted in new ways of thinking, but this was due to the "raw" and natural materials provided by Americans, not because of the admission of American scientists into European circles. American botanists contributed to European science not as botanists but as clients in an unequal exchange.[156]

Five

"A GREAT CURIOSITY"

The American Quest for Racial Refinement and Knowledge

The relish we [the professors at the College of Philadelphia now the University of Pennsylvania Medical College] have given him for your discoveries, has determined him to pursue the stream to its fountain in Edinburgh.—He wishes moreover to graduate in your university (where unfortunately for all the other universities in the world) degrees have a kind of exclusive preeminence.

—Benjamin Rush, letter of introduction for Benjamin Smith Barton to William Cullen, Professor of Medicine, University of Edinburgh (1786)

Coming to London, the great city, seeking order, seeking the flowering, the extension of myself that ought to have come in a city of such miraculous light, I had tried to hasten a process which had seemed elusive. I had tried to give myself a personality. It was something that I had tried more than once before, and waited for the response in the eyes of others. But now I no longer knew what I was.

—V. S. Naipaul, *Mimic Men* (1967)

When young Benjamin Smith Barton left Philadelphia for Edinburgh in the fall of 1786, among his most valued possessions were letters of introduction from physicians in America attesting to his academic worthiness. His "industry & Success" had enabled him to reach the top of his medical class at the fledgling college at Philadelphia.[1] One of the letters was written by Smith's preceptor, the Dr. Benjamin Rush, who had made the same transatlantic journey twenty years earlier. In June of that year, Rush had written his letter recommending Barton to his former professor at Edinburgh, the eminent William Cullen. Rush assured Cullen that he and Barton's other instructors at the College of Philadelphia had instilled in the aspiring physician a "relish" for Scottish medicine.[2] Because of their influence, this young American was "determined" to "pursue the stream to its fountain in Edinburgh."[3]

Rush did not exaggerate Barton's determination or ambition. In the Anglo-American medical world, Barton recognized that gaining a European degree ensured professional respect and success. American physicians in the postrevolutionary period had realized that even their patients showed "superior deference" to "European-trained" physicians and scientists.[4] Indeed, Barton was so confident that he chose to leave for Scotland just prior to completing his medical program in America.[5] Barton would be rewarded, after three years at Edinburgh, with a position on the medical faculty at the College of Philadelphia—just as his mentor Benjamin Rush had been before him.

Like countless other letters of recommendation in the early national period, Rush's words did more than simply vouch for a promising student. They also served the broader purpose of renewing and strengthening the personal and professional ties between Rush and his mentor, between the College of Philadelphia and the University of Edinburgh, and between the United States of America and the United Kingdom. Even if vast distances separated these places, the constant exchange of knowledge, objects, and bodies signified an enduring need for Americans to have formative experiences in and receive intellectual enrichment from Europe.

$\mathcal{B}$y the time Barton sailed, there was already a long-standing tradition of American medical students studying abroad.[6] Throughout the colonial period, strong ties kept North American and British scientific communities closely linked, with large numbers of Scottish doctors and teachers emigrating to work in the colonies.[7] The best-known Scottish émigré physicians included William Douglass of Boston, Cadwallader Colden of New York, John Kearsly of Philadelphia, and Charleston doctors John Lining, Alexander Garden, and Lionel Chalmers.[8] By the middle of the century, these medical professionals regularly sent their most promising colonial apprentices to Britain for further training. When they returned, these new physicians could expect to join the exclusive coterie of European-trained doctors working in the colonies.

The market aspect of this transatlantic movement of intellectual capital between the colony and the metropole was clear to astute colonials, such as Benjamin Franklin (see figures 5.1 and 5.2). Frustrated by the barriers he faced while attempting to rise to the top echelons of English society, Franklin

Figure 5.1 Portrait of Benjamin Franklin, after a drawing (1777) by Charles Nicolas Cochin. Franklin was a master at altering his appearance to fit the political occasion. Returning to France after the Declaration of Independence was signed, he played the part of a brilliant, witty, rustic, independent-minded American revolutionary. He made quite an impression. In what has become his most well-known "look," he was drawn by Cochin in a dull brown suit, spectacles, and a marten fur cap from Canada. His long hair was worn down rather than in a queue, as was the convention at the time among the elite. He was conscious of what he was doing, describing his appearance to his English friend Emma Thompson as "being very plainly dress'd, wearing my thin gray strait hair, that peeps out from under my only coiffure, a fine Fur Cap, which comes down to my Forehead almost to my spectacles. Think how this must appear among the Powder'd Heads of Paris!" *(American Philosophical Society)*

wrote to Scottish philosopher David Hume in 1762. In his letter, the ambitious colonial asserted that his talents would be rewarded more generously if he returned to the colonies "where from its Scarcity it [his talent] may probably come to a better Market."[9] The key to maximizing professional value, Franklin indicated, was to find a place in which "Scarcity" was in demand. In the provinces, professional training, especially in medicine, was in scarce supply and high demand. Thus, the knowledge acquired through higher education became a commodity like any other.[10]

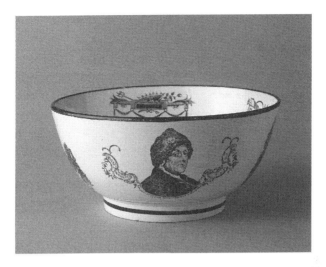

Figure 5.2 Transferware bowl decorated with a portrait of Benjamin Franklin. Although in his lifetime Franklin donned many guises, the image of him as a bespectacled rustic in a fur hat captured the imagination of people worldwide. It graced the surface of many objects. *(Winterthur Museum & Country Estate)*

In the 1760s, two colonial physicians, John Morgan and William Shippen, attempted to address this educational trade imbalance by establishing a domestic manufactures version of a medical college in Philadelphia.[11] The young men had made the pilgrimage from the colonies to study at the University of Edinburgh. Years later when they established the College of Philadelphia, the foreign trained physicians modeled it after their alma mater. The first class graduated in 1768 when there were only a total of forty students enrolled in the school.[12] Despite the fact that other medical colleges were established in the colonies during the eighteenth century, the number of American students studying abroad continued to increase.[13] As with Americans' other efforts in domestic manufacturing, New World medical faculties simply found their products eclipsed by their superior European counterparts.[14]

While the Revolution did not disturb the transfer of medical knowledge, it nonetheless transformed the political meanings of these asymmetrical exchanges. Like the missionaries and merchants of the early republic, men of science worried that their dependence was unbecoming a free people. Political independence encouraged Americans to devise strategies to explain lingering inequalities. All the same, ambitious, prospective doctors in the United States continued to "pursue the stream to its fountain" in Edinburgh.[15]

Examining Barton's Scottish sojourn and other Americans' deft navigation of late eighteenth-century transatlantic intellectual waters makes apparent the conventions governing the asymmetrical relationship between Europe and the United States. The patronage of British scholars and access to the knowledge they produced were among the commodities the American post-revolutionary cultural elite most coveted.[16] If Britons had the power to bestow their learning on Americans, what did these European intellectuals receive in exchange? While individual motivations obviously differed, by serving as the "fount of knowledge," these European intellectuals and their institutions of higher learning maintained their cultural hegemony over America long after formal political independence had been established. Like confirmed believers on a pilgrimage—in this case an intellectual one—Americans continued to travel across the Atlantic to pay homage to European academic authorities and receive the gift of learning. Yet no gift is entirely unconditional; if a person cannot reciprocate in kind when given an offering, then that relationship is marked as unequal.[17] In the postrevolutionary years, Americans continued to arrive as supplicants to European intellectuals, a compromising position for a free people who ultimately were attempting to unbecome British.

At this time, Britishness itself was a contested concept.[18] Within the Anglo-American world, triangulation of nonracialized peoples (English, Scottish, Welsh, Irish, and American) served as an organizing principle for social interactions. Scots inhabited a marginal position vis-à-vis the English—in many ways similar to the place Anglo-Americans occupied. This affinity between Americans and lowland Scots is exemplified by the close relationship between kindred spirits such as Franklin and Hume. Framed by a geography of relative location, however, American and Scottish affinities—while certainly present—did not alter the former colonists' subordinate station in transatlantic cultural hierarchies. Indeed, when Scots went abroad to make their fortunes in the empire, they became the principal colonizing figures. Even though Anglo-Americans also wore the mantle of colonial power, they did so primarily while oppressing Native American and enslaved African populations. But when among brethren from the British Isles, the colonials found themselves on the outside looking in.

Swimming to London, "Upstream": The Father, the Son, and the Fake

'Tis a pity that it is necessary for most Americans to leave their own Country to know how happy they were in it.

—Julia Rush to son James (1810)

> That great city [London] is an epitome of the whole world. Nine months
> spent in it will teach you more by your "eyes and ears," than a life spent in
> your native country.
> —Benjamin Rush to son James (1810)

What was it like for an American to arrive in Great Britain for medical training during the years after the Revolution? While obediently following in the footsteps of his esteemed father, James Rush reacted very differently to his new surroundings.[19] In 1768, when the young Benjamin Rush was studying in Britain, he seized the opportunity to view the throne of the king of England and eagerly persuaded his guide to allow him to sit on the throne, where he was awed for a "considerable time."[20] In contrast, shortly after James's arrival, he was "treated" to the spectacle of the celebration of King George III's coronation. Writing to the elder Rush from Edinburgh, he related: "I don't feel much enthusiasm on the occasion."[21] He explained to his mother his feeling of alienation during the celebratory rites of the British nation: "I have just left the street where drums horns and bagpipes are contending for sway in the empire of sounds; and have shut myself up in my room to write to my Mother, were I an enthusiastic Britton and not an American spectator I might enter into the spirit of what I have seen this morning, and attempt to describe it—But my views all took the course of *satire* or *censure.*"[22]

After a year at the University of Edinburgh, James was terribly disappointed with his experience. Frequent letters from his family in Philadelphia left him "melancholy" because they reminded him of the unbridgeable gaps between the experience of father and son: "When I compare your stay in this country with mine, it gives a palsy to my mind, and in a fit of shame I almost resolve never to go home."[23] In part, James's alienation stemmed from the disturbing realization that American science remained insignificant in the eyes of the British. He took personal and national offense at the lukewarm reception accorded his father's medical theories, finding that "nobody understands them, or wants to understand them." He also despaired of the prevailing British belief that nothing "useful in medicine should come from America."[24] Benjamin expected his son to return home "full of the knowledge," but James carped that his sojourn was a "waste of time" and money. He even pondered "putting up for the first packet that sails" back to America.[25]

At home, Americans with cosmopolitan aspirations could imagine themselves as somewhat equal players in the transatlantic world of science and medicine. When abroad, however, they were forced to confront the reality of their own and their nation's lower stature. As a British subject, the elder Rush had not been embittered by his marginality; as a citizen of the new nation, the younger Rush had an ambivalent reaction.[26] While Americans in the early national period wanted to reduce their dependency on Great Britain, they were also aware that completely severing ties with their former colonial masters was neither desirable nor possible.

The medical careers of Benjamin Rush, his student Benjamin Smith Barton, and James Rush illustrate the paths many doctors and scientists followed from America to Britain and back again before and after the Revolution.[27] After graduating from the College of New Jersey in 1760,[28] Benjamin Rush became the apprentice of Dr. John Redman of Philadelphia, spending the next five years assisting his teacher with patients.[29] Colonials frequently completed this type of apprenticeship prior to making the decision to pursue further training in Europe. When a new medical college in Philadelphia opened in 1766, Rush became one of its first students, attending William Shippen's lectures on anatomy and John Morgan's classes in chemistry.[30] Having exhibited an affinity for the medical arts, Rush could have earned his degree in Philadelphia with relative ease. Instead, he was advised to continue his studies at Edinburgh, with a prospective appointment to the chemistry department chair in Philadelphia on his return.[31] To his Edinburgh-trained mentors in Philadelphia, Rush could be of greater service to their fledgling medical school with a degree from the celebrated Scottish university.[32]

Heeding the advice of his teachers, Rush sailed for Great Britain in August 1766 and on arrival enrolled at the University of Edinburgh. Like other Americans who went abroad to study, Rush found himself ill prepared in the classical and philosophical learning "necessary to comprehend all that was taught in medicine."[33] To make up for his educational deficit, he spent his first summer and part of the autumn in Edinburgh acquiring knowledge of Latin, French, Italian, Spanish, and mathematics. After he managed to pass the requirements, Rush was able to pursue his studies in earnest. He embarked on vigorous self-experimentation, including vomiting special meals in order to understand the digestive processes of the human stomach.[34]

Rush took professional and personal advantage of his presence in Britain by eagerly collecting the latest medical knowledge and new social connections.[35] "[The] two years I spent in Edinburgh," Rush reflected in his autobiography, "I consider as the most important in their influence upon my character and conduct of any period of my life."[36] After his medical degree was conferred on June 19, 1768, Rush set off on an ambitious information-gathering tour of Europe. He traveled around England to investigate practical uses of chemical reactions. In France, he continued the pursuit of scientific, manufacturing, and medical knowledge by calling on scientists such as Antoine Baumé and Pierre Macquer, who worked on the practical applications of science.[37] The emphasis on everyday uses for science appealed to American medical professionals, who recognized that conducting purely theoretical research was not a practical undertaking in the peripheries of the British Empire.

Americans like Rush whose talents and affluence made it possible to obtain a foreign education could be relatively certain that they would be given leading positions in the American academy.[38] In 1769, Rush returned home with his Edinburgh diploma in hand and, as promised, was appointed a professor of chemistry at the College of Philadelphia.[39] Anglo-American professional networks were carefully nurtured by cultural and intellectual elites who depended upon them throughout their careers. These networks were based on personal relationships, many of which were established while studying abroad, that were constantly being challenged by the corrosive effects of time, distance, and political separation between Great Britain and America.

The prodigious volume of Rush's transatlantic correspondence and reading as well as his adherence to European professional practice helped to create and maintain these ties.[40] For cosmopolitan men like Rush, European influences were not limited to the realm of ideas (see figures 5.3 and 5.4). In a medical lecture he explained to his pupils that "loose dresses contribute to the easy and vigorous exercise of the mind...we find studious men are always painted in gowns, when they are seated in their libraries. Sometimes an open collar, and loose shoes and stockings, form a part of their picture," due to the "habits of mental ease and vigour which this careless form of dress creates."[41]

Throughout his life, Benjamin Rush sent letters, his best medical students, books he had written, and manuscripts he wanted published to his alma mater in Great Britain. Barton's departure for Edinburgh in 1786 provided Rush with both an occasion to pay tribute to his teacher William Cullen and to the superiority of Scottish medical knowledge. Three years earlier, as the formal peace between the United States and Britain was declared, Rush, the respected patriot and prominent supporter of the Revolution, explicitly reaffirmed his allegiance to his Edinburgh mentor. In 1783, Rush wrote to Cullen: "The events of the late war have not lessened my attachment to my venerable master. The members of the republic of science all belong to the same family. What has physic to do with taxation or independence?" For the rest of his life, Rush would declare his

Figure 5.3 Portrait of Benjamin Rush, painting by Thomas Sully (c. 1813–15). Rush sat for
this three-quarter length portrait shortly before he died in 1813. When he painted this portrait
Thomas Sully was considered to be at the height of his career having recently returned from study in
England *(American Philosophical Society)*.

"effusions of gratitude" and "obligations" to Cullen for his "friendship" and
"instruction." He told his teacher, "if I have been in any degree useful or
successful in my profession, I owe all these things to you."[42]

By sending his students to Edinburgh, Rush paid homage to his mentors
by recognizing his alma mater as the principal "seat of medical knowledge."
As he explained to Cullen, Rush and his colleagues had stoked Barton's
desire to study there. For Barton and other young, privileged Americans, the
time, expense, and effort of going abroad for their education reaped abun-
dant rewards, just as it had for Benjamin Rush's generation. Rush stressed to
Cullen that Barton had recognized the "exclusive preeminence" only an
Edinburgh degree could confer and had expressed a willingness to do whatever it took to obtain one (see figure 5.5).[43]

Figure 5.4 Portrait of Benjamin Rush, painting by Charles Willson Peale, oil on canvas, 127.6 x 101.6 cm. (1783 and 1786). This portrait connects the Philadelphian to European networks of scientific and medical knowledge through inclusion of material objects. Finely attuned to European culture, Rush is seen here wearing one of the "loose dresses" that he noted "contribute to the easy and vigorous exercise of the faculties of the mind." (Rush, "Manuscript Lectures of the Theory and Practice of Physick, 1790–1791," Benjamin Rush Papers, Historical Society of Pennsylvania.) The majority of the books proudly displayed behind him in this portrait were owned by Rush and upon his death his son James. They are now part of the collections of the Library Company of Philadelphia. These volumes on the latest scholarship in subjects ranging from political theory to moral philosophy and chemistry attest to his intellectual as well as sartorial connections to European society. *(Winterthur Museum & Country Estate)*

Rush's description of Barton's oceanic journey as an American's pursuit up the "stream" of scientific inquiry to its "fountain in Edinburgh" was especially apt. The metaphor of students journeying to the headwaters reflected the inequality of the relationships of exchange between American and British physicians. The current ran in one direction—from the Old World "downstream" to the former colonies. Barton's letters of introduction from Rush were therefore extremely valuable as objects of exchange and provided

Figure 5.5 Portrait of Benjamin Smith Barton, painting by Samuel Jennings (August 1789). This portrait was yet another attempt by Barton to establish himself as a respected member of the international scientific community. Barton's self-aggrandizing tendencies are evident here. He is shown holding a diagram drawn by someone else that he published in his first book, *Observations on Some Parts of Natural History* (1787). Like most of Barton's publications, this book was largely taken from other people's work. Barton, who failed to receive a degree, is placed in a natural setting in his land of origin rather than in a formal institutional setting. *(American Philosophical Society)*

a ticket into British social and intellectual circles, especially those within the orbit of the University of Edinburgh. In many respects, Barton's plan entailed exchanging a letter for a diploma—in effect, one promissory note for another—but, of course, this transaction was not about trading paper, sheepskins, or promises. Rather, this exchange revealed that only by operating within an established network of social relations across the Atlantic could Barton and other Americans have a chance to gain the highly prized Edinburgh degree.[44]

British medical schools, which could boast prestige and offered rigorous scientific training, established a standard unequaled in the United States. For the most part, American medical training remained an informal affair, requiring work as an apprentice to a practicing physician. As late as 1876, Dr.

Edward Clarke remarked that American medical schools did not "pretend to give a complete education, but only to supplement that which the student gets elsewhere."[45] In the early nineteenth century, the University of Edinburgh extended the length of its medical program from three to four years; American medical schools, by contrast, lowered graduation requirements. Few in number, these institutions did their best to accommodate students, reducing the academic term length from four months to twelve or thirteen weeks for students who needed to travel long distances. They suspended requirements to master (or even attempt) coursework in classical languages, natural history, and natural philosophy. Finally, these American schools eliminated the dissertation, long considered a focal point of European medical training. An 1810 article in the academic journal *Medical Repository* lamented that a medical diploma from an American school was as "little respected as the license of many of our country medical societies."[46]

Throughout the nineteenth century, American doctors continued to depend on overseas training, especially for technically demanding specialties such as surgery and anatomy.[47] Even after the Revolutionary War, Rush complained that in the United States the "professions of physic, surgery, and pharmacy are still blended together," forcing American doctors to work as general practitioners.[48] In 1795, Rush received a letter from his former student John Coxe, who was studying surgery in London, that underlined the instructional distance American schools had to close: "Indeed—but for the mere name acquired by crossing the sea—I am confident I should have acquired infinitely more advantage under Your instruction than here in an equal space of time—except in Surgery—which certainly is here in its greatest perfection."[49] Coxe's perceptive observation highlights the critical elements missing from American medical education: the immediate prestige and superior technical training they "acquired by crossing the sea" for study in Europe.[50] Indeed, those who made the journey gained recognition back home regardless of whether they formally earned a degree. In the decades following the Revolution, young Americans of Coxe's generation who made the transatlantic journey for medical training had to concede that British schooling carried an exalted reputation, something the new nation could not possibly match. American claims about the growing strength and viability of domestic training, if not merely the brave boasts of the weak, were certainly more hope than fact.

*I*n 1809, forty-three years after his father had gone to Edinburgh to study, and twenty-three years after Barton had embarked, James Rush sailed to the

British Isles to complete his medical education. The elder Rush had pressured his son to go to Edinburgh, convinced that he, too, would benefit immeasurably from the experience. But the younger Rush inhabited a different world from that of his father, for he was born of a generation who thought of themselves as proud citizens of a new nation rather than suppliant colonial subjects. As a "native of Philadelphia," James considered himself a patriotic American and had already earned a doctoral degree in medicine from the College of Philadelphia.[51] Despite the ambivalence he felt toward his expatriation, James knew his goal in Edinburgh was "to acquire that knowledge wh[ich] other countries furnish in greater abundance or with easier modes of attainment than his own."[52]

For members of America's scientific and cultural elite, James Rush *had* to leave the United States, because the two commodities medical study required—advanced scientific knowledge and equipment—were in short supply at home. Before financing his son's journey, Benjamin Rush drafted a detailed letter outlining what he wanted James to observe during his trip, which the younger Rush dutifully copied into his travel journal verbatim.[53] Benjamin stressed the "various curiosities of manufacturing mechanism" found in the United Kingdom, which "shews perhaps the most predominant character of civilized man." He pointed out to his son, "You have heard of the wealth of the country to which you are going" and counseled him to "observe the laudable the luxurious and the vicious modes in which it is expended."[54]

Many Americans studying and traveling overseas recorded their experiences in journals and diaries for the benefit of people back home. Their writings converted transatlantic travel into a material object, one that could be reproduced and shared among relatives and colleagues; these narratives could also be published, earning the temporary expatriate profits while enlightening a larger circle. And whereas American elites continued to travel in Great Britain for practical reasons as they had done during the colonial period, now this information was used to establish American cultural independence through emulation of Britain's social, cultural, and economic institutions. In his 1788 "Objects of Attention for an American," Jefferson encouraged Americans traveling overseas to observe and record foreign approaches to agriculture, mechanical arts, gardens, architecture, and politics.[55] James Rush was also instructed by both of his parents to keep a comprehensive record of his time abroad, highlighting the experiences that would aid in the nascent country's development, for the benefit of his "fellow citizens." The metaphors Rush employed in his regular letters to his son aptly described Americans' hunger for useful information from Britain. In one, he urged his son to "spread your sails to every wind that can convey to you new facts and opinions in Surgery" while in London. According to Rush, "It will be necessity for you to practice it in Order to assist you in getting into business. It will enable you moreover to <u>keep</u> your business when organised."[56] Rush's particular interest in studying insanity clearly informed his instructions to "Visit all public and humane institutions, particularly maniacal ones. Pry into their interior, as far as diet-dress-regime—and expense are concerned. Record every thing useful, especially where <u>numbers</u> are concerned in your journal. They will be choice new materials to work upon in promoting the happiness of your fellow citizens when you return."[57]

Alongside the desire to obtain valuable practical information from foreign sources was a lingering admiration of British culture and society. Despite the Rush family's unimpeachable patriotic pedigree, their fascination with the mother country was palpable. A devoted reader of travel narratives, James's mother Julia looked forward to receiving accounts of her son's experiences: "I anticipate a great deal of pleasure from your letters and descriptions of the numerous objects of curiosity in that superb metropolis. I have lately read the travels of Mr. Benjamin Silliman of Connecticut through England and Scotland, they are written in a very elegant style, and have afforded me much entertainment."[58] Her husband was no less enthusiastic; in yet another breathless letter he managed to convey his unalloyed enjoyment of the British capital:

> I refer you to my former letters for instructions how you are to employ your time in London. See! and examine everything curious in that great metropolis of the arts of the world during the Summer. Visit Oxford, and (if the excursion be not very expensive) Bath, also the palaces in the vicinity of London before the winter. Cultivate an acquaintance with physicians, apothecaries, & surgeons...obtain if possible an introduction to Dr. Dunstam of St Luke's hospital, and Mr. Haburn of Bethlehem, and collect all the facts from them upon the subject of Insanity that you can. "Be all eye—all ear—all grasp" in your intercourse with the citizens of London of all descriptions.[59]

As members of a new nation, Americans would have to become, to use the elder Rush's memorable exhortation, "all eye—all ear—all grasp."[60] This self-description matched Europeans' general impression of hungry American upstarts who came to the Old World in search of useful information.

*U*p to a point, Barton did everything according to the plans he and Rush had laid out before he had sailed to Edinburgh in 1786. He became a respected doctor in Philadelphia, and his foreign credentials marked him as a man with a superior education. But unbeknownst to his colleagues and patients, Barton had failed to earn his degree.[61] Aware that success in the United States had much to do with the cachet of a non-American degree, Barton was not inclined to disabuse anyone of the notion that he had actually received his degree from Edinburgh.[62]

Some of Barton's family knew he had not finished his degree. While still in Europe, he wrote to his elder brother William and explained that he planned to reenroll at Penn to earn his medical degree. However, on his return, the medical faculty in Philadelphia assumed the twenty-three-year-old Barton had received his degree and welcomed him to the staff.[63] Moreover, as he had spent the requisite time studying at the center of the medical world, Barton's expertise might have been enough to serve as a professor in the United States, his degree status notwithstanding. Many of Barton's peers in medicine who practiced and taught in the United States had studied abroad without obtaining their degrees. So Barton's failure to receive a doctorate from Edinburgh was not an aberration.[64] But unlike most of these colleagues, Barton did not even hold an American medical degree.

Barton began quietly trying to arrange an honorary degree from a less prestigious foreign university after nearly seven years as a professor at the University of Pennsylvania. He tried to use his European contacts to get a degree from the University of Gottingen. Failing that, he asked whether there were medical schools in Hamburg, or Brunswick, or Kiel, and if there were, would it be possible for him to purchase a degree from them. He finally obtained an honorary degree from the University of Kiel in 1796.[65]

After teaching so long on the Penn faculty, Barton obviously did not think it possible to enroll himself as a student in order to finish his degree, but his lack of credentials obviously bothered him. In fact, he lied to his European correspondent about the reasons he wanted a foreign degree. He wrote that it had been "several years since I received the degree of <u>Medical Doctor</u> from a university which, I confess, I do not much respect."[66]

That Benjamin Smith Barton, a man without a degree, was not only a respected doctor but a professor of medicine at the most prestigious medical school in the United States sheds light on what was at stake with regard to a foreign education. Though Benjamin Rush knew or at least suspected the truth about Barton's degree status, Barton went on to become one of the foremost physicians and scientists in the young republic. He did so by making the most of the influential contacts he had cultivated in Great Britain. Barton was almost a caricature of the ambitious emulation of Europe that characterized postcolonial educated Americans. But this emulation was not a social failing, nor was it an indication of a lack of dignity or pride, among Americans. Rather, there were pragmatic reasons for it. Fake degree or not, Barton had acquired knowledge that was plentiful across the ocean but scarce in America. The experience allowed him to make contacts in Europe, and most important of all, he was able during that time to cultivate transatlantic connections. It was these long-term relationships that made Barton worthy of a faculty position, just as they had made his mentor Rush an important scholar and intellectual. These relationships of exchange with overseas correspondents were the cultural practice of which a foreign university degree was merely the objectified form. In the end, the diploma was just a piece of paper if not for the scholarly relationships it embodied.

Postrevolutionary Americans in a "Geography of Value"

David Hosack, a respected physician and botanist, was another ambitious American man whose success owed much to his Edinburgh education. Born in New York in 1769, Hosack serves as an emblematic figure in this postrevolutionary generation of American elites, whose level of success was predicated on their ability to negotiate the transatlantic networks between America and Great Britain.[67] After over two years of undergraduate work at Columbia University, Hosack graduated from the College of New Jersey in 1789 and then earned an M.D. from the University of the State of Pennsylvania.[68] Shortly thereafter, he married a woman from New Jersey and established a medical practice in Alexandria, Virginia.[69] Enjoying professional success and his new marriage, Hosack nevertheless decided to advance his career by continuing his medical education in Britain. Despite his misgivings about leaving home, Hosack became "convinced that the distinction which our citizens at that time made between those physicians who had been educated at home and those who had had additional instruction from the universities of Europe" would prevent him from attaining the success he craved.[70] His explanation for his reluctant yet voluntary move is telling. Well aware of "how little property I had reason to expect from my parents," Hosack wrote that his "chief dependence was upon my own industry and unceasing attention to the profession I had chosen as the means of my subsistence; my ambition to excel in my profession did not suffer me to remain insensible under such distinction."[71] Ultimately, Hosack's ambitions carried the day, and the wistful newlywed headed across the Atlantic to the University of Edinburgh. "Although it was painful for me to think of leaving my family," Hosack wrote, "I took passage to Liverpool."[72]

Significantly, Hosack did not initially plan on earning another formal medical degree in Edinburgh. Just having traveled there would be enough for him to acquire the desired intellectual patina. This Scottish interlude would differentiate him from the majority of his fellow Americans. As Hosack's biographer puts it, "his major aim was . . . to return . . . with the added prestige of having studied at Edinburgh and London with whatever that might mean in the way of the latest and best available medical information."[73] Hosack "did not neglect to add 'polish' by attendance at the theater and by whatever contacts with the eminent were possible."[74]

As mentioned, when Americans went overseas, they often experienced the discomfort of realizing their own provinciality and ignorance.[75] Before arriving in the United Kingdom, Hosack considered himself a cultured gentleman; he bought imported books, purchased paintings, had portrait busts of friends, and maintained a well-stocked wine cellar. The painful moment of provincial reckoning occurred in the course of an otherwise pleasant afternoon wandering through the gardens of Blackford—the Scottish doctor Alexander Hamilton's estate near Edinburgh—as it became obvious to Hosack, and worse yet, to those around him, that the young American could contribute nothing to their polite conversation. "[M]orti-fied by my ignorance of botany with which other guests were conversant, I resolved, at that time, whenever an opportunity might offer, to acquire a knowledge of that department of science."[76] On his return to America, not only did Hosack go on to become one of the most successful physicians of his generation, he rose as one of the most distinguished botanists in the country and the founder of Elgin Gardens, the first botanical garden in the United States (see figure 5.6).[77] His experience in the former mother country and his subsequent ownership of learned books, lecture notes, and precious natural specimens (ironically, dried American plants European scientists had earlier acquired) made him an undisputed expert in botany (in his words), the "as yet untrodden field in this country." As his success shows, apparently, he had read the transatlantic natural history market cor-rectly, for his expertise was indeed a rare commodity when imported back to the United States.

At Hosack's alma mater, the College of New Jersey, President Samuel Stanhope Smith was desperately trying to close the educational gap with his British counterparts. He knew that the latest scientific knowledge and access to the centers of knowledge were commodities as precious as imported scientific glassware. European intellectuals such as the eminent

ELGIN GARDEN, 5th and 6th AVES., 49th and 51st STS., NEW YORK, C. 1812. (E-100)

Figure 5.6 Sepia Drawing of "View of Elgin Garden on Fifth Avenue" by Hugh Reinagle, 16 x 10.8.
[c. 1812]. David Hosack's Elgin Gardens. Named after his parents' hometown in Scotland, it was the first
botanical garden in the United States. Image published in I. N. Phelps Stokes and Daniel C. Haskell,
American Historical Prints: Early Views of American Cities, Etc. From the Phelps Stokes and Other
Collections (New York: New York Public Library, 1933). Image is on Plate 41-b facing page 44. *(Copy in
Sterling Memorial Library, Yale University)*

Scottish chemist John Maclean possessed, or rather embodied, the latest
scientific ideas and commanded high prices for their rarity. Maclean's
professional path highlights the logic of the geography of value: a commodity's worth—pecuniary, intellectual, cultural, civilizing—increased
as it moved from one location to another, from a place of abundance to
one of scarcity.

Just as Americans went to Britain to gain prestige and polish, American
colleges "imported" learned scholars from Great Britain to raise their
academic profiles and reputations. College presidents, boosters, board
members, and citizens worked hard to convince accredited individuals to
come to the United States, enticing them with promises of elevated esteem,
financial gain, and sometimes even an escape from political troubles back
home. Importation of European scholars had begun during the colonial
period and would continue throughout the nineteenth and twentieth cen-

turies. Benjamin Rush, key among those who prevailed upon Scottish academics to move to America universities, famously recruited the Scottish
minister John Witherspoon, a leading light in Edinburgh's intellectual and
religious circles. While studying at the University of Edinburgh, Rush had
visited the minister's home to persuade his wife (who reputedly became
physically ill at the thought of banishment to the colonies) to come to
America. Ingratiating and persistent, the young man managed to induce the
implacable Mrs. Witherspoon to become an expatriate.

The College of New Jersey boasted a number of émigré intellectuals
from Scotland. Crowing to a colleague, President Smith touted his most
prized intellectual acquisition, an "excellent professor in chemistry from
Scotland," John Maclean.[78] On his arrival in 1795, the young Glaswegian
was keenly welcomed at Princeton as a man whose highly desirable
European credentials militated against the American institution's own
sense of scholarly self-consciousness.[79] Just days after Maclean's formal
appointment, several periodicals published President Smith's glowing
letter extolling the Scottish scholar's accomplishments. In his missive,
Smith prominently emphasized that Maclean brought "the highest rec-
ommendations from Europe," "personal acquaintance" with important
overseas intellectuals, and "knowledge of the latest scientific information
from Great Britain and the Continent."[80]

The son of a Glasgow surgeon, Maclean was born five years before
America went to war with the British Empire.[81] When he arrived in the
United States, Maclean had already studied his craft in London, Edinburgh,
Glasgow, and Paris, during what has subsequently been deemed a definitive
phase in the revolution of chemical science in Europe.[82] Princeton would
bestow on him America's first professorship in chemistry. To American scientist Benjamin Silliman, he was "a man of brilliant mind, with all the acumen of his native Scotland." College leaders decided to make Maclean's
newly imported expertise in "sound natural history" the linchpin in their
curriculum. The institution had already exerted a great deal of effort and
money to buy scientific equipment from Britain but was now searching for
leading academics to instruct students on how to use these objects. Without
the one, the other would be of little worth—after all, mountains of rare
imported glassware could only be of help if students had knowledgeable
authorities to guide their use and applications in the latest European
scientific theories.

The leaders of the College of New Jersey recognized that Maclean not
only enhanced the school's academic standing but also was a sign of
America's intellectual and cultural advancement. As President Smith

explained, Maclean's value to the fledgling nation derived from his work on transforming chemical knowledge into "an object of cultivation" applicable to fields outside medicine. His work could be profitably employed in agriculture and manufactures, both "so useful in every country, but especially in a new one."[83] Moreover, he brought with him expertise in surgery and anatomy, historically the weakest areas in American medical training. By acquiring the European doctor, the university immediately became an exclusive center of expert scientific knowledge in the former colonies. Smith concluded by emphasizing that he was "well assured" young Americans could not obtain this type of knowledge "at present with more advantage at any place in America than the College of New Jersey."[84]

Analyzing the career trajectories of men such as David Hosack and John Maclean provides an explanation as to why so many educated, lowland Scots relocated to America throughout the colonial and early national periods.[85] They recognized that they could increase their value by transplanting themselves to a location of relative scarcity.[86] The changes in their value as they moved around on the transatlantic map serve to illuminate the close and complex relationship of Scotland and America vis-à-vis the larger British Empire.

The Significance of Scotland

Scotland represented a land of learning and opportunity for Americans. Visiting the Scottish capital of Edinburgh opened doors for students and exposed them to European culture and sophistication. And Scots, just by moving from one place to another, often rose straight to the top of their respective fields and of the social hierarchy in postcolonial America.[87] This positive view of Scotland contrasts with the prevalent English stereotypes circulating at the same time. Within the logic of the geography of value and the economy of relative location, Scottish-American connections in particular reveal the importance these mutual relationships of exchange had for both societies, especially considering their relative positions within the British Empire.

During the seventeenth and eighteenth centuries, Scotland held a marginal position within Great Britain, and its people were stereotyped as provincial, grasping upstarts. The German author Friedrich August Wedeborn observed in 1791 that the English hated the Scots more than any other Europeans.[88] This disdain was reflected in numerous satirical prints produced by English artists portraying Scotland as a wasteland and her people as bellicose savages and filthy, uncouth peasants. As with the Americans, English prejudice manifested itself in objects that supposedly reflected the Scots' lack of civility and refinement.[89] Food became a focal point for scorn. Scots were pictured eating oats, which Samuel Johnson's dictionary had defined as fit only for animals, as well as munching on an exclusive diet of haggis, sheep's heads, and dried fish.[90] Dr. Johnson commented that Scotland's "main riches lay in its manpower" and its "main export" was soldiers."[91] The success of Scots, in particular the Earl of Bute, became the principal source of English critics' most virulent diatribes. Despite his professional success, which culminated in his appointment as prime minister, Bute's Scottish background made him vulnerable to attack and ridicule by his critics.

To the even more provincial former colonies in North America, Scotland represented one of the most visible and accessible European centers of knowledge production. When Scottish elites traveled to the colonial outposts of the British Empire and, after 1783, the United States, they represented a link to Old World culture for many Americans. From an English point of view, Scottish provinciality could not be flatly equated with colonial American provinciality. While Scots may have been provincials in the eyes of the English, they were clearly British when they gazed out on the distant empire. Within an economy of relative location, this relative worth of Scottish identity explains why ambitious Scots traveled to the outskirts of the empire in search of opportunities.

After the Scottish and English parliaments passed the Acts of Union in 1707 creating the United Kingdom of Great Britain, Scots were entitled to serve as equal partners in colonizing foreign lands and profiting from the overseas imperial expansion. Scots could be found in every corner of imperial settlement; as soldiers and enterprising adventurers, they, in effect, comprised the vanguard of the British Empire. Scottish merchants placed great importance on access to existing English trade routes. From this perspective the British North American colonies were as much an imperial possession for the Scots as they were for the English.

Some scholars who have examined the special ties between America and Scotland ascribe their closeness to shared religious affinities and mutual recognition of their peripheral position in the British Empire.[92] While this common marginality was important, equally significant were what contemporaries perceived as critical differences between Old World Scotland and New World America. Emphasizing the exceptional, distinctive nature of late eighteenth-century "Scottishness" underestimates how the Scots actively took part in constructing a collective, national sense of "Britishness" that Americans did not share.[93] Moreover, cultural distinctions within Scotland allowed upper-class figures, such as Bute, to see themselves as lowland Scots, markedly different from the supposedly "barbaric" Highlanders—a differentiation similar to American elites of the East Coast and the South distinguishing themselves from the masses.

Examining this economy of relative location from the perspective of the United States, however, there were more similarities between London and Edinburgh, and between England and Scotland, than there were contrasts. Americans like Hosack who were eager to garner cultural polish and refinement visited both Scotland and England, conflating their cities and historical sites into a singular experience of Britain's civilized centers. Conversely, when visiting English cities, Scots often had to assert their equality, working aggressively to overcome English prejudice. While many Americans might have been aware of English prejudice toward the Scottish, these former colonials must also have realized that they ranked even lower in the British cultural hierarchy. Americans accepted Scottish superiority in training and technical knowledge. Proof of this belief was their active recruitment of Scottish ministers, doctors, educators, scientists, artists, and even artisans and tradesmen throughout the colonial and postrevolutionary periods.[94]

Emboldened by independence, elite Americans who were aware that they were cast as inferior members of western civilization aspired to achieving equality with Europe. In a cultural sense, the angst experienced in the postrevolutionary period in the United States manifested itself in a continual push to improve, a disdain for anyone deemed inferior, a ravenous hunger for material objects, and an inexhaustible ambition, driving its citizens to unchecked expansion, rampant speculation, and the exploitation of the land and labor of others.

Race, An American Commodity

One hot July day in 1796, curious citizens of Philadelphia pushed and shoved under the sign of the Black Horse that hung outside Mr. Leech's tavern on Market Street. They were all there to witness a "Great CURIOSITY": a man named Henry Moss who was born "entirely black," but who, after thirty-eight years, had miraculously "become as white and fair as any white person." According to a July 23 broadside, Moss's "natural colour began to rub off," and his "wool" was being replaced by "straight hair similar to that of a white person" (see figure 5.7). How, they wondered, could this be true? From eight

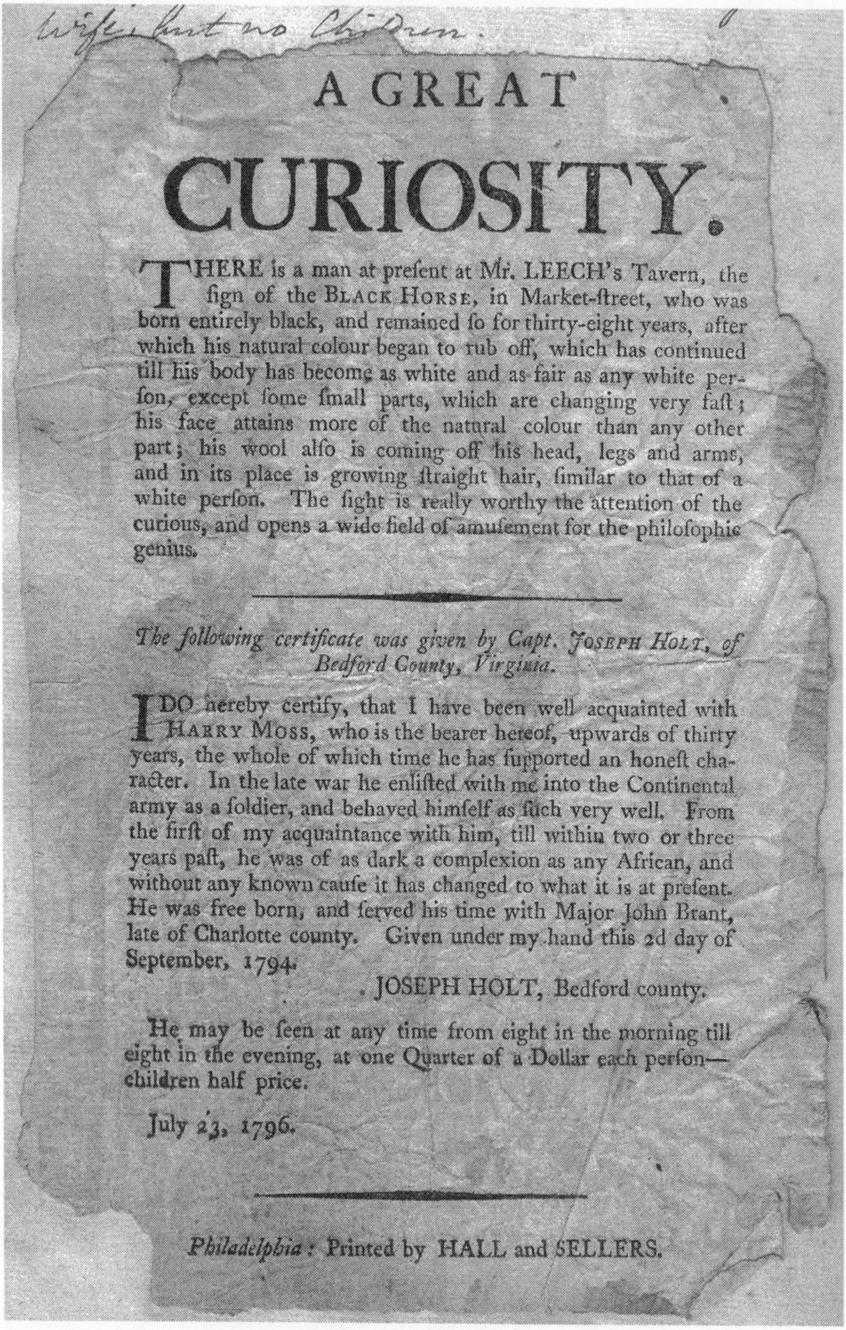

A GREAT

CURIOSITY.

THERE is a man at prefent at Mr. LEECH's Tavern, the fign of the BLACK HORSE, in Market-ftreet, who was born entirely black, and remained fo for thirty-eight years, after which his natural colour began to rub off, which has continued till his body has become as white and as fair as any white perfon, except fome fmall parts, which are changing very faft; his face attains more of the natural colour than any other part; his wool alfo is coming off his head, legs and arms, and in its place is growing ftraight hair, fimilar to that of a white perfon. The fight is really worthy the attention of the curious, and opens a wide field of amufement for the philofophic genius.

The following certificate was given by Capt. JOSEPH HOLT, of Bedford County, Virginia.

I DO hereby certify, that I have been well acquainted with HARRY MOSS, who is the bearer hereof, upwards of thirty years, the whole of which time he has fupported an honeft character. In the late war he enlifted with me into the Continental army as a foldier, and behaved himfelf as fuch very well. From the firft of my acquaintance with him, till within two or three years paft, he was of as dark a complexion as any African, and without any known caufe it has changed to what it is at prefent. He was free born, and ferved his time with Major John Brant, late of Charlotte county. Given under my hand this 2d day of September, 1794.

. JOSEPH HOLT, Bedford county.

He may be feen at any time from eight in the morning till eight in the evening, at one Quarter of a Dollar each perfon—children half price.

July 23, 1796.

Philadelphia : Printed by HALL and SELLERS.

Figure 5.7 Broadside advertising the display of Henry Moss who was billed as a thirty-eight-year-old man "born entirely black" who had turned "as fair as any white person" (1796). (*American Philosophical Society*)

in the morning until eight in the evening, Moss entertained visitors who plunked down half a shilling for the chance to view this "curiosity."

The public's preoccupation with Moss was insatiable. For two months, the Philadelphia physician Dr. Charles Caldwell recalled, the people of his city were utterly transfixed by the spectacle of Moss. As the doctor underscored in his *Autobiography*, "the cause of this singular change of complexion was a theme of wonder to everyone." Moss's name, Caldwell claimed, was as well known to periodical readers as that of John Adams, Thomas Jefferson, or James Madison. Although Caldwell may have been exaggerating, Moss's popularity would prompt him to take his show (his body) to several American cities, drawing crowds of curious onlookers.

Only secondhand glimpses of this common man's uncommon life survive from the period.[95] The "spectacle" Moss created not only piqued the interest of the average citizen but also garnered the attention of the new nation's leading intellectuals, who speculated, debated, and published their differing views on Moss's transformation. Although no extant documents written by Moss have been found, the social and cultural implications behind the differing theories about his changing color and Americans' keen interest illuminate much about pressing issues of the period: race relations, religion, slavery, and the unbecoming formation of an American national identity.

Caldwell was not the only physician captivated by Moss. Benjamin Rush also paid the admission fee for his chance to see Moss. The account of his visit in his letterbook was accompanied by a broadside advertising the show, pasted next to his entry for July 27, 1796. This advertisement was one of only two items the busy doctor and civic leader chose to paste into his book, the other being the eulogy for George Washington. Impressed by what he saw, Rush discussed the man who had "lately travelled through this city, and was exhibited as a show for money" in an article entitled "Observations Intended to Favour a Supposition That the Black Color (As It Is Called) of the Negroes Is Derived from the Leprosy," published in 1799 in the learned journal *Transactions of the American Philosophical Society*.[96] Moss's condition, Rush proposed, was caused by leprosy of the "Black Color (as it is called) of the Negroes." Barton was also fascinated by the man whom he described in an 1806 publication as a "white negro." Samuel Smith also commented extensively on Moss's case in an 1810 republication of his work *An Essay on the Causes of the Variety of Complexion and Figure in the Human Species*.[97]

The few facts about Moss's life that emerge from these men's records conflict in suggestive ways. Was Moss a slave or a free black man? Some describe Moss as a free black, a veteran of the Revolutionary War. Rush described Moss as a slave, but the broadside he pasted in his book maintained that Moss was born a freeman. As proof, the advertisement mentioned a "certificate given by Capt. JOSEPH HOLD, of Bedford County, Virginia," emphasizing that Moss "was free born." Smith argued that Moss was a slave who bought his freedom with the money he earned displaying himself to curious crowds. If this was true, white curiosity was a commodity that could be used by enslaved Africans to purchase that precious commodity, freedom.

Various explanations were proffered for Moss's miraculous changes in not just his skin color but also in what were considered by many racially significant markers, such as hair texture. As Rush explained, "the wool which formerly perforated the cuticle has been changed into hair." Moss became the textbook example when authors were speculating about racial variation. Barton attributed his change in skin color to a medical "affliction" (referred to by modern physicians as *Leucaethopia humana*) and—in the most influential work on Moss—used him to present his novel theories on how the natural and cultural environment affected skin color. Just as Moss aroused controversy concerning his freedom or enslavement, so, too, he transgressed racial categories in ways white Americans in the early national period found both intriguing and alarming.

Moss captured the national imagination in the very first years of the republic precisely because these new Americans were struggling with defining racial identity in the new nation. Recent scholars have linked race, specifically the notion of whiteness, to the cultural, economic, and political development of the nation. As scholar Dana Nelson explains, "whiteness— formerly associated primarily with British aristocratic elites—was increasingly extended, actually democratized, to define civic identity in the early national period."[98] The idea that environmental factors could change a man's race was a threatening concept to elite Anglo-Americans, residing as they did on the edge of the civilized world. Like all curiosities, Moss's unusual condition begged an explanation. But more than a theory explaining his medical condition, an examination of the intense curiosity he generated among the American people reveals a great deal about the new nation in this uncertain period.

As in other emerging nations, cultural conditions of the postrevolutionary United States were characterized by insecurity and instability. In this milieu, race—in particular skin color—took on new and charged meanings for white Americans. Contemporary debates about the origins of racial differentiation were not simply academic matters without social consequences; in the estimation of intellectuals such as Rush and Smith, the origin of racial difference determined the relationship between the races. Public curiosity about Moss and keen scientific interest in his condition expressed the racial anxiety experienced by white settlers in America. If black Africans and tawny Indians could become white when their environments changed from a condition of savagery to civilization, as some hypothesized was the case with Moss, could the opposite also happen? Would those who were born white become dark when they ventured into savage surroundings? Could Anglo-Americans just as easily become savages as refined Europeans?[99]

Citizens of the fledgling nation were pleased by European interest in the natural history of North America while at the same time they vehemently repudiated the accompanying pronouncements about the lack of civilization in the New World.[100] The concept of American degeneration held by European philosophers such as Buffon and the Abbé Raynal were serious national slights. Barton understood clearly what theories of degeneration implied about his nation and himself. Barton described the "puerile prejudices which disfigure and disgrace the writings of some of your most eminent European authors." The insult was also gendered, for degeneracy theories were taken to mean that the American nation—as symbolized by its animals, Indian inhabitants, and even white settlers—was less masculine than its European counterpart. Barton encapsulated a gender-bending Anglo-American reaction:

> But though nature shews the symptoms of her manhood here as much as she does in other portions of the globe, we Americans shall not dispute concerning our antiquity. We shall be content to claim an elevated place in the scale of human happiness and, surely, it will not be vanity, but it will merit our reverential gratitude to him who made us, if we venture to assert to the nations of the world, that we are the happiest of people.[101]

To reject Europe and free themselves from colonial dependencies, American elites feminized the desire for Old World objects and manners, "an admiration figured as both unmanly and unpatriotic."[102]

The need to uphold the United States as a nation both manly and civilized placed Americans in the paradoxical position of intellectually defending, and sometimes identifying themselves with, the very people they had killed, and dispossessed.[103] The common European belief in the inferior status of American civilization generated celebrations of the virtues of Native American culture at the same time domestic denigration and annihilation of indigenous populations continued. In his writings, Jefferson portrayed Indians in America as "a degraded yet basically noble brand of white man." He also presented an explanation for the so-called savagery of the American Indian. Jefferson argued that in order to form a fair estimate of the "genius and mental powers" of the savages, "great allowance [must] be made for those circumstances of their situation which call for a display of particular talents only." Jedidiah Morse presented a similar argument in *The History of America* (1795) when he asserted that the "character of the Indians is altogether founded upon their circumstances and way of life." He went on to explain that a "group of people who are constantly employed in procuring the means of a precarious subsistence, who live by hunting the wild animals, and who are generally engaged in war with their neighbours, cannot be supposed to enjoy much gaiety of temper, or a high flow of spirits."[104] Anglo-Americans used similar explanations to parry European charges of the nation's underachievement in the arts and sciences, arguing that the Revolutionary War had occupied all of their time and energy and prevented their pursuit of these achievements. Jefferson himself maintained, "When we shall have existed as a people as long as the Greeks did before they produced a Homer, the Romans a Virgil, the French a Racine and Voltaire, the English a Shakespeare and Milton, should this reproach be still true, we will enquire from what unfriendly causes it has proceeded."[105]

To many Europeans the most unique, interesting, and therefore defining aspect of the United States was the presence of Native Americans and enslaved Africans.[106] In sources as diverse as political cartoons, material objects, engravings, maps, and children's books, the most common iconographic representation of the British North American colonies and, later, the United States, was an image of an American Indian, a black slave, or—often—an ambiguous amalgamation of the two (see figure 5.8 and figure 1.1).[107]

Aware of this close identification with the "colored" people among them, white Americans imagined a need for a distinction between the white, civilized Americans and the "savage" Americans. Defenses against the theory of New World degeneration differed in strategies of counterattack.[108] What unified them all, however, was a reliance on the link between American "whiteness" and the materiality of civilization (see figure 5.9).[109]

Hume had argued thirty years before American independence that lightness of complexion indicated superiority of civilization.[110] It was the distinction of whiteness that American social thinkers would cling to as

Figure 5.8 British-made porcelain figurine representing "America," part of the popular "Four Continents" set. (*Winterthur Museum & Country Estate*)

independence exposed them to the probing glare of national comparison. The second distinction, based on the production of refined objects of culture, manufacture, and knowledge, found them lacking.

Embodying a legacy of European civilization, elite American intellectuals linked cultural aspirations to an object already in their possession: whiteness. Whiteness as an imagined, and consequently as a physical and legal property, became the one refined material good that they imported from Europe as part of their bodily migration. (It could, however, be "sullied," which explains the fear of miscegenation and climatic degeneration.) Like tea sets and refined objects of knowledge, whiteness was a property that joined people in London and New London together even as the upheavals of the Revolution and independence tore them apart politically.[111]

Thus, early racial theory in America reflected a triangular relationship among "civilized" Europeans, "uncivilized" Native Americans and blacks, and uncertain white Americans caught in between.[112] When Henry Moss put himself on display, he offered the American public an opportunity not only to see a curiosity but also to indulge their fears about just what kind of

Figure 5.9 "The Oracle," mezzotint by John Dixon (1774). In this popular image, England (Britannia), Scotland (Caledonia), and Ireland (Hibernia) are represented as classically dressed women with their weapons down while America, represented by a half-clad "savage," crouches in the corner in a threatening manner. (*Trustees of the British Museum*)

a nation they were now and were in the process of becoming. Moss was a source of fascination in a society in which race and nationality were tangled in fascinating ways. Whereas Americans, both literate and illiterate, turned out to see (and touch) Moss, Europeans interested in the United States and its racial puzzles turned to Samuel Smith, who produced one of the very few works by an American author read by Europeans at this time. In his *Essay on the Causes of the Variety of Complexion and Figure in the Human Species*, the author engaged the increasingly heated debates about the origins of humankind and the question of racial differentiation.[113] The topic had both scientific and religious significance. Those who believed that the divide between races ran deep enough to cut humans into different species also implicitly challenged the Mosaic account of man's common descent from

Adam and Eve. To Smith, this was heresy. Believing in the necessary unity of religious and scientific truth, he defended the Bible's account of humanity's origin by arguing that all people were indeed descended from common ancestors, but exposure to different "climates" and "states of society" had altered their physical appearances.[114] Smith also advanced the idea that exposure to the "savage state" roughened and coarsened features and darkened the complexion, while the civilized and highly cultivated state served to polish and refine features and lighten the skin. To be sure, the author was aware of the rather alarming implications of his theory, and inelegantly contorted his argument to avoid any intimation of possible white degeneration.[115]

An important part of Smith's argument in his *Essay* involved an explanation of how white Americans of western European extraction had maintained their superior level of "civilization" and physical "beauty" living side by side with Indian "savages" and African slaves in a dangerously uncultivated environment.[116] These whites' superiority, he argued, depended on their advanced degree of civilization. Smith assured readers that "society in America" was increasing in its "refinement." Plaguing his claims was the persistent and uncomfortable realization that the new nation's cultivation in the "arts of civilization" fell short of what could be found in Europe. Linking this scientific treatise to issues of an emerging national identity in the United States, Winthrop Jordan argues that Smith was "demonstrating to Europeans, particularly Englishmen, that the revolutionary republic was not going to fall apart at the seams and, indeed, that Americans were capable of polished accomplishments equal to those of the most cultivated nations of the Old World."[117] As a defensive measure, Smith insisted that even if the worst happened, and white Americans were to "sink into a state of savagism," their European decent would preclude a regression to savagery.[118]

Physical features, it was argued, were also influenced by what Smith called the "state of society," and Europeans, at least, were surfeited in the "arts of civilization." According to him, the "state of society" was determined by such factors as diet, clothing, lodging, manners, habits…objects of science, religion, interests, passions and ideas of all kinds, infinite in number and variety."[119] He contended that "each of these causes makes small variations on the human countenance" and that the "different combinations and results of the whole" as well as local climate "will be adequate to account for all the varieties that exist among mankind."[120] Smith's arguments exuded both the hope and fear of many white Americans in the early national period: hope that refinement was possible through acquisition of European arts and emulation of Old World manners; fear that proximity to the uncultivated environments surrounding them might also render white Americans uncivilized.

Smith looked to physical evidence to discern both the possibilities for a higher civilization and signs of degeneracy into savagery. As proof of the United States' civilized climate, Smith cited examples of Africans living in the nation. He stressed that the lighter skin of "domestic servants" (as opposed to "field slaves") was due to their working and living in closer proximity to civilized Americans of European extraction.[121] For him, Henry Moss portended a possible future for dark-skinned races should they remain closely associated with white Americans. Moss was not beset with disease; rather, physical proximity to civilized college presidents and refined doctors—exclusively of western European paternity—had turned this African American into someone who appeared more like them.

But what of Anglo-Americans who lived among Native Americans? Were they in danger of reverting to savagery? While conceding that the harsh natural conditions of North America did affect citizens of European extraction (most visibly by darkening their complexions), Smith assuaged readers' anxieties in an extended footnote: "The Anglo-Americans...will never resemble the native Indians. Civilisation will prevent so great a degeneracy either in the colour nor the features. Even if they were thrown back again into the savage state the resemblance would not be complete; because, the one would receive the impressions of the climate on the ground of features formed in Europe."[122] Those physical features—even when the Americans who possessed them were not surrounded by the civilized arts—would offer an impenetrable bulwark against the unbecoming degeneracy embodied by Native Americans.

Early American theories of white racial supremacy and the formal and informal policies and practices based on such theories created unity in a fractious society by promising those invested with citizenship entrée into the "imagined fraternity of white men," to use scholar Dana Nelson's words. The "nationalization of whiteness" she argues, "abstracted men's interests out of local issues and identities in an appeal to a nationally shared 'nature.'"[123]

Yet the pseudoscientific racial theories that took hold in America did more than that, they provided comforting explanatory tools for a people vulnerable to charges of being labeled inferior to Europeans. Just as "white manhood" erased regional and class differences, it had the potential to draw together white Americans and Europeans.[124] This racial formation linked white Americans to the civility that had been the property of Europeans—a superiority and civility not defined by geography. As Nelson writes:

"'Whiteness' became an 'American' property, certified, as Crèvecoeur so richly and suggestively summarized, 'in the broad lap of our great Alma Mater.'"[125]

Smith was concerned about the possibility of Africans becoming more civilized, since it reflected on the unity of mankind, but he was also addressing the possibility of the United States as a civilized place. Could savage peoples, born of uncivilized climates, be made more civilized? Unreservedly, his answer was yes. And if savages could become more civilized in the wild climate of America, then surely white Americans could as well. Smith also needed to reassure Anglo-Americans and Europeans that whites would not become savage, and it was here that white supremacy based on physical features functioned most clearly. It was whiteness, embodied in blood ties to Europe, that protected civilized status.

Transatlantic American intellectuals like Smith were determined to ensure that their European kith and kin—especially their British relatives—accepted them fully as cultural peers. Theories about New World degeneracy created an international intellectual debate that indirectly denigrated Anglo-Americans while also providing them with an issue that allowed them to contribute to the conversation. Widespread Enlightenment interest in the varieties of mankind therefore brought Americans into the transatlantic scientific debates regarding racial "others."[126] Thus, the second edition of Smith's *Essays,* published in 1810, is peppered with frequent retorts to the critical English reviewers who greeted his work with "contemptuous smiles." What the minister was most indignant about was their dismissal of his firsthand, scientific observations of his country and the favoritism they exhibited toward British travelers' "ignorant," impressionistic accounts. Seizing on one publication's tendentiousness, Smith groused:

> It is not much to the credit of the authors of the *[C]ritical [R]eview* in England that this remark, in the first edition of this essay, should have called forth their contemptuous smile. We often see these men at one time receiving with childish credulity the most ridiculous and extravagant tales transmitted by the ignorant travelers who have visited this country; at another, rejecting with obstinate skepticism, the most certain facts.[127]

How, Smith wondered, could these learned British thinkers reject the "most certain facts" of a fellow intellectual, who had lived his whole life in America? Or was being American the problem? For these European writers, perhaps, Smith's greatest strength appeared also to be his biggest weakness.

Despite his suspicions about travel narratives, Smith—the American provincial from New Jersey theorizing about all the world's people—was forced
to rely on Europeans' accounts for his information about non-American
societies.

Smith's colleagues in America responded to the subject of race with a
marked prolixity, prominently claiming in their transatlantic exchanges
intimate knowledge of African Americans and Native Americans. During
six years of medical training in Britain, the physician David Hosack had
made inroads to the British scientific community and kept abreast of pressing topics of scientific inquiry. In 1800, he wrote Benjamin Rush describing
the "very interesting work" of a Manchester surgeon who had "advanced
some new facts with regard to the negro." The study had caught the doctor's
attention because its topic afforded American scientists the chance to show-
case their insider knowledge. Like the Scots, Americans often looked out for
their compatriots when away from the land of their birth and shared
valuable information with fellow citizens. Hosack, identifying a potential
windfall for someone from home, explained to his mentor: "this subject [the
study of African Americans] can only be elucidated in this country where
we have an abundance of black subjects....I mention these things to you
that the Prof[esso]r of anatomy [at the University of Pennsylvania] may
give attention to it."[128] Hosack's letter described how Americans could parlay
their physical proximity to people of color into an advantage rather than a
source of shame.[129] Assuming the role of scientific observer automatically
distanced them from their subjects of study, a vantage point American intellectuals coveted.

The fascination of American men of letters with Henry Moss and David
Hosack's keen interest in questions of race reflected a fear that whites
might possibly turn black. The children who were conceived through
coerced sexual liaisons between enslaved women and white men were not
granted the rights of citizens because they took on the status of the
mother.[130] The very possibility their being deemed white was denied
through legal enforcement, for it would have signaled an acceptance that
whiteness was not the refined object that would protect Americans of
European descent against degeneracy. It was hoped and sometimes legis-
lated, that whiteness was an object that could be possessed but not lost or
transferred.

Whether or not Henry Moss was aware of the particular debates on racial
theory going on at the time, he was undoubtedly sensitive to the curiosity he
provoked and the money he could earn from it. His ability to profit by
putting himself up for display is an illustration of the value of the com-

modity of whiteness in American society at this time. In this context, the logic of the Naturalization Law of 1790 becomes manifest, especially with its restrictions on citizenship to "free white persons" (which remained on the federal books until 1952).[131] Necessitated by the proprietary practices of slavery, this legislation hinted at the hopes of some that the government could successfully secure the nation's racial borders as part of the project of nation building. Moss's case, less than a decade later, revealed the inherent difficulties and potential impossibility of that task. In the welter of national uncertainty and vulnerability, the irreducible object to protecting elite Americans' aspirations to civilization became whiteness—the foundational symbol of national belonging in postcolonial America.

Conclusion

THE LONG GOODBYE

Breaking with the British in Nineteenth-century America

In the four quarters of the globe, who reads an American book? or goes to
an American play? or looks at an American picture or statue? What does
the world yet owe to American physicians or surgeons? What new
substances have their chemists discovered? or what old ones have they
analyzed? What new constellations have been discovered by the telescopes
of Americans?—what have they done in the mathematics? Who drinks out
of American glasses? or eats from American plates? or wears American
coats or gowns? or sleeps in American blankets? ... Finally, under which of
the old tyrannical governments of Europe is every sixth man a slave, whom
his fellow-creatures may buy and sell and torture?

—Sydney Smith (1820)

The American is only the continuation of the English genius into new
conditions, more or less propitious. See what books fill our libraries. Every
book we read, every biography, play, romance, in whatever form, is still
English history and manners.

—Ralph Waldo Emerson (1856)

On August 24, 1814, rear-admiral of the British Royal Navy George
Cockburn and his men enjoyed a civilized meal in the President's Mansion,
which later became known as the White House, in Washington, D.C.[1]
According to the men who were with him, James Madison's dining parlor,
with its large, polished table, had been set for forty guests.[2] Wearied and far
from home, the Britons were grateful for the sumptuous feast. The men
imbibed "the several kinds of wine," stored "in handsome cut-glass
decanters.[3] Drawing from "the plate holders st[anding] by the fireplace,"
they used the imported "dishes and plates knives, forks, and spoons" to

consume the meal that the kitchen staff had just finished preparing.[4] Following dinner, the guests took in the rest of the mansion, admiring its furnishings, much of which had been acquired by George Washington during his presidency. Cockburn's delegation included the Scottish lieutenant Beauchamp Colclough Urquhart, whose family owned one of the largest Elizabethan estates in Great Britain. He, along with several of the others present, would have recognized the rarity of the objects surrounding them. After all, Washington had taken great pains to import the fashionable goods from Great Britain.

By most accounts, however, no one enjoyed the marshy, unpleasant city of Washington D.C., which had failed to develop in the fourteen years that it had served as the new nation's capital. The grandiose street plans laid out by Frenchman Pierre Charles L'Enfant only served to highlight the barrenness of the city, which was referred to as the "City of Magnificent Distances," "Wilderness City," and "City of Streets with No Houses."[5] The one home that dominated the sparse landscape was the President's Mansion. Expecting to see a déclassé, "republican" dwelling, the British visitors found a refined residence of twenty-three rooms furnished with crimson sofas, writing tables, and artwork on the walls. Not all of Cockburn's troops were generous in their assessment of the decor of the executive residence. In one English soldier's patronizing estimation, despite their "elegant and substantial repast," the surroundings were "considerably overdressed." "Having satisfied their appetites" and "partaken pretty freely of the wines," the men calmly proceeded to "set fire to the house which had so liberally entertained them"[6] (see figure C.1).

Earlier that evening, Admiral Cockburn sat in the chair belonging to the Speaker of the House, in a manner reminiscent of the awestruck Benjamin Rush sitting on the king's throne in the House of Lords in 1768.[7] While the Pennsylvanian had been profoundly moved by his experience, the admiral rose from his perch and asked rhetorically, "Shall this harbor of Yankee democracy be burned?" Within minutes of his orders, George Gleig, a British soldier, recollected, the city's "sky was brilliantly illuminated by the different conflagrations, and a dark red light was thrown upon the road, sufficient to permit each man to view distinctly his comrade's face."[8] A few hours later, the new nation's most symbolically significant residence would be engulfed in flames (see figure C.2). After a hurricane passing through the city extinguished the fire, all that remained of the landmark was its sandstone walls, erected by Scottish workmen. They would become the frame for the new structure, built shortly after the nation's second war with Great Britain had ended.[9]

Figure C.1 Engraving entitled "The Taking of the City of Washington in America." View from the Potomac River of the attack of the city of Washington, D.C., by British forces under Major General Ross, August 24, 1814. This battle took place during the War of 1812. The image was published in London by G. Thompson (October 14, 1814). *(Library of Congress)*

*T*his book opened with a description of a provincial home built on a wooded hilltop that its proprietor filled with imported and domestic goods designed to represent America as a unique blend of nature and civility. It closes with the British destroying another American home, also built on undeveloped land, that citizens hoped would someday be worthy of an established nation's capital city.

The War of 1812, which grew out of the clash between Great Britain and France and has been labeled the "second war for American independence," highlighted the vulnerability of the United States and its enduring struggle for respect and recognition from the former mother country.[10] The attitude of the British toward their former colonies was dismissive and condescending. President James Madison's official declaration of war was dismissed in the British Press. On July 25, 1812, the *Leicester Journal* published an article that described Madison's message as "the most laboured, peevish, canting,

Figure C.2 Engraving entitled "Capture of the City of Washington." A depiction of the destruction of the new nation's capital city of Washington, D.C., by British troops. The image was published in London by J. J. Gundee, 1815. *(Library of Congress)*

petulant, querulous and weak effusion, that ever issued from a man assuming the character of a statesman and the President, or elective quadrennial King, of a professedly Republican country."[11] But there was more to the British reaction than the understandable anger that would accompany such a declaration; there was also a measure of indignant shock that the United States would side with France. The outrage was borne not of distance but of a lingering expectation of familial loyalty from a society that shared Britain's language, history, blood lines, and religion. It was one thing for Americans to want their independence, quite another to side with Britain's despised enemy.[12]

Despite attempts on both sides to reestablish good relations, the tensions between Britain and the United States had been escalating in the years following the Revolution. Many Britons believed the New World's experiment with democracy would fail; their actions betokened their disinclination to acknowledge American independence in practice, despite the formal agreements made in political treaties. For instance, the British refusal to give up their forts in the Great Lakes region, one of the contributing factors in the War of 1812, was a concrete example of their disregard of national sovereignty and the terms of the peace negotiations.

The asymmetry that characterized Anglo-American relations in the years following the Revolution preoccupied several presidential administrations. While the U.S. government quickly dispatched John Adams to London as the first American ambassador in 1785, the British did not deem it necessary to send his counterpart until 1791. This did not go unnoticed by citizens who craved affirmation from their former mother country.[13] As the years passed, many registered anxiety over this slight. Thomas Mifflin of Pennsylvania, sounding somewhat like a child in need of recognition from a parent, asked a London correspondent in 1788: "If King George is really well-disposed towards us... why has he not sent a Minister Plenipotentiary to America during all these years since the Treaty of Peace?"[14]

The post was not an easy one to fill. Several British diplomats declined the position because they were loath to relocate to what his colleagues considered an insignificant New World outpost. The British foreign secretary, Francis Godolphin Osborne, the Duke of Leeds, explained to Gouverneur Morris in 1790 why he had not been able to convince anyone to take the job. Simply, the United States "was a long way off."[15] Eventually, twenty-eight-year-old George Hammond was convinced to relocate to the United States. Formal in his demeanor, as was expected of British diplomats, the young man found Americans' forthright manners rather off-putting: he was stared at, questioned, and subjected to visits from uninvited guests. In a private letter to the new foreign secretary, Lord Grenville, he described his position as "rather embarrassing."[16] Although Hammond considered the manners of his hosts distasteful, the country's most influential families showered the Englishman with invitations to teas and dinners. Their desire to gain his approval was so intense it led him to quip that "most of them are Tories at heart."[17] The same eagerness of Americans to ingratiate themselves with Britons had been noted at least as far back as the French and Indian War, when colonials wanted to impress British soldiers, but this sort of behavior was unbecoming a free people.[18]

In the years following the Revolution, Americans were subjected to other humiliating experiences that were unbecoming for a people hoping to prove themselves equals of the British. Widespread impressment—the "forcible enlistment (some would say kidnapping) of sailors—was another factor leading to the War of 1812.[19] In dire need of men to work their ships, members of the British Royal Navy boarded U.S. ships at will and captured anyone suspected of being British, and certainly those thought to have deserted. This practice reflected poorly on American authority because many of the British-born men who were impressed claimed to be natural-ized American citizens. The British refused to recognize these claims, justi-fying their actions by citing lax naturalization requirements and the ease with which forged or invalid documents could be obtained. The refusal to recognize the right of the U.S. government to define the terms with which they conferred citizenship status highlighted the tenuous position of the new nation.[20]

Placing a definitive label on people's identities was a highly subjective process.[21] This fluidity of identity recalls the period only a few decades ear-lier when Chinese officials in Canton had puzzled over the differences between Englishmen and these "new people" calling themselves Americans. From the Asian perspective of vast cultural difference between themselves and all westerners, there was little that separated these two peoples who shared language, blood, and material tastes. French diplomat Talleyrand remarked that he had "seen many Americans who wanted to pass for an Englishman but never an Englishman who wished to pass for an American."[22] The ultimate reward for social success was to "be taken for an Englishman or woman, rather than a representative of the breed of civi-lized Americans."[23]

The fear of reversion to colonial dependence remained on the minds of many Americans for decades. As the nation hovered between peace and war, President Madison stated that "Acquiescence in the practice and pretensions of the British Government…would *recolonize* our commerce…arrest our internal improvement, and strangle in the cradle, the manufactures which promise so vigorous growth."[24] Going to war did not save domestic manufac-tures. As they had done after the Revolution, British manufacturers raced to send their goods to America the moment peace was brokered, which devas-tated fledgling domestic manufactures. Despite the recent conflict, citizens who sought higher-quality, lower-priced imports avidly purchased imported goods, which had the added benefit of exuding cultural distinction. The preferences of American consumers for imported goods as much as the "practice and pretensions of the British Government" were responsible for the infanticide of American industries. Governed by the logic of the geog-raphy of value, these objects continued to mark their owners with distinc-tion even in the years that followed the fighting.[25]

Like other sites I have investigated in this book, the War of 1812 reveals a great deal about the triangular relations among the Old World Europeans (the French and especially the British), New World Anglo-Americans, and racially oppressed groups (African Americans and Native Americans).[26] In November 1812, the British commander of the empire's North American troops, Admiral Sir John Borlase Warren, suggested using disaffected racial minority groups against the United States.[27] If support from the Iroquois and the Creek could be solicited for the British effort, then (in the admiral's judgment) the land that had been taken from its Native American inhabitants could be returned—thereby creating a buffer zone against the possibility of future aggression by Americans attempting to enlarge the scope of the nation. More pragmatically driven than conscience ridden, the Earl of Bathurst, the British secretary of state for war and the colonies, explained his nation's willingness to ally with Native American tribes as a practical effort to prevent the United States from brokering a similar alliance.

Admiral Warren also believed that enslaved Africans could be easily enlisted to fight and would doubtless instill fear of slave insurrections in southern states. The nation's wartime enemy had comprehended its weaknesses and was poised to take strategic advantage of them. Falling along racial lines, those weaknesses were both defined and reinforced by the triangular relationship of Old World, New World, and the racially marginalized. In the years of dramatic change that followed the war, the United States would turn that tripartite relationship inward, attempting to find its separate identity in unbecoming ways that continued to marginalize racial minorities as a means to support the nation's ascendancy to a world power.

$\mathcal{W}$hen the Treaty of Ghent formally ended the Anglo-American conflict in December 1814, the United States was still an underdeveloped country. According to one historian, it "resembled economically developing countries of today," with rapid population growth, high birthrates, and an economy based on agriculture.[28] Put simply, the United States lacked the infrastructure needed for an expanding society to flourish. As in other developing countries, its expansion was underwritten by the sale of raw materials to purchase the manufactured goods required for everyday life.

Americans pinned their hopes for national glory on their natural resources and potential for expansion. From the nation's inception, they dreamed of building what Jefferson described as an "Empire of Liberty."[29] "We cannot but anticipate the period as not far distant," the Reverend Jedidiah Morse declared in his geography textbook for American youth, "when the AMERICAN EMPIRE will comprehend millions of souls, west of the Mississippi. Judging upon probable grounds, the Mississippi was never designed as the western boundary of the American empire. The God of nature never intended that some of the best part of his earth should be inhabited by the subjects of a monarch 4000 miles from them."[30]

The fulfillment of this dream was facilitated by the fact that the Erie Canal connected the Ohio River Valley and upstate New York. The consolidation of the domestic economy signaled the shift of the nation's focus from Europe to the American West. From the end of the War of 1812 to the beginning of the Civil War in 1861, Americans witnessed hitherto unexpected growth and change in a period variously labeled the "era of good feelings," "the Age of Jackson," and the antebellum period.[31] These decades saw tremendous growth and change resulting from the expansion in the Old Northwest and Southwest, commercial development, the development of domestic infrastructure, and religious revival.

Government policies supported internal development, and by 1851 the expansion (in the words of the seventh U.S. census report)

> [now] exhibit[ed] results which every citizen of the country may contemplate with gratification and pride. Since the Census of 1840, there have been added to the territory of the republic, by annexation, conquest, and purchase...and our title to a region...which before properly belonged to us, but was claimed and partially occupied by a foreign power, has been established by negotiation, and it has been brought within our acknowledged boundaries.[32]

In what might be seen as the nationalization of the frontier, the creation of a domestic infrastructure enabled Americans to ship the natural products of the expanding western hinterlands to cities such as New York and Philadelphia rather than directly to overseas trading centers in Scotland and England. While this change contributed to the development of a national economy, reorienting this economy of relative location—from across the Atlantic to the interior of the North American continent—did not end the demand for British imports. Indeed, the geography of value remained in place well after the War of 1812. Beyond whatever use-value products held—whether domestically produced or imported—they marked their owners with distinction, effectively allowing consumers to accrue cultural cachet. Despite how far Americans had come in asserting their independence, domestic and imported material objects (as well as people and ideas) were placed within a hierarchy of value in which imported goods still reigned supreme.[33]

Americans failed to meet the exalted "expectation of the world," in the decades immediately following independence according to Ralph Waldo Emerson. In his 1837 essay entitled "The American Scholar" he argued that the cause of the problem was that his countrymen had attempted in vain to emulate European culture: "We have listened too long to the courtly muses of Europe."[34] In the immediate postrevolutionary period new citizens failed to compete with foreign rivals using standards that were defined in Europe. After this emulative stage, American manufacturers, intellectuals, and artists began to strive for innovation in their domestic output rather than accuracy of imitation. This new phase inaugurated "America's romance with practicality."[35] This inventive moment marked the climax of the country's process of freeing itself from British cultural hegemony. If United States' postcolonial condition is taken as an acceptance of the cultural hierarchies of taste that ruled the colonial world, then in areas such as literature, education, and the arts and sciences, the lingering effects of marginality in the Atlantic world cast a long and unbecoming shadow on the United States.[36] This inventive moment in American manufacturing and cultural taste has often served as the starting point for scholarly narratives of the history of the young nation. But beginning these studies by celebrating newness and difference ignores the significance of Americans' desires to emulate more established cultures.[37]

The Continuing Confusion of the "American Mind"

Our close relationship to Old England was sometimes a little misleading to us juveniles. The conditions of our life were entirely different, but we read her descriptive stories and sang her songs as if they were true for us too. One of the first things I learned to repeat—I think it was in the spelling book—began with the verse:

> I thank the goodness and the grace
> That on my birth has smiled,
> And made me, in these latter days,
> A Happy English child.

—Lucy Larcom, *A New England Girlhood* (1889)

There were certain things I knew, though.... It was Salisbury. It was almost the first English town I had got to know, the first I had been given some idea of, from the reproduction of the Constable painting of Salisbury Cathedral in my third-standard reader. Far away in my tropical island, before I was ten. A four-color reproduction which I had thought the most beautiful picture I had ever seen.

—V. S. Naipaul, *The Enigma of Arrival* (1987)

Writing about her early nineteenth-century New England childhood, Lucy Larcom recalled for her readers the confusion caused by Americans' reliance on British cultural productions.[38] In her disarming style, Larcom's recollections highlight the ambiguity experienced by Americans living through the transition from colony to nation, invoking the tensions between political independence and the cultural dependence on Great Britain that continued throughout the nineteenth century. Like other postcolonial peoples, American children several decades after independence learned about the wider world from European authors.[39] The material objects that circulated the Atlantic drew geographically distant people together in a common cultural community. As the New England physician Benjamin Waterhouse observed, "Above all, books have united to make us feel as if we were but children of the same great family, only divided by the Atlantic Ocean."[40] Waterhouse's use of the familial metaphor unwittingly pointed to the ongoing asymmetrical nature of Anglo-American relations.

Americans' continuing engagement with British goods, people, and ideas shaped the nation's identity in its critical early years. Learning to recognize the mixed messages surrounding them, young readers would eventually come to realize that the "we" used in imported, reprinted, or pirated British books did not refer to American citizens.[41] Popular children's books, such as the *People of All Nations* and geographies of the day depicted Great Britain as the principal point of reference for Anglo-American consciousness.[42]

Emulating British culture, even at the expense of national pride, could elevate one's status within American society. Writing at the end of his life, Henry Adams, great-grandson of founding father John Adams, reflected in his well-known autobiography: "The true Bostonian always knelt in self-abasement before the majesty of English standards; far from concealing it as a weakness, he was proud of it as his strength."[43] With characteristic irony, Adams described Europeans' perceptions of his fellow citizens. "From an old-world point of view, the American had no mind; he had an economic thinking-machine which could work only on a fixed line. The American mind exasperated the European as a buzz-saw might exasperate a pine forest. The American mind...was not a thought at all; it was a convention, superficial, narrow, and ignorant; a mere cutting instrument, practical, economical, sharp, and direct."[44] Americans, often seen as inferior arrivistes, were considered mere pawns in larger imperial and geopolitical power games.[45] Whereas the "English mind," according to Adams, disliked the "French mind" and considered it "antagonistic, unreasonable, perhaps hostile," the French proved worthy adversaries of the British, people with "at least a thought."[46] Just as they had for generations, Americans desperately sought this elusive British respect: "British self-assertion, bluff, brutal, blunt as it was, seemed to Adams a better and nobler thing than the acuteness of the Yankee or the polish of the Parisian."[47]

Americans' eagerness for British approbation was made clear by their warm reception of the many British visitors who came to observe their society in the decades following the War of 1812.[48] The popularity of travel writing in Europe in the first half of the nineteenth century reflected its people's engagement with the United States as a laboratory for political and social experimentation. European social commentators looked to the New World for raw knowledge to support their social theories that, ultimately, illuminated more about themselves than about Americans.

While at first provincial Americans basked in the attention of such visitors, their pleasure was short-lived. A mirror was held up to them, and they recoiled from what they saw. British writers described American culture as characterized by greed, crude manners, and an overall lack of refinement.[49] In part, this can be understood as a by-product of Americans' unbecoming desire to win the approval and acceptance from their former mother country. In an 1844 speech, Ralph Waldo Emerson explained, "We are full of vanity, of which the most signal proof is our sensitiveness to foreign and especially English censure. One cause of this is our immense reading, and that reading chiefly confined to the productions of the English press."[50]

Keen to show off their secondhand knowledge of the United Kingdom, Americans made themselves vulnerable to ridicule.[51] In his serialized novel *Martin Chuzzlewit* (1843–44), which incorporated observations from his travels in America, Charles Dickens noted Americans' pride in their supposed familiarity with England, which combined misinformation and ignorance. When the blustering American General Choke insists that the Queen of England resides in the Tower of London, Chuzzlewit points out his mistake.[52] Choke defends "our intelligent and locomotive citizens"— even those who live in the "trackless forests of this vast Continent of the Western Ocean." The American general is proud of his inexact knowledge of London's precincts. Just as an imported English vase had value beyond its use, knowing about British geography added to their possessor's cultural capital. Chuzzlewit eventually demands of Choke, "Have you been in England?" to which the American replies, "In print I have, sir . . . not otherwise. We air [*sic*] a reading people here, sir. You will meet with much information among us that will surprise you, sir." As both insiders and outsiders of the powerful empire to which they had once belonged, Americans vacillated between defensiveness and celebration of their cultural hybridity. To critical European observers, and surely to African Americans and Native Americans, white Americans increasingly displayed the fictional General Choke's arrogance and ignorance, traits Europeans have continued to associate with Americans to this day.[53]

What Dickens observed was Americans' interstitial identity: neither fully British nor entirely indigenous, people in the throes of unbecoming.[54]

British visitors were fascinated by the crude, "uncouth" frontiersman, who emerged larger than life in the pages of these travelers' published accounts. This stereotypical figure provided proof of continuing English *cultural* if not economic and political superiority. In his travel narrative of the United States, *American Notes* (1842), Dickens described a frontiersman having a meal: "sitting down with so many fellow-animals to ward off thirst and hunger as a business; to empty, each creature, his Yahoo's trough as quickly as he can, and then slink sullenly away; to have these social sacraments stripped of everything but the mere greedy satisfaction of the natural cravings."[55] The rough and ragged backwoodsman (usually from the South or West) proved more interesting fodder for their publications than East Coast elites who had made it their business to emulate European mores and were "deemed to have much the same customs as London, with the same fashions, albeit one year out of date."[56]

Foreign visitors were not the only ones guilty of romanticizing frontier inhabitants and southern slave owners. As the nineteenth century progressed, regional fissures developed within the national polity.[57] Stereotypes were based on where inhabitants were seen to fit on the continuum of savage to civilized, in the same way that differences were said to have existed between those living in England and the "western settlers" of the North American colonies. For instance, writing in 1821, the Connecticut clergyman Timothy Dwight heaped criticism on Americans moving west, describing them in a manner reminiscent of the ways the British described immigrants to America. According to Dwight, these individuals "cannot live in regular society" and were "too idle, too talkative, too passionate, too prodigal, and too shiftless to acquire property or character."[58] Reverend Timothy Flint, a New Englander who resettled in the Mississippi Valley himself, concurred: "You will find, in truth, that he has vices and barbarism ... [and] His manners are rough."[59] In his waning years, Jedidiah Morse, who had dedicated his life to encouraging American autonomy from Britain, began to feel that he had more in common with his British counterparts than with the aggressive upstarts on the frontier.[60] His feelings were not unique.

As Americans began to shift their gaze from Europe to North America, some, most notably the Anglo-American elites of New England, began to view western "pioneers" as national outsiders, echoing the criticisms leveled against their own ancestors by previous generations of Britons. Many of the migrants were Dwight's own New England neighbors, simply transplanted "out west," away from their homes "back east" (a locution that still survives). Robert Baird's popular traveler's guide to "the West" defended these people.

"The characters and manners of the West," he wrote, "do not essentially differ from those of the population of the Atlantic states." Their "apparent
roughness" or "rudeness of manners" resulted from "the circumstances of a
people thrown together in a new country, often for a long time in settlements."[61] That Baird had to specially address tenacious stereotypes of western "backwardness" indicates that a domestic hierarchy of civility based on
regional location existed. Once again the concept of relative location applies,
as people's distance from the centers of power determined how others perceived their level of "civilization."[62]

Conflicting "Thoughts on American Genius"

> It is a peculiar sensation, this double-consciousness, this sense of always
> looking at one's self through the eyes of others, of measuring one's soul by
> the tape of a world that looks on in amused contempt and pity.
>
> —W. E. B. Du Bois (1897)

> The time is come to explode the European creed, that we are infantine in
> our acquisitions, and savage in our manners, because we are inhabitants of
> a new world, lately occupied by a race of savages.
>
> —Timothy Dwight (1787)

Caught between their history and their aspirations, elite Americans wanted to
possess "Britishness" (and the cultural cachet that accompanied it) while
simultaneously distancing themselves from their dependence on Great
Britain. After all, nations do require outsiders—people not connected to the
majority population by ethnicity, race, or language—in order to create
insiders: citizens joined together over time by these qualities.[63] Determining
just who were the outsiders was a complicated task for postrevolutionary
Americans; relatively recent settlers in a colony ruled by a distant empire and
now citizens of a democratic republic led by men from similar backgrounds
and classes.

Of course, the United States contained other nations within its geopolitical borders, ones that did not have to engage in unbecoming British because
they were historically established and already culturally distinct.[64] Sharing
neither language, culture, nor ethnicity with their colonizers, Native
Americans, along with enslaved Africans, became the structurally obligatory outsiders in contradistinction to whom individuals of western European
ancestry now asserted their superiority and their nationhood.[65] Thus racial
difference became the most valuable object to confer distinction and
national belonging on citizens with the proper complexions.[66] Just as

knowledge was embodied in British-made maps and botanical prints and took on greater value in a context of relative scarcity, so, too, the possession of another rare imported commodity in the context of the Americas—whiteness—endowed its owner with privilege and even identity.[67]

The story of unbecoming in the early American republic provides a counternarrative to the country's optimistic and confident projections about its future as a world power. From a domestic perspective, the founding fathers, many of them slave owners, stood at the top of a political and social hierarchy. When viewed from a transnational, postcolonial perspective, however, their relative economic and cultural disadvantages come into focus.[68] The experience of being judged by the standards of a distant metropole as inferior and uncivilized informed a wide variety of social practices in the young United States. Displays of arrogance, violence, and hubris stemmed from a position of marginality—as did more obvious gestures of insecurity. Patriotic pride in American strength often arose out of situations in which Americans were not in positions of power. Ultimately, postcolonial American racism can be understood as a function of perceived and real weakness—which is not to excuse injustice and violence against racial minorities but to illuminate a dimension of those practices within a transnational context.[69]

One danger of applying postcolonial theory to the United States is to "valorize [the] accomplishments linked with one racial group that, if anything, continued the colonial legacy of the imperial era."[70] It would indeed be misdirected to invoke postcolonial theory to present a "triumphal view of American history" that portrayed "white settlers as heroes who overcame the British Empire."[71] The point here is not to reiterate the narrative of American exceptionalism but to address the inequalities that are borne of imperialism.[72] It may be difficult for some people to think about historical protagonists, in particular celebrated founding fathers mimicking their European colonizers and, worse yet, getting it woefully wrong.[73] But although they enjoyed tremendous privilege within a domestic context, it was the particular burden of the postrevolutionary elite to be imbued with something akin to the double consciousness described so powerfully in the late nineteenth century by W. E. B. Du Bois.[74] By drawing links between the mentality of postrevolutionary slave owners and descendants of slaves, I hope to suggest that the racism so deeply engrained in American culture is at least in part a historical effect of postcolonial anxiety. As freeborn whites, American landed elites certainly enjoyed rights that were denied to other racialized groups, for instance, colonized Africans. But it would be a function of exceptionalist thinking to insist that former subjects of the

British Empire in the United States simply cast off the effects of their colonial past. The unstated assumption in this narrative is that Americans in the postrevolutionary period were not insecure because they possessed the one refined object that trumped all others: whiteness.

One may wonder what changes occurred during the decades after the War of 1812 that allowed European Americans to begin to abandon their culture of inferiority. Their transformation was not one of confident equality but rather was an aggressive assertion of superiority. After years of unsuccessful emulation and resentful adoration of the mother country, citizens of the ever-expanding nation played to their strengths: whiteness, which linked them to their Old World past; and nature, which allowed them to exploit their New World future (and, ironically, recalled the stereotypes of the colonial period). Americans continued to push westward, exploiting the land and labor of people of color and strengthening and expanding the national economy. In the fine arts, the Hudson River Valley School embraced the unique majesty of the New World landscape (see figure C.3). In the realm of literature and philosophy, members of the transcendentalist movement focused on nature as a uniquely American subject,

Figure C.3 "The Destruction of Empire," painting by Thomas Cole (1833–36), fourth scene of his five-part series "Course of Empire." This scene portrays the violent sack of the city amidst an impending storm. It served as a metaphor of the fate that awaited over-developed societies that became riddled with corruption and decay. *(Collection of the New-York Historical Society)*

in a uniquely American style.[75] In "Nature," considered by many the manifesto of this movement, Ralph Waldo Emerson explored America in its raw form, suggesting that the nation had finally left its past behind.[76] His speech "The American Scholar," dubbed America's "Intellectual Declaration of Independence" by Oliver Wendell Holmes, Sr., proclaimed: "We will walk on our own feet; we will work with our own hands; we will speak our own minds."[77]

American Origins: A Final Journey to the Mother Country

History has always been far more engrossed by problems of origins than by those of decline and fall. When studying any period, we are always looking for the promise of what the next is to bring.

—Johan Huizinga, *The Autumn of the Middle Ages* (1919)

After dedicating his life to persuading his compatriots to break free of the orbit of what he himself conceded was the "best of actual nations," Emerson had to pay homage to England.[78] The "American Scholar" traveled "back" there three times in his life. When he arrived in London, Emerson felt like he had come home: "The shop-signs spoke our language; our country names were on the door-plates; and the public and private buildings wore a native and wonted front."[79] Like the Britons who crossed the Atlantic in the other direction, he immediately recognized how the built environment reflected the shared history of the two nations. While visiting Stonehenge with Thomas Carlyle in 1847, Emerson conceded his admiration for the English who "have everything, and can do everything." After facetiously describing himself as "easily dazzled" and "accustomed to concede readily all an Englishman would ask," he stood before "the oldest religious monument in Britain" and in the "company of her latest thinker," expressed a longing for the land of his birth:

Meantime, I surely know, that, as soon as I return to Massachusetts, I shall lapse at once into the feeling, which the geography of America inevitably inspires, that we play the game with immense advantage; that there and not here is the seat and centre of the British race; and that no skill or activity can long compete with the prodigious natural advantages of that country, in the hands of the same race; and that England, an old and exhausted island, must one day be contented, like other parents, to be strong only in her children.[80]

Emerson charted the path along which the United States would ascend as a world power. Like Jefferson, his ideal vision of America melded New World nature with imported Old World civility. As both men realized, it would be the American continent's vast "geography" that would allow its people to "play the game with immense advantage." Of course this would only be possible once Americans managed to vanquish all competitors for the land and forced slaves to turn a profit from it.

There was one critical element Americans still needed to import from the mother country, according to Emerson: standing in England, looking back across the ocean to America, Emerson proclaimed that his nation would become the "seat and centre of the British race."[81] After generations of infantilizing metaphors issuing from overseas, Emerson managed to embrace the idea of America's youth and harness it to a message of national glory. The new nation would reach its potential only when "England, an old and exhausted island" finally stepped out of the way and accepted that it "must one day be contented, like other parents, to be strong only in her children." As Emerson envisioned it, Americans' possession of British racial superiority, coupled with the raw natural resources of the New World, would make them unstoppable. "No skill or activity can long compete with the prodigious natural advantages of that country, in the hands of the same race" as the British, he mused.[82]

Perhaps America would not have to unbecome British after all.

INTRODUCTION

1. Many of these artifacts were acquired by Lewis and Clark during their expedition in search of a northwest passage. See James P. Ronda, *Lewis and Clark among the Indians* (Lincoln: University of Nebraska Press, 1984).

2. For descriptions of Monticello's rooms, see Susan Stein, *The Worlds of Thomas Jefferson at Monticello* (New York: Abrams, 1993).

3. Monticello is translated into "little mountain" in Italian.

4. Andrea Palladio (1508–1580) was a Venetian architect who adapted styles of ancient Greece and Rome. His designs enjoyed a revival of popularity in the seventeenth and eighteenth centuries. Jefferson owned a set of Palladio's works—Andrea Palladio, *Andrea Palladio's architecture in four books: Containing a dissertation on the five orders & ye most necessary observations relating to all kinds of building. As also the different constructions of public and private houses, high-ways, bridges, market-places, xystes, & temples, with. their plans, sections, & elevations* (London: printed for Benjamin Cole, 1736)—as well as several other books by and about Palladio and referred to Palladio's work as his architectural bible. For a list of the architectural books in Jefferson's library, see James Gilreath and Douglas L. Wilson, eds., *Thomas Jefferson's Library: A Catalogue with the Entries in His Own Order* (Washington, D.C.: Library of Congress, 1989) and William Bainter O'Neal, *Jefferson's Fine Arts Library for the University of Virginia, with Additional Notes on Architectural Volumes Known to Have Been Owned by Jefferson* (Charlottesville: University of Virginia Press, 1956).

5. Thomas Jefferson to James Madison, September 20, 1785, in *The Papers of Thomas Jefferson*, ed. Julian Boyd et al., 33 vols. (Princeton, N.J.: Princeton University Press, 1950–), 8:535.

6. See Edmund Morgan, *American Slavery, American Freedom: The Ordeal of Colonial Virginia* (New York: Norton, 1975).

7. James Hemings was born in 1765 to Betty Hemings (c. 1735–1807), who came into the Jefferson family as part of the dowry of Martha Wayles Jefferson. He was the brother of Sally Hemings. *Papers of Thomas Jefferson*, 7:229. On his election to the presidency and inauguration in 1801, Jefferson asked Hemings to return to cooking for his family and guests as the first black chef in the White House. Hemings refused. Later that year, he committed suicide. A manuscript copy of this recipe in the handwriting of Jefferson's granddaughter Virginia is in the Trist-Burke Family Papers, MSS 5385-f, Albert and Shirley Small Special Collections Library, University of Virginia, Charlottesville. For a rich history of the family, see Annette Gordon-Reed, *The Hemingses of Monticello: An American Family* (New York: Norton, 2008).

8. When Jefferson assumed the post of minister plenipotentiary in Paris in 1784, he brought the nineteen-year-old Hemings with him, with the "particular purpose" of giving him cooking lessons. When he returned in 1789, Jefferson brought everything necessary to realize his dream of producing gourmet French cuisine in the kitchen at Monticello—olive oil, cooking equipment, recipes, seeds—and, most important, Hemings himself. Under French law Hemings could have obtained his freedom while abroad, but he chose to return to the United States with his master.

9. Jefferson finally relented and agreed to free James Hemings at a later date. He did this while serving as Secretary of State in Philadelphia, Pennsylvania, which was the temporary capital of the United States between the years of 1790–1800. The gradual abolition of slavery in America was begun in Pennsylvania in 1780. In a document dated September 15, 1793, Jefferson promised to grant Hemings his freedom on the condition that "the said James…shall continue until he shall have taught such persons as I shall place under him for the purpose to be a good cook… [and] he shall thereupon be made free." Thomas Jefferson to James Hemings, "Promise of Freedom," September 15, 1793, The Coolidge Collection of Thomas Jefferson manuscripts, 1705–1827, microfilm edition, 16 reels (Boston: Massachusetts Historical Society, 1977), reel 2. James recruited his brother Peter Hemings to take his job, thus subjecting his sibling to continual enslavement in the Jefferson household. It took James three years to instruct his brother in the delicate art of French cuisine. When Peter was sufficiently trained, Jefferson honored his promise and freed James on February 5, 1796.

10. See Benjamin Orlove, ed., *Allure of the Foreign: Imported Goods in Postcolonial Latin America* (Ann Arbor: University of Michigan Press, 1997). Paul Gilroy's study *The Black Atlantic: Modernity and Double Consciousness* (Cambridge, Mass.: Harvard University Press, 1993) was very influential in expanding scholars' analytical framework beyond the nation-state. For a study that looks at the American context specifically, see W. Jeffrey Bolster, *Black Jacks: African American Seamen in the Age of Sail* (Cambridge, Mass.: Harvard University Press, 1997).

This study is informed by the well-developed body of scholarship of transatlantic studies. For a useful collection of essays on the topic, see David Armitage and Michael J. Braddick, eds., *The British Atlantic World, 1500–1800* (New York: Palgrave Macmillan, 2002); for a review essay of the field see Nicolas Canny, "Writing Atlantic History: Or, Reconfiguring the History of Colonial British America," *Journal of American History* 86 (December 1999): 1093–1114.

11. Pierre Bourdieu elaborated upon the phrase "cultural capital" in several of his publications. The term was first used by Pierre Bourdieu and Jean-Claude Passeron in "Cultural Reproduction and Social Reproduction," in Richard Brown, ed., *Knowledge, Education, and Cultural Change; Papers in the Sociology of Education* (London: Tavistock Publications, 1973), 71–112. They later developed this concept in relation to other forms of capital. See Bourdieu, "The Forms of Capital," in John Richardson, ed., *Handbook of Theory and Research for the Sociology of Education* (Westport, Conn.: Greenwood Press, 1986), 241–258. For a more specific application of the concept to the topic of higher education, see *The State Nobility: Elite Schools in the Field of Power* (Oxford: Polity Press, 1996).

12. For an elegant meditation on the intellectual implications of studying the process of "becoming," see Robert Blair St. George, editor's introduction to *Possible Pasts: Becoming Colonial in Early America* (Ithaca, N.Y.: Cornell University Press, 2000), 4–5. St. George argues that the use of the word "actively displaces any lingering structuralist faith in colonies operating as steady-state, closed cultural systems, as 'being' in any

particular configuration over time." For elaborations on the theme of " 'becoming colo-nial in early America," see the essays in the collection and especially Michael Warner, "What's Colonial about Colonial America?" in *Possible Pasts: Becoming Colonial in Early America*, 49–72. On the process of identity formation in early America, see Michael Zuckerman, "The Fabrication of Identity in Early America," *William and Mary Quarterly*, 3rd ser., 34 (1977): 183–214. My thanks to Michael Zuckerman for helping me to develop my ideas on this point.

13. It is important to note that the definition of what it meant to be British was itself being contested at this time. Often immigrants have a fixed or static notion of the mother country that froze when they left "home." For more on the British Empire and British identity as it evolved and changed during this time, see Linda Colley, *Britons: Forging the Nation, 1707–1837* (New Haven, Conn.: Yale University Press, 1992); David Armitage, *The Ideological Origins of the British Empire* (Cambridge: Cambridge University Press, 2000); Kathleen Wilson, *The Sense of the People: Politics, Culture and Imperialism in England, 1715–1785* (Cambridge: Cambridge University Press, 1995), Colin Kidd, *British Identities before Nationalism: Ethnicity and Nationhood in the Atlantic World, 1600–1800* (Cambridge: Cambridge University Press, 1999). See also "AHR Forum: The New British History in Atlantic Perspective" and especially David Armitage, "Greater Britain: A Useful Category of Historical Analysis?" *American Historical Review* 104, no. 2 (April 1999): 427–445.

14. For instance, see St. George, "Massacred Language: Courtroom Performance in Eighteenth-century Boston," in *Possible Pasts: Becoming Colonial in Early America*, 327–356.

15. See Robert St. George's discussion in his introduction to *Possible Pasts: Becoming Colonial in Early America*.

16. For individual stories of how early Americans struggled in various cultural endeavors, see Joseph Ellis, *Founding Brothers: The Revolutionary Generation* (New York: Vintage Books, 2002), 10.

17. Jon Butler, *Becoming American: The Revolution before 1776* (Cambridge, Mass.: Harvard University Press, 2000).

18. I thank the anonymous reviewer of the manuscript for Oxford University Press for helpful input on this issue and with the book in general.

19. John Murrin, "A Roof without Walls: The Dilemma of American National Identity," in Richard Beeman, Stephen Botein, and Edward Carter, ed., *Beyond Confederation: Origins of the Constitution and American National Identity* (Chapel Hill: University of North Carolina Press, 1987), 334–338. See also T. H. Breen, "Ideology and Nationalism on the Eve of the American Revolution," *Journal of American History* 84 (June 1997): 13–39.

20. For classic studies on nationalism, see Benedict Anderson, *Imagined Communities: Reflections on the Origin and Spread of Nationalism* (London: Verso, 1983); Ernest Renan, "What Is a Nation?" in Homi Bhabha, ed., *Nation and Narration* (London: Routledge, 1990), 8–22; Etienne Balibar, "The Nation Form: History and Ideology," in Etienne Balibar and Immanuel Wallerstein, *Race, Nation, Class: Ambiguous Identities*, trans. Chris Turner (London: Verso, 1991), 86–106; E. J. Hobsbawm, *Nations and Nationalisms since 1780: Programme, Myth, Reality*, 2nd ed. (Cambridge: Cambridge University Press, 1992).

21. In his important study, David Waldstreicher considered the ambivalences of early national culture and politics. See *In the Midst of Perpetual Fêtes: The Making of American Nationalism, 1776–1820* (Chapel Hill: University of North Carolina Press,

1997). Other scholars have looked at the ambivalences of nationalism in the United States in new and complex ways. See, for instance, Sean Goudie, *Creole America: The West Indies and the Formation of Literature and Culture in the New Republic* (Philadelphia: The University of Pennsylvania Press, 2006), suggesting the use of the term "paracolonialism" to analyze the unique relationship between the emerging American nation and the West Indies. By making this distinction, he makes the point that one cannot simply import and apply postcolonial theory to the U.S. context. In *Fugitive Empire: Locating Early American Imperialism* (Minneapolis: University of Minnesota Press, 2005), Andy Doolen argues that in the eighteenth century, slavery, war, and territorial expansion were integral components of a continuing imperial context in America. Note also that the chronology of his study extends from the late colonial to the early national period. Ed White, *The Backcountry and the City: Colonization and Conflict in Early America* (Minneapolis: University of Minnesota Press, 2005), argues for the importance, in creating the nation, of the racialized backcountry developed in the colonial period. David Kazanjian, *The Colonizing Trick: National Culture and Imperial Citizenship in Early America* (Baltimore: Johns Hopkins University Press, 2004), looks at the cultural and political process through which America went from settler colony to neocolonial power. The work of earlier historians such as Richard van Alstyne and William Appleman Williams, see, for instance, *Contours of American History* (Cleveland: World, 1961), have obvious purchase here as well, insofar as they defined the new nation as imperial in its origins. See also Marc Egnal, *A Mighty Empire* (Ithaca, N.Y.: Cornell University Press, 1988); Francis Jennings, *The Creation of America: Through Revolution to Empire* (Cambridge: Cambridge University Press, 2000).

22. As Ashis Nandy has aptly observed, "colonialism never seems to end with formal political freedom." Nandy, *The Intimate Enemy: Loss and Recovery of Self under Colonialism* (Delhi: Oxford University Press, 1983), 3. Speaking of contemporary postcolonial situations, Ania Loombia notes that a "country may be both postcolonial (in the sense of being formally independent) and neo-colonial (in the sense of remaining economically and/or culturally dependent)." While one cannot "dismiss the importance of either formal decolonisation, or the fact that unequal power relations of colonial rule are reinscribed in the contemporary imbalances between 'first' and 'third' world nations." *Colonialism/Postcolonialism* (London: Routledge, 1998), 7.

23. Works by postcolonial scholars such as Partha Chatterjee's classic *Nationalist Thought and the Colonial World—A Derivative Discourse* (Minneapolis: University of Minnesota Press, 1993) argue that the discourse of independence in decolonizing movements is in fact derivative of what it seeks to repudiate, depending as they did on reproducing forms of nationalism for their success.

24. While I do not necessarily think that it should *not* be included along with other settler societies, I do not want this to be the focus of this study. Perhaps at this point, the political implications of my argument should be addressed. The fact that elite white slave owners felt oppressed by the structures of colonialism certainly does not "excuse" them from their own part in oppressing people of color. I do not feel it is the job of the historian to serve as judge and jury for people in the past; but I do think it is important to understand individuals in their entirety. I will argue in the Conclusion that racism in the postrevolutionary era was an expression of elite Americans' sense of inferiority and security as much as it was about their sense of superiority.

25. Michael Hechter, *Internal Colonialism: The Celtic Fringe in British National Development, 1536–1966* (Berkeley: University of California Press, 1975).

26. For an overview of this subfield of postcolonial studies, see Bill Ashcroft, Gareth Griffiths, Helen Tiffin, eds., *The Empire Writes Back: Theory and Practice in Post-Colonial Literatures*, 2nd ed. (New York: Routledge, 2002); Bill Ashcroft, Gareth Griffiths, Helen Tiffin, eds., *The Post-colonial Studies Reader* (London: Routledge, 1995).

27. Arthur Angel Phillips (1900–1985) was an Australian cultural critic who wrote an essay in the Melbourne-based journal *Meanjin* in 1950 that coined the phrase cultural cringe. In this essay he discussed internalized feelings of cultural inferiority that hindered Australian artists and intellectuals. He argued that the Australian public believed that the cultural productions of Europeans and especially Britons were by definition superior to domestic works. This dynamic forced ambitious locals to follow foreign trends or go abroad to study and gain professional experience. Those who had gone abroad or were of foreign origin were sought out for employment and promotion. As I will discuss in this book, the same phenomenon occurred in the early United States. See A[rthur]. A[ngel]. Phillips, *A. A. Phillips on the Cultural Cringe* (Carlton, Victoria: Melbourne University Publishing, 2006). For further work on the subject as it pertains to Australia, see Stephen Alomes, *When London Calls: The Expatriation of Australian Creative Artists to Britain* (Melbourne: Cambridge University Press, 1999); Ian Britain, *Once an Australian: Journeys with Barry Humphries, Clive James, Germaine Greer and Robert Hughes* (Melbourne: Oxford University Press, 1997).

28. [Timothy Dwight], "An Essay on American Genius," *New Haven Gazette and Connecticut Magazine,* February 1, 1787. See also the other essays by Dwight in the same periodical: [Dwight], "The Friend, No IV," April 13, 1786; "The Friend, No XI," June 22, 1786; "The Friend, No XII," July 6, 1786; "The Friend, No XV," October 4, 1787.

29. [Timothy Dwight], "An Essay on American Genius," *New Haven Gazette and Connecticut Magazine,* February 1, 1787.

30. See T. H. Breen, *The Marketplace of Revolution: How Consumer Politics Shaped American Independence* (New York: Oxford University Press, 2004). Breen's earlier articles on the argument on which he elaborated more fully in his books include: Breen, "An Empire of Goods: The Anglicization of Colonial America, 1690–1776," *Journal of British Studies* 24 (1986): 467–499 and Breen, "Narrative of Commercial Life: Consumption, Ideology, and Community on the Eve of the American Revolution," *William and Mary Quarterly* 50, 3rd ser. (1993): 471–501. See also the influential work of Carole Shammas, which examines the economy of the Anglo-American world. Shammas, *The Pre-Industrial Consumer in England and America* (New York: Oxford University Press, 1990), Shammas, "How Self-Sufficient Was Early America? *Journal of Interdisciplinary History* 13, 2 (Autumn 1982): 247–272; Shammas, "Consumer Behavior in Colonial America," *Social Science History* 6, 1 (Winter 1982): 67–86; Shammas, *A History of Household Government in America* (Charlottesville: University of Virginia Press, 2002).

31. For perspectives on consumption and the Atlantic world of goods, see Neil McKendrick, John Brewer, and J. H. Plumb, eds., *The Birth of a Consumer Society: The Commercialization of Eighteenth-Century England* (London: Europa, 1982); T. H. Breen, "'Baubles of Britain': The American and Consumer Revolutions of the Eighteenth Century," *Past and Present* 119 (May 1998): 73–104, and "Empire of Goods: The Anglicization of Colonial America, 1690–1776," *Journal of British Studies* 25 (1986): 467–499; Jean-Christophe Agnew, *Worlds Apart: The Market and the Theater in Anglo-American Thought, 1550–1750* (Cambridge: Cambridge University Press, 1986); John Brewer and Roy Porter, eds., *Consumption and the World of Goods* (London: Routledge, 1993); Cary Carson, Ronald Hoffman, and Peter J. Albert, eds., *Of Consuming Interests:*

The Style of Life in the Eighteenth Century (Charlottesville: University of Virginia Press, 1994); Cary Carson, "The Consumer Revolution in Colonial British America: Why Demand?," in *Of Consuming Interests*, 444–482; John Brewer, *The Pleasures of the Imagination: English Culture in the Eighteenth Century* (New York: Farrar Straus Giroux, 1997); John E. Crowley, *The Invention of Comfort: Sensibilities and Design in Early Modern Britain and Early America* (Baltimore: Johns Hopkins University Press, 2001); John Styles and Amanda Vickery, eds., *Gender, Taste, and Material Culture in Britain and North America, 1700–1830* (New Haven, Conn.: Yale University Press, 2006); Dena Goodman and Kathryn Norberg, eds., *Furnishing the Eighteenth Century: What Furniture Can Tell Us About the European and American Past* (New York: Routledge, 2007); Amanda Vickery, *Behind Closed Doors: At Home in Georgian England* (New Haven, Conn.: Yale University Press, 2009).

32. For a pioneering book by an American historian that uses material culture as primary evidence see Richard Bushman, *The Refinement of America: Persons, Houses, Cities* (New York: Knopf, 1992). There have been a number of studies that draw upon material culture to understand the past. See, for instance, Laurel Thatcher Ulrich, *The Age of Homespun: Objects and Stories in the Creation of an American Myth* (New York: Knopf, 2001); Phyllis Whitman Hunter, *Purchasing Identity in the Atlantic World: Massachusetts Merchants, 1670–1780* (Ithaca, N.Y.: Cornell University Press, 2001); Linda Baumgarten, *What Clothes Reveal: The Language of Clothing in Colonial and Federal America* (New Haven, Conn.: Yale University Press, 2002); Ann Smart Martin, *Buying into the World of Goods: Early Consumers in Backcountry Virginia* (Baltimore: Johns Hopkins University Press, 2008). I have taken an interdisciplinary approach to the study of material culture, broadly defined. A model of this is the scholarship of Robert St. George. See St. George, *Conversing by Signs: Poetics of Implication in Colonial New England Culture* (Chapel Hill: University of North Carolina Press, 1998); St. George, ed., *Material Life in America, 1600–1860* (Boston: Northeastern University Press, 1988); Most useful is St. George, editor's introduction to *Possible Pasts: Becoming Colonial in Early America* (Ithaca, N.Y.: Cornell University Press, 2000). The work of sociologist Pierre Bourdieu has also been important to my thinking about the social meaning of goods, especially his *Outline of a Theory of Practice,* trans. Richard Nice (Cambridge: Cambridge University Press, 1977), *The Logic of Practice,* trans. Richard Nice (Stanford, Calif.: Stanford University Press, 1990), *Distinction: A Social Critique of the Judgment of Taste,* trans. Richard Nice (Cambridge, Mass.: Harvard University Press, 1984), and *The Field of Cultural Production,* trans. Randal Johnson (New York: Columbia University Press, 1993). The work of anthropologists who theorize on the social meanings of the circulation of goods has also been extremely helpful to me. See the classic Mary Douglas and Baron Isherwood, *The World of Goods: Towards an Anthropology of Consumption* (New York: Norton, 1978) and especially the influential collection by Arjun Appadurai and Igor Kopytoff, eds., *The Social Life of Things: Commodities in Cultural Perspective* (Cambridge: Cambridge University Press, 1986).

33. For a study on performance from a multivalent perspective, see Joseph Roach's study *Cities of the Dead: Circum-Atlantic Performance* (New York: Columbia University Press, 1996). In this study Roach emphasizes cultural fluidity and hybridity and resists using fixed definitions of national boundaries as his point of reference. See also Sandra M. Gustafson, *Eloquence Is Power: Oratory and Performance in Early America* (Chapel Hill: University of North Carolina Press, 2000).

34. I am indebted to scholars in a wide variety of fields whose works have informed this book. These include, but are not limited to, studies in cartography, botany, the history

of science and medicine, cultural theory, ethnic studies, "Oriental" studies, decorative arts, and art history. I have engaged with these detailed studies in order to get a sense of each field's individual debates and concerns. This work brings together literatures that are not traditionally seen as related in order to allow their insights to inform each other in new ways. The notes in the chapters that follow will reflect my debt to their work.

35. A map is a drawing that represents a mental image of the world; a botanical print represents not an actual individual plant but a drawing that represents a category within a botanist's classificatory schemes, an abstract idea that links different plants into a species. Scientific knowledge in the eighteenth and nineteenth centuries was commonly embodied in a material form, such as a treatise, journal, or scholarly paper.

36. [Dwight], "Essay on American Genius," 1787. See Joseph Ellis, *After the Revolution: Profiles of Early American Culture* (New York: Norton, 1979).

37. *Oxford English Dictionary*, s.v. "unbecoming."

38. [Dwight], "Essay on American Genius."

39. Jedidiah Morse, *Geography Made Easy* (Boston: Thomas & Andrews, 1784), iii–iv.

40. [Dwight], "Essay on American Genius."

41. See Henry Ezekiel Jackson, *Benjamin West, His Life and Work* (Philadelphia: The J. C. Winston Co., 1900); Robert C. Alberts, *Benjamin West: A Biography* (Boston: Houghton Mifflin, 1978); and *Benjamin West, American Painter at the English Court: June 4–August 20, 1989* (Baltimore: Baltimore Museum of Art, 1989).

42. *Oxford English Dictionary*, s.v. "unbecoming."

43. Ibid.

44. See the Uniform Code of Military Justice U.S. (UCMJ, 64 Stat. 109, 10 U.S.C. Chapter 47) which is the foundation upon which military justice is based.

45. From a footnote in David Hume, "Of National Characters," 1753–54 edition (first published in 1748) in *David Hume: Essays: Moral, Political, and Literary,* T. H. Green and T. H. Grose, eds., 2 vols. (London, 1875), part I, essay XXI, "Of National Characters," 252. See also Winthrop Jordan's discussion of this passage in *White Over Black: American Attitudes toward the Negro, 1550–1812* (Chapel Hill: University of North Carolina Press, 1968), 253.

46. Thomas Bond, "Anniversary Oration (Philadelphia: American Philosophical Society [1782]), 8, 30–34; see Whitfield J. Bell, Jr., *Patriot-Improvers: Biographical Sketches of Members of the American Philosophical Society* (Philadelphia: American Philosophical Society, 1997), 1:42.

47. As one scholar put it, after the American Revolution, "a number of white Americans began to embark on serious studies of their own 'savages'" as their way to enter into the debates of the moral philosophers in Europe, who were accustomed to using fantastic "voyage literature" as their source of information on the New World. Ronald L. Meek, *Social Science and the Ignoble Savage* (Cambridge: Cambridge University Press, 1976), 218; Thomas Jefferson, *Notes on the State of Virginia*, ed. W. Peden (Chapel Hill: University of North Carolina Press, 1955), 62; R. H. Pearce, *The Savages of America* (Baltimore: Johns Hopkins Press, 1965), 91–96.

48. In this respect, Jefferson was careful to confine his refutation to "North America" rather than to the Western Hemisphere, which would have included the "swarthy" societies of Latin America. The case of the relations of creole settlers in Latin America to the metropolis is an interesting parallel to the case of Anglo settlers in America. I would argue that the fact that the strong parallels between Anglo-American and Spanish American creoles are not usually a subject of analysis is due to scholars' assumption that

whereas the former are "whites," the latter are not and this makes them inherently different. George Daniels notes that the fear and loathing of being "contemned by Europeans" was shared by Anglo-Americans and colonials in Latin America. Daniels, *Science in American Society: A Social History* (New York: Knopf, 1971), 135–136. As Don Carlos de Siguenza y Gongora wrote at the end of the seventeenth century, "In some parts of Europe, especially in the north, though being more remote, they think that not only the original Indian inhabitants of these [New World] countries but also those of us who were, by chance, born in them of Spanish parents either walk on two legs by divine dispensation or that, even by making use of English microscopes, they are hardly able to discover anything rational in us." Siguenza, *Libra Astronomica* (1690), quoted in Irving A. Leonard, *Don Carlos de Siguenza y Gongora: A Mexican Servant of the Seventeenth Century* (Berkeley: University of California Press, 1929), 62–63. Almost one hundred years later, Sr. Velasques de Leon commented: "The humility, fear, and difficulty which the Spanish Mexicans regularly have in producing their ideas is great, and much greater is the preoccupation of the Europeans with our barbarism. Why should they seek data from men whom they still visualized with bows and feather plumage as they depict us on their maps" (also quoted in Leonard, 63).

CHAPTER 1

1. An early American edition of a British book, *People of All Nations; An Useful Toy for Girl or Boy* (Philadelphia: Jacob Johnson, 1807) was made especially for young readers with small hands; this "toy book" measured one and three-fourths by two and one-fourth inches, contained sixty-three copper engraved plates, and was bound between stiff boards with a calf spine. These books (many of which are held in the extensive children's book collection of the American Antiquarian Society, Worcester, Massachusetts) were heavily read and used by readers, in contrast to some of the other books in the Society's collection in which the pages are not yet separated, indicating that no one ever read them. (There are no page numbers in this book.) Johnson went into business with a merchant partner, Benjamin Warner, in 1809, and they concentrated on publishing children's books, schoolbooks, stationery, and other popular titles. Although their focus was on the country trade, they set up a retail store at 147 Market Street in Philadelphia. Traveling extensively throughout the American West in places such as Kentucky and Tennessee, they set up other stores and extended wholesale accounts to country shopkeepers, booksellers, and printers. They favored dealing with fellow Quakers. See Rosalind Remer, *Printers and Men of Capital* (Philadelphia: University of Pennsylvania Press), 19, 142.

2. The text reads: "Otaheite is one of the Society Islands, in the South Pacific Ocean; the people are said to have mild features, with a pleasing countenance: they are very expert at making baskets." *People of All Nations* (1807), n.p.

3. The pattern in this book of depicting the "natives" rather than settlers as symbols of the British colonies in the Americas has one exception: the figure identified as a "West Indian," was neither a "native" nor a slave. The image portrays a white male planter in European dress. The caption reads "this is not one of the original natives of those islands, they were called Caribs. This appears to be an European, and accustomed to a maritime life." *People of All Nations*, n.p. This image of the West Indian planter in a suit and a large hat to keep out the sun was common in Britain; the most common stereotype portrays him negatively, with a jug in hand, and accuses him of having sexual relations with his African slaves.

4. Originally an iconic symbol of South America, by the eighteenth century this figure was commonly used to represent both the Northern and Southern hemispheres. This

figure often appeared in elaborate decorative cartouches of maps produced in the seventeenth and eighteenth centuries. Besides purely decorative elements such as scrolls and flourishes, cartouches included mythological figures, depictions of plants and animals, and pertinent information about the map such as its title, date of publication, printer's identifying information, dedications, map scales, and legends. Cartouches also functioned as a device to fill blank spaces on a map. In the seventeenth century, Dutch mapmakers elevated the art of map decoration with the introduction of the *carte à figures* "map with figures"; at this time, French was commonly used for trade communication among Europeans. This type of map contained vignettes of the region's "typical inhabitants in national costumes"; native peoples were "especially popular." This style of mapmaking was widely adopted and continued through the nineteenth century. Rebecca Stefoff, *The British Library Companion to Maps and Mapmaking* (London: British Library, 1995), 111, 116–117. See also Arthur Robinson, *The Look of Maps: An Examination of Cartographic Design* (Madison: University of Wisconsin Press, 1986), and R. A. Skelton, *Decorative Printed Maps of the Fifteenth to Eighteenth Centuries* (London: Spring Books, 1965). For work on the cultural implications of cartouches see Stephanie Pratt, "From the Margins: The Native American Personage in the Cartouche and Decorative Borders of Maps," *Word and Image* 12 (1996): 349–365; G. N. G. Clarke, "Taking Possession: The Cartouche as Cultural Text in Eighteenth-century American Maps," *Word and Image* 4 (1988): 455–474.

5. Common objects used to represent the American continent in maps of the period include corn, beavers, various species of New World trees, and fishing nets. Each of these items represented commercial activities.

6. *People of All Nations*, n.p.

7. Ibid.

8. As just one example, William Goldsmith's popular geography mentions two things in his description of the state of Georgia: its Indians and its native fruits. "The Creek Indians inhabit the middle part of this state, and are the most numerous and most civilized tribe in the United States. Oranges, figs, pomegranates and most of the tropical fruits flourish here." Rev. J. Goldsmith [Richard Phillips], *A general view of the manners, customs and curiosities of nations; including a geographical description of the earth: The whole illustrated by fifty-four maps and other engravings.: In two volumes. By the Rev. J. Goldsmith, Vicar of Dunnington, and formerly of Trinity College, Cambridge,* vol[s]. 1[–2], revised by the senior publisher: Sidney's Press (John Babcock and Son, New-Haven; and S. Babcock and Co., Charleston, 1825), 2: 48.

9. *People of All Nations* (1807), n.p.

10. Ibid., emphasis in original. Still today, the French refer to the English as "les rosbifs."

11. David Hume, Adam Smith, Adam Ferguson, and William Robertson were among the most influential of these Scottish thinkers.

12. Peter Laslett, editor's introduction and apparatus criticus to John Locke, *Two Treatises of Government: A Critical Edition*, 2nd ed. (London: Cambridge University Press, 1967), and John Locke, *An Essay Concerning Human Understanding* (Oxford: Clarendon Press, 1975). Quotes from *The Second Treatise of Civil Government* (1690), chap. 5, "Of Property," sec. 49.

13. As P. J. Marshall and Glyndwr Williams note, "To Locke, America, or most of it, was a wilderness—a land in its natural state, uncultivated, where a thousand acres were needed to yield the same sustenance to 'the needy and wretched inhabitants as ten acres in England.'" Marshall and Williams, *The Great Map of Mankind: British Perceptions of the World in the Age of Enlightenment* (London: Dent, 1982), 192.

14. See Colin Calloway, *White People, Indians, and Highlanders: Tribal People and Colonial Encounters in Scotland and America* (New York: Oxford University Press, 2008). See also Franco Venturi, *Utopia and Reform in the Enlightenment* (Cambridge: Cambridge University Press, 1971).

15. Edmund Burke to William Robertson, June 9, 1777, in *The Correspondence of Edmund Burke*,vol. 3, ed. George H. Guttridge (Cambridge: Cambridge University Press, 1961), 350–351.

16. See Hugh Honour, *The European Vision of America: A Special Exhibition to Honor the Bicentennial of the United States* (Cleveland: Cleveland Museum of Art, 1975), and Honour, *The New Golden Land: European Images of America from the Discoveries to the Present Time* (New York: Pantheon, 1975).

17. The primary reference work on the history of cartography is J. B. Harley and David Woodward, eds., *The History of Cartography*, 3 vols. (Chicago: University of Chicago Press, 1987); David Turnbull, *Maps Are Territory, Science Is an Atlas* (Chicago: University of Chicago Press, 1993); Mark Monmonier, *How to Lie with Maps*, 2nd ed. (Chicago: University of Chicago Press, 1996); Denis Wood, with John Fels, *The Power of Maps* (New York: Guilford Press, 1992). Significant works that look specifically at the Anglo-American context include D. W. Meinig's classic study *The Shaping of America: A Geographical Perspective on 500 Years of History*, vol. 1, *Atlantic America, 1492–1800* (New Haven, Conn.: Yale University Press, 1988); John Rennie Short, *Representing the Republic: Mapping the United States, 1600–1900* (London: Reaktion Books, 2001); Margaret Beck Pritchard and Henry G. Taliaferro, *Degrees of Latitude* (New York: Abrams, 2002). For work on the influence of the Enlightenment on mapping see Marshall and Williams, *Great Map of Mankind*; David N. Livingstone and Charles W. J. Withers, eds., *Geography and Enlightenment* (Chicago: University of Chicago Press, 1999), and Marie Claire Godlewska, *Geography Unbound: French Geographic Science from Cassini to Humboldt* (Chicago: University of Chicago Press, 1999).

18. Seymour Schwartz and Ralph Ehrenberg, *The Mapping of America* (New York: Abrams, 1980), 216. See also Benedict Anderson, "Census, Map, Museum," in Anderson, *Imagined Communities: Reflections on the Origin and Spread of Nationalism* (London: Verso, 1983), 163–164.

19. Charles O. Paullin, *Atlas of the Historical Geography of the United States* (Washington, D.C.: Carnegie Institution of Washington, 1932), 7.

20. Peter Jefferson, a cartographer and surveyor, was a resident of Abermarle County Virginia. Thomas Jefferson greatly admired his hardworking father and was encouraged by him to pursue his education. When Peter Jefferson died in 1757, he left Thomas, who was then fourteen, a good-sized estate consisting of five thousand acres and enough slaves to work the land (*Dictionary of National Biography*, s.v. "Jefferson, Thomas"). Joshua Fry was a former professor of mathematics at the College of William and Mary. The elder Jefferson and Fry had worked together previously while surveying the Virginia–North Carolina line and the boundaries of the Fairfax grant. See Edmund Berkeley and Dorothy Smith Berkeley, *Dr. John Mitchell: The Man Who Made the Map of North America* (Chapel Hill: University of North Carolina Press, 1974), 181.

21. Countless other maps that relied on data collected by colonial Americans and published in England supported British territorial claims. Just one example is *A Map of the British and French Dominions in North America with the Roads, Distances, Limits, and Extent of the Settlements,* which represented the disputed parts of the Ohio Valley as being controlled by Britain. The first of such maps was the one executed by Henry Popple in 1733 (nineteen by

twenty inches). Printed in London, this map was published as a series of twenty sheets. The British government came to be of the opinion that Popple's map was inaccurate and that Mitchell's map of 1755 was an improvement upon it. Paullin, *Atlas,* 13.

22. Among the important early non-Anglo maps of the newly formed United States are J. B. Eliot, *Carte du theatre de la guerre actuel* (Paris, 1778); Antonio Zatta, *Le Colonie unitie America settentrionale le di nuova projezione* (Venice, 1778); T. C. de Roeder, *Nauwkeurige Kaart Van De XIII Provintien Der Vereenigde Staaten Von Noord America* (Amsterdam, 1782).

23. For instance, Guillaume Delisle produced in 1718 an influential map, *Carte de la Louisiane et du Cours du Mississippi,* that established French claims in the Mississippi River valley and delta. This document angered the English, who countered with their own cartographic counterevidence in the form of Herman Moll's 1715 *New and Exact Map of the Dominions of the King of Great Britain on ye Continent of North America.* For further discussion see Schwartz, "European Claims in America," chap. 6 of Schwartz and Ehrenberg, *Mapping of America,* 133–155; especially 138, 140–142, 146.

24. As Benedict Anderson writes, "triangulation by triangulation, war by war, treaty by treaty, the alignment of map and power proceeded" (*Imagined Communities,* 173). Still today, the volume of map production of a region is related to the amount of strife in the area (Schwartz and Ehrenberg, *Mapping of America,* 142). For the European context of mapping in the eighteenth and nineteenth centuries, see James Scott, *Seeing Like a State* (New Haven, Conn.: Yale University Press, 1998).

25. The scholarship of J. B. Harley influenced many subsequent studies in this area. See Harley, "Power and Legitimization in the English Geographical Atlases of the Eighteenth Century," in John A. Wolter and Ronald E. Grim, eds., *Images of the World: The Atlas through History* (New York: McGraw-Hill, 1996); Mathew H. Edney, "Theory and the History of Cartography," *Imago Mundi* 48 (1996): 185–190; Mathew H. Edney, "Cartography without 'Progress': Reinterpreting the Nature and Historical Development of Mapmaking," *Cartographica* 30 (1994): 54–68; Robert A. Rundstrom, "Mapping, Postmodernism, Indigenous People and the Changing Direction of North American Cartography," *Cartographica* 28 (1991): 1–12. See also Norman Thrower, *Maps and Civilization: Cartography in Culture and Society* (Chicago: University of Chicago Press, 1996).

26. See Benedict Anderson, *Imagined Communities,* 163–164, and Jerry Brotton, *Trading Territories: Mapping the Early Modern* World (London: Reaktion Books, 1997).

27. According to historian Sara Gronim, maps in the early modern period, through the reliability of mathematics, were able to instill a certain confidence in maps as consistently "reliable representations of the physical world." This physical reliability was imparted to the social and political spheres; convention said that the physical world and its inhabitants could relate to one another as longitude does to latitude, and vice versa. "Geography and Persuasion: Maps in British Colonial New York," *William and Mary Quarterly* 58, no. 2 (April 2001): 373–374.

28. As Gronim writes, these natural markers "were intended to lend their credibility to humanly inscribed features, asking readers' assent to the social relations on the map." Ibid., 374.

29. Six years earlier, in 1748, his patron George William Fairfax, son of Lord Fairfax, brought Washington on a surveying trip to the unsettled areas of the Shenandoah valley. Landowners were often responsible for their own surveying needs. Given the shortage of professionals, many people learned the necessary skills by reading imported English manuals. An important guide that specifically touched on the British American context

was John Love, *Geodaesia; or, The Art of Surveying and Measuring of Land* (London, 1688), which was still being used in 1761.

30. See Martin Bruckner, *The Geographic Revolution in Early America: Maps, Literacy, and National Identity* (Chapel Hill: University of North Carolina Press, 2006), 26–27.

31. For a collection of 110 maps created or commented on by George Washington, see Lawrence Martin, ed., *The George Washington Atlas* (Washington, D.C.: U.S. George Washington Bicentennial Commission, 1932), vol. 1. See also *History of the George Washington Bicentennial Celebration*, vol. 1 (Washington, D.C.: U.S. George Washington Bicentennial Commission, 1932); Lawrence Martin, ed., *The George Washington Atlas*, (Richmond, Virginia: Virginia Surveyors Association, 1995).

32. Most cartographers derive the data for maps from previous documents. When a cartographer manages to utilize new information or make significant innovations to a map that is a significant improvement from its predecessors, it is deemed a "mother map." Paullin, *Atlas*, 7. Mitchell's work was finally displaced by that of Englishman Aaron Arrowsmith, whose *Map Exhibiting all the New Discoveries in the Interior Part of North America*, used Greenwich as the prime meridian. This map was first published as six sheets (fifty-seven by forty-nine inches) in 1795 and then again in 1802, 1811, and 1814, with additions on each reprinting. The 1814 version was the first of Arrowsmith's maps to include the findings of Lewis and Clark as well as Pike's explorations. Arrowsmith was ranked as one of the most important leaders in the field of cartography, and this map was used as a model for many mapmakers during the first half of the nineteenth century. See Paullin, *Atlas*, 14.

33. Berkeley and Berkeley, *Dr. John Mitchell*, 175. The birthplace of John Mitchell (1690?–1768) has been a matter of speculation among historians. See Herbert Thatcher, "Dr. Mitchell, M.D., F.R.S., of Virginia," *Virginia Magazine of History and Biography* 39 (1931): 126–135, asserting on the basis of Peter Kalm's statement that Mitchell was born in America.

34. Berkeley and Berkeley, *Dr. John Mitchell*, 175. This map is considered by cartographic scholars one of the most important maps from this period.

35. *American National Biography*, s.v. "John Mitchell."

36. John Mitchell's biographical details, or rather the lack thereof, prefigures the themes of future chapters in this book. The fluidity of identity—British and/or American—that he represents is one of the main concerns of this book. It is very difficult to identify several important individuals who lived during this period as American or English. Scholars do not identify such a subject's identity in a uniform fashion. Often an individual is described as "American" if he or she lived in America for any period during his or her lifetime, or at the time in question, regardless of where he or she was born. Conversely, it is typical of American scholars to refer to such a person as American only if he or she actually born in America: a mere sojourn in America does not an American make. If the conflicting information presented in museums scattered around the globe is any indication, the artist Benjamin West is a good example of a notable personality who falls into this ambiguous category of national identity. Though West was born in Newton Square, in the backwoods of Pennsylvania, in 1783, the British claim him for their own, since he was, after all, the historical painter to the court of King George III and later the surveyor of the king's pictures from 1791 to 1820. As the old adage goes, "Success hath many parents whilst failure is an orphan."

37. Schwartz and Ehrenberg, *Mapping of America*, 159–160.

38. For this point generally, see Benedict Anderson, *Imagined Communities*, especially chap. 10, "Census, Map, Museum."

39. The French also used it as a basis to counter the English claims to territory. French cartographers Jean Nicholas Bellin, Jean-Baptiste Bourguignon d'Anville, and Robert de Vaugondy adopted parts of Mitchell's work while adding their own perspective of where the proper boundaries between French and English land should be located. Schwartz and Ehrenberg, *Mapping of America*, 160–162.

40. Another map, *The Seat of War, in New England, by an American Volunteer,* was published in London in 1775 by Robert Sayer and John Bennett. Schwartz and Ehrenberg, *Mapping of America*, 184.

41. Some examples of objects that mixed textual and visual geographical information are these works: John Burgoyne, *A State of the Expedition from Canada: as laid before the House of Commons* (London: J. Almon, 1780), David Ramsay, *The History of the American Revolution* (Philadelphia: R. Aitken, 1789), Banastre Tarleton, *History of the campaigns of 1780 and 1781, in the Southern Provinces of North America* (London: T. Cadell, 1787), John D. Simcoe, *Journal of the Operations of the Queen's Rangers from the End of the Year 1777 to the Conclusion of the Late American War* (Exeter, England: 1787), and Charles Stedman, *History of the Origin, Progress, and Termination of the American War* (London: P. Wogan, P. Byrne, 1794). See Schwartz and Ehrenberg, *Mapping of America*, 157–216.

42. The *American Military Atlas*'s six maps included a map of North America by Samuel Dunn; a map of the northern colonies by Samuel Holland and Thomas Pownall; a map of the middle colonies after work by Joshua Fry, Peter Jefferson, and Lewis Evans; a map of the southern colonies after William de Brahm, Henry Mouzon, John Collett, and Bernard Romans; a map of the West Indies by Samuel Dunn; and a survey of Lake Champlain and Lake George drawn by William Brassier in 1762. Schwartz and Ehrenberg, *Mapping of America*, 190.

43. For instance, a map of the middle colonies was created after the work of Peter Jefferson.

44. William Faden (1749–1836), *The North American atlas, selected from the most authentic maps, charts, plans, &c. hitherto published* (London: printed for W. Faden, successor to the late Mr. Thomas Jefferys, 1777). Yale University Map Department at Sterling Memorial Library.

45. Schwartz and Ehrenberg, *Mapping of America*, 203–204.

46. Joseph F[rederick] W[allet] Des Barres, *Miscellaneous views and charts from the Atlantic Neptune* (London, 1777–81). This work contains seven maps and four colored plates. Also published for the British Royal Navy was Joseph F. W. Des Barres, Esq., *The Atlantic Neptune: published for the use of The Royal Navy of Great Britain* (London: Admiralty, 1775–81), and Joseph F. W. Des Barres, Esq., under the directions of the Right Honorable Lords Commissioners of the Admiralty, *The Atlantic Neptune: published for the use of the Royal Navy of Great Britain* (London: Admiralty, 1777).

47. Schwartz and Ehrenberg, *Mapping of America*, 202.

48. John Wallis (1781–1810) was a bookseller in London.

49. John Wallis, cartouche (etching) of *The United States of America laid down From the best Authorities* (London, April 3, 1783).

50. Buell's map was forty-three by forty-eight inches; it was published just ahead of the one William McMurray published in 1784, entitled *The United States according to the definitive Treaty of Peace signed at Paris, Sept[embe]r. 3d 1783*. See Ben A. Smith and James W. Vining, *American Geographers: 1784–1812* (Westport, Conn.: Praeger, 2003), and Walter Ristow, *American Maps and Mapmakers* (Detroit: Wayne State University Press, 1985).

51. Pritchard and Taliaferro, *Degrees of Latitude*, 294–295.

52. Not one to miss an opportunity to profit from his printing skills, Abel Buell (1742–1822) had previously been convicted of counterfeiting on a homemade press. He managed in 1800 to return to the good graces of the state by bringing home valuable information he acquired about the latest English textile equipment while on a trip to Great Britain. A modern reprint of Buell's 1784 map "A New and correct Map of the United States of North America" was published by the National Geographic Society (United States), Cartographic Division (Washington, D.C.: National Geographic Society, 1987). I consulted the copy owned by the Map Collection, Sterling Memorial Library, Yale University.

53. Buell depended heavily on the influential work of John Mitchell (1711–1768) and Lewis Evans (1700–1756). See their *Map of the British and French dominions in North America* (London, 1755). The second edition of Lewis Evans's map entitled *Geographical, historical, political, philosophical and mechanical essays: The first, containing an analysis of a general map of the middle British colonies in America; and of the country of the confederate Indians: a description of the face of the country; the boundaries of the confederates; and the maritime and inland navigations of the several rivers and lakes contained therein* was published by Benjamin Franklin and David Hall (Philadelphia: B. Franklin and D. Hall, 1755).

54. Other maps that appeared during this critical period traversed the Atlantic in the various stages of their production. For instance, *An Accurate Map of the State and Province of New-Hampshire in New England* by Colonel Joseph Blanchard and revised by Samuel Langdon, was originally engraved in England and then brought to America to be re-engraved; it was published in Boston in 1784. American-made maps remained crucially reliant on British precedents, techniques, and production.

55. Schwartz and Ehrenberg, *Mapping of America*, 205.

56. See Martin Bruckner, "Literacy for Empire: Geography, Education, and the Aesthetic of Territoriality," chap. 7 of *Geographic Revolution*, 238–263.

57. Gronim, "Geography and Persuasion," 374.

58. Mapmaking in the United States was not well established until the 1840s. Schwartz and Ehrenberg, *Mapping of America*, 219.

59. Ibid., 216.

60. Ibid., 222.

61. At the start of the nineteenth century, the Far West was of great interest to mapmakers. The Louisiana Purchase of 1803 further stimulated this interest worldwide. See Bruckner, "Native American Geographies and the Journals of Lewis and Clark," chap. 6 of *Geographic Revolution*, 204–237.

62. C. Vann Woodward argues that "from the very start the youth metaphor was built into European thinking about America." Despite long-term conflicts between France and Britain, they referred to one another as "peers and equals [who were] sometimes friendly, sometimes hostile." In contrast, when speaking of America the tone became one of superiority, admonition, and discipline: "Their words were sometimes those of age to youth, parent to offspring, master to apprentice, teacher to pupil." *The Old World's New World* (New York: New York Public Library, 1991), vii.

63. Robert Rogers, *A concise account of North America: containing a description of the several British colonies on that continent, including the islands of Newfoundland, Cape Breton, &c also of the interior, or westerly parts of the country by Major Robert Rogers* (London: Printed for the author, and sold by J. Millan, bookseller, 1765). Ralph Brown, "The American Geographies of Jedidiah Morse," *Annals of the Association of American Geographers* 31 (1941): 149. This article includes a useful bibliography of Morse's geographical works given in chronological order. It is adapted from a comprehensive list

of all of Morse's works compiled at Yale University by Winfield Shiras. Written in 1935, the document is entitled "A list of the works of Jedediah Morse, with notes," and is housed in the Library Shelving Facility of the Yale University Library.

64. "Discovery" referred to the initial moment of European contact. I am using the term as the people being studied here did.

65. Goldsmith, *General View*, 35.

66. Benedict Anderson notes that the "logo-map penetrated deep into the popular imagination, forming a powerful emblem for the anti-colonial nationalisms being born." Anderson, *Imagined Communities*, 175. Martin Bruckner discusses this document to show how the map of the U.S. shaped the "methodologies of formal literary instruction" and influenced "self-representation and political identification." Bruckner, *Geographic Revolution*, 139. The standard reference book on needlework is that of Betty Ring. See especially her work *Girlhood Embroidery: American Samplers and Pictorial Needlework, 1650–1850* (New York: Knopf, 1993).

67. Bruckner discusses the "geographic revolution" in early America from the 1680s to the 1820s with a focus on the relationship between geography and literary education. He argues at length about how this connection "influenced the textual practices surrounding the process of identity formation." Bruckner, *Geographic Revolution*, 3.

68. William Guthrie (1708–1770), received his degree from the University of Aberdeen, Scotland. He was the author of *A new system of modern geography: or, A geographical, historical, and commercial grammar; and present state of the several nations of the world* (London: J. Knox, 1770), which went through numerous editions, including *A New Geographical, Historical, and Commercial Grammar* (London: J. Knox, 1771); *A New Geographical, Historical, and Commercial Grammar* (London: J. Knox, 1774); *A New Geographical, Commercial, and Historical Grammar* (Edinburgh: Alexander Kincaid, 1792); *A New System of Modern Geography: or, A Geographical, Historical, and Commercial Grammar; and Present State of the Several Nations of the World*, 2 vols., 1st Amer. ed. (Philadelphia: Mathew Carey, 1794–1795). See William Sprague, *The Life of Jedidiah Morse, D.D.* (New York: Anson D. F. Randolph, 1874), 192.

69. Geography is defined as "The science which has for its object the description of the earth's surface, treating of its form and physical features, its natural and political divisions, the climate, productions, population, etc., of the various countries. It is frequently divided into mathematical, physical, and political geography, subterranean geography (geology). *Oxford English Dictionary*, s.v. "geography."

70. As indicated in note 8, the pseudonymous author of this geography, "Rev. J. Goldsmith," is identified in its title as "vicar of Dunnington, and formerly of Trinity College, Cambridge." Goldsmith, *General View*, title page.

71. The remainder of the advertisement provided information on where these geographical materials were sold in the United States and what other types of objects were sold alongside them. The placement of the advertisement in this book suggests that it was assumed that readers would also be likely customers for these other costly imported "fancy articles." The work was sold by purveyors of "fancy articles—ladies and gen'ts dressing cases furnished complete; work boxes, gold paper and every article in the Fancy Stationary line." Goldsmith, *General View*, 290.

72. *A peep at the various nations of the world; with a concise description of its inhabitants. Embellished with several neat Engravings* (New York: S. King, c. 1825), 6.

73. Jedidiah Morse, *American Universal Geography, or a view of the present state of all the empires, kingdoms, states and republicas of the known world, and of the United States in particular* (Boston: Thomas and Andrews, 1793), 1:vi–vii.

74. Ibid.

75. Sprague, *Life of Jedidiah Morse*, 192. Sprague's biography was published for Morse's sons, who did not live to see it published. Although lacking in critical scholarly analysis, it includes many important letters of which many have not survived. Judging from comparisons with the transcripts of the letters that do survive, they seem to have been transcribed faithfully. For Morse's religious views, see especially Joseph Phillips, *Jedidiah Morse and New England Congregationalism* (New Brunswick, N.J.: Rutgers University Press, 1983), and James King, *Jedidiah Morse, a Champion of New England Orthodoxy* (New York: Columbia University Press, 1939).

76. For different scholarly perspectives on Webster, see V. P. Bynack, "Noah Webster's Linguistic Thought and the Idea of an American National Culture," *Journal of the History of Ideas* 45, no. 1 (Jan.–Mar., 1984): 99–114; Joseph Ellis, *After the Revolution: Profiles of Early American Culture*, chap. 6 (New York: Norton, 1979); Jill Lepore, *A Is for American: Letters and Other Characters in the Newly United States* (New York: Knopf, 2002).

77. Noah Webster, "On the Education of Youth in America" (1788), in Webster, *A Collection of Essays and Fugitiv [sic] Writings on Moral, Historical, Political and Literary Subjects* (Boston, [1790]), reprinted as Document 26 in Philip Kurland and Ralph Lerner, eds., *The Founders' Constitution* (Chicago: University of Chicago Press, 1987), 679–680.

78. Ibid.

79. Morse, *American Universal Geography*, 1:vi–vii.

80. Jedidiah Morse, *Geography Made Easy: Being a Short, but Comprehensive System of that very Useful and Agreeable Science* (New Haven, Conn.: Meigs, Bowen & Dana, 1784).

81. For a biography that attempts to use psychological evidence to understand the life of Morse see Richard Moss, *The Life of Jedidiah Morse: A Station of Peculiar Exposure* (Knoxville: University of Tennessee Press, 1995). See also Brown, "American Geographies of Jedidiah Morse."

82. Guthrie, *A New System of Modern Geography: or, A Geographical, Historical, and Commercial Grammar; and Present State of the Several Nations of the World*, 2 vols., 1st Amer. ed. (Philadelphia: Mathew Carey, 1794–1795). Turner (1753–1788), was a graduate of Oxford University. His *New and Easy Introduction to Universal Geography* (London, 1780) was of "an elementary character"; it was written as a series of letters. It reached its thirteenth edition in 1808. Bolstered by his success with that book, Turner wrote *An Easy Introduction to the Arts and Sciences* (London, 1783), which was also widely used as a standard schoolbook for several years. Over the years, Turner made some additions and corrections to this book, and by 1811 it had reached its fourteenth edition. *Dictionary of National Biography*, s.v. "Richard Turner." Bruckner discusses the connection between the two works by Morse and Turner in *Geographic Revolution*, 115.

83. This refers to the fourth edition of Guthrie's work, which was published in London in 1774.

84. Morse goes on to note: "But they are more to be valued on account of their prudent behaviour, thorough cleanliness, and tender affection for their husbands and children, and all the engaging duties of domestic life." Morse, *Geography Made Easy*, 184. Many editions of Guthrie's book quoted the same passage, therefore Morse could have used any number of them. Guthrie died in 1770, so additions to his work made after that date were made by unnamed editors or the publisher. See Guthrie, *New Geographical, Commercial, and Historical Grammar* (London: J. Knox, 1774), 185.

85. Morse to Christoph Daniel Ebeling, May 27, 1794, Morse Family Papers, Manuscripts and Archives, Yale University Library; emphasis in original.

86. Morse, *Geography Made Easy*, 5.

87. Jedidiah Morse to Richard Price, August 28, 1784, Morse Family Papers, Manuscripts and Archives, Yale University Library. Richard Price (1723–1791) was a Welsh political philosopher and Dissenting minister. He gained recognition through his pamphlets, including one supporting the cause of the American rebels and another supporting the beginning of the French Revolution. He had many transatlantic connections, including Jefferson, Rush, Adams, and Franklin. See *The Correspondence of Richard Price*, ed. D. O. Thomas and W. Bernard Peach, 3 vols. (Durham, N.C.: Duke University Press, 1983–94).

88. The public was eager for a geography of America. The last one of any significance was Robert Rogers, *Concise Account of America*, 1st ed. (London: J. Milan, 1765). With the dramatic political changes occurring in the country, this text had become inadequate and outdated.

89. Jedidiah Morse, Jr., to Jedidiah Morse, Sr., January 8, 1785, Morse Family Papers, Manuscripts and Archives, Yale University Library.

90. Historian and politician David Ramsay (1749–1815) was born the son of immigrant Irish Protestant farmers in Pennsylvania. He was a graduate of the College of New Jersey (now Princeton University) in 1765 and received medical training at the College of Philadelphia (1770–1773), where he studied under Benjamin Rush. Among Ramsay's most important writings are *An Oration on the Advantages of American Independence* (1778), *History of the Revolution of South Carolina* (1785), *The History of the American Revolution* (1789), *A Manuscript on the Means of Preserving Health, in Charleston and the Adjacent Low Country* (1790), *An Oration in Commemoration of American Independence* (1794), *A Sketch of the Soil, Climate, Weather, and Diseases of South Carolina* (1796), *A Review of the Improvements, Progress and State of Medicine in the Eighteenth Century* (1801), *The History of South Carolina* (1809), *Memoir of the Life of Martha Laurens Ramsay* (1811), and *The History of the United States* (1816–17). *American National Biography*, s.v. "David Ramsay."

91. Sprague, *Life of Jedidiah Morse*, 202.

92. Even then, as I will discuss in chapter 5, Barton had gone overseas to study and had taken much from European sources.

93. Histories of the American Revolution were similarly considered political. See David Ramsay, *The history of the revolution of South-Carolina, from a British province to an independent state*, 2 vols. (Trenton: Isaac Collins, 1785); *The History of the American Revolution*, 2 vols. (Philadelphia: R. Aitken, 1789). Subsequent editions were also published in 1793, 1795, and 1811.

94. The production of a domestic geography was described by Americans as nation building. Until then, Americans were reading British geographies and using imported texts in the schoolroom. What messages, then, were Americans teaching their children, the first "generation" of people born as American citizens, about the new nation? Americans already depended on the former mother country for many things; it seemed particularly humiliating to have to rely on it for a description of American herself.

95. Morse's piece was published in the *New Haven Gazette and Connecticut Magazine* 2 (1787): 222.

96. Jedidiah Morse, *The American Geography; or, A View of the Present Situation of the United States of America* (Boston: Thomas & Andrews, 1789), v.

97. Brown, "American Geographies of Jedidiah Morse," quote from 146.

98. Morse, *American Geography*, preface, vi.

99. See Sprague, *Life of Jedidiah Morse*, 203. Brown estimates that fifteen copies were sold—in a country that had 3,929,214 people, according to the 1790 census. Brown, "American Geographies of Jedidiah Morse," 176.

100. The abridgment was published in Boston by Thomas & Andrews in 1790. It was a duodecimo volume consisting of 322 pages. Jedidiah Morse, *Geography made easy: being an abridgement of the American geography. To which is added, a geographical account of the European settlements in America; and of Europe, Asia and Africa. Illustrated with eight neat maps and cuts. Calculated particularly for the use and improvement of schools in the United States* (Boston: Isaiah Thomas & Ebenezer T. Andrews, 1790). A copy is housed in the Beinecke Rare Book and Manuscript Library, Yale University.

101. Sprague, *Life of Jedidiah Morse,* 203.

102. Historians can trace the popularity of Dwight's book through looking at the spread of its publication and distribution by state and the many editions it went through by year: Nathaniel Dwight, *A short but comprehensive system of the geography of the world: by way of question and answer: principally designed for children, and common schools,* was first printed in Connecticut around 1795—(Hartford: Hudson & Goodwin, 1795[?]), and (Hartford, Conn.: Elisha Babcock, 1795)—and then published in Boston in 1796 (Manning & Loring, 1796), and was sold in Boston by David West and by S. Hall, B. Larkin, J. White, E. Larkin, J. West, and W. P. Blake. It was also available in Salem and Newburyport, Massachusetts, as well as Portsmouth, New Hampshire, and Portland, Maine. It was published again in Connecticut in 1796 (Hartford: Hudson & Goodwin, 1796). The second Connecticut edition (Hartford: Hudson & Goodwin, 1796), like the previous edition, sold throughout Connecticut. The first Albany edition, which was reprinted from the second Connecticut edition (Albany: Charles R. & George Webster, 1799), was sold throughout New York state. Following the fourth edition (Boston: Manning and Loring, 1797) came the second Albany edition, again reprinted from the second Hartford edition (Albany: Charles R. and George Webster, 1799); the third Connecticut edition (Hartford: Hudson & Goodwin, 180[?]); the fourth Connecticut edition (Hartford: Hudson and Goodwin, 1800); the sixth edition (Boston: Manning & Loring, 1801); the first New Jersey edition (Elizabethtown: J. Woods, 1801); a Pennsylvania edition (Philadelphia: Mathew Carey, 1802); the fifth Connecticut edition (Hartford: Hudson & Goodwin, 1802); the second New Jersey edition (Elizabethtown: J. Woods, 1803); another Massachusetts edition (Northampton: S. & E. Butler, 1805); and so forth (for a more complete list see Brown, "American Geographies of Jedidiah Morse."

103. Sprague, *Life of Jedidiah Morse,* 204–205. Christoph Daniel Ebeling (1741–1817), a professor of Greek and History at the Gymnasium in Hamburg, Germany, was recognized as an authority on America. While writing his book *Erdbeschreibung und Geschichte von Amerika: die Vereinten Staaten von Nordamerika* [*The Geography and History of America: The United States of America*] (Hamburg, Germany: C.E. Bohn, 1793–1794), Ebeling obtained many important maps of North America.

104. Ebeling to "Rev. Sir" June 26, 1794, as cited in Brown, "American Geographies of Jedidiah Morse," 149–155.

105. See, for instance, Sprague, *Life of Jedidiah Morse,* and Brown, "American Geographies of Jedidiah Morse."

106. Brown, "American Geographies of Jedidiah Morse," 148. Evans produced an important map in 1755 entitled *Analysis of a Map of the Middle British Colonies in America,* 2nd ed. (Philadelphia, 1755). The prime meridian passes through Philadelphia, and notations on the bottom margin indicate the longitude west of the meridian of London. Evans consulted "actual surveys," astronomical observations, maps, notes, journals, books, and reports of traders and travelers. The information about the eastern seaboard is much more accurate than that about the western lands, which at the

time were not settled by Europeans. This map was notable for its size, twenty-six by nineteen inches; it was frequently pirated. Its closest rival was Mitchell's map (Paullin, *Atlas,* 13).

107. Jedidiah Morse to Christoph Daniel Ebeling, Hamburg, Germany, May 27, 1794, Morse Family Papers, Manuscripts and Archives, Yale University Library.

108. Morse, *American Universal Geography,* 1:v–vi.

109. Ibid., 1:v–vi.

110. Ibid.

111. Ibid., 1:vi–vii.

112. The first volume of the second edition of Morse's *American Universal Geography* concentrated on the "Western Continent," with the vast majority of it being devoted to the United States. It can properly be considered a second edition of his 1789 work. In the four years that had passed since the publication of the first edition of this work, many changes had taken place in the new nation. Morse found that many additions and corrections were needed. See Sprague, *Life of Jedidiah Morse,* 207.

113. Brown, "American Geographies of Jedidiah Morse," 148.

114. Ibid., 206.

115. Ibid., 207.

116. Morse, *American Universal Geography,* 1:vi–vii.

117. Ibid.

118. Jedidiah Morse, "To the Friends of Science" (Philadelphia: Robert Aitken, 1787). Other extant examples of requests for geographical information include one that was distributed in New York during the following year. See also Jedidiah Morse, [request for geographical information], dated June 23, 1788, Morse Family Papers, Manuscripts and Archives, Yale University Library.

119. Many of examples of these responses are in the Morse Family Papers, Manuscripts and Archives, Yale University Library. See, for instance, John May, October 3, 1789; S. Blackburn, April 6, 1789; and J. Buckminster, Portsmouth, February 4, 1789.

120. Jedidiah Morse, "Geographical Queries," undated, Morse Family Papers, Manuscripts and Archives, Yale University Library.

121. Jedidiah Morse, "To the Friends of Science" (broadside dated Philadelphia, August 7, 1787) (Philadelphia: Robert Aitken & Son, 1787).

122. St. George Tucker to Jedidiah Morse, Philadelphia, February 14, 1792, Morse Family Papers, Manuscripts and Archives, Yale University Library; Jedidiah Morse to William Livingston, New Haven, October 26, 1789, with note by Livingston, Livingston Family Papers, Massachusetts Historical Society, Boston; Brown, "American Geographies of Jedidiah Morse," 165.

123. A great deal of the voluminous correspondence he carried out with average citizens from across the country is preserved in the Morse Family Papers, Manuscripts and Archives, Yale University Library.

124. See the editor's comments by David Waldstreicher in Thomas Jefferson, *Notes on the State of Virginia,* ed. Waldstreicher (New York: St. Martin's Press, 2002), 21.

125. Jedidiah Morse, "To the Friends of Science."

126. Brown, "American Geographies of Jedidiah Morse," 146.

127. The 1789 and 1793 editions were significant works that subsequently went through numerous republications.

128. Brown, "American Geographies of Jedidiah Morse," 147.

129. Ibid., 148. By 1819, Morse's work had gone through seven editions. A French version was published in 1795 and a Dutch edition between 1793–1796.

130. Jedidiah Morse, Charlestown, to Richard Price, London, April 6, 1789, Morse Family Papers, Manuscripts and Archives, Yale University Library. Morse was introduced to Price by Ezra Stiles. In this letter he mentions that he had been in touch with John Stockdale, "book-seller, Picadilly, London."

131. Richard Price, Hackney, to Jedidiah Morse, May 18, 1789, Historical Society of Pennsylvania, emphasis in original. As Price explained to Morse, international copyright laws did not exist. It was not until 1790 that laws in the United States were regularized. Before that, they only applied within a single state. Price himself suffered from this as his work *Observations on the Importance of the American Revolution* was copied. See also the Morse to Price, August 28, 1789, and Price to Morse, March 29, 1790, Morse Family Papers, Manuscripts and Archives, Yale University Library.

132. Morse mentions writing to Stockdale in a letter to Richard Price, dated Charlestown, April 6, 1789, Morse Family Papers, Manuscripts and Archives, Yale University Library. Morse was introduced to Stockdale by David Ramsay.

133. Published as Jedidiah Morse, *The American Geography*, 2nd ed. (London: John Stockdale, 1792).

134. John Stockdale to Jedidiah Morse, October 3, 1794, Jedidiah Morse Papers, Manuscripts and Archives Division, New York Public Library.

135. Ibid.

136. John Stockdale to Jedidiah Morse, April 1, 1795, and April 29, 1796, Morse Family Papers, Manuscripts and Archives, Yale University Library. The publisher had reprinted one thousand copies of Morse's book in a small duodecimo size.

137. John Stockdale to Jedidiah Morse, March 16, 1793, Jedidiah Morse Papers, Manuscripts and Archives Division, New York Public Library.

138. See James Freeman, *Remarks on the American Universal Geography* (Boston: Belknap and Hall, 1793).

139. Stockdale, editor's preface to *American Geography, Jedidiah Morse* (London: John Stockdale, 1794), iii.

140. Winterbotham was convicted in 1793 of seditious statements made in his sermons and convicted and sentenced to serving time in Newgate Prison in November of that year. William Winterbotham, *An historical, geographical, commercial, and philosophical view of the American United States, and of the European settlements in America and the West-Indies* (London: J. Ridgway, etc., 1795). See Brown, "American Geographies of Jedidiah Morse," 197.

141. John Stockdale, London, to Jedidiah Morse, October 3, 1794, Jedidiah Morse Papers, Manuscripts and Archives Division, New York Public Library. John Stockdale to Jedidiah Morse, April 29, 1796, Morse Family Papers, Manuscripts and Archives, Yale University Library.

142. Reid and his partners Charles Smith and Levi Wayland, booksellers and stationers in New York City, formed a partnership with printers John Tiebout and Edward O'Brien, also of New York City, to publish three thousand copies of Winterbotham's volume by subscription. See John D. Gordan, III, "Morse v. Reid: The First Reported Federal Copyright Case," *Law and History Review* 11, no. 1 (1993): 23–25.

143. Ibid., 21–41. Kent, who was a professor of law at Columbia at the time, was a Yale classmate of Morse.

144. John Stockdale, London, to Jedidiah Morse, October 3, 1794, Jedidiah Morse Papers, Manuscripts and Archives Division, New York Public Library. John Stockdale, London, to Jedidiah Morse, April 29, 1796, Morse Family Papers, Manuscripts and Archives, Yale University Library.

145. Benjamin Rush, Philadelphia, to Jedidiah Morse, June 15, 1769 [error; actual date 1796], Jedidiah Morse Papers, Manuscripts and Archives Division, New York Public Library.

146. Morse's *Gazetteer* was published in 1797 and reprinted in Great Britain in 1798. Charles Dilly to Jedidiah Morse, June 4, 1799, Morse Family Papers, Manuscripts and Archives, Yale University Library.

147. Jedidiah Morse to Christoph Daniel Ebeling, May 27, 1794, Morse Family Papers, Manuscripts and Archives, Yale University Library; emphasis in original.

148. Morse to W. Livingston, October 26, 1787, William Livingston Family Papers, Massachusetts Historical Society.

149. In the winter of 1786–87, Morse traveled to Georgia. The trip was recorded in the notes President Stiles made of the October 25, 1786, meeting of the Corporation of Yale College. Stiles wrote: "Mr. Tutor Morse desiring to be absent [during] Spring in order to make the Tour of the States to Georgia for perfecting a new Edition of his Geography, we elected the Rev[eren]d Abiel Holmes Tutor." Evert A. Duyckinck and George L. Duyckinck, *Cyclopaedia of American literature: embracing personal and critical notices of authors, and selections from their writings: from the earliest period to the present day: with portraits, autographs, and other illustrations in two volumes*, vol. 1 (New York: Charles Scribner, 1856), 161.

150. Morse, *The American Geography*, 2nd ed. (London: John Stockdale, 1792), 383.

151. Isaac Weld, Jr., *Travels through the states of North America, and the provinces of upper and lower Canada, during the years 1795, 1796, and 1797* (London: Printed for John Stockdale, 1807), 168.

152. David Waldstreicher describes the often conflicting regional variations on national identity that vie with one another for dominance and the integral role print culture in the early national period played in these debates. Waldstreicher, *In the Midst of Perpetual Fetes: The Making of American Nationalism, 1776–1820* (Chapel Hill: University of North Carolina Press, 1997). See also Peter Onuf, "Federalism, Republicanism, and the Origins of American Sectionalism," in Edward Ayers, ed., *All Over the Map: Rethinking American Regions* (Baltimore: Johns Hopkins University Press, 1996), 11–37.

153. St. George Tucker, *A Letter from St. George Tucker, Esq. To The Reverend Jedidiah Morse* (Richmond, 1795; reprint, Richmond: William Byrd Press for the Institute of Early American History and Culture, 1953), 17. During his lifetime St. George Tucker (1752–1827) established himself as an author, jurist, and poet. He enrolled in the College of William and Mary in 1771 and soon thereafter was accepted as a law student. For general information on Tucker, see *American National Biography*, s.v. "St. George Tucker."

154. Tucker, *A Letter from St. George Tucker, Esq. To The Reverend Jedidiah Morse*, 6.

155. L. H. Butterfield, foreword to St. George Tucker, *A Letter from St. George Tucker, Esq. To The Reverend Jedidiah Morse*, viii.

156. Tucker's American edition of Sir William Blackstone's *Commentaries on the Laws of England* first became popular in Virginia and later spread to readers across the east coast of the United States. St. George Tucker, *Blackstone's Commentaries: With Notes of Reference, to the Constitution and Laws, of the Federal Government of the United States, and of the Commonwealth of Virginia*, 5 vols. (Philadelphia: W.Y. Birch and A. Small, 1803).

157. St. George Tucker, *A Dissertation on Slavery: With A Proposal for the Gradual Abolition of It, in the State of Virginia* (Philadelphia: Mathew Carey, 1796), 156–157, and *A Letter to a Member of the General Assembly of Virginia on the Subject of the Late*

Conspiracy of the Slaves; with a Proposal for their Colonization (Baltimore: Bonsal & Niles, 1801).

158. Tucker, *Letter from St. George Tucker to Jedidiah Morse*, 4.

159. Jay was sent to resolve many important issues that resulted from the Revolutionary War. Among the most important concessions given to the Americans was the British promise to leave the Northwest Territory as promised in 1783. They also allowed trade with the Caribbean and India in exchange for limits on cotton exports. Jefferson and his followers strongly opposed strengthening trade ties with Britain because among other things, they feared it would be to the advantage of their political rivals and they favored strengthening the nation's relationship with France. This treaty was seen by contemporaries and modern scholars as re-creating America's special relationship with Great Britain. See James Roger Sharp, *American Politics in the Early Republic: The New Nation in Crisis* (New Haven, Conn.: Yale University Press, 1993), 113–137; Stanley Elkins and Eric McKitrick, *The Age of Federalism* (New York: Oxford University Press, 1993), 303–373; Joseph Charles, *Origins of the Party System* (Williamsburg, Va.: Institute of Early American History and Culture, 1956).

160. L. H. Butterfield, foreword to Tucker, *Letter from St. George Tucker to Jedidiah Morse*, viii. Jack Greene has argued that in the colonial period, the British were more aware of the differences between various American colonial identities than the colonists themselves. Perhaps because they dealt more often with both groups, men in London could more clearly make this distinction. "The Constitution of 1787 and the Question of Southern Distinctiveness," in Greene, *Imperatives, Behaviors, and Identities: Essays in Early American Cultural History* (Charlottesville: University Press of Virginia, 1992), 327–347.

161. James Freeman, *Remarks on the American Universal Geography* (Boston: Belknap and Hall, 1793). It seems turnabout is fair play: Morse had previously attacked Freeman, a religious liberal, for a collection of children's songs he published. See Phillips, *Jedidiah Morse and New England Congregationalism*, 36–37.

162. Robert Davidson, *Geography Epitomised [sic]; or a Tour Round the World: Being a Short but Comprehensive Description of the Terraqueous Globe: Attempted in Verse By an American* ([London]: Philadelphia: printed by J[oseph] Crukshank, London, 1784, re-printed and sold by T. Wilkins, Philadelphia, 1786). Subsequent publications of the book included versions published in Burlington, New Jersey (by Neale & Lawrence, 1791); Leominster [Massachusetts?] (C. Whitcomb, 179[?]); Morristown, New Jersey (Henry P. Russell, 1803); and Stanford, New York (Daniel Lawrence, 1803). See also Thomas Greenleaf, *Geographical Gazetteer of the Towns of the Commonwealth of Massachusetts* [no title page. Boston: Printed by Greenleaf and Freeman, 1784–1785]. A gazetteer is a reference book that lists settlements and natural features and their exact locations in alphabetical order. See Brooke Hindle, *The Pursuit of Science in Revolutionary America* (New York: Norton, 1956), 317. Thomas Greenleaf (1755–1798) "was a printer and publisher who was born in Abington, Massachusetts, the son of Joseph Greenleaf, a justice of the peace and popular writer, and Abigail Payne." *American National Biography,* s.v. "Greenleaf, Thomas."

163. William Channing Woodbridge (1794–1845), born in Medford, Massachusetts, the son of a clergyman and educator, entered Yale College at thirteen years of age. In 1817, he took a position at the recently founded American Asylum for the Deaf and Dumb in Hartford. *Dictionary of National Biography,* s.v. "William Channing Woodbridge."

164. William Woodbridge, *Rudiments of geography, on a new plan designed to assist the memory by comparison and classification: with numerous engravings of manners, cus-*

toms and curiosities: accompanied with an atlas exhibiting the prevailing religions, forms of government, degrees of civilization, and the comparative size of towns, rivers, and mountains (Hartford: S. Goodrich, 1822) (unless otherwise noted, all subsequent citations are to this edition). This work went through up to nineteen editions spanning two decades, including the following, all published in Hartford: Oliver D. Cooke & Sons, 1825; O.D. Cooke, 1826; Oliver D. Cooke & Co., 1828; Oliver D. Cooke & Co., 1829; Beach and Beckwith, 1835; and J. Beach, 1838. "Preparatory lessons," questions, and atlases were included in the text. Oliver D. Cooke also separately published *School Atlas to Accompany Woodbridge's Rudiments of Geography* in 1827 and 1828.

165. Other objects reflect this ambiguity as well. For instance, how would one label a tall clock made from American wood and English mechanical pieces or a painting done by an American-born painter in the employ of the British monarch?

166. The majority of children's books of this period did not record the significant political changes. *The New England Primer* was first published in the late seventeenth century—issues of it were published in 1683 and 1690; however, the first extant version was published in 1727. Other eighteenth-century primers include *Tom Thumb's Play Book* and *The American Primer.*

167. Goldsmith, *General View.*

168. J. Goldsmith [Richard Phillips], *A view of the character, manners, and customs of the North- Americans: comprehending an account of the northern Indians, of the inhabitants of Oonalashka and Nootka Sound, of the Five Indian Nations of Canada, of the inhabitants of the United States, &c.: in which are displayed all the remarkable curiosities which are to be found in those countries* (Philadelphia: Johnson and Warner; J. Bouvier, printer, 1810).

169. Philips (1767–1840) defined the function of geographies in his introduction to Goldsmith, *General View.* According to Philips, maps were important because they exposed people to the "science that teaches the 'natural and artificial' divisions of the earth's surface, the relative positions of places, the productions and curiosities of countries, and the manners and customs of their inhabitants," iii.

170. Ibid., iii.

171. Ibid., 15.

172. Ibid., 24; my emphasis.

173. The author wrote that Scotland boasted a "valiant, hardy, industrious, well-informed, and temperate race of people." Ibid., 25. For more on the construction of British identity, see Linda Colley, *Britons* (New Haven, Conn.: Yale University Press, 1992).

174. The narrative follows how the "English government out-witted" Spain by engaging to take a large amount of her wines, which "induced [Spain] to admit the importation of English manufactures, on paying a light duty,—and this destroyed [Spain's] internal industry." Spain had "possessed large tracts of country in America, celebrated for silver," but these valuable New World possessions, "instead of enriching, has contributed to enervate and impoverish" Spain. At the end of this exposition, readers are told that the mistakes of other European colonial powers were instructive for the English people. "Spain presents a picture, which should be a warning both to government and people." He goes on to say, "But this was not all that led her to idleness and poverty...while the people become idle, the clergy became industrious in *systematising beggary*—just as the clergy are now doing in America,—and the immense wealth thus acquired enabled them to bid a bounty for hypocrisy, to overawe the government, and to establish the inquisition:—and, as like causes produce like effects, we may anticipate the same things in America.—But the fault does not rest entirely with *our* clergy:—the people in many

instances have been very parsimonious towards them, and their services have not been half compensated—with strict economy, they have been so embarrassed with debts as to unfit them for the pulpit—Had they received that liberal support to which their services justly entitle them, in all probability there would have been less cause of complaint. It is to them we are indebted for the best traits in our character:—by their precepts and example we become more mild—more sociable—more just—and more friendly to each other. So long as the Sabbath is to be sanctified we cannot dispense with their services;—and he who faithfully and honestly labours at the altar is as justly entitled to support, as he who labours at the plough." Goldsmith, *General View*, 23.

175. Ibid., 285.

176. Ibid., 307, 308–311.

177. Students using this book took Great Britain as a point of reference in exercises that instructed them to draw meridians and parallels for a map of Great Britain when given its latitude and longitude. Each colonial settlement had its own time—sufficient as late as the advent of railroads in the nineteenth century, which made standardization a necessity. To calculate exact sun time, one must figure out longitude. The first observatory to do authoritative work on this was in Greenwich. Therefore, their calculations were used on maps and nautical charts. The British, on January 13, 1848, became the first to adopt a standardized time for their entire nation. Until the late 1870s, no other nation did so. This could not work for the United States, of course, as it is spread out so widely. Robert E. Riegel, "Standard Time in the United States," *American Historical Review* 33 (October 1927): 84.

178. Woodbridge, *Rudiments of Geography,* 47. Europe is the only place mentioned. He admits that the compilation was made with maps from "a number of the best works of American and English geographers and travelers." This is the second edition, due to the "great and unexpected demand that exhausted the first edition immediately after its publication, and the approbation it has received from instructors of youth and gentlemen of high respectability." In this second edition, the author noted his debt to the *Edinburgh Gazetteer* from which he "derived much aid" and "some other recent publications, which he could not before obtain" (x).

179. Joseph C. Hart, *An abridgment of geographical exercises, for practical examinations on maps written for the Junior Department on the New-York high schools, and adopted by the public school society. Accompanied by an atlas of fourteen maps,* 2nd ed. (Philadelphia: J. Grigg and A. Finley, 1827), 22.

180. Goldsmith, *General View,* 42–43.

181. Ibid., 40–41.

182. The Senior Editor continues: "were her farmers to erect *spring-houses* and *ice-houses,* which can be done on every farm, and at little expense, their dairies would yield to them 10 per cent more profit, without estimating the great convenience to themselves.— In Pennsylvania, they are very common, although living-springs and stone are not so plenty there as in New England." Ibid.

183. For instance, Richard Phillips describes Great Britain as a "Limited Monarchy" in which the "will of sovereign is subordinate to and restrained by certain laws" and a "Military Republic" as a "government under name republic, in which supreme power is usurped by some of the chiefs of the army; such as that of France was a few years since, and such was that of Great Britain in the time of Cromwell. Rev. J. Goldsmith, [Richard Phillips], *A General View of the Manners, Customs, and Curiosities of Nations,* vol. 1 (Philadephia: Johnson & Warner, 1810), xliii.

184. Among the works Goldsmith consulted were Thomas Anburey, *Travels Through the Interior Parts of America* (London: Printed for W. Lane, 1789); Aeneas Anderson's *A*

Narrative of the British Embassy to China (London: J. Debrett, 1795); Cadwallader Colden's *The History of the Five Indian Nations Depending on the Province of New-York in America* (New York: Bradford, 1727); David Collin's *An Account of the English Colony in New South Wales,* 2 vols. (London: Printed for T. Cadell, Jr., and W. Davies, 1798–1802). He notes that in "compiling these accounts of manners, customs, curiosities and c. of other nations, the following works, among a multitude of others have been consulted and are *the authorities* relative to the several countries on which the fact and anecdotes are inserted." Goldsmith, introduction to *General View,* 1:v.

185. In 1820, Woodbridge journeyed to southern Europe in order to regain his failing health and on this trip decided to write a geography. In July 1821, he returned to Connecticut and devoted his time to preparing his highly successful *Rudiments of Geography.* He also worked with Emma Willard, a teacher at the Female Seminary at Troy, New York, on *Universal Geography, Ancient and Modern* (1824), which was also very successful and had a large number of imitators. Woodbridge returned to Europe later the same year when his health failed once again. He first went to England in order to secure in London publication of *Woodbridge's Geography* (1827). See *American National Biography,* s.v. "William Channing Woodbridge." See Amy DeRogatis, "Moral Geography: The Plan of Union Mission to the Western Reserve, 1787–1833" (Ph.D. Dissertation: University of North Carolina at Chapel Hill, 1998) and DeRogatis, *Moral Geography: Maps, Missionaries, and the American Frontier* (New York: Columbia University Press, 2002).

186. See Benedict Anderson's discussion of the significance of maps in the colonial and postcolonial contexts. Anderson, "Census, Map, Museum," chap. 10 of *Imagined Communities,* rev. ed. (London: Verso, 1991): 163–185.

187. Woodbridge, *Rudiments of Geography,* 5th ed. (Hartford: Oliver D. Cooke & Sons, 1825), 50.

188. Zachariah Allen, *The Practical Tourist, or Sketches of the State of the Useful Arts, and of Society, Scenery, &c. &c. in Great-Britain, France and Holland* (Boston: Richardson, Lord & Holbrook, 1832), 70–71.

189. Ibid.

190. Ibid., 71.

191. Woodbridge, *Rudiments of Geography.*

192. Ibid.

193. Ibid.

194. J[ohn]. Pershouse to J[ames]. P[ershouse], dated Kingswinford [Pennsylvania], December 10, 1805, John Pershouse Correspondence and Papers, 1749–1899, Manuscripts Collection, American Philosophical Society, Philadelphia. The correspondence in this collection consists mainly of letters between John Pershouse and his brother James who was living in England. The collection also contains an interesting travel journal kept by John Pershouse in the years 1800–1838 that includes his observations about American life. John Pershouse began his career as a merchant near Manchester, England, before coming to America. Although he had not originally intended to stay in the United States, he was involved in a dry goods importation business and real estate ventures in the Philadelphia area between 1801–1815. After that, he left the United States for his native England but returned two years later. As a longtime resident of the new nation, the comparisons he makes between American and British society have more depth than that of other British travelers' accounts. For more on Pershouse, see James Tagg, "John Pershouse's American Sojourn, 1801–1815: The Prospect of Becoming Modern in the New Republic," *Journal of the Early Republic* 5, 1 (Spring 1985): 59–93.

195. Ibid.

196. See Billy G. Smith, ed., *Down and Out in Early America* (University Park, Penn.: Pennsylvania State University Press, 2004); Billy G. Smith, *The "Lower Sort": Philadelphia's Laboring People, 1750–1800* (Ithaca, N.Y.: Cornell University Press, 1990); Terry Bouton, *Taming Democracy: "The People," the Founders, and the Troubled Ending of the American Revolution* (New York: Oxford University Press, 2007).

197. Goldsmith, *General View,* 290.

198. Benjamin Martin, *The Description and Use of Both the Globes, the Armillary Sphere, and Orrery,* 2nd ed. (London: Bigg and Cox, 1773), iii.

199. Goldsmith, *General View,* 291.

200. Ibid.

201. Samuel Stanhope Smith to Sam[ue]l Bayard, Esq., December 26, 1796, Samuel Stanhope Smith Collection, Firestone Library, Princeton University.

202. Ibid.

203. The collection of the Library of Congress, Geography and Map Division, contains several of Wilson's globes, including a thirteen-inch terrestrial globe (1811), three copies of his three-inch globes, and six of his thirteen-inch terrestrial and celestial globes.

204. The first phrase is a reference to Benedict Anderson's *Imagined Communities* and the second is from Eric Hobsbawm and Terence Ranger, eds., *The Invention of Tradition* (Cambridge: Cambridge University Press, 1992), a collection of essays.

205. See Jean-Christophe Agnew, "Coming Up for Air," in Brewer and Porter, *Consumption and the World of Goods,* 19–39.

CHAPTER 2

1. William Stephens Smith (1755–1816), who served as John Adams's secretary, married John Adams's eldest daughter Abigail "Nabby" Adams Smith (1765–1813). *American National Biography,* s.v. "Smith, William Stephens."

2. Lafayette found out about Jefferson's request through the French Foreign Ministry, through which Jefferson had to apply to bring the forbidden article into France. O'Brien interprets Lafayette's tone as teasing, but Jefferson did not find the matter amusing in the least. Thomas Jefferson to Marie Joseph Paul Yves Roch Gilbert du Motier, Marquis de Lafayette, November 3, 1786, in *The Papers of Thomas Jefferson,* ed. Julian P. Boyd et al., 33 vols. (Princeton, N.J.: Princeton University Press, 1954), 10:397–398. See William Howard Adams, *The Paris Years of Thomas Jefferson* (New Haven, Conn.: Yale University Press, 2000), 202; Conor Cruise O'Brien, *The Long Affair: Thomas Jefferson and the French Revolution, 1785–1800* (Chicago: University of Chicago Press, 1996), 32.

3. For a discussion about the significance of public and private debt in the lives of the founding generation, see Herbert E. Sloan, *Principle and Interest: Thomas Jefferson and the Problem of Debt* (New York: Oxford University Press, 1995).

4. We have many modern-day examples of this, including the boycotting of table grapes and clothing made in sweatshops in protest of unfair labor practices—and the various incarnations of "buy American" campaigns meant to stimulate domestic production and therefore strengthen the U.S. economy.

5. From a social science perspective, Craig Calhoun defines asymmetrical exchange in the following terms: "Symmetrical exchange describes a marriage system in which the men of one group may marry the women of a second group, and vice versa. Asymmetrical exchange reflects an element of non-reciprocity, as when men from one

group are barred from marrying women of a second group and must seek wives from a third group. In such systems, there emerges a distinction between wife-givers and wife-takers." See Craig Calhoun, ed., *Dictionary of the Social Sciences* (Oxford: Oxford University Press, 2002), 252–253.

6. Interestingly, historians from earlier in the twentieth century recognized this phenomenon. Subsequent generations of scholars ignored this aspect of early American history, perhaps as a result of the United States' subsequent ascendancy as a world power. See, for instance, John Allen Krout and Dixon Ryan Fox's synthetic history, *The Completion of Independence, 1790–1830* (New York: Macmillan, 1944).

7. Benjamin Franklin, to Mary Stevenson, letter dated Philadelphia, March 25, 1763, in *The Papers of Benjamin Franklin*, vol. 10, ed. Leonard W. Labaree (New Haven, Conn.: Yale University Press, 1959), 232–233; William Eddis (1738–1825), letter to unnamed recipient dated Annapolis, [Maryland,] June 8, 1770, in Eddis, *Letters from America*, ed. Aubrey Land (Cambridge, Mass.: The Belknap Press of the Harvard University Press, 1969), 32. Historian Kenneth Silverman noted the "vast inverse proportion of territory to accomplishment between England and her American colonies." Silverman, *A Cultural History of the American Revolution* (New York: Crowell, 1976), 9.

8. *The Power and Grandeur of Great-Britain, Founded on the Liberty of the Colonies, and the Mischiefs Attending the Taxing of Them* (New York: James Parker, 1768), copy in Rare Books and Manuscripts, The Huntington Library, San Marino, California. See also T. H. Breen, "Narrative of Commercial Life: Consumption, Ideology, and Community on the Eve of the American Revolution," *William and Mary Quarterly*, 3rd ser., 50 (1993): 473–474; John J. McCusker and Russell R. Menard, *The Economy of British America, 1607–1789* (Chapel Hill, N.C.: Omohundro Institute for Early American History and Culture, 1991), 310.

9. *Power and Grandeur of Great-Britain*, 5; also quoted in Breen, "Narrative of Commercial Life," 473–474, n. 11.

10. Eddis, *Letters from America*, 74. The quote goes on to say, "In vain is encouragement held forth to induce ingenious artisans to emigrate from their original situations. On their arrival either the allurements which tempted them deceive their expectations, or the natural wish to obtain a permanent establishment supersedes every other consideration, and induces a great majority of these adventurers to purchase lands which comparatively bear no price, and the purchasers are reduced to rely on time and industry to recompence their assiduity," 75.

11. McCusker and Menard, *Economy of British America*, 310.

12. Various governmental regulations restricting trade in particular types of commodities such as iron were adopted.

13. By 1775, Scottish factors had established a dominant role in the American economy. The *Oxford English Dictionary* defines "factor" as "one who buys and sells for another person; a mercantile agent; a commission merchant. Also in combination, as corn-, cotton-, produce-, wool-, etc. factor." "Scottish Commerce and the American War of Independence," Economic History Review 9, no. 1 (1956): 123–131.

14. [William Knox], *The Interest of the Merchants and Manufacturers of Great Britain, in the Present Contest with the Colonies, Stated and Considered* (London, 1774), quoted in McCusker and Menard, *Economy of British America*, 310.

15. British manufacturers were not the only ones to increase their productivity over the eighteenth century. North American exports grew from approximately a quarter of a million pounds a year at the turn of the century to around a million and a half pounds

per year between 1771 and 1775. During the period 1768–1772, Great Britain took in 55 percent of the value of all American exports. See James F. Shepard, "British America and the Atlantic Economy," in Ronald Hoffman, ed., *The Economy of Early America: The Revolutionary Period, 1763–1790* (Charlottesville: Published for the United States Capitol Historical Society by the University Press of Virginia, 1998), 8.

16. For more on the mercantile system and the development of the American economy see McCusker and Menard, *Economy of British America*; McCusker, "British Mercantilist Policies and the American Colonies," in Stanley Engerman and Robert Gallman, eds., *The Cambridge Economic History of the United States*, vol. 1 (Cambridge: Cambridge University Press, 1996), 337–362; John Crowley, *The Privileges of Independence: Neomercantilism and the American Revolution* (Baltimore: Johns Hopkins University Press, 1993). For an essay collection that discusses various aspects of early American economy, see Cathy Matson, ed., *The Economy of Early America: Historical Perspectives and New Directions* (University Park: Pennsylvania State University Press, 2006). See also Hoffman, *Economy of Early America*.

17. As much as 90 percent of the goods from the mother country consumed by the colonists were either manufactured or semi-manufactured commodities. Colonials purchased around half of England's exports of goods such as copperware, ironware, glassware, earthenware, silk goods, flannels, printed cotton, and linen goods. In addition, between two-thirds and three-quarters of all exported English cordage, iron nails, beaver hats, and linen and woolen goods landed in British North America. T. S. Ashton, editor's introduction to Elizabeth Schumpeter, *English Overseas Trade Statistics, 1697–1808* (Oxford: Oxford University Press, 1960), 10.

18. *Power and Grandeur of Great-Britain*. See note 12.

19. Per capita demand grew as individual levels of wealth and income increased, and colonists turned to others for goods they had heretofore made themselves. Between 1720 and 1770, per capita imports to the British North American colonies from Great Britain rose by about 50 percent. The rise in demand was spread fairly evenly throughout this period, with a slight increase in rate between 1750 and 1770 as compared to the first thirty years. Per capita colonial imports from the metropolis grew by more than one-third between 1700 and 1770, at an annual compound rate of about 0.4 percent. For an estimation of the retail costs of these imports, see Carole Shammas, "How Self-sufficient Was Early America?" *Journal of Interdisciplinary History* 13 (1982): 263–265. The figures are from McCusker and Menard, *Economy of British America*, 279.

20. Specifically, the years referred to here are 1607–1775. This was fueled by a significant growth in the colonial population and improvements in communication and transportation, particularly the coastwide trade that stimulated absolute demand. A thorough study of English ledgers has yet to be completed. These records are important for my purposes, because they provide evidence of what American colonists imported from London and other British ports. The colonial naval officer shipping lists are not useful for this purpose because for the most part they did not record the contents of the bales and boxes imported from the mother country. My thinking on this subject is informed by McCusker and Menard, *Economy of British America*, esp. 277–294. Probate records and archaeological digs indicate that people of all socioeconomic strata purchased more expensive items with which to serve their food and set their tables. Poorer consumers switched from handmade wooden plates to pottery, while their richer neighbors traded up from rough pottery to finer, imported wares (286).

21. Michael Zakim, "Sartorial Ideologies: From Homespun to Ready-Made," *American Historical Review* 106, no. 5 (2001): 1560. See also Zakim, *Ready-Made Democracy:*

A History of Men's Dress in the American Republic, 1760–1860 (Chicago: University of Chicago Press, 2003).

22. It should be noted here that the labels "luxuries" and "necessities" are themselves socially constructed. Quote from Stanley Elkins and Eric McKitrick, *The Age of Federalism: The Early American Republic, 1788–1800* (New York: Oxford University Press, 1993), 20. See also John Crowley, *The Invention of Comfort: Sensibilities and Design in Early Modern Britain and Early America* (Baltimore: Johns Hopkins University Press, 2001).

23. Benjamin Rush to [probably] Jacob Rush, January 26, 1769, in *Letters of Benjamin Rush*, ed. L. H. Butterfield, vol. 1 (Princeton, N.J.: Princeton University Press, 1951), 74–75. Also quoted in Michael K. Brown, "Piecing Together the Past: Recent Research on the American China Manufactory 1769–1772," Proceedings of the American Philosophical Society 133, no. 4 (1989): 559.

24. Susan Gray Detweiler, *George Washington's Chinaware* (New York: Abrams, 1982), 9.

25. Eddis, *Letters from America*, 75.

26. Bonnin was born in Antigua in 1741; educated at Eton, he came to America from England in 1769. Morris was born in Philadelphia. *(Philadelphia) Pennsylvania Gazette*, September 5, 1771. It is said the Bonnin probably learned the trade at the Bow Factory in England. The partners applied to the Pennsylvania Assembly for a loan. For additional biographical information, see Graham Hood, *Bonnin and Morris of Philadelphia: The First American Porcelain Factory, 1770–1772* (Chapel Hill: University of North Carolina Press, 1972), and Brown, "Piecing Together the Past."

27. *(Philadelphia) Pennsylvania Gazette*, August 1, 1771. Both Hood and Brown attribute the authorship of this broadside to Bonnin. See Hood, *Bonnin and Morris of Philadelphia*, 18–19, and Brown, "Piecing Together the Past," 562.

28. Ibid.

29. See essays in Francis J. Puig and Michael Conforti, eds., *The American Craftsman and the European Tradition 1620–1820* (Minneapolis, Minn.: Minneapolis Institute of Arts; Hanover, N.H.: Distributed by University Press of New England, 1989), especially Gary B. Nash, "A Historical Perspective on Early American Artisans," 1–13, and Barbara McLean Ward, "The European Tradition and the Shaping of the American Artisan," 14–22. Also see essays in Catherine E. Hutchins, ed., *Shaping a National Culture: The Philadelphia Experience, 1750–1800* (Winterthur, Del.: Henry Francis du Pont Winterthur Museum, 1994), in particular David L. Barquist, "'The Honours of a Court' or 'the Severity of Virtue': Household Furnishings and Cultural Aspirations in Philadelphia," 313–333.

30. *(Philadelphia)* Pennsylvania Gazette, August 1, 1771.

31. Benjamin Franklin to Deborah Franklin, letterbook draft, letter dated January 28, 1772, Rare Books and Manuscripts, American Philosophical Society. Humphrey Marshall mentions the manufactory as well. Marshall writes: "Our Collonies [sic] is Gone into the Importation of Goods by accounts more Largely than Ever. However I hope their remains Such a Sprerit [sic] to promote Industry and frugallity [sic] among the ablest of the farmers that they Will Purchase But as few of their Goods and they Can Well avoid. Our China Manefactury [sic] I hope will Improve and the Making of Derible[?] flint Glass Seems to make noise among us." Humphrey Marshall to Benjamin Franklin, letterbook draft, letter dated West Bradford Chester County Pensilvania the 27th. of the 11th. mo 1771, Rare Books and Manuscripts, American Philosophical Society.

32. Benjamin Franklin to Deborah Franklin, letterbook draft, letter dated London, January 28, 1772, Rare Books and Manuscripts, American Philosophical Society.

33. *(Philadelphia) Pennsylvania Gazette*, August 1, 1771.

34. Joseph Shippen, Jr., to Edward Shippen, Esqr., February 26, 1771, typescript letter, original manuscript unlocated, Shippen Papers, Manuscript Group 375, New Jersey Historical Society, Newark, also quoted in Brown, "Piecing Together the Past," 562.

35. Josiah Wedgewood, *An address to the workmen in the pottery, on the subject of entering into the service of foreign manufacturers* (Newcastle: J. Smith, 1783), 8.

36. *(Philadelphia) Pennsylvania Gazette* (May 5, 1773). On April 20, 1774, another notice was published in the *Pennsylvania Gazette* that announced the sale of Bonnin's property: "by virtue of a writ to me directed, will be sold by public vendue and signed by William Dewees, Sheriff." The notice informs the public that the lot "containing by computation one acre and an half" will be sold along with "sundry implements used in the business of China making." Apparently, Bonnin's estate was seized by the sheriff.

Reputedly, by the turn of the nineteenth century, the former factory was "famous as a sailor's brothel and riothouse on a large scale." John F. Watson, *Annals of Philadelphia, Being a Collection of Memoirs, Anecdotes, and Incidents of the City and its Inhabitants From the Days of the Pilgrim Founders* (Philadelphia: E. L. Carey & A. Hart, 1830), 680, also quoted in Brown, "Piecing Together the Past," 555.

37. Susan Myers, "The Business of Potting, 1780–1840," in Myers, ed., *The Craftsman in Early America* (New York: Norton, 1984), 190–233.

38. Eddis, *Letters from America*, 73.

39. The number of sheep per capita in eastern Massachusetts declined by almost one-fourth during the four decades preceding the Stamp Act. The textile manufacturing industry in America was minuscule in comparison to that in Great Britain. Another contributing factor was that Great Britain was much more technologically advanced and techniques common in Europe were not yet introduced in America. For a comparative overview of textiles see Mary Schoeser and Celia Rufey, *English and American Textiles* (New York: Thames and Hudson, 1989), 11.

40. See Linda Baumgarten, *What Clothes Reveal: The Language of Clothing in Colonial and Federal America* (New Haven, Conn.: Yale University Press, 2002), especially chap. 3, "Homespun and Silk: American Clothing," 76–105.

41. This is a product of the colonial revival movement of later years. For an interesting discussion of this movement, see Laurel Thatcher Ulrich, *Age of Homespun: Objects and Stories in the Creation of an American Myth* (New York: Knopf, 2001).

42. Baumgarten, *What Clothes Reveal*, 78.

43. There are many different spellings of "osnaburg," including "ozenbrig," "oznabrig," and "osnaburgh." This coarse, unbleached linen or hempen cloth first made in Osnabruck, Germany, was commonly used for trousers, sacks, and bags. In America, it was used for overalls and farmers' clothing. Cambric was a fine white linen cloth in plain weave. Definitions of textiles can be found in Schoeser and Rufey, *English and American Textiles*. Examples of the types of linen textiles used in this period can be found in the collections of Colonial Williamsburg, Williamsburg, Virginia, including a man's shirt most likely owned by a resident of New Jersey around 1800 and a shift owned by Ann Van Rensselaer, of Albany, New York. This fabric was used for garments that had to be washed frequently, such as undergarments and bedding. See also Baumgarten, *What Clothes Reveal*, 78.

44. Baumgarten, *What Clothes Reveal*, 78.

45. Ibid.

46. Ibid.

47. It should be remembered that British consumers were also subject to laws that restricted their consumption habits. The vagaries of these protectionist laws created

different rules for the types of objects that could be legally consumed in various locations within the Anglo-American world. From early in the eighteenth century, certain East Indian textiles were banned from use in mainland Great Britain as a means of protecting the domestic woolen industry. A law passed in 1720 forbade wearing and using imported Indian cotton textiles in Britain. Prized for their "brilliant, colorfast hues and luxurious polished surface finish," these fabrics were only allowed to land in Britain for reexport to the colonies. As a result, colonial consumers could purchase a wide array of colorful alamodes, lustrings, wrought silks, and calicoes from the East Indies that were not available in the home markets. While enforcement of this law eased as the century progressed, it could still be invoked. The famous London furniture maker Thomas Chippendale did not manage to escape the wrath of custom officials, who seized Indian chintz from his workshop where he was creating bed hangings for his celebrated patrons. Ibid., 79.

48. See T. H. Breen, *The Marketplace of Revolution: How Consumer Politics Shaped American Independence* (New York: Oxford University Press, 2004).

49. Rush on Dr F[ranklin], April 19, 1788, Rare Books and Manuscripts, Library Company of Philadelphia.

50. Franklin subscribed to vegetarian principles very early in his life but gave them up when he ran away to Philadelphia. The habit also allowed him to save money that could be used to buy important things such as books. In Paris he dined well on copious amounts of both meat and liquor and on a particularly celebratory occasion on October 1, 1778, "drank a good deal of champagne." His personal inventory for 1782 included twelve hundred bottles of French wine. Karen Hess, "Historical Notes," in Hannah Glasse, *The Art of Cookery Made Plain and Easy; Excelling any Thing of the Kind ever yet published* (reprint; Bedford, Mass.: Applewood Books, 1997), v–vi. Yale University owns several editions of this popular cookbook, whose dates of publication range from the mid-eighteenth century through the first decades of the nineteenth century. Editions of the book were published in America and in Great Britain. See for example an early English edition: Hannah Glasse, *The art of cookery, made plain and easy; which far exceeds any thing of the kind ever yet published; By a lady* (London: printed for the author; and sold at Mrs. Ashburn's, a China-Shop, 1747). For an edition published in Scotland, see Hannah Glasse, *The art of cookery, made plain and easy. To which are added one hundred and fifty new receipts, a copious index, and a modern bill of fare* (Edinburgh: A. Donaldson, 1774). For an example of a later American edition, see Hannah Glasse, *The art of cookery made plain and easy: excelling any thing of the kind ever yet published; also, the order of a bill of fare for each month, in the manner the dishes are to be placed upon the table, in the present taste by Mrs. Glasse. New ed. with modern improvements* (Alexandria, Va.: Printed by Cottom and Stewart, 1812).

51. Franklin, *The Private Life of the Late Benjamin Franklin* (London: J. Parsons, 1793), 78. The impulse to both emulate and repudiate the former mother country is one that commonly characterizes postcolonial societies. My thinking about this complex phenomenon is greatly informed by the work of Gayatri Chakravorty Spivak, Gyan Prakash, and others in the Subaltern Studies Group, who write about a very different yet, in my opinion, not unrelated subject. The phrasing I use in this sentence is inspired by that of Spivak, who noted that the philosophical position of postcolonial criticism entails saying an "impossible 'no' to a structure, which one critiques, yet inhabits intimately." "The Making of Americans, the Teaching of English, the Future of Colonial Studies," *New Literary History* 21 (1990): 28. Gyan Prakash provides a commentary on Spivak's point in his useful historiographic review essay "Subaltern Studies as Postcolonial

Criticism," *American Historical Review* 99, no. 5 (December 1994): 1475–1490. This was the leading essay in a special issue devoted to the work of the Subaltern Studies Group.

52. Franklin, *Private Life of the Late Benjamin Franklin*, 78 (my emphasis).

53. Ibid.

54. Benjamin Franklin to Deborah Franklin, letterbook draft, letter dated January 28, 1772, Rare Books and Manuscripts, American Philosophical Society.

55. The gendered meanings of Franklin's statement about consumption, freedom, and the colonial's place in the emerging eighteenth-century world of goods is important to note. For more on this see Mary Louise Roberts, "Gender, Consumption, and Commodity Culture," *American Historical Review* 103 (June 1998): 817–844.

56. Benjamin Franklin to Deborah Franklin, February 19, 1758, in *Papers of Benjamin Franklin*, vol. 7, ed. Leonard W. Labaree (New Haven, Conn.: Yale University Press, 1963), 381.

57. Ibid.

58. Europeans ridiculed Americans for their lack of knowledge of how to properly display and utilize the latest fashionable items. George Washington had no idea where to place the gift he received from a compatriot who had just returned from Europe. Brissot de Warville and Moreau de Saint-Mery were scandalized by the fact that Americans left their floors carpeted during the stifling hot summer months. Brissot de Warville haughtily pronounced: "A carpet in summer is an absurdity." Jacques Pierre Brissot de Warville, *Travels in The United States of America Performed in 1788*, vol. 1 (London: R.S. Jordan, 1794), 270. Similarly, American women were ridiculed by European observers for their overenthusiastic embrace of fashion. If bows on gowns were all the rage in the metropole, then the Americans would cover their entire dresses with them, thinking that more was surely better.

59. Benjamin Franklin to Deborah Franklin, letterbook draft, letter dated London, Feb. 19, 1758, Rare Books and Manuscripts, American Philosophical Society.

60. Richard Bushman, *The Refinement of America: Persons, Houses, Cities* (New York: Knopf, 1992); see also John Kasson, *Rudeness and Civility: Manners in Nineteenth-century Urban America* (New York: Hill and Wang, 1990). See also the classic study by Norbert Elias, *The Civilizing Process* (New York: Pantheon Books, 1978). This work has influenced many subsequent studies including my own.

61. Samuel Adams to Arthur Lee, October 31, 1771, in *The Writings of Samuel Adams*, ed. Harry Alonzo Cushing, vol. 2 (New York: Putnam, 1905), 267. This description was originally brought to my attention by T. H. Breen's aptly titled "'Baubles of Britain': The American and Consumer Revolutions of the Eighteenth Century," *Past and Present* 119 (1988): 73–104.

62. Adam Smith, *The Theory of Moral Sentiments* (London: A. Millar, 1760), 1.3.16.

63. For the theoretical basis of this analysis, see the collection of essays in Arjun Appadurai, ed., *The Social Life of Things* (Cambridge: Cambridge University Press, 1986).

64. Kenneth Silverman notes: "Each fresh accession of some major element of European culture brought confident visions of an American Empire." *Cultural History of the American Revolution*, 11.

65. For more on the idea and its influence on American culture, see William Andrews, "The *Translatio Studii* as a Theme in Eighteenth-century American Writing" (Ph.D. diss., University of Pennsylvania, 1971).

66. This theory also had empire-building (*translatio imperii*) and religious (*translatio religii*) components. These notions were linked with the millenarian religious convictions

in the westward march of enlightenment, empire, and the arts. See Michael Sletcher, "The Rise of Heterodoxy and Civic Education in Seventeenth-Century New England: A Transatlantic Study of the First Puritan Seminary in America" (Ph.D. diss., Cambridge University, 2002), especially chap. 4. For a discussion of the concept as it pertains to millennial beliefs in America, see Ruth H. Bloch, *Visionary Republic: Millennial Themes in American Thought, 1756–1800* (Cambridge: Cambridge University Press, 1985).

67. Jedidiah Morse, *American Universal Geography; or, A View of the Present Situation of the United States of America* (Boston: Thomas and Andrews, 1793), 630. A portion of this quote also appears in William Appleman Williams, *The Contours of American History* (Cleveland: World, 1963), 179. Williams misattributes the passage to Morse's earlier work Jedidiah Morse, *The American Geography; or, A view of the present situation of the United States of America* (London: Printed for J. Stockdale, 1792). It was also republished Jedidiah Morse, *The American Geography; or, A view of the present situation of the United States of America* (London: Printed for J. Stockdale, 1792).

68. Labaree, *Papers of Benjamin Franklin*, 10:232–233; Silverman, *Cultural History of the American Revolution*, 9.

69. *Works of John Adams*, ed. Charles Francis Adams, vol. 9 (Boston: Little, Brown, 1856), 600. According to Silverman, this belief had the "reassuring familiarity of a motto or the ending of a fable. This view was expressed in "newspapers, correspondence, and daily conversation." Silverman, *Cultural History of the American Revolution*, 9.

70. Eddis, *Letters from America*, 32.

71. Eddis noted that "store keepers of various denominations were encouraged to pursue the path which industry had pointed out. Warehouses were accordingly erected and woolens, linens, and implements of husbandry were first presented to the view of the labourous planter. As wealth and population increased, wants were created, and any considerable demands, in consequence, took place for the various elegancies as well as the necessities of life." Eddis, *Letters from America*, 100–101. This passage was also commented upon by T. H. Breen in "The Meaning of Things: Consumption and Ideology in the Eighteenth Century," in John Brewer and Roy Porter, eds., *Consumption and the World of Goods* (London: Routledge, 1993), 252. Many historians have found Eddis's observations on American society useful. James Axtell argues that Native Americans simultaneously embraced and resisted the influence of European goods in their lives. See Axtell, *The Invasion Within: The Contest of Cultures in Colonial North America* (New York: Oxford University Press, 1985).

72. In 1744, Franklin hailed the publication of Cicero's *Cato Major* as the "first Translation of a *Classic* in this *Western World*." Silverman puts it succinctly: "being the first, it portended the rest. Thus Franklin perceived the book as a 'happy Omen, that Philadelphia shall become the Seat of the American Muses.' Throughout the century (and to this day), Americans prided themselves on firsts," *Cultural History of the American Revolution*, 10.

73. Silverman, *Cultural History of the American Revolution*, 10.

74. For more on the subject, see Silverman, *Cultural History of the American Revolution*.

75. Gottlieb Mittelberger, *Journey to Pennsylvania* (Cambridge, Mass: Harvard University Press, 1960), 88–89. This quote was originally found in John Styles, "Manufacturing, Consumption and Design in Eighteenth-Century England," in John Brewer and Roy Porter, eds., *Consumption and the World of Goods* (London: Routledge, 1993), 527. Styles originally located this quote in T. H. Breen, "An Empire of Goods: The

Anglicization of Colonial America, 1690–1776," *Journal of British Studies* 25, no. 4 (October 1986): 489.

76. *Joshua Johnson's Letterbook 1771–1774—Letters from a merchant in London to his partners in Maryland*, ed. Jacob M. Price (London: London Record Society, 1979), xv.

77. Ibid., 8, 43–45.

78. Ibid., 21.

79. The work of William Hogarth depicting common scenes from middle-class life was also extremely popular on both sides of the water. As just one example, his series "The Idle and Industrious Prentice," was advertised in American papers from its initial publication in 1747 through 1771, after his death 1771. Silverman, Cultural History of the American Revolution, 12. For more on Hogarth, see Ronald Paulson, *The Art of Hogarth* (London: Phaidon Press, 1975), Mark Hallett, *Hogarth* (London: Phaidon Press, 2000), and Hallett, *The Spectacle of Difference: Graphic Satire in the Age of Hogarth* (New Haven, Conn.: Yale University Press, 1999).

80. Benedict Anderson discusses how the rise of print culture created a sense of shared identity in *Imagined Communities: Reflections on the Origins and Spread of Nationalism* (London: Verso, 1983).

81. See Carrie Rebora, *John Singleton Copley in America* (New York: Metropolitan Museum of Art, 1995), 248.

82. Revere had been trained by his father, a goldsmith, and most likely inherited his father's business at the time of his death in 1754.

83. For work on the politics of objects see Zakim, "Sartorial Ideologies," 1553–1586. See also Breen, "'Baubles of Britain'"; John J. McCusker, "The Current Value of English Exports, 1697 to 1800," *William and Mary Quarterly*, 3rd ser., 28 (October 1971): 623–627; Thomas M. Doerflinger, "Farmers and Dry Goods in the Philadelphia Market Area, 1750–1800," in Hoffman, *Economy of Early America*, 167–172; Max George Schumacher, "The Northern Farmer and His Markets during the Late Colonial Period" (Ph.D. diss., University of California, 1948), 140–142; Carole Shammas, *The Pre-industrial Consumer in England and America* (New York: Oxford University Press, 1990), 98–99, 269; Richard L. Bushman, "Shopping and Advertising in Colonial America," in Cary Carson, Ronald Hoffman, and Peter J. Albert eds., *Of Consuming Interests: The Style of Life in the Eighteenth Century* (Charlottesville: Published for the United States Capitol Historical Society by the University Press of Virginia, 1994), 233–251; Beverly Lemire, *Fashion's Favourite: The Cotton Trade and the Consumer in Britain, 1660–1800* (New York: Oxford University Press, 1991), 12–42, 100–114. For Revere, see Claudia Kidwell, introduction to Joan L. Severa, *Dressed for the Photographer: Ordinary Americans and Fashion, 1840–1900* (Kent, Ohio: Kent State University Press, 1995), ix–x.

84. The aspiring artist's sizeable clientele consisted mostly of merchants, clergymen, and their wives. One curator suggests that Copley was influenced by the European tradition of portraying artisans with the objects and tools of their craft or by images from the Northern Renaissance of goldsmiths, bankers, and jewelers. Rebora, *John Singleton Copley in America*, 248.

85. Albert Boime, "Art in the Age of Revolution," in Boime, *A Social History of Modern Art*, vol. 1 (Chicago: University of Chicago Press, 1987), 3–184.

86. The two men's relationship was documented in a 1773 broadside: "The People being informed by Col. Hancock, that Mr. Copley, Son-In-Law to Mr. Clarke, Sen. had acquainted him that the Tea Consignees did not receive their Letters from London till last Evening, and were so dispersed, that they could not have a joint Meeting early enough to make their Proposals at the Time intended; and there-fore were desirous of a

further Space for that Purpose." "At a meeting of the people of Boston and the neighboring towns at Faneuil-Hall" (Boston: Edes and Gill, November 29, 1773).

87. Both men were sons of immigrants to America. Copley's parents immigrated to America from Ireland; his mother was from Quinville and his father from Cork. Paul Revere's father was Apollos Rivoire (also known as Paul Revere, Sr.), a French Huguenot.

88. In-depth studies have been devoted to the social and cultural significance of portraiture. See especially Margaretta M. Lovell, *Art in a Season of Revolution: Painters, Artisans, and Patrons in Early America* (Philadelphia: University of Pennsylvania Press, 2005). See also Wayne Craven, *Colonial American Portraiture: The Economic, Religious, Social, Cultural, Philosophical, Scientific and Aesthetic Foundations* (Cambridge: Cambridge University Press, 1986), 341. For additional background on the portrait in American society, see Richard H. Saunders and Ellen G. Miles, *American Colonial Portraits, 1700–1776* (Washington, D.C.: Smithsonian Institution Press, 1987).

89. According to Emily Neff, the realism of his portraits is created by an "attention to the minutiae of patterned lace, his polished wood and metal surfaces, brilliant fabrics, and lustrous pearls, rendered with the precision of a master carver, tailor, or jeweler." Neff, "Copley's 'Native' Realism and His English 'Improvement'," in Neff, *John Singleton Copley in England* (London: Merrell Holberton, 1995), 12–13. The pictorial brilliance of the fabrics in Copley's portraits was considerably toned down after the anti-imperial protests began. See Rebora, *John Singleton Copley in America*. For a classic reference work on portraiture and painting in America in this period, see James Thomas Flexner, *American Painting: The Light of Distant Skies, 1760–1835* (New York: Harcourt, Brace, 1954); and Flexner, *America's Old Masters* (New York: Viking Press, 1939), *First Flowers of Our Wilderness* (Boston: Houghton Mifflin, 1947), and *A Short History of American Painting* (Boston: Houghton Mifflin, 1950). For a more recent survey, see Craven, *Colonial American Portraiture*. For a useful exhibition catalog see Saunders and Miles, *American Colonial Portraits*. For interpretive pieces, see Lovell, *Art in a Season of Revolution: Painters, Artisans and Patrons in Early America* (Philadelphia: University of Pennsylvania Press, 2007); T. H. Breen, "The Meaning of 'Likeness': American Portrait Painting in an Eighteenth-century Consumer Society," *Word and Image* 6, no. 4 (October–November 1990): 325–350.

90. Pro-American petitions were raised by groups within Britain between 1766 and 1775 by those who depended on colonial customers. Barlow Trecothick, a member of Parliament from London, organized petitions from twenty-five trading towns. These documents noted the economic hardship that resulted from the decrease in exports to North America and asked for the Stamp Act's repeal. Petitions to the House of Commons were made again in 1775 by leaders from manufacturing regions in Britain complaining of the interruption of trade and demanding relief from the dire situation. These efforts were too late, for by this time, nonimportation laws had gone into effect, and news was arriving about the Continental Congress's adoption of nonexportation acts. See Jacob Price, "Who Cared about the Colonies?" in Bernard Bailyn and Philip Morgan, eds., *Strangers within the Realm* (Chapel Hill: University of North Carolina Press, 1991), 412–414.

91. *The Boston Gazette, and Country Journal*, no. 698 (August 15, 1768), front page.

92. Benjamin Franklin to Lord Howe, Philadelphia, July 20, 1776, copy in Rare Books and Manuscripts, The Huntington Library, San Marino, California. Franklin must have been fond of the metaphor of the cracked vase, for his use of it was also mentioned by Silas Deane, letter from Ghent, February 1, 1782: "You say that You had long endeavored with unfeigned, & unwearied zeal to preserve from breaking that fine and noble china

Vase, the British Empire, for that You knew that being once broken, the separate parts could not retain even their share, of the Strength, & Value that existed in the whole, and that a perfect reunion of those parts could scarce ever be hoped for;—America and Great Britain are by dear purchased experience convinced of the truth of Your Observation." Copy in Rare Books and Manuscripts, University of Pennsylvania Library, Philadelphia, Pennsylvania.

93. Hutchinson had two sons who were agents of the British East India Company.

94. The name Boston Tea Party was originally a derisive one meant to mock the events of December 16, 1773. On the significance of the decision to dress as Native Americans, see Philip Deloria, *Playing Indian* (New Haven, Conn.: Yale University Press, 1999), especially 6–7, 31–32. Deloria discusses the materiality of "playing Indian": "Their feathers, blankets, headdresses, and war paint point to the fact that images of Indianness have often been translated into material forms."

95. See Alfred Fabian Young, *The Shoemaker and the Tea Party: Memory and the American Revolution* (Boston: Beacon Press, 1999).

96. Accounts of the historic event were published in the nineteenth century. For instance, see [Benjamin Bussey Thatcher], *Traits of The Tea Party; Being a Memoir of George R. T. Hewes, with a History of That Transaction; Reminiscences of the Massacre, and the Siege, and Other Stories of Old Times. By a Bostonian* (New York: Harper & Brothers, 1835); [James Hawkes], *A Retrospect of The Boston Tea-Party, with a Memoir of George R. T. Hewes, a Survivor of the Little Band of Patriots who Drowned the Tea in Boston Harbour in 1773. By a Citizen of New York* (New York: S. S. Bliss, 1834); C. A. Wall, *The Historic Boston Tea Party of December 16, 1773* (Worcester, Mass.: F. S. Blanchard & Co., 1896).

97. It was at this time that "Americans first focused their attention on why British authorities had redefined the rules that had governed the empire for as long as anyone could remember." Breen, "Narrative of Commercial Life," 472–473.

98. Bushman, *Refinement of America*, shows how the culture of refinement expanded into the daily lives of the lower classes in America from the mid-eighteenth century. He notes that by 1768, "29 percent of the poorest inventories and 57 percent of the middling group had some indication of tea in the household. In the highest categories, 83 to 85 percent…listed tea or tea services" (184).

99. Adam Smith, *Wealth of Nations*, vol. 2 (London: W. Strahan and T. Cadell, 1776), 582, quoted in McCusker and Menard, *Economy of British America*, 310.

100. The Tea Act was passed by the British Parliament on May 10, 1773, in order to allow the British East India Company (BEIC) to sell tea to British colonies without having to pay any taxes to the British government. The BEIC was close to financial ruin by 1772 due to instability in India and the amount of taxes they had to pay to the British government. By doing away with these high taxes, the Tea Act served to strengthen the BEIC's monopoly on the colonial tea trade by allowing it to sell excess tea at considerably lower prices. After it was passed, the BEIC only had to pay the Townshend Duties. These duties were part of the Townshend Acts, which were a series of acts that were passed by Parliament beginning in 1767. They were designed to generate revenue from the British North American colonies to support their administration. American colonists rigorously opposed these acts which established that Parliament had the right to tax the colonies. Although the colonists' protests helped to get the hated Acts partially repealed, the duty of 3 pence per pound of tea was retained in order to reaffirm the right of Parliament to legislate for Americans. This right had been expressed by Parliament in the Declaratory Act of 1766. Alvin Rabushka, *Taxation in Colonial America* (Princeton, N.J.: Princeton University Press, 2008), 758.

101. The phrases are taken from an article entitled "'Messieurs Edes & Gill, Please to insert the following, Tea! How I shudder at thy fatal Stream!," *Boston-Gazette, & Country Journal*, no. 698 (August 15, 1768).

102. Benjamin Rush [probably] to Jacob Rush, January 26, 1769, in *Letters of Benjamin Rush*, 1:74–75, quoted in Brown, "Piecing Together the Past," 559. (See note 23 here.)

103. David Waldstreicher puts it well: "When the Americans seemed to act rebelliously just as they began to exult, more than ever, in their Britishness, it seemed as if the empire might be falling apart at the moment of its greatest triumph." See Waldstreicher, *Runaway America* (New York: Hill and Wang, 2004), 147. For more on the idea of the increasing Anglicization of America in the years leading to the Revolution, see John Murrin, "Anglicizing an American Colony: The Transformation of Provincial Massachusetts" (Ph.D. diss., Yale University, 1966); T. H. Breen, "Ideology and Nationalism on the Eve of the American Revolution: Revisions Once More in Need of Revising," *Journal of American History* 84, no. 1 (1997): 13–39.

104. John Adams to Abigail Adams, Falmouth, July 6, 1774, in *Familiar Letters of John Adams and His Wife Abigail Adams, During the Revolution*, ed. Charles Francis Adams (New York: Hurd & Houghton, 1876), 18.

105. General Nathaniel Heard to General George Washington, June 5, 1777, in *The Papers of George Washington: Revolutionary War Series*, vol. 9, *March–June 1777*, ed. Philander D. Chase (Charlottesville: University Press of Virginia, 1999), 610–611.

106. As cited in John Kuo Wei Tchen, *New York before Chinatown* (Baltimore: Johns Hopkins University Press, 1999), 4. Tchen provides an insightful analysis of this material in his book.

107. George Washington to David Brooks, September 22, 1779, in *The Writings of George Washington from the Original Manuscript Sources, 1745–1799*, ed. John C. Fitzpatrick (Washington, D.C.: Government Printing Office, 1931), 16:321.

108. "The general's careful deliberations on the apportioning of tea exemplified his proper role as a patriarch rewarding his officers," just as his ownership of Wedgwood and china "certainly reminded him and his officers, in the heat of battle, of his status and authority." Tchen, *New York before Chinatown*, 4.

109. See, for example, Robert F. Dalzell, Jr., and Lee Baldwin Dalzell, *George Washington's Mount Vernon: At Home in Revolutionary America* (New York: Oxford University Press, 1998).

110. Tchen makes a distinction between what he labels "patrician Orientalism," centered on the need of elites to maintain a level of material acquisition that emulated European elite tastes, and a related but more widespread "commercial Orientalism" (what Tchen has also called "hotel lobby Orientalism") that traded on the various market values of things Chinese. The lobbies and finest suites of the best Philadelphia hotels, for instance, have been dominated since the Revolution by Oriental vases, watercolor paintings, and chinoiserie. See Tchen, *New York before Chinatown*, xxi–xxii.

111. Marquis de Chastellux, *Travels in North America in the Years 1780–1782 by the Marquis de Chastellux*, vol. 1, trans. Howard C. Rice, Jr. (Chapel Hill: University of North Carolina Press, 1963), 280.

112. George Washington to John Mitchell, Camp at Middle brook, February 17, 1779, in *Papers of George Washington*.

113. In terms of quantity, he ordered "not less I conceive, than what follows of each article will do: 2 large Tureenes, 3 dozn. Dishes, sized 8 dozn. Shallow Plates, 3 dozn. Soup Ditto, 8 Table drinking Mugs, 8 Ditto Salts. and some pickle plates. The whole to be

very carefully packed." He also ordered "Six tolerably genteel but not expensive Candlesticks all of a kind and three pair of Snuffers to them. I wish for as much fur as will edge a Coat, Waistcoat, and Breeches and that it may be sent to me as soon as possible. Let this be accompanied by 2 pounds of Starch." Mitchell, who was in Philadelphia, sent his reply on February 21 of the same year. The final purchase was recorded in the last inventory after the death of Martha Washington in 1802.

114. Detweiler, *George Washington's Chinaware*, 9. This is not to imply that the goods did not take on a different political meaning after the Revolution. Even a century after independence, there is evidence of Americans urging manufacturers to replace "Queen's Ware" with "creamware." The editors of a publication called the *Crockery Journal* supported this, "as we Americans do not propose to do homage to foreign potentates." See David Buten, *Eighteenth-century Wedgwood* (New York: Main Street Press, 1980), 17.

115. Josiah Wedgwood to Thomas Bentley, March 12, 1767, in *Letters of Josiah Wedgwood*, Katherine Euphemia, Lady Farrer, ed., vol. 1 (Manchester: E. J. Morten, 1906), 127.

116. This plan prescribed that the focus of the presentation was on the food itself rather than on ornamental centerpieces as was done on the Continent. The shared serving dishes covered the table in a balanced and symmetrical setting. Diana diZerega Wall, "Family Dinners and Social Teas: Ceramics and Domestic Rituals," in Catherine E. Hutchins, ed., *Everyday Life in the Early Republic* (Winterthur, Del.: Henry Francis du Pont Winterthur Museum, 1994), 262–263. The British influence continues today; the old English plan is used by many American families, particularly for celebratory meals such as Christmas and Thanksgiving.

117. For a detailed study of Washington's chinaware, see Detweiler, *George Washington's Chinaware*. Both of Martha Washington's husbands made the purchasing decisions for their households.

118. Quote from Tchen, *New York before Chinatown*, 5. "Chinamen" and "chinawomen" were the eighteenth-century terms for those who sold china. Around one hundred of these merchants are known to have worked in London for a good portion of the eighteenth century. Their numbers reached a peak in the 1760s. They also sold objects such as tea, snuff, chocolate, arrack, fans, lacquered cabinets, and tea tables. See also Aubrey J. Toppin, "The China Trade and Some London Chinamen," *English Ceramic Circles Transactions* 3 (1935): 26–27, 45. See Tchen's comments on the conflation of various Asian cultures by Europeans and Americans in John Kuo Wei Tchen, "Believing Is Seeing: Transforming Orientalism and the Occidental Gaze," in Tchen, *Asia/America: Identities in Contemporary Art* (New York: New Press, 1994), 12–25.

119. George Washington to Richard Washington, December 6, 1775, George Washington Papers, Manuscripts Division, Library of Congress. The episode is discussed in Tchen, *New York before Chinatown*, 5–6.

120. See Pierre Bourdieu, *Distinction: A Social Critique of the Judgement of Taste*, trans. Richard Nice (Cambridge, Mass.: Harvard University Press, 1984). Objects meant more to colonials than to the British because they were so crucial in establishing their levels of civility and cultural attainment.

121. Washington demonstrated his awareness of the connection between respect and material sophistication years before. He assumed a good deal of debt in order to improve Mount Vernon after his engagement but *before* his marriage to the much wealthier widow Martha Custis. This was a way to elevate himself to her social level and avoid speculation that he was more enamored with the money than the woman.

122. George Washington to Richard Washington, December 6, 1775, George Washington Papers, Manuscripts Division, Library of Congress.

123. Ibid. See note 125.

124. Peter Lyons to John Norton & Sons, July 15, 1771, in *John Norton and Sons Merchants of London and Virginia Being Their Papers from the Counting House for the Years 1750–1795*, ed. Frances Norton Mason (Newton Abbot, England: David & Charles, 1968), 168.

125. Peter Lyons to John Norton & Sons, September 25, 1771, in *John Norton and Sons*, 188–189.

126. See Zakim, "Sartorial Ideologies," 1566.

127. See Frank K. Prochaska, *The Eagle and the Crown: Americans and the British Monarchy* (New Haven, Conn.: Yale University Press, 2008). During a heated debate, the newly formed Congress of the United States of America questioned the use of ceremonial titles, after a Senate bill addressed some members as "Honorable." In the House of Representatives, members voted to have the word struck without even considering the issue. Politicians in the early national period reposed great political meaning in the diction of their official business. They expressed concerns about using words like 'splendor' and the phrase 'His most gracious Speech,' because their use could possibility carry monarchical implications. While the issue of word usage may seem trivial to modern readers, to a generation struggling to achieve the delicate balance of separation from the parent country and continued participation in the civilized world, it was anything but. European observers recorded Americans' anxieties about minute social and cultural details surrounding minor social occasions. See Joanne Freeman, *Affairs of Honor: National Politics in the New Republic* (New Haven, Conn.: Yale University Press, 2001). Freeman notes that French minister Comte de Moustier commented Americans' cultural insecurities, describing the nation's leaders as being tense as "a tight rope." Freeman, 39. Commenting on the politicization of everyday life, Freeman notes that politicians in the early republic felt that cultural practice, like the constitutional framework, shaped the nation. I wish to thank Frank Prochaska for sharing his work and his expertise so generously.

128. I conducted research at his family home in Scotland and was unable to find any acknowledgment of his right to the title there. William Alexander's (1726–1783) claim to the vacant title in the peerage of Scotland was based on the fact that he was the eldest male relative of the first earl's grandfather. He unsuccessfully fought this case while in London around 1756. On returning to his native America, he was appointed surveyor-general of the Province of New Jersey and was a member of the Provincial Council. He counted Washington among his friends and asked him to give away his daughter at her wedding. Born of privilege, he made his early fortune in slave trading, iron manufacturing, and land speculation. There are several works on his life. The best researched and most up to date is Paul David Nelson, *William Alexander, Lord Stirling* (Tuscaloosa: University of Alabama Press, 1987). Others include William Duer, *The Life of William Alexander* (New York: Wiley, Putnam, 1847); Ludwig Schumacher, *Major-general the Earl of Stirling* (New York: New Amsterdam, 1897); Charles Ditmas, *The Life and Service of Major-general William Alexander Also Called the Earl of Stirling* (Brooklyn: Printed for the [Kings County Historical] Society, 1920); Alan Valentine, *Lord Stirling* (New York: Oxford University Press, 1969): George Danforth, "The Rebel Earl" (Ph.D. diss., Columbia University, 1955).

129. See Carol Borchert Cadou, *The George Washington Collection: Fine and Decorative Arts at Mount Vernon* (Manchester, Vt.: Hudson Hills Press, 2006), 14. For instance, immediately after his marriage to the wealthy widow Martha Custis, he ordered a set of cutlery through Robert Cary, the agent of his wife's late husband. He had his crest engraved on each piece, adding significantly to the cost. What is significant is that he

continued to do so after the Revolutionary War, even as he began to embrace the new Federalist styles.

130. By the eighteenth century, Americans were engaged in what scholars such as David Waldstreicher have deemed an "Anglo-American politics of celebration." See Waldstreicher, _Runaway America_, 23; see also Richard Bushman, _King and People in Provincial Massachusetts_ (Chapel Hill: University of North Carolina Press, 1985). I wish to thank David Waldstreicher for his support of this project from its inception to its completion.

131. The phrase is borrowed from Fox, _The Completion of Independence, 1790–1830_. Benjamin Rush used it to describe the task of cultural separation that Americans faced in the aftermath of their Revolutionary War victory. The book was part of the series "A History of American Life in Twelve Volumes" that was edited by Arthur M. Schlesinger and Dixon Ryan Fox. Carl Becker served as the consulting editor on the series.

132. See Norman S. Buck, _The Development of the Organization of Anglo-American Trade, 1800–1850_ (New Haven, Conn.: Yale University Press, 1925).

133. According to figures compiled by Timothy Pitkin, in 1790–1800 the average consumption of tea in America annually was 2,545,504 pounds. In 1800–1812, that figure increased to 3,771,194 pounds. Pitkin, _A Statistical View of the Commerce of the United States of America_, 2nd ed. (New York, 1817), 247–248, quoted in Jean McClure Mudge, _Chinese Export Porcelain for the American Trade, 1785–1835_, 2nd ed. (Newark: University of Delaware Press, 1962), 232 n.

134. For a definition of asymmetrical exchange from a social science perspective, see note 5.

135. See James Axtell, "Dressing for Success on the Mohawk Frontier: Hendrick, William Johnson, and the Indian Fashion," in Peter C. Mancall and James Hart Merrell, eds., _American Encounters: Natives and Newcomers from European Contact to Indian Removal, 1500–1850_ (New York: Routledge, 2000), 324–350.

136. As Americans made the transition from subjects to citizens, their extensive material and cultural reliance on Britain became increasingly vexing, with American elites addressing this tension by separating imported objects from politics. Pierre Bourdieu developed a theoretical model that asserts that social formations are organized around a "hierarchically organized series of fields (the economic field, the educational field, the political field, the cultural field, etc.), each defined as a structured space with its own laws of functioning and its own relations of force." According to Bourdieu, each field operates separately, yet all of them are "structurally homologous." See Randal Johnson, editor's introduction to Bourdieu, _The Field of Cultural Production: Essays on Art and Literature_ (New York: Columbia University Press, 1993), 6. For the most part, scholarship has been organized in a way that replicates this false split. Political historians do not often study material culture, and decorative art scholars could do more to situate the objects they study in historical context. These omissions have obscured insights into the postcolonial experience in America.

137. Today, Americans put great stock in originality and invention, but this was not always true. The best example of this is from the 1980s, when Americans derided Japan for copying all of America's innovations. They also dismissed out of hand the Japanese claim that they had "improved" on inventions such as the car, videocassette recorder, and stereo sound system. This was what Americans did with British technology in the early republic and through the nineteenth century. Doron Ben-Atar explores this issue in _Trade Secrets: Intellectual Piracy and the Origins of American Industrial Power_ (New Haven, Conn.: Yale University Press, 2004).

138. Zakim, "Sartorial Ideologies," 1568; Jack Greene, *Intellectual Construction of America: Exceptionalism and Identity from 1492 to 1800* (Chapel Hill: University of North Carolina Press, 1993), 71, 78, 102–104, 114–116.

139. Not all sources reflect such a positive opinion of the attractiveness of Washington's homespun suit as the one just quoted.

140. The epigraph is from J. Leander Bishop, *A History of American Manufactures from 1608 to 1860*, vol. 1 (Philadelphia: Edward Young and Co., 1866), 8.

141. The quote is from Benjamin Rush to [probably] Jacob Rush, January 26, 1769, in L. H. Butterfield, ed., *Letters of Benjamin Rush*, vol. 1 (Princeton, N.J.: Princeton University Press, 1951), 74. Also in *Pennsylvania Journal* 1374 (April 6, 1769).

142. Rush, "A Speech Delivered in Carpenter's Hall," *Pennsylvania Evening Post* I (April 11 and 13, 1775), also quoted in John F. Kasson, *Civilizing the Machine: Technology and Republican Values in America, 1776–1900* (New York: Grossman, 1976), 9–10.

143. Benjamin Rush to son James, May 1, 1810, Box 11, Benjamin Rush Collection, Library Company of Philadelphia. See note 28. Because historians understandably consider the Revolution a watershed event, most scholarly treatments of the period are designed to highlight contrasts between the late colonial and early national economies rather than the continuities that were equally important. Economic historians McCusker and Menard have observed a similar phenomenon in their field. They state: "economic historians have neglected the years of the war and its immediate aftermath. Indeed, apart from military, diplomatic, and political aspects, the period from 1776 to 1789 is among the least studied in American history." Indeed the economic and cultural continuities between the colonial and postrevolutionary periods in American history have largely been overlooked. McCusker and Menard, *Economy of British America*, 358.

144. Benjamin Rush to son James, May 1, 1810, Box 11, Benjamin Rush Collection, LCP. In that same letter Rush encouraged his son to stay longer in England and wrote that it would be *"perfectly convenient* to me to support you till next Spring in London. "In order to do that," he informed James, "I shall remit to your bankers in Liverpool £200 Sterling by next packet. And more shall be sent if necessary to defray the expense of your voyage home." Leonard Tennenhouse suggests that people thought in terms of a "separation of the nation as a political entity from the nation as a culture." This understanding helps clarify why American authors made greater efforts after the Revolution than they had before to maintain an English cultural identity for and "put the stamp of Englishness on the new nation." This was accomplished by "reproducing those aspects of Englishness that do not require one to be in England so much as among English people." Tennenhouse, *The Importance of Feeling English: American Literature and the British Diaspora 1750–1850* (Princeton, N.J.: Princeton University Press, 2007), 1–18.

145. My analysis follows the arguments made by Bushman, *Refinement of America*.

146. See the work of Karen Halttunen, *Confidence Men and Painted Women: A Study of Middle-class Culture in America, 1830–1870* (New Haven, Conn.: Yale University Press, 1986).

147. For a study of tavern life in early America and its significance as political space, see Peter Thompson, *Rum Punch and Revolution: Taverngoing and Public Life in Eighteenth-century Philadelphia* (Philadelphia: University of Pennsylvania Press, 1999).

148. For the theoretical basis of this analysis, see Arjun Appadurai, ed., *The Social Life of Things: Commodities in Cultural Perspective* (New York: Cambridge University Press, 1986).

149. All this happened in a relatively short period of time. Europeans were introduced to Chinese tea by the early seventeenth century.

150. In the late eighteenth century, William Winterbotham (1763–1829) provided his readers with the following description: "Among the aromatic shrubs of China, that

which furnishes tea holds the first rank. It is not, however, known by this name in the country, but is called *tcha*"—and "By corruptoin [*sic*] in some of maritime provinces, *tha*, from which derived our word tea." See W[illiam] Winterbotham, *An Historical, Geographical, and Philosophical View of the Chinese Empire; Comprehending A Description of the Fifteen Provinces of China, Chinese Tartary; Tributary Sates; Natural History of China, Government, Religion, Laws, Manners and Customs, Literature, Arts, Sciences, Manufactures, &c. To which is added, A Copious Account of Lord Macartney's Embassy, Compiled from Original Communications*, 2 vols. (Philadelphia: Richard Lee, 1796), 263.

151. For more on this see Detweiler, *George Washington's Chinaware*, 9.

152. See Bushman, *Refinement of America*, 184.

153. In America, it was generally not considered proper for women to drink at public houses unless they were travelers recovering from the day's tiring journey. In these instances, women were served watered-down or highly sugared alcoholic beverages. Women did drink alcohol-based medicines for their health, and many who regarded spirits as "vulgar" regularly consumed highly alcoholic "cordials" or "stomach elixirs." These practices also varied from region to region and between urban and rural settings in America. On the East Coast, ladies drank in mixed company at society dinners, suppers, and evening parties. In the backcountry, whiskey was passed along in bottles without as much concern for either age or sex. The majority of women's alcoholic drinking occurred privately in their homes.

154. In England during the early eighteenth century, people preferred to drink coffee and alcohol in public houses, which became the center of political, social, literary, and commercial life into the first half of the nineteenth century. Men commonly drank coffee in public spaces with other men, rather than in mixed company. By contrast, in both Great Britain and her American colonies, tea was taken at home during breakfast or socially in afternoon gatherings that included both sexes. Brian Cowan, *The Social Life of Coffee: The Emergence of the British Coffeehouse* (New Haven, Conn.: Yale University Press, 2005).

155. Anne Home Shippen Livingston and Ethel Armes, eds., *Nancy Shippen, Her Journal Book; The International Romance of a Young Lady of Fashion of Colonial Philadelphia with Letters to Her and about Her* (Philadelphia: Lippincott, 1935), 199.

156. Bishop, *History of American Manufactures*, 211.

157. Joy and Hopkins to George Washington, 1784. See also Kathryn C. Buhler, *Mount Vernon Silver* (Mount Vernon, Va.: Mount Vernon Ladies' Association of the Union, 1957), 44.

158. George Washington to Bushrod Washington, Rocky Hill, September 22, 1783, in Washington, *Writings* (from the "Letter Book" copy, George Washington Papers, Manuscripts Division, Library of Congress).

159. See P. J. Marshall, "Britain without America; A Second Empire?" in Marshall, ed., *The Eighteenth Century*, vol. 2 of *The Oxford History of the British Empire* (Oxford: Oxford University Press, 1998), 576–595. Marshall notes that the disintegration of the Spanish and Portuguese empires created further opportunities for trade at this time.

160. The rate consumption of earthenware in the United States grew from 908,714 pieces in 1765 to 1,207,435 pieces in 1770 and then down to 143,942 pieces in 1775. The amount grew in each five-year period after that—to 1,798,710 pieces in 1780; 2,014,040 pieces in 1785; 2,900,316 pieces in 1790; 9,013,269 pieces in 1795—and by 1800 had risen to 9,914,911 pieces. British earthenware exports increased by over 300 percent in the two decades after independence, and by 1812 Staffordshire potters were sending 40–50 percent their wares to the United States—and would do so every year until 1865.

See J. Potter, "Atlantic Economy, 1815–1860: The U.S.A. and the Industrial Revolution in Britain," in L. S. Pressnell, ed., *Studies in the Industrial Revolution Presented to T. S. Ashton* (London: Athlone Press, 1960), 236–281; see especially 278.

161. I have based these paragraphs on the figures given in the tables by Schumpeter, *English Overseas Trade Statistics, 1697–1808*, 63–69.

162. Exports to British North America grew from a quarter of a million pounds to the peak of 2.1 million pounds sterling in 1765–1770. The boycott of British goods during the revolutionary conflict decreased that amount to 835,000 pounds sterling in the following five years. However, after the end of the war, the growth rate of British exports to the United States outpaced that of imports from the United States.

163. "Mr. Brougham," quoted in Bishop, *History of American Manufactures*, 211–212.

164. During the nineteenth century, consumers were presented with ever-increasing amounts of texts about objects in the forms of catalogs and advertisements. See Joseph Corn, "Textualizing Technics: Owner's Manuals and the Reading of Objects," in Ann Smart Martin and J. Ritchie Garrison, eds., *American Material Culture: The Shape of the Field* (Winterthur, Del.: Henry Francis du Pont Winterthur Museum, 1997): 169–194. In the late nineteenth century, fiction writers and anthropologists engaged with objects to extract social meanings. See Neil Harris on Henry James and William Dean Howells, "The Drama of Consumer Desire," in Otto Mayr and Robert Post, eds., *Yankee Enterprise: The Rise of the American System of Manufacturers* (Washington, D.C.: Smithsonian Institution Press, 1981), 189–216. On anthropologists "reading objects," see Curtis Hinsley, "Collecting Cultures and Cultures of Collecting," Museum Anthropologist 16, no. 1 (1992): 12–20. The classic work is by anthropologist Mary Douglass, who explicated the symbolic significance of goods that formed a language of communication. Mary Douglass and Baron Isherwood, *The World of Goods: Toward an Anthropology of Consumption* (New York: Norton, 1979).

165. [Rudolph Ackermann, ed.], *The Repository of Arts, Literature, Commerce, Manufactures, Fashions and Politics*, 1st ser., London, no. 11 (November 1809), unnumbered hand-colored plate following p. 52.

166. Schoeser and Rufey, *English and American Textiles*, 4.

167. [Ackermann], *Repository of Arts*, 1st ser., London, no. 11 (November 1809), unnumbered plate following p. 344.

168. Ibid.

169. Pierre de la Mésangère, *Meubles et Objets de Goût* (Paris: A. Calavas, 1796–1830).

170. *The Selected Letters of Josiah Wedgwood*, ed. Ann Finer and George Savage (London: Cory, Adams & Mackay, 1965), 58, 159.

171. Ibid.; see also Arlene Palmer Schwind, "The Ceramic Imports of Frederick Rhinelander, New York Loyalist Merchant," *Winterthur Portfolio* 19, no. 21 (1984): 21–36; Christina H. Nelson, "Transfer-printed Creamware and Pearlware for the American Market," *Winterthur Portfolio* 15, no. 2 (January 1980): 93–115.

172. George Miller, Ann Smart Martin, and Nancy S. Dickinson, "Changing Consumption Patterns: English Ceramics and the American Market from 1770 to 1840," in Catherine E. Hutchins, ed., *Everyday Life in the Early Republic* (Winterthur, Del.: Henry Francis du Pont Winterthur Museum, 1994), 219–220.

173. Margaret Hall, *The Aristocratic Journey: Being the Outspoken Letters of Mrs. Basil Hall Written During a Fourteen Months' Sojourn in America, 1827–1828*, ed. Una Pope-Hennessy (New York: Putnam, 1931), 289. Modern decorative arts scholars have questioned the prevailing assumption that Americans received shoddy merchandise from Great Britain. See Arlene Palmer Schwind, "The Ceramic Imports of Frederick

Rhinelander, New York Loyalist Merchant," *Winterthur Portfolio* 19, no. 1 (1984): 21–36, arguing that the opposite was true.

174. See *Klinkowstrom's America, 1818–1820*, trans. and ed. Franklin D. Scott (Evanston, Ill.: Northwestern University Press, 1952), 170.

175. Ibid.

176. Liverpool potters emblazoned their wares with rousing scenes of the colonies' defeat of the mighty empire. Staffordshire potters followed suit, and soon there were so many competitors that each manufacturer began to use different borders to distinguish their wares from one another. Important firms include Wedgwood, the Herculaneum Pottery of Liverpool, and Neale and Company.

177. See Baumgarten, *What Clothes Reveal*, 87.

178. Jug, Henry Francis du Pont Winterthur Museum, Winterthur, Delaware, accession number 58.1198 (A). A similar jug is in the Mariners' Museum, Newport News, Virginia, as cited in Nola O. Hill, "American History on Liverpool and Staffordshire," *Antiques* 64 (October 1953): 290.

179. Transferware of this type depicting American victories in both the Revolution and the War of 1812 was available in the American market in the late eighteenth and early nineteenth centuries. Examples at the Winterthur Museum are "His Excellency George Washington," accession number 59.586; "The Gallant Defense of Stonington," accession number 64.1715; "Captain Hull of the Constitution," accession number 67.14; "Lawrence and Decatur," accession number 67.19. For studies on transferware pottery from a material culture perspective, see Nelson, "Transfer-printed Creamware and Pearlware." For a general work on British transferware from a material culture perspective, see Cyril Williams-Wood, *English Transfer-printed Pottery and Porcelain: A History of Over-glaze Printing* (London: Faber & Faber, 1981).

180. Detweiler, *George Washington's Chinaware*, 8–9.

181. William Turner, *Transfer Printing on Enamels, Porcelain and Pottery: Its Origin and Development in the United Kingdom* (London: Chapman and Hall, 1907), 82–83, copy in Rare Books and Manuscripts, The Huntington Library, San Marino, California.

182. In 1953 Nola O. Hill asserted that "in their effort to stimulate trade the Liverpool potters [were] at times almost traitors to their country." Hill, "American History on Liverpool and Staffordshire," 290.

183. See James Deetz, *In Small Things Forgotten: The Archaeology of Early American Life* (Garden City, N.Y.: Anchor Books, 1977).

184. Henry Bromfield to his father, letter dated July 23, 1784, Henry Bromfield Papers, in Bromfield Family Papers (1731–1830), Massachusetts Historical Society, Boston, Massachusetts. Henry Sr. was the brother of merchants John and Thomas Bromfield. The family had been merchants in Boston for two generations prior and before that had been large landowners in England and Wales. Henry Bromfield, Sr., accompanied his son at that outset of this trip to England, where he engaged in business in London with his brother Thomas, before returning to America ahead of Henry Jr. Kenneth Wiggins Porter, *The Jacksons and the Lees: Two Generations of Massachusetts Merchants, 1765–1844*, vol. 1 (New York: Russell & Russell), 6 and 189.

185. Henry Bromfield to his father, March 3, 1790, Henry Bromfield Papers, in Bromfield Family Papers (1731–1830), Massachusetts Historical Society, Boston, Massachusetts.

186. Ibid.

187. Ibid.

188. Ibid.

189. Hams were a common item Americans abroad requested of contacts back home. For instance, merchant Joshua Johnson writes—also mentioning the complication of the duty on hams—"I find that the duty on hams is taken off so that, if any of my friends would be so polite as to present me with one now and then, you may assure them there is no danger from the Customs House officers." Note that Johnson also mentions the complication of the duty on hams. Johnson, *Joshua Johnson's Letterbook*, 4.

190. Henry Bromfield, Jr. to his father, July 23, 1784, Massachusetts Historical Society, Boston, Massachusetts.

191. Ibid.

192. Ibid.

193. Henry Bromfield, Jr. to his father, letter dated March 26, 1804, Henry Bromfield Papers, in Bromfield Family Papers (1731–1830), Massachusetts Historical Society, Boston, Massachusetts.

194. Books were commonly procured in London for customers, friends, and relatives in America. For instance, see Johnson, *Joshua Johnson's Letterbook*, 8; 13–18.

195. The monetary amounts of the gifts are given in case of necessity at customhouse, where I am told there is great expense." Henry Bromfield, Jr., letter dated, March 3, 1790, Henry Bromfield Papers, in Bromfield Family Papers (1731–1830), Massachusetts Historical Society, Boston, Massachusetts.

196. Henry Bromfield, Jr., letter dated September 29, 1791, Henry Bromfield Papers, in Bromfield Family Papers (1731–1830), Massachusetts Historical Society, Boston, Massachusetts; see also Henry Bromfield, Jr., letter dated November 6, 1793, Henry Bromfield Papers, in Bromfield Family Papers (1731–1830), Massachusetts Historical Society, Boston, Massachusetts.

197. Henry Bromfield, Jr., letter dated July 15, 1795, Henry Bromfield Papers, in Bromfield Family Papers (1731–1830), Massachusetts Historical Society, Boston, Massachusetts.

198. Ibid.

199. Henry Bromfield to his family, letter dated May 10, 1805, Bromfield Family Papers, Massachusetts Historical Society, Boston, Massachusetts.

200. Ibid.

201. Invented in 1802, the banjo clock had with a small gilt bracket that enabled one to hang it on a wall. This new, affordable item was created by Simon Willard of Roxbury, Massachusetts. Both clocks and pencils used wood, a resource that certainly was plentiful in America. In the period after the Revolution, the things Americans attempted to produce domestically tended to be made for those wanting inexpensive items such as the banjo clock. Willard made four thousand clocks in 1802–1840. In 1812, William Monroe, a cabinetmaker from Concord, Massachusetts, manufactured the first lead pencils produced in the United States. Gorton Carruth, *The Encyclopedia of American Facts and Dates, Selected for the White House Library* (New York: Harper & Row, 1987), 125, 147.

202. Doron Ben-Atar, "Alexander Hamilton's Alternative: Technology Piracy and the Report on Manufacturers," in Doron Ben-Atar and Barbara Oberg, eds., *Federalists Reconsidered* (Charlottesville: University of Virginia Press, 1998), 41–60; the quote appears on page 44.

203. Ben-Atar notes: "even the most patriotic Americans realized that habit and structural economic patterns originating in colonial relationships fostered dependence on European imports and hindered the young nation's technological development. Revolutionary calls for cutting off all connections to the Old World were contradicted by

the recognition that for all the patriotic pride and talk of self-sufficiency, the United States had to emulate European discoveries" (*Trade Secrets*, 84–85). The development of American industry depended on transatlantic guidance, whether in the form of the advice of British immigrants, letters from friends and family in Britain, or visits to the centers of industry in England. See also Rowland Berthoff, *British Immigrants in Industrial America* (Cambridge: Cambridge University Press, 1953).

204. Doron Ben-Atar and Barbara Oberg, "Introduction: The Paradoxical Legacy of the Federaists," in Ben-Atar and Oberg, *Federalists Reconsidered*, 5–6.

205. The term Yankee was first used by the British as a term of derision; it was later embraced with pride by the Americans. The British were also the authors of the song "Yankee Doodle." The name comes from the Dutch name *Janke*, which combines a diminutive of "John" (Jan) with *kees*, a diminutive of *kaas* (cheese). The name was used by the Dutch as a term for pirates. Ben-Atar mentions this in his introduction to *Trade Secrets*, xv.

206. Ben-Atar, *Trade Secrets*, xv.

207. Benjamin Rush did the same when he was there as a student and looking for practical applications of chemistry.

208. Ben-Atar, *Trade Secrets*, 86. As Ben-Atar notes, unfortunately for Americans, attempts to importing machines on the sly were not always successful.

209. Zachariah Allen, *preface to The practical tourist, or sketches of the state of the useful arts, and of society, scenery, &c. &c. in Great-Britain, France and Holland* (Boston: Richardson, Lord & Holbrook, 1832), copy in Rare Books and Manuscripts, American Antiquarian Society, Worcester, Massachusetts. Allen wrote: "In the midst of importunate cares, and in the hurried pursuits of business, the notes of the 'Practical Tourist' have been prepared for publication, with the sincere desire that they may, to some readers at least, be found useful." He took the notes for this book during a tour he made in 1825. "A few of the following sketches may already have met the eye, as they were handed to the editor of a public journal at his request, to be inserted in his columns." See also Allen, *The Science of Mechanics, as applied to the Present Improvement in the Useful Arts in Europe, and in the United States of America: Adapted as a Manual for Mechanics and Manufacturers, and Containing Tables and Calculations of General Practical Utility* (Providence, R.I.: Hutchens & Cory, 1829), copy in Rare Books and Manuscripts, The Huntington Library, San Marino, California. Allen compiled information for this work as well as taking a tour "through the most interesting districts of England and France" during which "my attention was principally directed to the latest improvements in mechanical inventions in those countries" (lv). In a note on the same page, he quotes a journal article: "Youthful nations (observes a late writer in the *Quarterly Review*) 'will be quicker than Europe, and in our own vigorous children in the United States of America we already see the generations that in reason and industry are destined to stand beside Englishmen.'"

210. Allen contrasted himself with European travelers who "commonly preferred to breathe the pure air of a beautiful country, where the works of a munificent Creator are offered for contemplation and enjoyment; or to indulge exclusively in the pleasures afforded to taste and intellect, by the examination of splendid buildings, paintings, statues and libraries" (*Practical Tourist*, 5–6).

211. Ibid.

212. Ibid., 83.

213. Ibid., 68.

214. Arlene Palmer, *Glass in Early America* (New York: Norton, 1993), 6.

215. Brooke Hindle and Steven Lubar, *Engines of Change: The American Industrial Revolution, 1790–1860* (Washington D.C.: Smithsonian Institution Press, 1986), 25.

216. Although Stiegel established networks of agents to sell his wares, he had to close his factory in 1774 and was sentenced to debtor's prison.

217. Amelung noted that he "had letters of recommendation from those great men, Franklin and Adams, and the American Consul at Paris, to the first men in this country, viz. to his Excellency General Mifflin, President of Congress, Thomas Johnson, Esq. William Paca, Esq. and Charles Corroll, of Carrollton, Esq. and a great number to the first mercantile houses, which would be too tedious to mention; all those letters will prove that I had the character of a worthy and honest man in Germany, and kept the same until I left it." John F. Amelung, *Remarks on Manufactures, Principally on the New Established Glass-House, near Frederick-Town, in the State of Maryland* (No city listed: Printed for the Author, 1787), 12. This document was reprinted in *Journal of Glass Studies* 18 (1976): 130–135. The copy that is reproduced in the *Journal of Glass Studies* (from the collection of the Charleston Library Society) is of particular interest because it includes handwritten notes by the author himself from the year 1790. This special bicentennial edition of the Journal of Glass Studies provides the most detailed scholarship on early American glassmaking and John Frederick Amelung in particular. It is divided into three parts: the history of the New Bremen Manufactory and John Frederick Amelung, archaeological excavations of the site, and chemical analyses of Amelung glassware.

218. Amelung's quote is found on John F. Amelung, *Remarks on Manufactures*, 12. On June 3, 1790, the first Congress to meet after the Constitution was ratified discussed loaning Amelung $8,000 in order to bring hundreds of glassworkers to the United States. They felt "a manufactory attended with so much difficulty in its commencement, so important in its consequences to the United States, and of such general utility to the whole Union, ought to receive the assistance and protection of the United States." In the end, however, opponents stopped the loan. Ben-Atar, *Trade Secrets*, 104. For further discussion of Amelung's business venture, see Chapter 5, "Official Orchestration of Technology Smuggling," in Ben-Atar, *Trade Secrets*, 104–109.

219. On the closing of the New Bremen factory, see Dwight P. Lanmon and Arlene M. Palmer, "The New Bremen Glassmanufactory," *Journal of Glass Studies* 18 (1976): especially 36–38 and Lanmon and Palmer, "The Amelung Postscript," *Journal of Glass Studies* 18 (1976): 39–43.

220. Palmer, *Glass in Early America*, 9.

221. Phineas Bond to the Duke of Leeds, *American Historical Association Annual Report* 1 (Washington, D.C.: Government Printing Office, 1896), 630–631, as quoted in Dwight P. Lanmon and Arlene M. Palmer, "Foreword," *Journal of Glass Studies* 18 (1976): 9.

222. Ibid., 10–11.

223. Of course, the two were related, as imported workers with skill and knowledge served to advance American technology. See Daniel Creamer, "Recruiting Contract Laborers for the Amoskeag Mills," *Journal of Economic History* 1 (May 1941): 42–56; also see Ben-Atar, *Trade Secrets*, 202 n. 262.

CHAPTER 3

1. For a contemporary account on the launching of the *Empress of China*, see *Salem (Massachusetts) Gazette,* March 4, 1784, report with New York dateline, February 26, 1784. The *Edward* was carrying the ratified version of the agreement made at the Treaty of Paris that was signed on September 3, 1783. The Continental Congress had formally ratified it on January 14, 1784. See *Peace and the Peacemakers: The Treaty of*

1783, Ronald Hoffman and Peter J. Albert (eds.) (Charlottesville, Virginia: Published for the United States Capitol Historical Society by the University Press of Virginia, 1986).

2. Philip Freneau, "On the First American Ship (Empress of China, Capt Greene) that Explored the Route to China and the East-Indies, After the Revolution," first published by the author in *Poems Written Between the Years 1768 & 1794* (Monmouth, N.J.: Philip Freneau, 1795); the poem was reprinted by Freneau in his newspaper the *Time-Piece and Literary Companion,* April 17, 1797.

3. The *Empress of China* reached Macao on August 23, six months and a day from departure, and dropped anchor in Whampoa Reach on August 28, 1784, as reported in Samuel Shaw, Journal Notes, handwritten manuscript, Massachusetts Historical Society, Boston, Massachusetts, 162–163 (for convenience, I will cite from the published version hereafter: Samuel Shaw, *The Journals of Major Samuel Shaw, The First American Consul at Canton with the Life of the Author by Josiah Quincy,* ed. Josiah Quincy [Boston: William Crosby and H. P. Nichols, 1847]), 163–164. Regarding tardiness of the Chinese in recognizing the Americans as politically distinct from the British, see Philip Chadwick Foster Smith essay "Philadelphia Displays 'The Flowery Flag,'" in Jean Gordon Lee, *Philadelphians in the China Trade, 1784–1844* (Philadelphia: Philadelphia Museum of Art, 1984), 4. See also Jean McClure Mudge, *Chinese Export Porcelain for the American Trade, 1785–1835,* 2nd ed. (Newark: University of Delaware Press, 1981), 35.

4. George Washington to Marquis de Lafayette, October 30, 1783, George Washington Papers,1741–1799, ser. 4, General Correspondence: 1697–1799, Library of Congress.

5. As the eighteenth century progressed, restrictive legislation increased. In 1750, for instance, colonists were prohibited from manufacturing or exporting certain textiles, and the Iron Act was passed, which banned the production of finished iron goods in the colonies. Laws such as the Woolen Act of 1699 prohibited intercolonial trading of goods such as wool and woolens. In 1718, a law was passed that prohibited the free migration of skilled British artisans. The Hat Act of 1732 banned the exportation of American-made hats from the colony in which they were made.

6. Joseph B. Felt, *The Annals of Salem,* 2 vols., 2nd ed. (Salem, Mass.: W. & S. B. Ives, 1845–1849); *(Salem) Gazette,* August 21, 1783.

7. R. W. Van Alstyne, *The Rising American Empire* (Oxford: Blackwell, 1960). See especially chap. 8, "The Lure of East Asia," 170–194.

8. Benedict Anderson, *Imagined Communities: Reflections on the Origin and Spread of Nationalism* (London: Verso, 1983).

9. Robert Morris, a successful merchant who was also serving as the U.S. superintendent of finance, assumed half of the financial responsibility, and Daniel Parker & Company took the other. The company consisted of three men, including John Holker, Jr. (1755–1828), of Philadelphia, who was the son of a British émigré to France. Holker moved to Philadelphia during the Revolutionary War as an agent of the French Royal Marines. Daniel Parker, originally from Massachusetts, had been an artillery officer in the American Continental Army during the war. Third was William Duer, a speculator from New York. Of the partners, Holker provided most of the capital and credit. Parker, it seems, falsified the company's financial records and misappropriated more than 10 percent of the *Empress's* cash purchasing power in Canton; in July 1784, he fled to Great Britain, leaving his partners in the lurch. The quote was published in the Federalist newspaper the *New York Packet* as noted in John Kuo Wei Tchen, *New York before Chinatown* (Baltimore: Johns Hopkins University Press, 1999), 34.

10. David Howard and John Ayers, *Masterpieces of Chinese Export Porcelain from the Mottahedeh Collection in the Virginia Museum* (London: Sotheby Parke Bernet, 1980), 30.

11. *Independent Gazetteer; or the Chronicle of Freedom* (Philadelphia), February 28, 1784.

12. John Barry (1745–1803), a captain in the American Continental Navy, commanded the *Asia* on its 1787–1789 voyage to China. Samuel Shaw (1754–1794) was an officer in the Revolutionary War and was the supercargo on the *Empress of China*. John Green (1736–1796), who received a captain's commission in the American Continental Army, was the commanding officer of the *Empress of China*. Thomas Truxtun (1755–1822), a privateer in the Revolutionary War, served as captain on the *Canton's* two voyages to China. Shaw was appointed secretary of the Society of Cincinnati and was the author of the original draft of its constitution. Shaw, *Journals*, 111.

13. Josiah Quincy (ed.), in Shaw, *Journals*, 111.

14. Terry Bouton describes the dramatic self-fashioning that took place among the officers of the American Continental Army. Although many came from "modest social backgrounds," during the war they came to believe that they had "risen dramatically in social rank" because the war had exposing them to the "manners of Old World gentility as they rubbed elbows with allied officers in the French army, some of whom held aristocratic titles." This experience and elevation of their expectations made them loathe to return to their former lives. Bouton, *Taming Democracy* (New York: Oxford University Press, 2007), 65.

15. John White Swift to John Swift, December 3, 1784, Hildeburn Papers, Historical Society of Pennsylvania, Philadelphia, Pennsylvania.

16. John Green Papers, Philadelphia Maritime Museum (now known as the Independence Seaport Museum), quoted in Smith, "Essay," 70.

17. Ibid.

18. The Congressional committee consisted of James Monroe of Virginia, George Partridge of Massachusetts, and Hugh Williamson of North Carolina. The document was dated January 30, 1784. The sea letters of the *Empress of China* are housed in the John Green Papers, Philadelphia Maritime Museum (now known as the Independence Seaport Museum).

19. John Green Papers, Philadelphia Maritime Museum, quoted in Smith, "Essay," 69.

20. The seal of the United States of America was formally adopted on June 20, 1782. It appeared on gold, silver, and copper coins issued by the U.S. government throughout the 1780s. Americans in Canton would give coins to the Chinese porcelain makers to use as models for their designs. Many porcelain pieces survive that are decorated with different eagles of varying attractiveness. See Mudge, *Chinese Export Porcelain*, 143–145.

21. Daniel Parker, for himself and Owners of the Ship, *Empress of China*, New York, captain's orders, to James Green, January 25, 1784, John Green Papers, Philadelphia Maritime Museum, also quoted in Smith, "Essay," 68.

22. Shaw, *Journals*, 162.

23. Ibid., 154–155.

24. Ibid., 153.

25. Ibid., 164.

26. "Letter to John Jay, May 19, 1785," *American Museum* 1 (March 1787): 194–197. This interest was not a new phenomenon. This periodical was among the most important ones in America that dealt with issues of foreign policy during the late eighteenth century. Robert Morris, financier and eventual backer of the *Empress*, expressed interest in the trade as early as 1783; Robert Morris to John Jay, November 27, 1783, in *The Correspondence and Public Papers of John Jay*, ed. Henry P. Johnston, 4 vols. (New York:

Putnam's, 1890–1893), 3:96–97. Ship owners provided their supercargoes with detailed directives regarding which items to buy, for the success of their costly venture depended on their prowess.

27. Shoemaker, "E. Rawle Shoemaker Commonplace Book, 1783–1785 quoted in Lee, *Philadelphians and the China Trade*, 18. The commonplace book belonged to Rebecca Rawle, who was married to Edward Shoemaker. See Rawle Family Papers 1682–1921, ser. 2, Rebecca Warner Rawle Shoemaker, box 7, and ser. 6, Related Families, box 12, Historical Society of Pennsylvania, Philadelphia, Pennsylvania.

28. John White Swift, purser of the "Empress of China," to his father, John Swift, resident of Philadelphia, letter dated Canton, December 3, 1784, reprint in "Notes and Queries," *Pennsylvania Magazine of History and Biography* 9, no. 4 (1886): 485; also quoted in John W. Swift, P. Hodgkinson, and Samuel W. Woodhouse, "The Voyage of the *Empress of China*," *Pennsylvania Magazine of History and Biography* 63, no. 1 (1939): 29.

29. The ship is recorded in Kenneth Scott Latourette, *Voyages of American Ships to China, 1784–1844* (New Haven, Conn.: Connecticut Academy of Arts and Sciences, 1927), 240.

30. Smith, "Essay," 247, and Lee, *Philadelphians and the China Trade*, 27–28, and *Hazard's United States Commercial and Statistical Register, Containing Documents, Facts, and Other Useful Information 1839–1840* (Philadelphia: W. F. Geddes, 1840), 3.

31. The delegates to the Stamp Act Congress adopted a flag that was decorated with nine alternating red and white stripes meant to represent the nine participating colonies. Popularly known as the "Rebellious Stripes," this flag was the first collective representation of revolutionary America. It borrowed its design elements from the British flag of the time and that of the British East India Company. See Leora Auslander, *Cultural Revolutions: Everyday Life and Politics in Britain, North American, and France* (Berkeley: University of California Press, 2009), 84.

32. All ships wishing to trade in Canton were required to first stop in Macao and obtain a pass, which was referred to as a "chop." Americans were aware of how others saw them. They reported: "'The Chinese called our men 'the new people.'" Quoted in entry for January 15, 1787, in Joseph B. Felt, *Annals of Salem*, 2:291.

33. *Fan guei* is in pinyin, the recognized standard for the Romanization of Chinese.

34. J. K. Fairbank and S. Y. Teng, "On the Ch'ing Tributary System," *Harvard Journal of Asiatic Studies* 6, no. 2 (June 1941): 172, quoted in Mudge, *Chinese Export Porcelain*, 30.

35. Shaw, *Journals*, 180.

36. See Frederic Wakeman, Jr., "Canton Trade and the Opium War," in Denis Twitchett and John K. Fairbank, eds., *The Cambridge History of China*, 13 vols. (Cambridge: Cambridge University Press, 1978–2009), vol. 10, pt. 1, 163–212; see especially 174. Chinese sovereignty was severely damaged by the First Opium War (1839–1842). See Jean Chesneaux, Marianne Bastid, and Marie-Claire Bergère, *China from the Opium Wars to the 1911 Revolution*, trans. Anne Destenay (New York: Pantheon, 1976); R. Keith Schoppa, *The Columbia Guide to Modern Chinese History* (New York: Columbia University Press, 2000); Hsin-pao Chang, *Commissioner Lin and the Opium War* (Cambridge, Mass.: Harvard University Press, 1964).

37. W[illiam] Winterbotham, *An Historical, Geographical, and Philosophical View of the Chinese Empire Comprehending a Description of the Fifteen Provinces of China, Chinese Tartary, Tributary States; Natural History of China; Government, Religion, Laws, Manners and Customs, Literature, Arts, Sciences, Manufactures, &c. To which is added, A Copious Account of Lord Macartney's Embassy, Compiled from Original Communications,*

2 vols. (London: J. Ridgway, and W. Button, 1795; reprint, Philadelphia: Richard Lee, 1796), 2:197. For biographic information on George Macartney, see Roland Thorne, "Earl George Macartney (1737–1806)," in *The Oxford Dictionary of National Biography*, ed. H. C. G. Matthew and Brian Harrison (Oxford: Oxford University Press, 2004); online ed., ed. Lawrence Goldman, May 2009, http://www.oxforddnb.com/view/article/17341 (accessed January 31, 2010). For biographic information on William Winterbotham, see Susan J. Mills, "Winterbotham, William (1763–1829)," in *The Oxford Dictionary of National Biography*, ed. H. C. G. Matthew and Brian Harrison (Oxford: Oxford University Press, 2004), http://www.oxforddnb.com/view/article/29771 (accessed January 31, 2010).

38. Ibid., 197.

39. Ibid.

40. Ibid., 262–263.

41. Ibid., 233.

42. George Staunton, *An authentic account of an embassy from the King of Great Britain to the Emperor of China; including cursory observations made, and information obtained, in travelling through that ancient empire, and a small part of Chinese Tartary. Together with a relation of the voyage undertaken on the occasion by His Majesty's ship the Lion, and the ship Hindostan, in the East India Company's service, to the Yellow Sea, and Gulf of Pekin; as well as of their return to Europe; with notices of the several places where they stopped in their way out and home; being the islands of Madeira, Teneriffe, and St. Jago; the port of Rio de Janeiro in South America; the islands of St. Helena, Tristan d'Acunha, and Amsterdam; the coasts of Java, and Sumatra; the Nanka Isles, Pulo Condore, and Cochin China. Taken chiefly from the papers of His Excellency the Earl of Macartney, Sir Erasmus Gower, and other gentlemen in the several departments of the embassy*, 3 vols., 2nd ed. (London: John Stockdale, 1798), copy in Beinecke Rare Book and Manuscript Library, Yale University, 2:6–7. Several other editions of George Staunton's work were published on both sides of the Atlantic. See, for instance, George Staunton, *An authentic account of an embassy from the King of Great Britain to the Emperor of China*, 3 vols. (London: Printed for G. Nicol, bookseller to His Majesty, Pall-Mall, 1797); George Staunton, *An authentic account of an embassy from the King of Great Britain to the Emperor of China* (Dublin, Printed for P. Wogan [et al.], 1798); George Staunton, *An authentic account of an embassy from the King of Great Britain to the Emperor of China* (Philadelphia: Printed for Robert Campbell, by John Bioren, 1799); this particular account by Staunton was mainly based upon information contained in the papers of George Macartney.

43. Winterbotham, *Historical, Geographical, and Philosophical View*, 2:233.

44. Ibid., 193.

45. Ibid., 197.

46. J. L. Cranmer-Byng, "Lord Macartney's Embassy to Peking in 1793 from Official Chinese Documents," *Journal of Oriental Studies* 6, nos. 1–2 (1957–58): 162. Cranmer-Byng's work presents the Chinese perspective on Macartney's mission and presents readers with Chinese documents in translation; it is valuable because it works with Chinese language materials. It is reprinted in *Britain and the China Trade, 1635–1842*, selected and with an introduction by Patrick Tuck (London: Routledge, 1999), vol. 7.

47. Cranmer-Byng, "Lord Macartney's Embassy," 163.

48. Preface to *Journal of Oriental Studies*, 6.

49. Winterbotham, *Historical, Geographical, and Philosophical View*, 2:197.

50. Cranmer-Byng, "Lord Macartney's Embassy," 163–164.

51. Macartney suggested that the East India Company send their "very finest cloths" rather than the "coarser woolens"; Macartney, *Journal of Oriental Studies*, 105.

52. Macartney, December 29, 1793, *Journal of Oriental Studies*, 208.

53. Cranmer-Byng, "Lord Macartney's Embassy," 178.

54. Quoted in E. H. Pritchard, "The Instructions of the East India Company to Lord Macartney on His Embassy to China and His Reports to the Company, 1792–94. Part II: Letter to the Viceroy and First Report," *Journal of the Royal Asiatic Society of Great Britain & Ireland* no. 3 (July 1938): 395–396, and Cranmer-Byng, "Lord Macartney's Embassy," 178.

55. Quoted in Pritchard, "Instructions," 395–396, and Cranmer-Byng, "Lord Macartney's Embassy," 178.

56. Shaw, *Journals*, 183. For the importance of mapping and size as the indicator of the potential power of the new nation, see chapter 1 here.

57. Native Americans were sometimes able to use the British and French rivalry to their advantage in a similar manner. However, by the end of the French and Indian War, which was fought in North America between 1754 and 1763, the British had assumed dominance in the area, rendering the strategy less effective. See Richard White, *The Middle Ground: Indians, Empires, and Republics in the Great Lakes Region, 1650–1815* (Cambridge: Cambridge University Press, 1991).

58. France's entry into the war of American independence early in 1778 changed the nature of the war and Britain's view of the conflict. As John Shy writes, "with France still the main threat, a new British government was ready to negotiate a peace with the Americans." Shy, "The American Colonies, 1748–1783," in P. J. Marshal, ed., *The Oxford History of the British Empire: The Eighteenth Century* (Oxford: Oxford University Press, 2001), 322; and Stephen Conway, "Britain and the Revolutionary Crisis," in ibid., especially 340–341.

59. Shaw, *Journals*, 181.

60. Shaw, *Journals*, quoting the British representative, 181.

61. Shaw, *Journals*, 181–182.

62. Ibid., 181.

63. Ibid.

64. See ibid., 136–39; 151.

65. See ibid., and Cranmer-Byng, "Lord Macartney's Embassy," 178.

66. First eight and then eventually thirteen western nations had factories in Canton. They were located on a quarter-mile area along the riverfront. They included Great Britain, the Netherlands, France, Sweden, Denmark, and later Spain, Greece, the Imperialists, and the United States of America. Each factory flew the flag of its owner's country. Michel Beurdeley, *Chinese Trade Porcelain*, trans. Diana Imber (Rutland, Vt.: Tuttle, 1963), 18 (originally published as *Porcelaine de la Companie des Indes* [Fribourg, Switzerland: Office du Livre S.A., 1963]).

67. Shaw, *Journals*, 179.

68. Ibid., 179–180.

69. Ibid., 180–181.

70. The "imperialists" refers to the Imperial East India Company, which was also known as the Ostend Company (referred to in Dutch as Oostendse Compagnie and in German as Ostender Kompanie). The Austrian private trading company was granted a charter in 1717 by the emperor of the Holy Roman Empire to trade between Ostend in the Austrian Netherlands and the East and West Indies. See Thomas Randall, late vice-consul at Canton, to [Alexander] Hamilton, on the trade with China, August 14, 1791, in *Industrial and Commercial Correspondence of Alexander Hamilton Anticipating*

His Report on Manufactures, ed. Arthur Harrison Cole (Chicago: A. W. Shaw, 1928), 130 n. 4, citing H. B. Morse, *Chronicles of the East India Company*, 5 vols. (Oxford: Clarendon Press, 1926–1929), 1:161. Randall's letter dated August 14, 1791, in which he comments on, among other things, the sale of sea otter skins is also published in Alexander Hamilton, *The Papers of Alexander Hamilton*, 9, Harold Syrett, ed. (New York: Columbia University Press, 1965), 38–54. Randall was eventually able to parlay his second posting as supercargo on the *Empress* into the vice-consulship at Canton.

71. Randall to [Alexander] Hamilton, on the trade with China, August 14, 1791, 130.

72. Ibid., 132.

73. Ibid., 142.

74. William P. Elting Notebook, 1797–1803, Massachusetts Historical Society.

75. William Hunter, *The "Fan Kwae" at Canton before Treaty Days, 1825–1844* (London: Kegan Paul, Trench & Co., 1882; reprint, Taipei: Ch'eng-wen, 1965), 98–101, quoted in Smith, "Essay," 39–40.

76. Specie in this sense refers to "hard money" or coins of precious metal, usually gold or silver.

77. Winterbotham, *Historical, Geographical, and Philosophical View*, 1:41.

78. Ibid., ix.

79. Hunter, *"Fan Kwae" at Canton*, 19–21.

80. Randall to [Alexander] Hamilton, on the trade with China, August 14, 1791, 131.

81. Shaw, *Journals*, 174. To resolve this problem, a *"fiador* is nominated in the co-hoang [*sic*], and the vessel's business done on their joint account" (174). Each foreign ship entering the port also had to secure a comprador to provide them with supplies, and when the ship was too small for profit, the comprador, "besides being paid for all supplies, will have a douceur of a hundred or a hundred and fifty taels. This must be submitted to, as the government derives a stated revenue from every ship, of whatever size, which the comprador has permission to supply" (175).

82. Smith, "Essay," 32.

83. Laboratory analyses by staff at the Winterthur Museum of the enamel decoration on this bowl revealed that the American flag was added by a different hand after the rest of the painting had been completed.

84. For a list of items purchased on the maiden voyage of the *Empress of China* to Canton, consult the records of Frederick Molineux who served as the Captain's Clerk on that trip. During the journey, Molineux recorded the purchases made on the account of Captain John Green in a small blue cloth bound book (that has since been unbound) labeled "RECEIPTS." The second half of the book is written primarily by Samuel Hubbart who sailed with Captain Green on the second voyage of the *Empress of China*. The item is listed under John Green, "Receipts, Canton in China, 1784–1786," Rare Book and Manuscripts Library, University of Pennsylvania, Philadelphia. These records were published in two sources including Samuel Woodhouse, "The Voyage of the Empress of China," *Pennsylvania Magazine of History and Biography* 63:1 (January 1939): 30–36, and Philip Chadwick Foster Smith, *The Empress of China* (Philadelphia: The Philadelphia Maritime Museum, 1984), 259–265.

85. Tchen noted the complexity of these relations: "The confident revolutionary nation and the power it had broken with found a common antagonist in an 'oriental' empire resisting the 'Occident.' Directly engaging China and the Chinese forever complicated America's occidental identity." Tchen has pointed out the significance of the China trade to the "formation of American identity and the contradictions embodied by the founding generation who both strove to be British gentlemen and Revolutionary Americans." Tchen, 26.

86. Freneau was referring to ormulu ware, the most expensive type of porcelain. However, this type of ware never gained popularity in the United States because it was much too costly for the vast majority of American consumers. Jonathan Goldstein, *Philadelphia and the China Trade, 1682–1846: Commercial, Cultural, and Attitudinal Effects* (University Park: Pennsylvania State University Press, 1978), 33.

87. Philip Freneau, "On the First American Ship."

88. For statistics regarding the average consumption of tea in America between 1790–1800 and 1800–1812 see chapter 2, note 133.

89. Until steam power was adopted by the American textile industry, imported nankeen was used to make everyday clothes. This durable, brownish yellow cloth was brought into the country by the thousands of tons. It could be procured in white or blue for a higher price.

90. Of all of the objects brought into the United States via the China trade, porcelain ones have survived in the largest numbers, due to their durability, their cost, and the care people put into preserving them over generations. Therefore, material culture scholars and museums have done the most work on cataloging and identifying these items.

91. Tchen, *New York before Chinatown*, 5.

92. Morris to Harrison, June 13, 1787, Brinton-Coxe Collection, Historical Society of Pennsylvania; also quoted in catalog entry for Morris, in Lee, *Philadelphians and the China Trade*, and Lee, *Philadelphians and the China Trade*, 63.

93. The *Alliance* returned laden with goods on September 17, 1788. This voyage was experimental in several respects. The ship took a new route to China. It sailed east from the Cape of Good Hope and along the southern coast of Australia. Two islands were "discovered" along this route and were dubbed "Morris" and "Alliance." The June departure was unconventional because it was out of season. Morris to Harrison, June 13, 1787, Brinton-Coxe Collection, Historical Society of Pennsylvania.

94. The *Empress* also brought home tea, nankeen, silk, muslins, and gunpowder. Captain John Green's abstract of the manifest is reproduced in Smith, "Essay," app. C, 266 (the manifest itself remains privately held, but Winterthur and the Historical Society of Pennsylvania have microfilm copies, Microfilm M105 and item no. 81.83, respectively).

95. Nancy Ellen Davis, "The American China Trade, 1784–1844: Products for the Middle Class" (Ph.D. diss., George Washington University, 1987).

96. Marley R. Brown III, "Ceramics from Plymouth: 1621–1800—The Documentary Record," in Ian Quimby, ed., *Ceramics in America* (Winterthur, Del.: Henry Francis du Pont Winterthur Musuem, 1974).

97. Chinese artists were extremely skillful at copying decorative designs.

98. See Alfred Tamarin and Shirley Glubok, *Voyaging to Cathay: Americans in the China Trade* (New York: Viking Press, 1976).

99. Shaw was himself wary of being duped: "The knavery of the Chinese, particularly those of the trading class, has become proverbial" (Shaw, *Journals*, 183). Hence the importance of having an experienced supercargo.

100. Winterbotham, *Historical, Geographical, and Philosophical View*, 1:270.

101. "Instructions to Unidentified China Trade Supercargo," Philadelphia Maritime Museum, as quoted in Smith, "Essay," 31.

102. See Sue Ellen Gronewold, "Yankee Doodle went to Canton," *Natural History* 93 (1984): 72.

103. Randall to [Alexander] Hamilton, on the trade with China, August 14, 1791, in Cole, ed., *Industrial and Commercial Correspondence*, 131.

104. On the importance of ginseng in China see E. N. Anderson, *The Food of China* (New Haven, Conn.: Yale University Press, 1988), 113, 230, 235–236, and Edward H. Schafer, "T'ang," in K. C. Chang, ed., *Food in Chinese Culture: Anthropological and Historical Perspectives* (New Haven, Conn.: Yale University Press, 1977), 111–112.

105. [Samuel Shaw], "Remarks on the Commerce of America with China," *The American Museum, or, Universal Magazine* 7 (March 1790): 126.

106. Beginning in the Middle Ages and continuing until the twentieth century westerners used the term "Tartary" to refer to the vast region in central and northern Asia that was ruled by the Mongols during the thirteenth and fourteenth centuries. Winterbotham, *Historical, Geographical, and Philosophical View,* 1:291.

107. Ibid., 290.

108. Ibid., 291.

109. Ibid.

110. Ibid., 291–292. The plant grew at latitude 30–47 degrees north and longitude 10–20 degrees east, reckoning from the meridian of Peking.

111. [Samuel Shaw], "Remarks on the Commerce of America with China," 127.

112. John White Swift to his father, Canton, December 3, 1784. Hildeburn Papers, Historical Society of Pennsylvania, quoted in John W. Swift, P. Hodgkinson, and Samuel W. Woodhouse, "The Voyage of the *Empress of China,*" *Pennsylvania Magazine of History and Biography* 63, no. 1 (1939): 29.

113. [Samuel Shaw], "Remarks on the Commerce of America with China," 127.

114. A native of Connecticut, Edwards (1703–1758) was a Congregational minister considered by scholars to be among America's most influential theologians. He conducted missionary work to Native Americans, wrote influential sermons, and preached widely. See Jonathan Edwards, *The Works of Jonathan Edwards,* vol. 16, *Letters and Personal Writings,* ed. George S. Claghorn (New Haven, Conn.: Yale University Press, 1998), 543. For a comprehensive electronic source see *The Works of Jonathan Edwards Online,* Jonathan Edwards Center, Yale University.

115. Amos Porter, *The China Journal of Amos Porter, 1802–1803* (Greensboro, Vt.: Greensboro Historical Society, 1984), 1.

116. The ship *Amethyst* is listed in Latourette, *Voyages of American Ships to China, 1784–1844. Transactions of the Connecticut Academy of Arts and Sciences* 28 (April 1927): 243. The *Amethyst* was owned by Sullivan Dorr (1778–1858). Early in life, Dorr was engaged in the fur trade on the northwest coast of the United States; at the age of twenty, he went to Canton to follow mercantile pursuits. Much of his business was for the firm of J. & J. Dorr, based in Boston and owned by his brothers, Jonathan and Joseph. He stayed in Canton for five years (1799–1803) and on returning to the states settled in Providence and became a prosperous merchant. He resided in a home he built in 1811 on the northeast corner of Benefit and Bowen Streets.

117. Porter, *China Journal,* 12.

118. Ibid., 12.

119. Ibid.

120. Ibid., 23.

121. Ibid.

122. Samuel Eliot Morison, *The Maritime History of Massachusetts* (Boston: Houghton Mifflin, 1941), 44.

123. Randall, 135.

124. Ibid.

125. Ibid.

126. Ibid. At "garbled," the editor notes: "an archaic phrase meaning pick out the best."

127. There was no American equivalent to the British East India Company or the Dutch East India Company (Vereenigde Oost-Indische Compagnie), which was first established in 1602. Unlike that of European nations, the American trade with China was not regulated, so every trader involved was at liberty to do as he wished. Beurdeley suggested that their style was more in line with "sixteenth-century merchant adventurers than the formal naval gentlemen of eighteenth-century England." Beurdeley, *Chinese Trade Porcelain*, 130. For more on the East India Company, see Philip Lawson, *The East India Company: A History* (London: Longman, 1993). For a study on the business practices of the Company and their involvement in the tea trade, see Hoh-cheung Mui, *Management of Monopoly: A Study of the English East India Company's Conduct of Its Tea Trade, 1784–1833* (Vancouver, B.C.: University of British Columbia Press, 1984). For background on the British presence in Asia, see P. J. Marshall, "The British in Asia: Trade to Dominion, 1700–1765," in *The Oxford History of the British Empire*, Volume II, *The Eighteenth Century*, P. J. Marshall, ed. (Oxford: Oxford University Press, 1998), 487–507. For a study of the previous period of English trade in Asia, see P. J. Marshall, "The English in Asia to 1700," in *The Origins of Empire: British Overseas Enterprise to the Close of the Seventeenth Century*, Volume I in Nicholas Canny, ed., *The Oxford History of the British Empire* (Oxford : Oxford University Press, 1998), 264–285. There have also been museum exhibitions on the British East India Company that focus on the objects of the China Trade. See Anthony Farrington, *Trading Places: The East India Company and Asia, 1600–1834* (London: The British Library, 2002) and Margaret Christman, *Adventurous Pursuits: Americans and the China Trade, 1784–1844* (Washington, D.C.: National Portrait Gallery, 1984).

128. For more on the Pacific world, see Donald Denoon with Stewart Firth et al., eds., *Cambridge History of the Pacific Islanders* (New York: Cambridge University Press, 1997); Alan Frost and Jane Samson, eds., *Pacific Empires: Essays in Honour of Glyndwr Williams* (Vancouver: University of British Columbia Press, 1999). For more specific studies of the American arrival in the Pacific, see James R. Gibson, *Otter Skins, Boston Ships, and China Goods: The Maritime Fur Trade of the Northwest Coast, 1785–1841* (Kingston, Montreal: McGill-Queen's University Press, 1992) and Arrell Gibson, with the assistance of John Whitehead, *Yankees in Paradise: The Pacific Basin Frontier* (Albuquerque: University of New Mexico, 1993).

129. These pieces are extant in museum collections in places throughout New England, Great Britain, the American Northwest Coast, Hawaii, Australia, and other Pacific island locations. There is a wealth of ethnographic studies on these objects and collections in which they reside. See, for instance, Nicholas Thomas, *Entangled Objects: Exchange, Material Culture, and Colonialism in the Pacific* (Cambridge, Mass.: Harvard University Press, 1991) and Patrick V. Kirch and Jean-Louis Rallu, eds., *Growth and Collapse of Pacific Island Societies: Archaeological and Demographic Perspectives* (Honolulu: University of Hawaii Press, 2007).

130. For recent works on the life of John Ledyard (1751–1789) see Edward Gray, *Ledyard: In Search of the First American Explorer* (New Haven, Conn.: Yale University Press, 2007), and Bill Gifford, *The Making of John Ledyard* (New York: Harcourt, 2007). For Ledyard's own writings, see his *Journal of Captain Cook's last voyage to the Pacific Ocean, on Discovery; performed in the years 1776, 1777, 1778, 1779, illustrated with cuts and a chart, shewing the tracts of the ships employed in this expedition. Faithfully narrated from the original* (London: E. Newbery, 1781). It was later reprinted in the United States: Ledyard, *A journal of Captain Cook's last voyage to the Pacific Ocean and in quest of a north-west*

passage, between Asia & America; performed in the years 1776, 1777, 1778, and 1779. Illustrated with a chart, shewing the tracts of the ships employed in this expedition. Faithfully narrated from the original ms. of Mr. John Ledyard (Hartford, Conn.: printed and sold by Nathaniel Patten, a few rods North of the Court-House, 1783). For an account of his later journeys see Ledyard, *Journey through Russia and Siberia, 1787–1788: The Journal and Selected Letters,* ed. Stephen D. Watrous (Madison: University of Wisconsin Press, 1966). For a nineteenth-century account of his life, see the account by the prolific Jared Sparks (1789–1866), *The life of John Ledyard, the American traveller; comprising selections from his journals and correspondence* (Cambridge, Mass.: Hilliard and Brown, 1828).

131. Ebenezer Dorr to Capt Samuel B. Edes, Commander of the Snow Pacific Trader, Boston, Sept 11, 1799, Dorr Family Papers, Massachusetts Historical Society.

132. For an insightful article on the issues discussed here, see David Igler, "Captive-Taking and Conventions of Encounters on the Northwest Coast, 1789–1810," *Southern California Quarterly* 91:1:3–5. For work on global exchanges in the Pacific, see Igler, "Diseased Goods: Global Exchanges in the Eastern Pacific Basin, 1770–1850," *American Historical Review* 109, No. 3 (June 2004): 693–719. Gary Okihiro's *Pineapple Culture: A History of the Tropical and Temperate Zone* (Berkeley: University of California Press, 2009) is an innovative study of a historically significant Pacific plant.

133. *Comic Album: Or, A Book for Every Table* (London: Orr & Co., 1842), quoted in C. Pagani, "Chinese Material Culture and British Perceptions of China," in Tim Barringer and Tom Flynn, eds., *Colonialism and the Object: Empire, Material Culture and the Museum* (London: Routledge, 1998), 32. For studies on foreign trade in Canton that focus on the changes that took place in the nineteenth century, see John K. Fairbank, *Trade and Diplomacy on the China Coast: The Opening of the Treaty Ports, 1842–1854* (Cambridge, Mass.: Harvard University Press, 1953); W. E. Cheong, *Mandarins and Merchants: Jardine Matheson & Company, a China Agency of the Early Nineteenth Century* (London: Curzon Press, 1979); and Jonathan Spence, *The Search for Modern China,* 2nd ed. (New York: W.W. Norton, 1999).

134. Tchen, *New York before Chinatown,* 5.

CHAPTER 4

1. William Bartram (1739–1823), born in Philadelphia, as a young man studied Latin, French, and the classics at Philadelphia Academy. His journeys are not well documented, but he gathered specimens in North and South Carolina, Alabama, Louisiana, Georgia, Florida, and Mississippi. He developed relationships with Creek, Cherokee, and Seminole tribes, who proved essential to his research, as they helped him locate and collect specimens. See *Dictionary of National Biography,* s.v. "Bartram, William."

2. Bartram noted that after the "stately bird" was caught, "[w]e had this fowl dressed for supper and it made excellent soup." Given the choice, it seems the naturalist preferred other dishes: "as long as I can get any other necessary food I shall prefer his [the Sandhill Crane's] seraphic music in the ethereal skies." William Bartram, *Travels through North & South Carolina, Georgia, East & West Florida, the Cherokee country, the extensive territories of the Muscogulges, or Creek Confederacy, and the country of the Chactaws; containing, an account of the soil and natural productions of those regions, together with observations on the manners of the Indians* (Philadelphia: Printed by James & Johnson, 1791), 220–221. This incident is also discussed in Judith Magee, *The Art and Science of William Bartram* (University Park: Pennsylvania State University Press, 2007), 109.

3. Sir Joseph Banks (1743–1820), Baronet of Revesby Abbey, Lincolnshire, attended Harrow School and Eton College, where he developed a love of botany while studying the classical curriculum; he came into his inheritance in 1761 and was thus given the financial freedom to pursue the study of natural history. But because he trained under a Linnaean scholar, Banks must be understood as more than a simple gentleman collector. He served as a naturalist on expeditions to Newfoundland and Labrador, as well as on the expedition of HMS *Endeavour* to Australia, New Zealand, etc., captained by James Cook. Bank's fame from his role in this expedition was widespread. George III became his patron, and in 1773 Banks was appointed director of the Royal Botanical Gardens at Kew. He was subsequently elected president of the Royal Society of London and served in this capacity from 1778 until 1820. See *Dictionary of National Biography*, s.v. "Banks, Sir Joseph."

4. William Bartram to Robert Barclay, November 1788, quoted in David Rembert, Jr., "The Botanical Explorations of William Bartram in the Southeast," paper presented at the Bartram Trail Conference Symposium, 1991.

5. William Bartram's drawings are scattered throughout collections in Britain. Some were purchased by Sir Joseph Banks after the death of William Bartram's patron John Fothergill in 1780 and are part of the Natural History Museum, London. The Natural History Museum also houses the William Bartram Drawings Collection, which includes sixty-eight botanical drawings. Most of these were sent by Bartram to Fothergill in the years 1772–1776. Others that had been in the possession of Peter Collinson made their way into the collection of Edward Smith-Stanley (1775–1851), the thirteenth Earl of Derby. Over forty of Bartram's drawings are held at Knowsley Hall, the ancestral home of the Earl of Derby. See Joseph Ewan, *Botanical and Zoological Drawings, 1756–1788* (Philadelphia: American Philosophical Society, 1968), 31–32; see also Rembert, "Botanical Explorations."

6. See Richard Drayton, *Nature's Government: Science, Imperial Britain, and the Improvement of the World* (New Haven, Conn.: Yale University Press, 2000).

7. For studies on the practice of natural science in the colonial era, see Susan Scott Parrish, *American Curiosity: Cultures of Natural History in the Colonial British Atlantic World* (Chapel Hill: University of North Carolina Press, 2006).

8. There is a striking parallel between the role of Anglo-American naturalists and that of the Asian Indian artists employed by British colonial officials in India to gather and draw initial sketches of botanical specimens.

9. While the difference in status between an Anglo-American and an Indian from India may seem stark, their structural position within the hierarchy of the international production of scientific information is in fact not so disparate. Both groups were recruited by Europeans to toil in the field in order to gather information that would be processed and published in Europe. As discussed in this chapter, "native" informants in both locations most often were not given credit for their work. The production of J. D. Hooker, *Illustrations of Himalayan Plants* is a good example of the multilayered hierarchical process of botanical print production. Both it and Hooker's *Rhododendrons of Sikkim-Himalaya* feature excellent hand-colored lithographs based on rough sketches by teams of unnamed Indian artists. During his time in Calcutta, James F. Cathcart, a Scottish man who was working for the Bengal Civil Service employed a team of at least six Indian artists to produce botanical sketches. Historical accounts describe him as the quintessential colonial master at the outer regions of the empire. He was "occupying a large house, surrounded by a broad verandah... on the floor of which living plants of all kinds were piled in profusion. He had already established a corps of Indian collectors, who scoured the neighboring forests, descend-

ing to 2,000 feet, and ascending to 8,000, bringing every plant that was to be found in flower; and in his house were two artists busily at work … he intended to procure more artists." Hooker, *Illustrations of Himalayan Plants, Chiefly Selected from Drawings Made for the Late J. F. Cathcart, esquire. The descriptions and analyses by J.D. Hooker. The plates executed by W. H. Fitch* (London: L. Reeve, 1855), iii. The Royal Botanic Gardens, which also hired native East Indian artists, had amassed nearly a thousand drawings of little-known flora executed by these artists and was intending to publish them in a book at the time that Cathcart died suddenly in 1851. His friend Sir Joseph Dalton Hooker completed the book in tribute to him. In order to do this, Hooker recruited talented botanical engraver Walter Hood Fitch, who "corrected the stiffness and want of botanical knowledge displayed by the native artists who executed most of the originals." Hooker, *Illustrations of Himalayan Plants*, iii.

10. The term "scientist" began to be used in the nineteenth century. Before that, the term "philosopher" was used as a general term or more specific designations such as "botanist" and "physician." For this reason I use the term "naturalist" rather than "scientist" in this book.

11. Brooke Hindle, *The Pursuit of Science in Revolutionary America* (New York: Norton, 1956).

12. Adam Smith, *The Wealth of Nations* (London: Penguin Classics, 1986). For classic studies of the Enlightenment see Peter Gay, *The Enlightenment: An Interpretation* (New York: Norton, 1969), and Henry May, *The Enlightenment in America* (New York: Oxford University Press, 1976).

13. Francis W. Pennell, "Benjamin Smith Barton as Naturalist," *Proceedings of the American Philosophical Society* 86, no. 1 (1942): 109.

14. The study was published in Edinburgh in 1787, while Barton was a medical student there. Benjamin Smith Barton, *Observations on Some Parts of Natural History,* pt. 1 (Edinburgh, 1787).

15. The two unpublished essays that Barton wrote while he was a student in Edinburgh in the years 1786–1788 are in the Collections of the Royal Medical Society, Mss. Manuscripts, 22:171–180, 207–213; 23:1–17, as cited by Whitfield Bell, Jr., *Early American Science Needs and Opportunities for Study* (Williamsburg, Va.: Institute of Early American History and Culture, 1955), 46. See also Frank Spencer, "Two Unpublished Essays on the Anthropology of North America by Benjamin Smith Barton," *Isis* 68, no. 4 (Dec., 1977): 567–573.

16. Historian Whitfield Bell, Jr., described Barton as "able, ambitious, industrious, apparently not without charm." Bell, "Benjamin Smith Barton, M.D. (Kiel)," *Journal of the History of Medicine and Allied Sciences* 26, no. 2 (1971): 200.

17. Banks was president from 1778 to 1820.

18. See correspondence, meeting minutes, and committee reports in "The Royal Society of Arts, London. Selected materials relating to America, 1754–1806" (film), 2 reels, Manuscript Collections, American Philosophical Society, Philadelphia.

19. Among the people Barton sent questionnaires to were John Heckewelder, David Zeisberger, Henry M. Brackenridge, and Christopher Miller. Barton collected information about North American Indian tribes from a Mr. McGee, who served as an interpreter for the tribes. Barton, [untitled], February 4, 1799, and "Journal Concerning Indians," Violetta Delafield-Benjamin Smith Barton Collection (1783–1817), American Philosophical Society. See also Pennell, "Benjamin Smith Barton as Naturalist," 112.

20. For an informative discussion of the dissemination of information in the eighteenth and nineteenth centuries see Richard D. Brown, *Knowledge Is Power: The Diffusion*

of Information in Early America, 1700–1865 (New York: Oxford University Press, 1989). Specifically, chapter 8 of Brown's study, "William Bentley and the Ideal of Universal Information in the Enlightened Republic," focuses on an American who served as a nexus of foreign and domestic information for his compatriots in a manner similar to Barton.

21. Banks was much more circumspect in his relations with the French, who were Britain's scientific superiors and closest rivals. As John Gascoigne argued, "relations with France, Europe's premier scientific nation and Britain's ancient and persistent foe, called for much more complex scientific diplomacy." Gascoigne, Science in the Service of Empire: Joseph Banks, the British State and the Uses of Science in the Age of Revolution (Cambridge: Cambridge University Press, 1998), 152–153. Scientific diplomacy was as duplicitous as any other. Although willing to accept the material gestures of friendship in the form of plant cuttings for his precious Kew Gardens from eager postcolonial Americans, Banks's disdain for Americans and American philosophy was known to those in London. He diplomatically said little about this in public. "A Review of Some Leading Points in the Official Character and Proceedings of the late President of the Royal Society," London and Edinburgh Philosophical Magazine 56 (1820): 161–174, 241–257. Gascoigne, Science in the Service of Empire, 43–44.

22. The Philadelphia Medical and Physical Journal, Collected and Arranged By Benjamin Smith Barton, M.D., Professor of Materia Medica, Natural History, and Botany, in the University of Pennsylvania, vol. 1 (Philadelphia: John Conrad, 1805), iii–iv.

23. Founded in 1798, the Missionary Society of Connecticut was the first major voluntary missionary society in America. Though in most historical texts the society refers to itself as the MSC, I have followed the convention of historians in labeling it the CMS. Colin Goodykoontz, Home Missions on the American Frontier (Caldwell, Id.: Caxton, 1939), 114. According to James Rohrer, it was the "largest and most influential orthodox missionary agency." In the two decades after its founding, Rohrer notes that the Society employed a total of 148 missionaries to work in Vermont, New York, Pennsylvania, and the territory northwest of the Ohio River. Rohrer, Keepers of the Covenant: Frontier Missions and the Decline of Congregationalism, 1774–1818 (New York: Oxford University Press, 1995), 11–12. William Warren Sweet concurs that the CMS was the most important state missionary society in New England because of its size and the span of its missionary work in the frontier areas where New Englanders were migrating. According to Sweet, the CMS commissioned and supported 276 missionaries between 1798 and 1859. The CMS took in $252,512.83, and it was estimated that almost five hundred churches were organized through its work. Sweet, Religion on the American Frontier, vol. 3, The Congregationalists (Chicago: University of Chicago Press, 1939), 67. The best secondary sources on the CMS include those studies listed above. See also Ronald H. Norricks, "To Turn Them From Darkness: The Missionary Society of Connecticut on the Early Frontier, 1798–1814," Ph.D. diss., University of California, Riverside, 1975. Other studies also contain useful discussions of the activities of the CMS as well as broader treatments of the history of missionary societies in America. They include: Charles L. Chaney, The Birth of Missions in America (South Pasadena, Calif.: William Carey Library, 1976); Oliver Wendell Elsbree, The Rise of the Missionary Spirit in America, 1790–1815 (Williamsport, Penn.: The Williamsport Printing & Binding Co., 1928); Charles Roy Keller, The Second Great Awakening in Connecticut (New Haven, Conn.: Yale University Press, 1942); and Richard D. Shiels, "The Connecticut Clergy in the Second Great Awakening," Ph.D. diss., Boston University, 1976.

24. The LMS was an interdenominational organization formed in 1795 by British evangelical Methodists, Presbyterians, Independents, and Episcopalians who organized to send missions to remote areas of the globe. Ruth Bloch, *Visionary Republic: Millennial Themes in American Thought, 1756–1800* (Cambridge: Cambridge University Press, 1985), 220. For more information on the activities of British missionary societies such as the LMS, see Niel Gunson, *Messengers of Grace: Evangelical Missionaries in the South Seas, 1797–1860* (Melbourne: Oxford University Press, 1978), and Stephen Neill, *Christian Missions* (Baltimore: Penguin Books, 1964).

25. See Bloch, *Visionary Republic*, and Bloch, "Battling Infidelity, Heathenism, and Licentiousness: New England Missions and the Post-revolutionary Frontier, 1792–1805," 46–47, also published in Frederick Williams, ed., *The Northwest Ordinance: Essays on Its Formulation, Provisions, and Legacy* (East Lansing: Michigan State University Press, 1989); *Rohrer, Keepers of the Covenant*; William R. Hutchison, *Errand to the World: American Protestant Thought and Foreign Missions* (Chicago: University of Chicago Press, 1987). The CMS, like the foreign missionary societies Hutchison discusses, had strong ties to coworkers in Britain. These organizations "maintained strong ties and active correspondence with their European (overwhelmingly this meant British) counterparts." For the foreign missionary societies, the "obligations of a general Anglo-American community were stressed along with those of Protestantism at large, and almost as much as those of the specially favored Americans." This commitment to an Anglo-American alliance was repeatedly communicated in everything from promotional publications to public sermons. Hutchison, *Errand to the World*, 44. The articles published in the *Connecticut Evangelical Magazine* (Hartford, Conn.) (hereafter *CEM*) reflect the strength of these transatlantic religious networks. For instance, see the article entitled "Christian Unity," which made a call for a "visible union to be sought by all his followers in this world" who are "directed to unite and incorporate themselves into one visible society, which is called a church." "Christian Unity," *CEM* 4, no. 8 (February 1804), 302. One piece entitled "The records of the Connecticut Missionary Society" is available on microfilm: *Missionary Society of Connecticut Papers, 1759–1948*, microfilm edition, 20 microfilm reels (Glen Rock, N.J.: Microfilming Corporation of America, 1976). This microfilm series includes minutes, reports, correspondence, sermons, and published items including the *Connecticut Evangelical Magazine*. The first series of the magazine was entitled the *Connecticut Evangelical Magazine*; it was published from July 1800 to June 1807. There was a second series of the magazine that was renamed the *Connecticut Evangelical Magazine and Religious Intelligencer*. This series was published from January 1808 to December 1815. The entire run of both of the series are available on microfilm.

26. See C. Vann Woodward's argument about the inequality of the relationship of Old World and New in *The Old World's New World* (New York: Oxford University Press, 1991).

27. Abel Flint served as secretary of the CMS for several years in the early nineteenth century. Thomas Howeis to Abel Flint, January 31, 1801, *Missionary Society of Connecticut Papers, 1759–1948*, microfilm edition, London Missionary Society Letters, reel 13.

28. George Burder, "Extract of a Letter from the Secretary of the London Missionary Society, to the Trustees of the Missionary Society of Connecticut, dated, London, August 22, 1803," *CEM* 4, no. 7 (January 1804): 277–278.

29. LMS to CMS, August 22, 1803, *Missionary Society of Connecticut Papers, 1759–1948*, microfilm edition. While acknowledging their work among the "vacant churches" of the transplanted New Englanders on the frontier, Burder certainly supported the LMS's priority of sending missions to the Indian tribes.

30. Issues of the *CEM,* which were regularly sent to the LMS, consistently high-lighted the activities of David Bacon, who between 1800 and 1804 went on the Society's only mission to the American Indians. In 1800, Bacon traveled to Detroit as a CMS missionary and preached to both European American settlers and Indians. Like many other missionaries, Bacon was inspired by the life of David Brainerd, who half a century earlier had worked, in the words of Rohrer, "ineffectively" for a few years among the Indians of New York, New Jersey, and Pennsylvania before succumbing to tuberculosis. Rohrer, *Keepers of the Covenant,* 109–110. During Bacon's tour of duty, he ran into difficulty supporting himself and his wife and child on the $200-a-year salary he drew from the CMS. To make matters worse, he also had to use his salary to pay for an Indian translator. For three years, Bacon's repeated requests for more money were turned down by the CMS. David Bacon to Abel Flint, February 11, 1803, *Missionary Society of Connecticut Papers, 1759–1948,* quoted at 125. See, for example, "Religious Intelligence," *CEM* 1, no. 3 (September 1800): 118–119; "Religious Intelligence: Missionaries," *CEM* 1, no. 4 (October 1800): 158–160; "Religious Intelligence: Missionaries," *CEM* 1, no. 5 (November 1800): 197–199; David Bacon, "Religious Intelligence: Missionaries," *CEM* 1, no. 6 (December 1800): 274–278; "Religious Intelligence: Missionaries," *CEM* 2, no. 7 (January 1801): 280; "Religious Intelligence," *CEM* 2, no. 4 (October 1801): 156–160; Article 5—No Title, *CEM* 3, no. 4 (October 1802): 159; "Religious Intelligence," *CEM* 3, no. 9 (March 1803): 359–360; "Attempts to Christianize the Indians in New-England," *CEM* 4, no. 1 (July 1803): 5–15; "Religious Intelligence," *CEM* 6, no. 8 (February 1806): 319–320. Indeed, even though the annual "narrative on the subject of missions" for the year 1803 was buried at the back of the March 1804 issue, the editors decided to break the narrative in the middle so that they could begin the April issue with a report on Bacon's activities. *CEM* 4, no. 9 (March 1804): 328–336, and *CEM* 4, no. 10 (April 1804). This notice-able emphasis on the CMS's single Indian mission is interesting, in light of the fact that all agreed that Bacon's sincere efforts had failed to make a lasting impression. In fact, the trustees recalled Bacon from the field in 1804 against his wishes, reassigning him to work among whites in Connecticut. The magazine consistently placed as the lead story on its front page a serial account by Cotton Mather of Reverend John Eliot's activities among natives in Natick, Massachusetts—a mission that had taken place over a century earlier during the late 1600s. After Bacon returned from the field in 1804, the CMS no longer had any active missionary efforts among Native American tribes about which to write. In order to satisfy readers' interest in the topic, they began to publish serialized accounts of seventeenth- and eighteenth-century missionary efforts. Serialization in the *CEM* represented the editors' embrace of emergent market strat-egies to further their religious endeavors. For an explication of how Anglo-American religious leaders engaged in the emerging consumer society and used market strategies to spread the Word, see Harry Stout, *The Divine Dramatist: George Whitefield and the Rise of Modern Evangelicalism* (Grand Rapids, Mich.: Eerdmans, 1991). The disparity between the widespread publication of stories about past Indian missions and the CMS's actual work among native tribes was not necessarily disingenuous. However the focus on Bacon was indicative of the self-consciousness of the CMS concerning their lack of work among natives.

31. It is important to note that since the seventeenth century when Puritans embarked on their "errand into the wilderness," there had been a concern about saving the Indians in the New World. William Hutchison writes, however, that, "Insofar as the errand had looked to the saving or improving of others, it had involved a fitful concern

about the Indians, and a somewhat steadier sense of obligation toward England and Protestant Europe." Hutchison, *Errand to the World*, 6.

32. CMS to LMS, July 12, 1803, *Missionary Society of Connecticut Papers, 1759–1948*, reel 13.

33. CMS to LMS, July 12, 1803, *Missionary Society of Connecticut Papers, 1759–1948*.

34. In 1803, the CMS issued *Summary of Christian Doctrine*, a pamphlet containing the basic tenets of the Congregational faith. They also published and distributed materials for the edification of young children, such as Joseph Emerson's *Evangelical Primer*. The Book Committee of the CMS also sent newly formed congregations hundreds of Bibles and the *Hartford Selection of Hymns*. Jack T. Ericson, ed., *Missionary Society of Connecticut Papers, 1759–1948: A Guide to the Microfilm Edition* (Glen Rock, N.J.: Microfilming Corporation of America, 1976), 7.

35. *Connecticut Evangelical Magazine and Religious Intelligencer* (Hartford, Conn.) (hereafter *CEMRI*), new ser., 6, no. 7 (July 1813): 280.

36. Because a relationship between two unequal parties is always one of subordination, the rhetoric of patronage can edge suspiciously close to a patronizing language. The British were well aware of how their American children looked up to them as a model. In a letter dated November 10, 1802, Joseph Hardcastle, LMS Secretary to CMS, Hardcastle responded to the CMS professions of admiration by humbly acknowledging that "the Lord is employing us as instruments, however unworthy, of promoting his cause and interest, in the world, and of furthering his blessed designs and eternal purposes."

37. Inspired by the Second Great Awakening, the American Board of Commissioners for Foreign Missions was the first American Christian foreign mission agency. It was founded by individuals who had recently graduated from Williams College in Williamstown, Massachusetts. Although it was Congregationalist, it sponsored missions undertaken by members of other denominations such as Presbyterians. There were strong links between the CMS and the ABCFM. At the founding of the latter, CMS president John Treadwell was a board member and president. Hutchison, *Errand to the World*, 43. The quote in the text is taken from an article "Religious Intelligence: Domestic," *CEMRI*, new ser. 4, no. 11 (November 1811): 419–420. The article discussed in detail Adoniram Judson's "special mission to England" "to confer with the Directors of the London Missionary Society." The instructions given to him by the board of the ABCFM were published in the newspaper. For a relatively recent study of the Judson family, see Joan Jacobs Brumberg, *Mission for Life: The Story of the Family of Adoniram Judson, the Dramatic Events of the First American Foreign Mission, and the Course of Evangelical Religion in the Nineteenth Century* (New York: Free Press, 1980).

38. LMS to CMS, July 12, 1803, and LMS to CMS, August 22, 1803, *Missionary Society of Connecticut Papers, 1759–1948*, reel 13.

39. LMS to CMS, July 12, 1803, *Missionary Society of Connecticut Papers, 1759–1948*, reel 13.

40. CMS to Revs. C. Strong and N. Williamson, July 5, 1800, "Outgoing Correspondence, 1798–1861" (file), *Missionary Society of Connecticut Papers, 1759–1948*, reel 14.

41. CMS to Rev. John Sergeant, February 22, 1802, *Missionary Society of Connecticut Papers, 1759–1948*, reel 14.

42. CMS to J. Sergeant, February 22, 1802, *Missionary Society of Connecticut Papers, 1759–1948*, reel 14.

43. Rohrer's research supports Reverend Waterman's objections, noting that the CMS had a surplus of funds during this period. Between 1798 and 1825, the Permanent Fund generated more than $35,000 in interest alone for missionary efforts. Rohrer, *Keepers of the Covenant*, 66.

44. *CEM* 4, no. 1 (July 1803): 27–28.

45. CMS to Rev. Joseph Badger, February 24, 1804, *Missionary Society of Connecticut Papers, 1759–1948*, reel 14.

46. CMS to the LMS, March 20, 1805, *Missionary Society of Connecticut Papers, 1759–1948*, reel 14.

47. Ibid.

48. Modern accounts of the CMS do not stress the role of the LMS in shaping activities of the Americans such as the decision to create a Book Committee. Jack Ericson (editor of *Missionary Society of Connecticut Papers, 1759–1948: A Guide to the Microfilm Edition)* simply states that the "trustees were not content with merely sending missionaries to the new settlements; they also *realized* that the settlers lacked all types of reading materials and particularly religious books and Bibles"; my italics. In dropping the British out of the story, not only does such a reading reflect how American scholars have overlooked transnational influences on the lives of Americans in the postrevolutionary era, it indicates how such episodes have been interpreted from a progressive perspective of American exceptionalism. Any action that differentiated Americans from the British was a sign of the increasing independence of American religious institutions from the British. Erickson, *Missionary Society of Connecticut Papers*, 6.

49. *CEM* 1, no. 1 (July 1800): 5.

50. See Henry Lowood, "The New World and the European Catalog of Nature," in Karen Ordahl Kupperman, ed., *America in European Consciousness, 1493–1750* (Chapel Hill: University of North Carolina Press, 1995), 299.

51. As historian Brooke Hindle writes: "The Americans, whether such assiduous collectors as Bartram or competent classifiers of the capacity of [Alexander] Garden and [John] Mitchell, depended upon the intellectual stimulus they received from Europe. Their raw material was found in America but it was only from Europe that encouragement to exploit it was derived. It was inevitable that the knowledge to understand and apply American raw material must come from Europe." Hindle, *Pursuit of Science*, 58.

52. Peter Collinson (1694–1768), botanist, was born to a Quaker family of cloth merchants in London who had extensive trade connections with America. He developed friendships with Americans Benjamin Franklin, Alexander Garden, Cadwallader Colden, and John Bartram. Collinson organized a system in which Bartram supplied North American seeds and plants to British patrons in return for an annual subscription. Collinson supported botany in other ways such as lending Mark Catesby the money to publish his *Natural History of Carolina. Dictionary of American Biography,* s.v. "Peter Collinson." Physician and botanist John Fothergill (1712–1780) was born to a Quaker family in Yorkshire, England. He had a great interest in natural history due to the influence of a patron who also convinced him to pursue a medical education at the University of Edinburgh. While a student there he joined the newly established Medical Society (later the Royal Medical Society of Edinburgh). Fothergill earned his M.D. in 1736 with a thesis on the use of emetics. An enthusiast of botany, Fothergill was a close friend of Collinson and through that connection became friends with Americans such as Franklin. Fothergill became involved with American affairs and wrote a pamphlet entitled *Considerations Relative to the North American Colonies* (1765), which argued for the repeal of the Stamp Act and the just treatment of Americans. In the conclusion of

this work he writes, "Remember, my Countrymen, that the *Americans* are not a con-
quered, but a free People; descended from freeborn *Englishmen* for the most Part, and
those who are of another Progeny, have acquired the like Sentiments, by Proximity and
Acquaintance. They are People of the like Passions with ourselves, and look upon oppres-
sive Power, with the same Spirit of Intolerance; while their Generosity and Affection, to
those who treat them kindly, is like the Region they inhabit, vast, and whose Limits are
hitherto unknown." John Fothergill, *Considerations Relative to the North American
Colonies* (London: Printed by Henry Kent, 1765), 46. In 1775 he participated in an effort
to prevent a war with America. *Dictionary of American Biography*, s.v. "John Fothergill."

53. Collinson sent a glass tube needed to conduct electrical experiments as well as
an account, published in Germany, that explained how to repeat experiments in
electricity. Both books and glassware were material objects of science that Americans
imported from Britain. This example also highlights the fact that at this time, Americans
commonly imported books from other European nations through British contacts.
Collinson and Fothergill also supported the effort to publish Franklin's work. In 1751,
Fothergill wrote the preface for a collection of letters by Franklin entitled *Experiments
and Observations on Electricity*. Hindle, *Pursuit of Science,* 74–79. Collinson also sent
Edward Cave some of Franklin's letters. Cave published them in *Gentleman's Magazine*
20 (1750): 34–35.

54. Of course, British society was transformed by its contact and connections to
America and other distant lands as well. See Gascoigne, *Science in the Service of Empire.*

55. The full title of the book donated by Fothergill is *An experimental history of the
materia medica, or of the natural and artificial substances made use of in medicine:containing
a compendious view of their natural history, and account of their pharmaceutical properties, and an estimate of their medicinal powers* (London: printed by H. Baldwin, for the
author; and sold by R. Willock, 1761). It is held in the collections of the Pennsylvania
Hospital Clinical Library, Philadelphia, Pennsylvania. Hindle, *Pursuit of Science,* 114.

56. There are two dates pertinent to the founding of the American Philosophical
Society and John Bartram (1699–1777) was involved in both efforts. The first effort at
organization took place in 1743, and in 1767 there was an effort to revive the struggling
organization. According to often-quoted American nationalist lore, Swedish naturalist
Carl Linnaeus, known as the father of modern scientific classification, called John
Bartram 'the greatest natural botanist in the world.'" Interestingly, the original source of
this well-quoted compliment cannot be found. See Robert McCracken Peck, "William
Bartram: Sowing with the Harvest," in Catherine Hutchins, ed., *Shaping a National
Culture: The Philadelphia Experience* (Winterthur, Del.: Henry Francis DuPont
Winterthur Museum, 1994), 209 n. 4.

57. As I will discuss later in this chapter, Miller's book provided the most popular
model on which many American gardens were based.

58. Peck, "William Bartram," 202.

59. My discussion of the careers of John and William Bartram has been informed by
Thomas Slaughter, *The Natures of John and William Bartram* (New York: Knopf, 1996).

60. John Bartram wanted the name of Sir Hans Sloane, president of the Royal Society,
engraved in the goblet so that when his friends drank from it, "they may see who was my
benefactor." As Slaughter writes, John Bartram's "need didn't stop at a lie, which is what
this vessel was.... The engraving was even antedated to memorialize a friendship that
never existed, as if Sloane had really bought a chalice and inscribed personal sentiments
instead of passing along cash for plants to a merchant representing the colonist who
found them in the woods." Slaughter, *Natures of John and William Bartram,* 99.

61. Gascoigne, *Science in the Service of Empire* discusses the importance of botanical collecting to the British imperial project. For an "official" history of Kew Gardens, see Ray Desmond, *Kew: The History of the Royal Botanic Gardens,* with a foreword by Professor Sir Ghillean Prance (London: Harvill Press, 1995).

62. Collinson's patronage gave him ownership of Bartram's intellectual property, which would later prove frustrating to the young American hopeful.

63. "Small Mud Tortoise," print of drawing by William Bartram, in Bartram, *Botanical and Zoological Drawings.* One of Bartram's earliest illustrations in the collection, executed sometime between 1755 and 1756 and entitled "Magnolia Warbler, Dendroica magnolia," was finished when William was drawing birds for Edwards and trees for Collinson, in what some have called his "stump and Magpie" period.

64. George Edwards, *Gleanings of natural history: exhibiting figures of quadrupeds, birds, insects, plants, &c* (London: Royal College of Physicians, 1758–1764), copy in Beinecke Rare Book and Manuscript Library, Yale University.

65. Edwards, *Gleanings of Natural History,* 174; emphasis in original.

66. Edwards furthered his reputation in the British-centered world of natural history scholarship using materials Bartram gathered and drew in the field.

67. Edwards supplied the deficiency of Sir Hans Sloane's pronouncements on the thrush, noting that Slone had labeled this bird "simply the Thrush, and says they frequent the woody mountains, etc. but whether or no it be a bird of passage, he doth not inform us." Edwards refers readers to Sloane's *History of Jamaica,* 2:305. Edwards, *Gleanings of Natural History,* 184.

68. Edwards refers to Catesby's *Hist[ory]. of Carolina,* 1:31. Edwards, *Gleanings of Natural History,* 184.

69. European ornithologists had long puzzled over where swallows wintered. Most speculated that these birds hid in caves or hibernated in the mud during the winter. Bartram's permanent residency in North America was crucial in overturning this notion. The American took great pleasure in being able to provide observations that served as evidence that would dispel this belief. He provided a lengthy account of his observations of the migratory patterns of large flocks of swallows. In his studies, he saw these birds flying south over the Carolinas and then returning to nest in Pennsylvania in the spring. In 1791, Bartram published these findings in his most famous work, *Travels through North and South Carolina, Georgia, East and West Florida, the Cherokee country, the extensive territories of the Muscogulges or Creek confederacy, and the country of the Chactaws. Containing an account of the soil and natural productions of those regions; together with observations on the manners of the Indians* (Philadelphia: James & Johnson, 1791). The book was quickly published overseas in London and Dublin. See Bartram, *Travels through North and South Carolina, Georgia, East and West Florida* (Philadelphia, Printed by James and Johnson, 1791, London, Reprinted for J. Johnson, 1792); Bartram, *Travels through North and South Carolina, Georgia, East and West Florida* (Dublin: For J. Moore, W. Jones, R. M'Allister, and J. Rice, 1793); Bartram, *Travels through North and South Carolina, Georgia, East and West Florida* 2d ed. in London (Philadelphia, Printed by James and Johnson, 1791, London, Reprinted for J. Johnson, 1794). In this work, Bartram makes it a point to explain why European writers had been thus far silent on the subject of migration, noting that the knowledge required to answer the question could only "be acquired by travelling and residing the whole year at least in the various climates from north to south." William Bartram's book influenced British society in an unintended manner. Romantic poets such as William

Wordsworth and Samuel Taylor Coleridge found his book inspiring because of Bartram's deep understanding and connection with the natural world. For Bartram's contribution to the knowledge of the migratory habits of the swallow, see Bartram, *Travels*, 272. In *The Book of Nature*, Margaret Welsh discusses how naturalists living year round in America enjoyed the "advantages of residency." In a subsection entitled "Besting the Europeans" she writes that Alexander Wilson (who was born and raised in Scotland, but proudly adopted America as his new home) hoped that the scientific work produced in America would "succeed on European terms." Wilson "boasted that the homegrown 'elegance' of domestic typesetting, binding, and paper quality was 'not inferior' to English rivals. In this era of fervid promotion of U.S. manufactures, Wilson went so far as to apologize for the imported watercolors but took pains to note that the rags from which the paper was made were American." See Welsh, *The Book of Nature: Natural History in the United States 1825–1875* (Boston: Northeastern University Press, 1998), 27–29. See also Bruce Silver, "William Bartram's and Other Eighteenth-century Accounts of Nature," *Journal of the History of Ideas* 39, no. 4 (1978): 601; Andrew J. Lewis, "A Democracy of Facts, an Empire of Reason: Swallow Submersion and Natural History in the Early American Republic," *William and Mary Quarterly* 62, no. 4 (2004): 663–696.

70. Edwards had edited the very Catesby study he was critiquing.

71. Edwards, *Gleanings of Natural History*, 174.

72. Ibid. For further evidence of the same sentiment, see also the commentary on "The White-Throated Sparrow, and the Yellow Butterfly," in which he writes: "I have never seen the bird; but thought Mr. Bartram's drawing of it very curious, and have reason to be satisfied as to his veracity and accuracy." Edwards, *Gleanings of Natural History*, 198–199.

73. George Edwards's public acknowledgment of William Bartram's contributions to his work was integral to the development of the young American's career. In several of his commentaries on various North American birds, Edwards mentions his reliance on the preserved specimen and written descriptions Bartram sent to him. The fact that Bartram lived permanently in North America was important because some observations, such as those about the migration patterns of many bird species, could only come from a year-round resident of North America. As Joseph Ewan notes, Edwards "quoted William's notes on Pennsylvania birds, especially migrants." For instance the "Little Thrush" was from a specimen William had sent to Edwards. See Ewan, *Botanical and Zoological Drawings*, 19–20.

74. For example, in "The White-Throated Sparrow and the Yellow Butterfly," Edwards had to trust Bartram's "neat drawing in colours" because the actual specimens were not sent along with it to England. On another print, Edward notes: "The Fly was brought from Carolina, and engraved on the plate from nature." Edwards, *Gleanings of Natural History*, 174, 198–199.

75. Edwards, *Gleanings of Natural History*, 195.

76. The artifact is mentioned in Bartram's *Travels,* a well-received book that was republished several times. For instance, one edition was published in Philadelphia by James & Johnson in 1791 and reprinted in London by J. Johnson in 1792; another reprint was issued in Dublin by J. Moore, W. Jones, R. M'Allister, and J. Rice in 1793; the second edition was published in London by James & Johnson in 1791 and reprinted in London by J. Johnson in 1794.

77. See my earlier discussion (chapter 1) on mapping and the significance of the concept of empty cartographic space to describe America during the colonial periods and the early republic.

78. Many of the dried specimens Bartram collected and sent to England still reside in the collections of the British Museum of Natural History. Peck, "William Bartram," 204; Bartram, *Botanical and Zoological Drawings*.

79. William's younger brother John, Jr. (1743–1812), managed the financial side of the business.

80. Manasseh Cutler (1742–1823) graduated from Yale College in 1765. Among other things, he a founder of Ohio University and the Ohio Company, and was a Congregational minister. A learned man, Cutler was interested in botanical research, medicine, law, and astronomy. A Federalist, he served two terms as a representative from Massachusetts from 1801–1804.

81. See W. P. Cutler and J. P. Cutler, eds., *The Life, Journals, and Correspondence of Reverend Manasseh Cutler L.L.D.*, 2 vols. (Cincinnati: R. Clarke, 1888), 1:258.

82. Slaughter, *Natures of John and William Bartram*, 81. Bartram's garden was more analogous to modern nurseries that grow plants for sale rather than a decorative garden. It is estimated that during the colonial period, John Bartram provided Europe with one-third of the total of all American plants sent there, making him a successful salesman of nature. American amateur collectors, like Bartram, would pull plants from the ground, send their finds to British middlemen, such as Collinson, who would take them to rich gentlemen in England to put in their beautifully grand formal gardens.

83. For more on the symbolic and social meanings of gardens, see Richard Bushman, *The Refinement of America: Persons, Houses, Cities* (New York: Knopf, 1992), 127–131. My overall project has been greatly informed by Bushman's study, particularly on its emphasis in analyzing social relations in this period through the prism of material culture. See also Tamara Thornton, *Cultivating Gentlemen: The Meaning of Country Life among the Boston Elite, 1785–1860* (New Haven, Conn.: Yale University Press, 1989). I thank Ann Fabian for bringing this work to my attention.

84. The title of the book noted specifically that it was intended for use in England. Philip Miller, *The gardeners dictionary*, 2nd ed., corr[ected]. (London, 1733), copy in Beinecke Rare Book and Manuscript Library, Yale University. See also the fifth and sixth editions of this immensely popular book, both entitled *The abridgement of the Gardeners dictionary: containing the best and newest methods of cultivating and improving the kitchen, fruit, flower garden, and nursery; as also for performing the practical parts of husbandry: together with the management of vineyards, and the methods of making wine in England. In which likewise are included, directions for propagating and improving, from real practice and experience, pasture lands and all sorts of timber trees*, and published in London: printed for the author; and sold by John Rivington; A. Millar, J. Whiston, and B. White, H. Woodfall, 1763 and 1771, respectively, copies in Beinecke Rare Book and Manuscript Library, Yale University. The continued popularity of this work is reflected in its numerous republications as well as supplementary books by Miller, for instance *The gardeners kalendar: directing what works are necessary to be performed every month in the kitchen, fruit, and pleasure-gardens, as also in the conservatory and nursery by Philip Miller. The thirteenth edition, adapted to the new style, with a list of the medicinal plants to which is prefixed, A short introduction to the science of botany, illustrated with copper plates* (London: Printed for the author and sold by John Rivington in St. Paul's Church-Yard, 1762), copy in Beinecke Rare Book and Manuscript Library, Yale University. *Figures of the most beautiful, useful, and uncommon plants described in the Gardeners dictionary, exhibited on three hundred copper plates, accurately engraven* [sic] *after drawings taken from nature. With the characters of their flowers and seed-vessels, drawn when they were in their greatest perfection. To which are*

added, their descriptions, and an account of the classes to which they belong, according to Ray's, Tournefort's, and Linnaeus's *method of classing them* (London: 1760), copy in Beinecke Rare Book and Manuscript Library, Yale University. Books based on Miller's work were also written by other authors, including Don George, *A general system of gardening and botany. Founded upon Miller's Gardener's dictionary, and arranged according to the natural system* (London: C. J. G. and F. Rivington, 1831–1837), copy in Beinecke Rare Book and Manuscript Library, Yale University.

85. During this period in English history, the individual was increasingly coming to be seen as a commodity. It followed that it was the owner's responsibility to improve and cultivate property. "Hence, the garden was a valuable place in which cultivation of nature (one form of property improvement) could lead to improvement of human beings (another form of property). In this system, the owner of the landscape garden made statements about his responsibility and cultivation through the garden, and simultaneously showed a respect for property." Chandra Mukerji, "Reading and Writing with Nature: A Materialist Approach to French Formal Gardens," in John Brewer and Roy Porter, eds., *Consumption and the World of Goods* (London: Routledge, 1993), 453.

86. A print drawn from the seacoast of Cape Fear, North Carolina, includes the ruby-throated hummingbird that can be used to document William's development as an artist. He sent a rendering of this specimen to his patron Collinson twenty years previously that was much less developed artistically—a testament to his determination to improve his skills.

87. Fothergill was the owner of the largest privately owned botanic garden in England, located at Upton, Essex, near London. He constantly craved the taste of new American specimens. On Fothergill's death, Sir Joseph Banks acquired his collection, and favorite colleagues, such as Daniel Solander, were given free access to them for their own studies.

88. With new British explorations, British naturalists were swept away by the flora and fauna from the East, which they considered much more exotic that those of America. To William Bartram's utter disappointment, his drawings, as well as the manuscript he prepared for his patron—a compendium of his life's work—languished unpublished in Britain.

89. For further information on the naming of the species, see Joseph Ewan, "French Naturalists in the Mississippi Valley," in J. F. McDermott, *French in the Mississippi Valley* (Urbana, Ill.: University of Illinois Press, 1965), 159–174.

90. Francis Harper, "Some Works of Bartram, Daudin, Latreille, and Sonnini, and Their Bearing upon North American Herpetological Nomenclature," *American Midland Naturalist* 23, no. 3 (May, 1940): 692–723.

91. Francois Marie Daudin (1774–1804) wrote the eight-volume *Histoire naturelle, générale et particulière, des reptiles; ouvrage faisant suite à l'Histoire naturelle générale et particulière, composée par Leclerc de Buffon, et rédigée par C.S. Sonnin* (Paris: F. Dufart, 1802–1803), copy in Beinecke Rare Book and Manuscript Library, Yale University.

92. After his initial plan to take the manuscript and run to Europe was foiled, Barton eventually illustrated his *Elements of Botany* (published in Philadelphia in 1803) with prints he took from Bartram's works. Benjamin Smith Barton, *Elements of Botany* (Philadelphia, 1803), copy in Seeley G. Mudd Library, Yale University.

93. Whitfield Bell, Jr., *Patriot-Improvers: Biographical Sketches of Members of the American Philosophical Society* (Philadelphia: American Philosophical Society, 1997).

94. For instance, almost if not all of the titles in mathematics issued in America during the eighteenth century were reprints of British textbooks.

95. Hindle, *Pursuit of Science*, 36–101.

96. Alison to Stiles, July 10, 1761, Stiles Papers, quoted in Winthrop D. Jordan, *White over Black: American Attitudes toward the Negro, 1550–1812* (Chapel Hill: University of North Carolina Press, 1968), 99.

97. Humphry Marshall's work *Arbustrum Americanum: The American Grove, or, an Alphabetical Catalogue of Forest Trees and Shrubs, Natives of the American United States, Arranged According to the Linnaean System* (Philadelphia: Joseph Crukshank, 1805), copy in Library Company of Philadelphia.

98. Marshall, *Arbustrum Americanum*, title page.

99. On manufacturing as a cultural process in the early republic, see Laura Rigal, *The American Manufactory: Art, Labor, and the World of Things in the Early Republic* (Princeton, N.J.: Princeton University Press, 1998).

100. Ibid., 5.

101. Christine Chapman Robbins, "David Hosack's Herbarium and Its Linnaean Specimens," *Proceedings of the American Philosophical Society* 104, no. 3 (1960): 293.

102. For the most eloquent expression of Hosack's intentions, see David Hosack to Benjamin Rush, September 8, 1794, Rush Letterbook, bound vol. 27, Library Company of Philadelphia.

103. Ibid.

104. Londoner Sir James Edward Smith studied medicine in Edinburgh and later received his medical degree from Leiden University in 1788. He had purchased the Linnaean collections in 1784. According to Robbins, "His prestige was due, in large part, to his ownership of the famous Linnaean Herbarium."

105. David Hosack to Benjamin Rush, September 8, 1794, Rush Letterbook, bound vol. 27, Benjamin Rush Papers, Library Company of Philadelphia.

106. Benjamin Smith Barton, *Collections for an Essay towards a Materia Medica of the United-States* (Philadelphia: Robert Carr, 1801), copy in Library Company of Philadelphia.

107. Ibid., iii–iv.

108. Ibid.

109. Ibid.

110. Benjamin Smith Barton to Joseph Banks, May 26, 1793, Benjamin Smith Barton Papers, page [folder] 12, Historical Society of Pennsylvania.

111. James Rush to Benjamin Rush, March 29, 1810, Rush Correspondence, box 11, Benjamin Rush Papers, Library Company of Philadelphia.

112. The phrase is adapted from Matthew 23:24 (King James Version). My thanks to James Green for bringing the biblical reference to my attention. James Rush to Benjamin Rush, March 29, 1810, Rush Correspondence, Benjamin Rush Papers, Library Company of Philadelphia.

113. Benjamin Waterhouse to J[ames]. E[dward]. Smith, Cambridge, Mass., July 24, 1811, quoted in Lady [Pleasance Reeve] Smith, ed., *Memoir and Correspondence of the Late Sir James Edward Smith, M.D.* (London: 1832), 2:174. See also Brooke Hindle, ed., *Early American Science* (New York: Science History, 1976), 202. James Edward Smith (1759–1828) was born in Norwich, England. He was a botanist and founder of the Linnean Society. Benjamin Smith Barton, "Miscellaneous Facts and Observations," *Philadelphia Medical and Physical Journal* 1 (1805): 158–159. See also Benjamin Smith Barton, Introduction to *Fragments of the Natural History of Pennsylvania*, pt. 1 (Philadelphia, 1799).

114. Samuel Stanhope Smith, circular letter, 1790, Samuel Stanhope Smith Collection, 1772–1817, Department of Rare Books and Special Collections, Manuscripts Division, Firestone Library, Princeton University.

115. Ibid.

116. Ibid.

117. Ibid.

118. Alice Walters, "Conversation Pieces: Science and Politeness in Eighteenth-century England," *History of Science* 35 (1997): 121–154.

119. Samuel Stanhope Smith, circular letter, 1790, Samuel Stanhope Smith Collection, 1772–1817, Princeton Library Collections, Department of Rare Books and Special Collections, Manuscripts Division, Firestone Library, Princeton University.

120. As George Daniels noted of the period, "allowing students free use of laboratory materials could not be entertained seriously." Daniels, *Science in American Society: A Social History* (New York: Knopf, 1971), 129.

121. Ibid.

122. A resident of Charleston, South Carolina, Stephen Elliott served as president of the Literary and Philosophical Society of South Carolina. Elliott's comment is quoted in an article by William Jackson Hooker, "On the Botany of America," *American Journal of Science and Arts* 9 (1825): 263–284, quote on 276. The article focuses to a large extent on the research that Europeans had done on the topic of North American botany. There was also discussion about "what renders the botany of North America peculiarly interesting to the British naturalist." Hooker, "On the Botany of America," 264. John Krout and Dixon Fox note: "America presented a magnificent challenge to the [scientific] field worker"; Krout and Fox, *The Completion of Independence, 1790–1830* (New York: Macmillan, 1944), 320.

123. English botanist and zoologist Thomas Nuttall (1786–1859) studied in America between 1808 and 1841. The fruits of his labor included the following publications: Thomas Nuttall, *The Genera of North American Plants* (Philadelphia, 1818); Thomas Nuttall, *An Introduction to Systematic and Physiological Botany* (Cambridge, 1827). For more on Nuttall's life, see Elias Durand, *Memoir of the Late Thomas Nuttall* (Philadelphia: C. Sherman & Son, 1861); Jeannette E. Graustein, *Thomas Nuttall, Naturalist; Explorations in America, 1808–1841* (Cambridge, Mass.: Harvard University Press, 1967).

124. Krout and Fox, *Completion of Independence,* 318. Scottish ornithologist and naturalist Alexander Wilson (1766–1813) collected drawings of bird life and subscribers during his wide-ranging travels across the nation. Alexander Wilson, *American Ornithology; or, The natural history of the birds of the United States: illustrated with plates engraved and colored from original drawings taken from nature,* 9 vols. (Philadelphia: Bradford and Inskeep, 1808–1814). I consulted the copies housed in the Beinecke Rare Book and Manuscript Library, Yale University. For various perspectives on Wilson's life, see Clark Hunter, ed., *The Life and Letters of Alexander Wilson* (Philadelphia: American Philosophical Society, 1983); George Ord, *Sketch of the Life of Alexander Wilson, author of the American ornithology* (Philadelphia: H. Hall, 1828) and Cantwell, Robert, 1908–1978; *Alexander Wilson: Naturalist and Pioneer, a Biography* (Philadelphia: Lippincott, 1961).

125. Henry Muhlenberg (1753–1815), as he signed his letters in English and as he was known to his friends, Lutheran clergyman and botanist, was born Gotthilf Heinrich Ernst Muhlenberg in Trappe, Pennsylvania, the son of Heinrich (also known as Henry) Melchior Muhlenberg, a patriarch of the Lutheran church in America, and Anna Maria Weiser, the daughter of the Indian interpreter Conrad Weiser. See *American National Biography,* s.v. "Muhlenberg, Henry." See also Herbert H. Beck, "Henry E. Muhlenberg," *Castanea: The Journal of the Southern Appalachian Botanical Club* 3, no. 4 (April 1938): 41–53.

126. Henry Jr. had an international education. He first attended school at his birthplace, and later in Philadelphia when the family moved there in 1761. When he was nine

years old he was sent with his two older brothers to Halle, in Saxony, to continue his studies and prepare for the ministry. The brothers were enrolled in an orphanage school where his father had been a teacher. At this time, an equivalent advanced education was not available in the United States. See chapter 4 for a more detailed discussion about Americans' reliance upon European institutions of higher learning.

127. Muhlenburg relied on his European contacts for medical supplies as well as scientific advice. He drew upon his connections in Halle in order to provide his congregation with necessary medical supplies.

The Revolutionary War allowed Muhlenberg to enter the field of botany since the British occupation of Philadelphia gave him a year of enforced leisure in New Hanover, Pennsylvania. It was at this time that he took up his studies in earnest. Prior to this forced hiatus, Muhlenburg's father pressured him to devote more time to his parish and less to plants. Botany was considered a hobby rather than a vocation. Like many other men of science in America he had to hold down other jobs as their means of employment.

128. "Botany in the United States," *North American Review* 13 (1821): 100–134; William Darlington, comp., *Reliquiae Baldwinianeae: Selections from the Correspondence of the Late William Baldwin with Occasional Notes, and a Short Biographical Memoir compiled by William Darlington* (Philadelphia: Kimber and Sharpless, 1843), 20–21.

129. "From the observed natural phenomena of the New World would come other evidence modifying scientific theories of the Old." Krout and Fox, *Completion of Independence,* 319.

130. James DeKay, *Anniversary Address Delivered before the New York Lyceum* (New York, 1826); Krout and Fox, *Completion of Independence,* 318.

131. For the political and national importance of natural science and the uniquely American use of empirical evidence and "fact," see Andrew J. Lewis, "A Democracy of Facts, an Empire of Reason: Swallow Submersion and Natural History in the Early American Republic," *William and Mary Quarterly* 62, no. 4 (2004): 663–696.

132. Thomas Jefferson was also aware of the way Europeans received credit for scientific discoveries and inventions that Americans made. In a note to his *Notes on the State of Virginia,* Jefferson complained of how two famous American inventions were known by the names of the Britons who introduced them to Europe: "There are various ways of keeping truth out of sight. Mr. Rittenhouse's model of the planetary system has the plagiary appellation of an Orrery; and the quadrant invented by Godfrey, an American also, and with the aid of which the European nations traverse the globe, is called Hadley's quadrant." Jefferson, *Writings,* ed. Merrill D. Peterson (New York: Library of America, 1984), 191.

133. [Georges Louis Leclerc] Comte de Buffon, *Historie Naturelle, Générale et Particuliére,* 36 vols. (Paris, 1749–88). The primary propositions of the theory of degeneration included (a) fewer species of animals exist in the New World as opposed to the Old; (b) in instances where the same or similar species of animal are found in the New World and the Old, the animals of the Old are larger than in the New; (c) domesticated animals that were transported from the Old to the New World are smaller than their progenitors; (d) animals that are found only in the New World tend to be smaller than their counterparts in the Old World; (e) all forms of life, both animal and human, in the New World tend to be "degenerate." See I. Bernard Cohen, *Science and the Founding Fathers: Science and the Political Thought of Jefferson, Franklin, Adams, and Madison* (New York: Norton, 1995), 74. Jefferson's scientific efforts to dispute the Frenchman's claims were seen by many Americans as a patriotic effort to strengthen the nation's inter-

national reputation. One of his projects was to present fossils of mammoths as proof of the robust nature of America's animal life.

134. For a discussion on the context of Buffon's work, see Philip Sloan, "The Gaze of Natural History," in Christopher Fox, Roy Porter, and Robert Wolker, eds., *Inventing Human Science: Eighteenth-century Domains* (Berkeley: University of California Press, 1995), 112–151 and especially 126–141.

135. Historians such as I. Bernard Cohen have puzzled over how "Jefferson allowed his patriotic enthusiasm to outrun his scientific judgment" when he held David Rittenhouse up as a candidate of excellence "second to no astronomer living." Cohen, *Science and the Founding Fathers*, 79. Although I do not believe there is such a thing as an "objective" scientific opinion, I do think Cohen's comment is salient for the argument I am making. The sentence from which Cohen is quoting asserts "that in genius he must be the first, because he is self-taught." Jefferson, *Writings*, 190. Jefferson's comment in defense against Raynal's indictment of American genius is representative of the attempt by Anglo-Americans to change the standard of intellectual evaluation to reward, or at least make exceptions for those who are "self-taught." The application of this standard would, of course, work out in favor of American intellectuals, the majority of whom were "amateurs" who dabbled in scientific experimentation in their spare time.

136. Guillaume-Thomas François Raynal (1713–1796) was the author of *Histoire Philosophique et Politique des Etablissements et du Commerce des Europeens dans les deux Indes*, 4 vols. (Amsterdam, 1770), expanded to 12 vols. (Paris, 1820–21). For a full bibliographic listing of Raynal's works, see J. M. Quérand, *La France Littéraire ou Dictionnaire Bibliographique* (Paris: Didot Frères, 1835). William Douglass's book on North America, which was positively reviewed by William Robertson in the *Edinburgh Review in* 1755, also suggested that the rudest and most imperfect form of society could be found in America rather than, as previously thought, in the Highlands and Islands of Scotland (these include the Shetland, Orkney, and the Inner and Outer Hebrides Islands). He described America as the "youngest Brother and meanest of Mankind." The review appears in the *Edinburgh Review* 2 (1755–56), article 11. W[illiam] D[ouglass], *A Summary, Historical and Political, of the first Planting, Progressive Improvements, and present state of the British Settlements in NORTH-AMERICA*. The first, second, and third parts of this work were published in Boston in 1747, 1749, and 1750, respectively; in 1755, a two-volume reprint of the entire work was published in London; it was this edition Robertson reviewed in the *Edinburgh Review*. William Robertson (1721–1793) was a major figure in the Scottish Enlightenment. Robertson was an accomplished historian, clergyman, and the principal of the University of Edinburgh.

137. Jefferson provided Raynal's original quote in the French: " 'On doit etre etonne' (he says) que l'Amerique n'ait pas encore produit un bon poete, un habile mathematicien, un homme de genie dans us seul art, ou une seule science,' 7. Hist. Philos. p. 92 ed Maestricht. 1774." Jefferson, *Writings*, 190.

138. Jordan, *White over Black*, 477.

139. John Sullivan (1740–1795) also charged Jefferson for "salting and tending" the animal to "prevent putrefaction." Jefferson "paid a tanner for fleshing the skin" and had the "expense of a box and putting up the skeleton" … "dressing the skin to preserve it with the hair on free from worms, etc." Nevertheless, the specimen was damaged. Anna Clark Jones, "Antlers for Jefferson," *New England Quarterly* 12 (1939): 340–341.

140. In a letter to Sullivan dated January 7, 1785, Jefferson noted: "Could I choose the manner in which I would wish them to be preserved, it should be to leave the bones of the legs and hoofs in the skin and the bones of the head also, with the horns [*sic*] on";

quoted in ibid., 337. A year later, a letter from Sullivan described the failure to carry out Jefferson's instructions: "I found that everything I had done toward procuring for you the skeleton of a moose would not answer your expectations." Bones were not left in the skin or "proper care taken to preserve or dress the skins with the hair on, so that no proper resemblance of the animal could be had" (339). Jefferson had to write to Buffon explaining that "The skin of the moose was drest with the hair on, but a great deal of it has come off, and the rest is ready to drop off."

141. John Sullivan to Thomas Jefferson, April 16, 1787, April 26, 1787, May 9, 1787, in *The Papers of Thomas Jefferson,* ed. Julian Boyd et al., 33 vols. (Princeton, N.J.: Princeton University Press, 1950–), 11: 295–297, 11:320–321, 11:359, respectively; Thomas Jefferson to Sullivan, October 5, 1787, 12:208. The correspondence regarding the moose began in 1784. Others included in the discussion were John McDuffee and William Whipple.

142. Thomas Jefferson to Comte de Buffon, October 1, 1787, in ibid., 12:194–195.

143. Thomas Jefferson to Sullivan, October 5, 1787, in ibid., 12:208–209.

144. Joseph Kastner, *A World of Naturalists* (London: John Murray Publishers, 1978), 125.

145. Among the most important of these were Cornelius de Pauw, *Recherches Philosophiques sur les Americans*, translated as *Scientific Research on the Americans*, vols. 1 (Berlin: Chez Georges Jacques Decker, 1768) and 2 (Berlin: Chez Georges Jacques Decker, 1769), and [Guillaume Thomas Francois] Abbé Raynal, *Histoire Philosophique et Politique des Etablissements et du Commerce des Europeens dans les deux Indes,* translated as *Philosophical and Political History of the Settlements and Trade of the Europeans in the East and West Indies,* 4 vols. (Amsterdam, [s.n.], 1770, and Maestricht: J.E. Dufour, 1774).

146. See Kastner, *World of Naturalists*, 125.

147. Garden to Linnaeus, dated Charleston, North Carolina, January 2, 1760, in James Edward Smith, ed., *A Selection of the Correspondence of Linnaeus and Other Naturalists, from the Original Manuscripts* (London: Longman, Hurst, Rees, Orme, and Brown, 1821), 1:297–302. See also Margaret Denny, "Linnaeus and His Disciple in Carolina: Alexander Garden," *Isis* 38 (1948): 173. In *Pursuit of Science,* Hindle argues that Americans went into certain areas of scientific investigation by the more powerful British scientists' "request, rather than by inclination." For instance, when Alexander Garden of Charleston initiated a correspondence with Linnaeus he was snubbed by the eminent scientist. However, after waiting in silence for four long years, Garden was asked to collect the fish, reptiles, and insects of South Carolina and send them to Europe for Linnaeus's use. Not only did Garden immediately jump to fulfill the request, he furnished both specimens and detailed descriptions. Carolus Linnaeus, whose birth name was Carl von Linné (1707–1778) was a Swedish botanist who is best known for establishing the modern system of binomial nomenclature.

148. Thomas Pennant, *Arctic Zoology,* 2 vols. (London: Printed by H. Hughs, 1784–1785), copy in Beinecke Rare Books and Manuscripts, Yale University. Born in Wales, naturalist Thomas Pennant (1726–1798) was nominated by Carolus Linnaeus to the Royal Swedish Society of Sciences and to the Royal Society.

149. Pennant, introduction to *Arctic Zoology.*

150. Ibid.

151. Ibid.

152. This correspondence is found in the Benjamin Smith Barton Papers, Historical Society of Pennsylvania; see, for instance, Thomas Pennant to Barton, October 17, 1790, page [folder] 2. Pennant's increasing frustration can be tracked in Pennant to Barton,

November 3, 1791, page [folder] 6; Pennant to Barton, March 26, 1792, page [folder] 7; and Pennant to Barton, June 14, 1792, page [folder] 8. Barton had a reputation for this sort of unsavory practice among his colleagues. His dealings with Wilhelm Gottlieb Tilesius von Tilenau (1769–1857) provide another example. After answering "all questions of Mr. Smith Barton" and sending him "every Work of the *Imperial Akademic* [sic], he wish'd for," Tilesius "never was favoured with a single Line afterwards." In 1806, after returning from a voyage around the world, Tilesius wrote to Barton complaining that the American had failed to reciprocate his gestures of goodwill by sending him the preliminary notes for Barton's new edition of his work *Arctic Zoology*. However, Tilesius's letter and admonishments came to no avail. In a letter to American Casper Wistar, Tilesius concluded: "I am now bound to think I never shall receive them through Mr. Barton." Wilhelm Gottlieb Tilesius to Casper Wistar, October 1813, Casper Wistar Papers (1794–1817), American Philosophical Society. Caspar Wistar (1761–1818) was born in Philadelphia to a Quaker family. His educational path was similar to many other American men of science discussed in *Unbecoming British*. Like many other prominent physicians of his generation, he studied under Dr. John Redman and later with New York physician Dr. John Jones who had come to Philadelphia. In 1779 Wistar became a medical student at the University of the State of Pennsylvania (later the University of Pennsylvania). In 1782, after he earned his Bachelor of Medicine, Wistar went to England and Scotland to further his education; he graduated from the University of Edinburgh with a Doctorate of Medicine in 1786.

153. Keir B. Sterling, editor of a reprint of Benjamin Smith Barton, *Notes on the Animals of North America* ([1793]; reprint, New York: Arno Press, 1974), concurs that Pennant would have "quoted liberally" from these notes for the new edition of his *Arctic Zoology* had Barton sent them in time. Barton worked on this manuscript, which he described as an informal collection of notes and observations between 1792 and 1793. Pennant's new edition of *Arctic Zoology* for which these impressions were intended was published in February and March of 1793. Barton's manuscript notes arrived in late July or early August of that same year. Until this 1974 reprint, *Notes on the Animals of North America* was unpublished. Sterling, "Introduction," unnumbered pages.

154. Benjamin Smith Barton to Thomas Pennant, June 29, 1793, Violetta Delafield–Benjamin Smith Barton Collection (1783–1817), American Philosophical Society, reprinted in Benjamin Smith Barton, *Notes on the Animals of North America*, ed. Keir B. Sterling (New York: Arno Press, 1974). This is a reprint of Barton's original manuscript, "Notes on the Animals of North America" [1793], which was prepared at the request of Thomas Pennant. Barton, "Notes on the Animals of North America," Violetta Delafield–Benjamin Smith Barton Collection, 1783–1817, American Philosophical Society.

155. Hindle, *Pursuit of Science,* 58.

156. Parrish is concerned primarily with how knowledge from America as geographic space made an impact in European Enlightenment thought. This is distinct from my argument in this book that the politically independent Americans were themselves insecure clients on the cultural periphery of the British Empire. See Susan Scott Parrish, *American Curiosity* (Chapel Hill: University of North Carolina Press, 2006). Parrish offers a description of how Americans were able to successfully enter into and affect European thought: "*American Curiosity* argues for the critical importance of the Americas in shaping Enlightenment methods and systems" (15). See Parrish's introduction and text generally for discussion of Americans entering into the world of European epistemology (5).

CHAPTER 5

1. Benjamin Rush, letter of introduction for Benjamin Smith Barton to William Cullen, June 17, 1786, Miscellaneous Manuscripts Collection, American Philosophical Society, Philadelphia.

2. The official name of the institution changed several times. In 1779, during the Revolutionary War, the state of Pennsylvania seized the College of Philadelphia because it was considered a Tory institution. At this time its name was changed to the University of the State of Pennsylvania. The new organizational structure was based upon egalitarian ideals such as a nonsectarian faculty and Board of Trustee members of all denominations. In 1791, the institution was made private and at that point it became known as the University of Pennsylvania.

3. Benjamin Rush, letter of introduction for Benjamin Smith Barton to William Cullen, June 17, 1786, Miscellaneous Manuscripts Collection, American Philosophical Society.

4. See William and Mabel Smallwood, *Natural History and the American Mind* (New York: Columbia University Press, 1941), 151–152.

5. Benjamin Rush noted in his letter of recommendation that Barton's class would be graduating at the end of the year, but Barton's "preference of a diploma from Edin[burg]h" would prevent his "sharing with them in the honours of the university of Pennsylvania." Benjamin Rush, letter of introduction for Benjamin Smith Barton to William Cullen, June 17, 1786, Miscellaneous Manuscripts Collection, American Philosophical Society.

6. In the seventeenth century, American colonials went to Europe to study. Paris and Leiden were the most common destinations.

7. A different version of this chapter was published in "'To Pursue the stream to its fountain': Race, Inequality, and the Post-colonial Exchange of Knowledge Across the Atlantic," *Explorations in Early American Culture* 5 (2001): 173–229. I wish to express my gratitude to the McNeil Center, University of Pennsylvania, Philadelphia, Pennsylvania, for allowing me to reprint this material and for its fellowship support.

8. In the eighteenth century, American universities were connected by patterns of migration and institutional patronage to Scottish and English Dissenting universities. Though Harvard was originally patterned after Emmanuel College of Cambridge University, it was connections to Scottish and English Dissenting academies that became most significant there, as well as at other American universities. These networks were strengthened because patronage was extended to Americans by prominent English dissenters and because Scottish teachers and physicians were more willing than their English counterparts to emigrate to the colonies. Brooke Hindle, *The Pursuit of Science in Revolutionary America* (New York: Norton, 1956), 86; Francis Packard, "Medicine and the American Philosophical Society," *Proceedings of the American Philosophical Society* 86, no. 1 (1942): 93–94; Deborah C. Brunton, "The Transfer of Medical Education: Teaching at the Edinburgh and Philadelphia Medical Schools," in Richard B. Sher and Jeffrey R. Smitten, eds., *Scotland and America in the Age of the Enlightenment* (Edinburgh: Edinburgh University Press, 1990), 242–258; Deborah Brunton, "Edinburgh and Philadelphia: The Scottish Model of Medical Education," in Jennifer Carter and Donald Withrington, eds., *Scottish Universities: Distinctiveness and Diversity* (Edinburgh: John Donald Publishers, 1992), 80–86; George Pryde, *The Scottish Universities and the Colleges of Colonial America* (Glasgow: Jackson, Son & Company, 1957). For the networks of Scottish physicians to the British West Indies in the eighteenth century, see Douglas

Hamilton, "Smallpox at Paradise: Scots in Medical Practice in the West Indies" (Ph.D. diss., University of Aberdeen, 1999), chap. 4.

9. Franklin to Hume, May 19, 1762, in *The Papers of Benjamin Franklin*, vol. 10, ed. Leonard W. Labaree (New Haven, Conn.: Yale University Press, 1959), 84; letter also quoted in Gordon Wood, *The Radicalism of the American Revolution* (New York: Vintage Books, 1991), 77. Benedict Anderson provides a more general discussion about the frustrations colonial elites experienced when attempting to rise within the imperial hierarchy in chapter 4, "Creole Pioneers," in *Imagined Communities*.

10. Gordon Wood observes that although Franklin was widely recognized for his scientific work, he was denied access to the "topmost sphere" of English politics. However brightly his scientific achievements may have shone in the eyes of British and European philosophes, they counted for very little in the eyes of the 'great People' at the center of British imperial power." Even the most talented colonials experienced barriers when they entered the metropolis. Wood continues: "it was not until the late 1760s, when all his hopes for English preferment seemed squashed, that Franklin began to think of himself as an American. The first part of his *Autobiography* was written at the moment in 1771 when his grandiose English political and social ambitions seemed most lost, and it became a kind of justification of his failure, a salve for his disillusionment…a vindication of the American Revolution and the changes it had made in the old patronage society." Wood, *Radicalism of the American Revolution*, 77.

11. In 1762, London physician John Fothergill wrote a letter of recommendation to James Pemberton on Shippen's behalf. The letter urged the support of the Pennsylvania legislature to "erect a school for Physic amongst you." Fothergill to James Pemberton, April 7, 1762, Pemberton Papers, 47, Historical Society of Pennsylvania, Philadelphia, Pennsylvania. When Morgan returned to America in 1765, he, too, carried an important letter of British support. Thomas Penn, the proprietor of Pennsylvania, recommended to the Board of Trustees that Morgan be put in charge of the project to found the school. Thomas Penn to Board of Trustees, February 15, 1765, quoted in Francis R. Packard, *History of Medicine in the United States* (New York: Hoeber, 1931), 1:346–347, as discussed in Hindle, *Pursuit of Science*, 115. With the Board behind him, Morgan took control of the movement, explaining his ideas in a two-day presentation that was published as *Discourse upon the Institution of Medical Schools in America delivered at a public anniversary commencement, held in the College of Philadelphia May 30 and 31, 1765: With a preface containing, amongst other things, the author's apology for attempting to introduce the regular mode of practicing [sic] physic in Philadelphia* (Philadelphia: Printed and sold by William Bradford, 1765). Morgan felt this accomplishment would bring honor to the "reputation of my country," for it would indicate "what a Spirit for cultivating Science prevails in this Western World." Morgan to Sir Alexander Dick, March 28, 1768 [copy], American Philosophical Society, as cited in Hindle, *Pursuit of Science*, 116.

12. The school was officially inaugurated in 1766. When its first class graduated in 1768, there were forty students enrolled in the program. *Pennsylvania Gazette*, [Philadelphia] June 30, 1768.

13. See J. B. Morrell, "The University of Edinburgh in the Late Eighteenth Century: Its Scientific Eminence and Academic Structure," *Isis* 62, no. 2 (Summer 1971): 158–171. See also John D. Comrie, *History of Scottish Medicine* (London: published for the Wellcome Historical Medical Museum by Baillière, Tindall & Cox, 1932), 1:340; Samuel Lewis, "List of the American Graduates in Medicine in the University of Edinburgh from 1705 to 1866," *New England Historical and Genealogical Register* 42 (1888): 159–165; and Hindle, *Pursuit of Science*, 114.

14. In 1765, five Americans graduated from colonial institutions. In that same year, the same number graduated with medical degrees from the University of Edinburgh with many more of their countrymen attending classes at the famed medical school for at least one year without earning a formal degree. John C. Greene, "American Science Comes of Age, 1780–1820," *Journal of American History* 55, no. 1 (June 1968): 24.

15. During this period, Edinburgh remained the most popular destination for American students. Many American students also attended institutions in other European locations, including the Netherlands.

16. According to a study by Robert W. I. Smith, *English-speaking Students of Medicine at the University of Leyden* (Edinburgh: Oliver and Boyd, 1932), at least twenty-three Americans studied medicine in Leiden during the seventeenth and eighteenth centuries, and at least fifteen of these received their degrees. (These numbers exclude the many students from the West Indies.) Smallwood, *Natural History and the American Mind*, 60–61. Until later in the nineteenth-century, relatively few Americans went to France to study medicine. For a study that focuses on the medical profession in nineteenth-century America see John Harley Warner, *The Therapeutic Perspective: Medical Practice, Knowledge, and Identity in America, 1820–1885* (Cambridge, Mass.: Harvard University Press, 1986).

17. This insight was developed by the early twentieth-century French anthropologist Marcel Mauss, who observed that gifts, which might seem "disinterested and spontaneous…are in fact obligatory and interested." Mauss, *The Gift: Forms and Functions of Exchange in Archaic Societies* (1922) (London: Routledge, 1990), 1.

18. See Linda Colley, *Britons: Forging the Nation, 1707–1837* (New Haven, Conn.: Yale University Press, 1992), and Kathleen Wilson, *The Sense of the People: Politics, Culture, and Imperialism in England, 1715–1785* (Cambridge: Cambridge University Press, 1995).

19. The quotations in the epigraphs to this section are from Julia Rush (mother) to James Rush, May 2, 1810, 19, and Benjamin Rush to James Rush, Philadelphia, May 1, 1810, both in Rush Correspondence, box 11, Benjamin Rush Papers, Library Company of Philadelphia.

20. As Gordon Wood has described it: "No metropolitan Englishman could have matched the awe felt by the Pennsylvanian Benjamin Rush when in 1768 he first saw the king's throne in London. It was as if he were 'on sacred ground,' and he 'gazed for some time at the throne with emotions that I cannot describe.'" According to Wood, "Rush pleaded with his reluctant guide to let him sit upon it 'for a considerable time,' even though the guide said that visitors rarely did so. The experience was unsettling, to say the least: 'I was seized with a kind of horror…and a crowd of ideas poured in upon my mind.' This was all a man could want in this world; 'his passions conceive, his hopes aspire after nothing beyond this throne'"; Wood, *Radicalism of the American Revolution*, 15.

21. Full quote: "—We have it in expectation to celebrate the anniversary of his majesty's coronation for the completion the fiftieth year. I think [Joseph?] Denny & Co, could not do a more consistent act, than to send a representative to light a candle at the illumination. As I dont [*sic*] feel much enthusiasm on the occasion, if this deputy will come to Edinburgh, he may have the honour of—greasing his fingers in his majesty's service, at my window, and I'll thank him much for easing me of the trouble.—The paper will inform you better than I can, how, <u>precious ministerial</u> blood can be shed in duty." James Rush, Edinburgh, to Benjamin Rush, September 28, 1809, Rush Correspondence, box 11, Benjamin Rush Papers, Library Company of Philadelphia. There are several studies on the intense antagonism between the Federalist and Republican parties that James Rush makes reference to in this quote. For examples of

some recent studies, see Stanley Elkins and Eric McKitrick, *The Age of Federalism: The Early American Republic, 1788–1800* (New York: Oxford University Press, 1993); William Dowling, *Literary Federalism in the Age of Jefferson: Joseph Dennie and The "Port Folio," 1801–1812* (Columbia: University of South Carolina Press, 1999); Doron Ben-Atar and Barbara Oberg, eds. *Federalists Reconsidered* (Charlottesville: University Press of Virginia, 1998).

22. James Rush to Julia Rush, October 25, 1809, Rush Correspondence, box 11, Benjamin Rush Papers, Library Company of Philadelphia; emphasis added. James went on the describe the procession consisting of "companies of free masons and magistrates … [a] procession conducted with expense[,] and thousands were the hearty amens," and commenting: "I thought it was very pretty to express by means of decorated citizens, the happiness and prosperity of a county; but I saw that a lane of supplicating beggars, form'd an eloquent reverse—" Describing the "famous jubilee day—morning being fired and drum'd away, afternoon and eve with appropriate amusements" at 5 oclock a great dinner was given and according to James, the "only thing" one needed to get in was "25 shillings." He added: "The illumination of the city did not take place—But some of the public buildings were hung with lights, and struck with crowns that glittered in red and blue and white.—a display of fire works , and battles among the multitude with crackers … concluded the whole of this grand affair[;] that which pleas'd me more than any thing else, was a large torch flaming from the high dark walls of the castle—such were the doings in Edinb[urg]h—the papers will give you an account of those in London. With it my letters will bear no comparison. And it is natural The incense that is burnt under the nostril of the saint should be more aromatic—." It is interesting to note that in such transatlantic correspondences, overseas Americans frequently tell their correspondents back home to refer to newspapers for a better account of current events. James to Julia Rush, October 25, 1809, Rush Correspondence, box 11, Benjamin Rush Papers, Library Company of Philadelphia.

23. James Rush to Benjamin Rush, March 29, 1810, Rush Correspondence, box 11, Benjamin Rush Papers, Library Company of Philadelphia.

24. Ibid.

25. J. Rush to B. Rush, March 29, 1810, Rush Correspondence, box 11, Benjamin Rush Papers, Library Company of Philadelphia.

26. See note 54 here. Wood, *Radicalism of the American Revolution*, 15.

27. Originally, on receiving his bachelor of arts degree from the College of New Jersey in September 1760, Rush had intended to become a lawyer. His earliest mentor, Reverend Samuel Finley, who was married to Rush's aunt, advised against it and suggested medicine as a career. Finley said the "practice of law was full of temptations." Recalling the decision later in his autobiography, Rush wrote: "On what slight circumstances do our destinies in life seem to depend!" Rush, "Autobiography," unpublished manuscript copy, Benjamin Rush Papers, Library Company of Philadelphia, 35. (This work was not published in Rush's lifetime.) His friends from college were against his decision, and he wrote that he had questioned it at times, though he noted that he eventually came to believe divine providence had steered him in the right direction.

28. In the spring of 1759, at the age of fifteen, Rush entered the junior class at the College of New Jersey. At the time, Reverend Samuel Davies had just succeeded Reverend Jacob Green as president of the College. Several years before, Davies had been sent to Great Britain by the trustees of the College to "solicit contributions to build and endow the College." He was successful in this endeavor, and as Rush wrote later in his autobiography, "From his intercourse when abroad with the most eminent Scholars and Divines

among the dissenters, he enlarged his mind and became better qualified for the station he was now to fill. He seemed to be made for it. To a handsome person, he united the most elegant and commanding manners. He was truly dignified, but at the same time affable and even familiar in his intercourse with his pupils." Ibid., 35.

29. John Redman (1722–1808) was a graduate of the University of Leiden in the Netherlands (1748) and one of the leading physicians in Philadelphia at the time. He served for twenty-nine years as a consulting physician to Pennsylvania Hospital and was a founder and first president of the College of Physicians of Philadelphia. Among his pupils were the physicians John Morgan, Caspar Wistar, and Benjamin Rush. He was trained under the influence of Herman Boerhaave and later took up the ideas of William Cullen. *Dictionary of American Biography*, s.v. "John Redman"; *Annals of Medical History* 8 (1926): 213–223; and Rush, "Autobiography," unpublished manuscript copy, Benjamin Rush Papers, Library Company of Philadelphia, 37 n. 31. Rush's apprenticeship with Redman went from February 1761 to July 1766.

30. William Shippen, Jr., was encouraged to inaugurate his lecture series by Fothergill, the noted London physician who supported the development of scientific pursuits in America (see chapter 4).

31. *Dictionary of American Scientists*, s.v. "Benjamin Rush," 616.

32. It consisted of luminaries such as the physicians William Cullen (1710–1790), Joseph Black (1728–1799), John Gregory (1724–1773), John Hope (1725–1786), and Alexander Monro, II (1733–1817). The biographies of each of these men can be found in the *Dictionary of National Biography*. For more on the University of Edinburgh's worldwide reputation in this period, see Rush, "Autobiography," unpublished manuscript copy, Benjamin Rush Papers, Library Company of Philadelphia, 42; J. D. Comrie, *The History of Scottish Medicine to 1860* (London: Baillière, Tindall & Cox, 1927); F. R. Packard, "How London and Edinburgh Influenced Medicine in Philadelphia in the Eighteenth Century," *Annals of Medical History*, new ser., 4 (1932): 219–244.

33. American students overseas often found that they were not adequately prepared for study in Great Britain. Although they had been star pupils in America, within the context of the metropole, they did not shine so brightly. Ambitious and unwilling to admit their deficiencies, men like Rush hired tutors in order to catch up to their British classmates. The classical languages seemed to give them the most difficulty. Benjamin Rush's studies of classical languages notwithstanding, several years later Charles Caldwell observed his "extremely limited" knowledge of "ancient languages," mathematics, astronomy, and chemistry. It seems Rush had only learned enough to prevent embarrassment, and after returning home did not continue to cultivate his knowledge of the ancient languages. In Caldwell's characteristically critical and frank opinion, Rush's learning was limited to his profession as a physician and did not extend to that of a well-rounded philosopher. "To the literature of the ancients he was a stranger. Even the works of the physicians of Greece and Rome he never read except in translation." Caldwell, *Autobiography* (Philadelphia: Lippincott, Grambo, 1855), 148. Even the most highly educated Americans were deficient in their knowledge of the classic languages in comparison to their British counterparts. In reaction to this intellectual disadvantage, after the Revolution influential American leaders worked to abolish Latin altogether and to try to remake standards of education. However, it took time and ideological work for this new standard to gain legitimacy, especially in the minds of Americans who had accepted British standards for so long.

34. Rush's dissertation on the human digestive process reflected his special interest in chemistry. He concluded that the acidity of the stomach contents was the result of the

fermentation process. He was mistaken in this theory, and several years later in 1804 he realized this. His realization was based on new evidence presented by his student John R. Young. *Dictionary of American Scientists*, s.v. "Benjamin Rush," 616.

35. Rush was very successful in creating a powerful network of supporters during his time in Great Britain. His mentor, the celebrated professor William Cullen (1710–1790), held the chair of the institutes of medicine (physiology) at Edinburgh. Cullen was known as an amiable and generous teacher. He had a strong philosophical bent and had served as a professor of chemistry until the year Rush arrived in Edinburgh, when he stepped into the position of chair of the institutes of medicine. Cullen was a popular lecturer on campus and chose to give his lessons in English rather than Latin, which was contrary to the custom of the day. This period was also instrumental in Rush's development of his medical theories. He was greatly influenced by Cullen's belief that life is an expression of "nervous force." For additional information on Rush's work, see *The Autobiography of Benjamin Rush: His "Travels through Life" Together with His Commonplace Book for 1789–1813*, ed. George W. Corner (Princeton, N.J.: Princeton University Press, 1948), app. 1, 361–366. This edition—based on original manuscripts located at the American Philosophical Society and the Library Company of Philadelphia, which I used in preparing this chapter—is helpful because of the supplementary information it provides.

36. Rush, "Autobiography," unpublished manuscript copy, Benjamin Rush Papers, Library Company of Philadelphia, 43. This high regard for his experience in Edinburgh was reflected in several letters from Benjamin Rush to his son James, Rush Correspondence, box 11, Benjamin Rush Papers, Library Company of Philadelphia.

37. Antoine Baumé (1728–1804) was known for practical chemical innovations in manufacturing processes involving dying, silk making, and the purification of saltpeter, as well as inventing the Baumé scale hydrometer. Pierre Macquer (1718–1784), another French chemist, was known for his development of practical medical and industrial processes such as the manufacturing of porcelain.

38. Speaking of a later period, C. L. R. James notes the same colonial system operating in the British Empire, which offered the "best" Jamaican students an opportunity to study at the "best" schools in Britain as a way to prepare them for leadership roles back in their colonial communities. C. L. R. James, *Beyond a Boundary* (Durham, N.C.: Duke University Press, 1993).

39. His position there marked the formal beginning of chemistry in the colonies.

40. For the importance of transatlantic letter writing between men of science, see Konstantin Dierks, "Letter Writing, Masculinity, and American Men of Science, 1750–1800," in *Explorations in Early American Culture*, vol. 65 (supplemental issue) of *Pennsylvania History* (Philadelphia: Pennsylvania Historical Association, 1998), 167–198. Benjamin Rush, "Manuscript Lectures of the Theory and Practice of Physick, 1790–1791," Benjamin Rush Papers, Historical Society of Philadelphia, 336, also discussed in Brandon Fortune with Deborah Warner, *Franklin and His Friends: Portraying the Men of Science in Eighteenth-Century America* (Washington, D.C.: Smithsonian National Portrait Gallery, 1999), 62.

41. Rush wrote about this topic in "Manuscript Lectures of the Theory and Practice of Physick, 1790–1791," 336, Benjamin Rush Papers, HSP. See Benjamin Rush, "On the Influence of Physical Causes in Promoting an Increase of the Strength and Activity of the Intellectual Faculties of Man," in *Two Essays on the Mind* (New York: Brunner/Mazel, 1972), 96, as quoted by Fortune and Warner, eds., *Franklin and His Friends*, 62 and 166 n. 23.

42. Rush to William Cullen, September 16, 1783, in *The Letters of Benjamin Rush*, ed. L. H. Butterfield (Princeton, N.J.: Princeton University Press, 1951), 1:310.

43. See Fortune and Warner, *Franklin and His Friends,* 103–106.

44. One historian of science has put it succinctly: "Even though the old state of dependence persisted long into the nineteenth century, it was no longer accepted gracefully; it was in fact, considered by a growing number of native scientists to be a blemish upon the good name of the republic." George Daniels, *Science in American Society: A Social History* (New York: Knopf, 1971), 133.

45. Lectures at American medical institutions commonly ran for only three or four months of the year. Clarke points out with pride that the American physicians who were "fortunate enough to add to their American a European education" were in fact "in every way the peers of European physicians and surgeons." While Clarke acknowledges the superiority of European medical education, he goes on to say: "Hence we are not ashamed to present our medical schools, with all their shortcomings and imperfections, as substantial contributions to the practical medicine of this century. And, moreover, we can justly point to graduates of these schools, some of whom have, and others of whom have not, been fortunate enough to add to their American a European education, as in every way the peers of European physicians and surgeons." Quote appears in the chapter by Edward H. Clarke entitled: "Practical Medicine," in Edward H. Clarke, Henry J. Bigelow, Samuel D. Gross, T. Gaillard Thomas, and J. S. Billings, *A Century of American Medicine, 1776–1876* (1876; reprint, Brinklow, Md.: Old Hickory Bookshop, 1962), 1–72; the quote appears on pages 18–19.

46. *Medical Repository* 13 (1809–1810): 176.

47. As late as 1876, an American medical survey lamented: "It is safe to affirm that there is not a medical man on this continent who devotes himself exclusively to the practice of surgery." Samuel D. Gross, "Surgery," in Clarke et al., *Century of American Medicine,* 117.

48. This trend of lowering requirements found in American medical schools was reflected in American colleges as well. Institutions of higher learning in the United States suffered a period of "great retrogression" in the early nineteenth century. For a study of the transformations and tumult American colleges faced as a result of the social and ideological changes brought by the Revolution, see Rodney Hessinger, "'The Most Powerful Instrument of College Discipline'": Student Disorder and the Growth of Meritocracy in the Colleges of the Early Republic" (Ph.D. diss., Temple University, 1999), chap. 3.

49. John Coxe to Benjamin Rush, July 17, 1795, Rush Letterbook, bound vol. 27, Benjamin Rush Papers, Library Company of Philadelphia.

50. Ibid.

51. James Rush, "Journal of a Voyage Across the Atlantic in the year 1809," Rush Correspondence, box 13, Benjamin Rush Papers, Library Company of Philadelphia.

52. Ibid.

53. Ibid.; Benjamin Rush to James Rush, Rush Correspondence, box 11, Benjamin Rush Papers, Library Company of Philadelphia.

54. James Rush, "Journal of a Voyage Across the Atlantic in the year 1809," Rush Correspondence, box 13, Benjamin Rush Papers, Library Company of Philadelphia.

55. Thomas Jefferson, "Travelling notes for Mr. Rutledge and Mr. Shippen," June 3, 1788, in *Thomas Jefferson: Writings,* ed. Merrill D. Peterson (New York: Library of America, 1984), 659–660.

56. Benjamin Rush to James Rush, Philadelphia, February 27, 1810, Rush Correspondence, box 11, Benjamin Rush Papers, Library Company of Philadelphia.

57. Benjamin Rush to James Rush, February 7, 1810, Rush Correspondence, box 11, Benjamin Rush Papers, Library Company of Philadelphia; emphasis in the original.

58. Julia Rush to James Rush, May 27, 1810, Rush Correspondence, box 11, Benjamin Rush Papers, Library Company of Philadelphia.

59. Benjamin Rush to James Rush, June 8, 1810, Rush Correspondence, box 11, Benjamin Rush Papers, Library Company of Philadelphia.

60. Ibid.

61. The sudden departure of a successful student from the institution he traveled across the sea to attend, right before he was supposed to graduate, raises many questions. It seems Barton left Edinburgh late in the winter of 1788 with money that belonged to several prominent societies and physicians, including the Royal Medical Society, the Speculative Society, and that of a prominent Edinburgh physician known for his patronage of overseas Americans. For scholarly investigations into this scandal see Whitfield Bell, Jr., "Benjamin Smith Barton, M.D. (Kiel)," *Journal of the History of Medicine and Allied Sciences* 26, no. 2 (1971): 197–203; Theodore Jeffries, "A Biographical Note on Benjamin Smith Barton (1766–1815), *Isis* 60 (1969): 231–232; Edgar Fahs Smith, "Benjamin Smith Barton," Address at the University of Pennsylvania, delivered in 1916 and reprinted in *Papers of the Lancaster County Historical Society*, 28: 59–66, 1924; Francis W. Pennell, "Benjamin Smith Barton as Naturalist," *Proceedings of the American Philosophical Society* 86 (1943): 108–122, especially 110. I found evidence of this incident in various manuscript collections, including Benjamin Smith Barton Papers, Historical Society of Pennsylvania; Violetta W. Delafield Collection, Benjamin Smith Barton Papers, American Philosophical Society; and Benjamin Rush Papers, especially "Drs. Barton, Coxe, Hosack & Miller," Rush Correspondence, bound vol. 27, Benjamin Rush Papers, Library Company of Philadelphia.

62. Barton returned the United States on the ship *Apollo* in 1789.

63. Bell, "Benjamin Smith Barton," 197–203.

64. Francis Packard, "Medicine and the American Philosophical Society," *Proceedings of the American Philosophical Society* 86, no. 1 (September 1942): 93–94.

65. Benjamin Smith Barton to Scheling, May 11, 1796, Benjamin Smith Barton Papers, Historical Society of Pennsylvania. Barton added the initials "M.D." above this letter's signature, as if an afterthought.

66. Ibid.

67. David Hosack, born August 31, 1769, in New York City, was the first son of Alexander and Jane Hosack of Elgin, Scotland. His paternal grandfather was born at Cromarty, and his grandmother Isabel Dunn had come from Elgin, Morayshire, where Alexander was born. Alexander joined the British army in 1755 at nineteen and was stationed in Ireland and then Halifax, Nova Scotia. Hosack's father came to America from Elgin, Scotland, via a tour in the British army.

68. See note 2 above.

69. Hosack was married to Catharine "Kitty" Warner on April 14, 1791, in Princeton, New Jersey, by Samuel Stanhope Smith. It is surmised by his biographer, Christine Robbins, that Hosack chose this location because at the time Alexandria, Virginia, was generally believed to be the location of choice for the new national capital. Robbins, *David Hosack: Citizen of New York* (Philadelphia: American Philosophical Society, 1964), 22. Hosack's teachers studied in Edinburgh as well. They included Adam Kuhn (who received his medical degree from the University of Edinburgh in 1767); Benjamin Rush (1768); and Samuel Bard (1765), who lived in New York. Others in New York with whom Hosack most likely was personally acquainted were John Richardson Bayard Rodgers (1785) and Samuel Latham Mitchill (1786).

70. Alexander E. Hosack, "Memoir of the Late David Hosack by His Son," in S. D. Gross, ed., *Lives of Eminent American Physicians and Surgeons of the Nineteenth Century*

(Philadelphia, 1861), 289–337, quoted in Christine Chapman Robbins, "David Hosack's Herbarium and Its Linnaean Specimens," *Proceedings of the American Philosophical Society* 104, no. 3 (June 1960): 294.

71. Hosack, "Memoir," 289–337, quoted in Robbins, "David Hosack's Herbarium and Its Linnaean Specimens," ibid.

72. Ibid.

73. Ibid.

74. Robbins, *David Hosack: Citizen of New York*, 26.

75. Julie Flavell notes this phenomenon during the colonial period in " 'The School for Modesty and Humility': Colonial American Youth in London and Their Parents, 1755–1775," *Historical Journal* 42, no. 2 (1999): 377–403; see also William Sache, *The Colonial American in Britain* (Madison: University of Wisconsin Press, 1956).

76. Robbins, *David Hosack*, 26.

77. Elgin Gardens was named after Hosack's parents' hometown in Scotland.

78. Samuel Stanhope Smith, circular letter, January 19, 1796, and Smith to Sam[ue]l Bayard, December 26, 1796, both in the Samuel Stanhope Smith Collection, 1772–1817, box 1, C0028, Princeton Library Collections, Firestone Library.

79. Rush, a 1760 graduate of the College of New Jersey, was a booster of the College and talked Maclean into going to Princeton knowing it would be beneficial to his alma mater. He was instrumental in convincing many Scottish intellectuals to migrate to American institutions of higher education. The most famous of his "recruits" was the famous Scottish minister John Witherspoon. While studying medicine at the University of Edinburgh, the "ingratiating" young Rush (as he is referred to by L. H. Butterfield) was summoned by Witherspoon to persuade his wife to come to America. It was said that she got physically ill at the thought of relocating to the New World. Butterfield notes that Rush's tactics mirrored that of the Americans sent to Britain to raise funds for religious organizations. The stance he took was that America was like a child in the woods in need of Scottish guidance. "The young daughter of the Church of Scotland, helpless and exposed in this foreign land, cries to her tender and powerful parent for relief." L. H. Butterfield, *John Witherspoon Comes to America* (Princeton, N.J.: Princeton University Library, 1953), xii.

80. Quoted by John Maclean, Jr., the tenth president of the College, in his *Memoir of John Maclean, M.D., the First Professor of Chemistry in the College of New Jersey*, 2nd. ed. (Princeton, N.J.: Princeton Press, 1885), 21. Copy in the Harvey Cushing/John Hay Whitney Medical Library, Yale University.

81. His father, also named John Maclean, was the son of Archibald Maclean, minister of the parish of Kilfinichen, Scotland. His mother was Agnes Lang of Glasgow. Shortly after his parents were married, his father went to Canada as a surgeon in the British army and was serving General James Wolfe in 1759 when Quebec was won from the French. There is a story, perhaps apocryphal, that John Sr. was the third man to scale the Heights of Abraham in the attack on Quebec. After ending his service in the army, he returned to Glasgow and practiced surgery there until his death. Both he and Agnes died relatively early; David, the youngest of their children (born in 1771), was raised by a guardian.

82. Maclean studied in Paris during the height of the careers of famous men such as Antoine-Laurent de Lavoisier (1743–1794), Claude Louis Berthollet (1748–1822), and Antoine François, comte de Fourcroy (1755–1809). While in Paris, he embraced the new system of chemistry that was developing there.

83. Samuel Stanhope Smith, letter dated Princeton, October 26, 1795, published in *Woods Newark Gazette and New Jersey Advertiser*, November 11, 1795, as quoted in John

Maclean, *A Memoir of John Maclean, M.D., The First Professor of Chemistry in the College of New Jersey, By His Son, John Maclean, The Tenth President of the College* (Princeton, N.J.: Printed at the "Press" Office, 1876), 21.

84. Ibid.

85. There are several studies that note this trend. For a good overview see William R. Brock and Helen Brock, *Scotus Americanus* (Edinburgh: University of Edinburgh Press, 1982). While beyond the scope of this book, the significance of this practice in the Atlantic world cannot be exaggerated, especially in light of its relationship to slavery and the triangular trade. See Sidney Mintz's influential work *Sweetness and Power: The Place of Sugar in Modern History* (New York: Penguin Books, 1986); Richard Dunn, *Sugar and Slaves; the Rise of the Planter Class in the English West Indies, 1624–1713* (Chapel Hill: University of North Carolina Press, 1972).

86. In the case of slaves, people did not transport themselves; they were forcibly transported. Native Americans were forced to move as the geopolitical boundaries around them changed.

87. Americans' dependence and their sense of colonial and postcolonial inferiority increased within the rubric of a newly constructed British identity. This is clearly distinct from the notion that Americans and Scots shared a common provinciality. Certainly, long before the 1707 Union with England, many Scots had seen themselves as equal to the English. This was not the case with the Americans, who were now struggling to form an independent nation. As Michael Fry notes, Scots "stood among those in the forefront of European colonization in North America." See "Introduction," *Scotland and the Americas, 1600 to 1800* (Providence, R.I.: John Carter Brown Library, 1995), xvii. The essays in *Scotland and the Americas* make this point. See especially, David Armitage, "The Darien Venture," in *Scotland and the Americas, 1600 to 1800* (Providence, R.I.: John Carter Brown Library, 1995), 3–14; Ned Landsman, "Immigration and Settlement," in *Scotland and the Americas, 1600 to 1800* (Providence, R.I.: John Carter Brown Library, 1995), 15–26; and Robin Fabel, "Scots in Georgia and the British Floridas," in *Scotland and the Americas, 1600 to 1800* (Providence, R.I.: John Carter Brown Library, 1995), 39–52.

88. [Gebhard] F[riedrich]. A[ugust] Wendeborn, *A view of England towards the Close of the Eighteenth Century*, LL.D., translated from the original German, by the author himself, 2 vols., vol. 1 (London: Printed for G. G. J. and J. Robinson, Pater-noster-Row, 1791), copy in Henry E. Huntington Library, San Marino, California, 1:374, also quoted in Michael Duffy, *The English Satirical Print, 1600–1832: Englishman and the Foreigner* (Cambridge: Chadwyck-Healey, 1986), 18.

89. See ibid. Duffy notes that "the general picture was of filthy, bloodthirsty brutes, destitute of civilisation" (19).

90. As quoted in ibid., 18–19. Haggis is a traditional Scottish dish of organ meat, oatmeal, and spices encased in a sheep's stomach and boiled with vegetables.

91. Ibid., 19.

92. This argument was outlined in the influential article by John Clive and Bernard Bailyn, "England's Cultural Provinces: Scotland and America," *William and Mary Quarterly* 11 (1954): 200–213. The argument was later developed and refined by scholars as in the following: Ned Landsman, *Scotland and Its First American Colony, 1683–1765* (Princeton, N.J.: Princeton University Press, 1985), Landsman, "Scotland, the American Colonies and the Development of British Provincial Identity," in Lawrence Stone, ed., *An Imperial State at War: Britain from 1689 to 1815* (London: Routledge Press, 1994), and Landsman, "The Legacy of British Union for the North American Colonies: Provincial

Elites and the Problem of Imperial Union," in John Robertson, ed., *A Union for Empire: Political Thought and the British Union of 1707* (Cambridge: Cambridge University Press, 1995), 297–317.

93. This perspective reflects the work of Scottish historians such as Andrew Mackillop and Douglas Hamilton who are studying the relationship of Scotland and the British Empire. See Andrew Mackillop, *More Fruitful than the Soil, Army, Empire and the Scottish Highlands, 1715–1815* (East Linton: Tuckwell Press, 2000); Andrew Mackillop, "Europeans, Britons and Scots: Scottish Sojourning Networks and Identities in India, c.1700–1815," in Angela McCarthy, ed., *A Global Clan: Scottish Migrant Networks and Identities since the Eighteenth Century* (London: Tauris Academic Studies, 2006); Andrew Mackillop, "Accessing Empire: Scotland, Europe, Britain, and the Asia Trade, 1695–c.1750," *Itinerario* 29, no. 3 (November 2005): 7–30; Douglass Hamilton, *Scotland, the Caribbean and the Atlantic World, 1750–1820* (Manchester: Manchester University Press, 2005).

94. Historian Andrew Hook asserts: "There is no evidence that Philadelphians regarded Scottish culture itself as in any sense 'inferior'; on the contrary, respect and admiration for Scotland's cultural achievements clearly continued to grow in Philadelphia throughout the eighteenth century." Hook, "Philadelphia, Edinburgh and the Scottish Enlightenment," in Richard B. Sher and Jeffrey R. Smitten, eds., *Scotland and America in the Age of Enlightenment* (Edinburgh: Edinburgh University Press, 1990), 232–233. Speaking specifically of Philadelphia and Edinburgh in the eighteenth century, Hook puts it succinctly: "There is no question as to which city was more likely to learn from the other" (232).

95. Benjamin Smith Barton, "Facts Relative to Henry Moss, a White Negroe, Now in This City," in *Early Proceedings of the American Philosophical Society* (Philadelphia: American Philosophical Society, 1884), 241–256; see Charles Caldwell, *The Autobiography of Charles Caldwell, M.D.*, ed. Harriot W. Warner (Philadelphia, 1855), 163–164, 268–289. Samuel Stanhope Smith, *Essay on the Causes of Variety of Complexion and Figure in the Human Species*, 2nd ed., ed. Winthrop Jordan (1810; reprint, Cambridge: Cambridge University Press, 1965), 58–59. John Mortimer, "Some Account of the Motley Coloured, or Pye Negro Girl and Mulatto Boy," *American Philosophical Society Transactions 3* (1787): 292–395. See also Winthrop Jordan's discussion of Moss in his classic study *White over Black: American Attitudes toward the Negro, 1550–1812* (Chapel Hill: University of North Carolina Press, 1968), 521–522; Joann Pope Melish, *Disowning Slavery: Gradual Emancipation and "Race" in New England, 1780–1860* (Ithaca, N.Y.: Cornell University Press, 1998), in particular her comments on the "white negro," 137–150.

96. Benjamin Rush, "Observations Intended to Favour a Supposition That the Black Color (As It Is Called) of the Negroes Is Derived from the Leprosy," *Transactions of the American Philosophical Society* 4 (1799): 289–297.

97. Samuel Stanhope Smith, *An Essay on the Causes of the Variety of Complexion and Figure in the Human Species*, 2nd ed., enl. and improved (New-Brunswick, N.J.: J. Simpson; New York: Williams and Whiting, 1810 [New Brunswick]: J. Deare).

98. Dana Nelson, "Consolidating National Masculinity: Scientific Discourse and Race in the Post-Revolutionary United States," in Robert Blair St. George, ed., *Possible Pasts: Becoming Colonial in Early America* (Ithaca, N.Y.: Cornell University Press, 2000): 201–215. The quote appears on page 203. In her study *The Word in Black and White: Reading "Race" in American Literature, 1638–1867*, Nelson offers a theoretically informed account of Anglo-American notions of white superiority. She traces the beginning of

this concept to the scientific revolution of the middle Renaissance. The eighteenth-century Enlightenment is part of this intellectual genealogy and, according to Nelson, "kept Man rationally and squarely at the top rung of the ladder, and the story of (European) man's hierarchical superiority became 'common sense.'" Nelson, *The Word in Black and White: Reading "Race" in American Literature, 1638–1867* (New York: Oxford University Press, 1992). The quotes appear on page 9.

99. Dana Nelson was part of a group of scholars whose work in the 1990s began to look at "how the abstracted category of 'white manhood' could take hold and become a lived, common reality that superseded the locality, class, and ethnicity of identity in the early nation. Rather than treating 'race' as a corollary to culture—as ethnicity—these scholars analyze race and, more specifically, whiteness as a structure or system of privilege and identity, of discrimination and exclusion." The extension of white identity to embrace more people, while being sure to exclude others, "developed in part to manage the divisive effects of interclass and interregional rivalry that characterized the period." The fears of dependency and rivalry were projected onto the newly excluded groups. Nelson, "Consolidating National Masculinity: Scientific Discourse and Race in the Post-Revolutionary United States," in Robert Blair St. George, ed., *Possible Pasts: Becoming Colonial in Early America* (Ithaca, N.Y.: Cornell University Press, 2000), 201–215. The quote appears on page 203. See also Nelson, *Nature's Body: Gender and the Making of Modern Science* (Boston: Beacon Press, 1993). In this work Nelson traces the way science was masculinized during the Enlightenment.

100. Barton effused to Joseph Banks that Banks's opinion regarding the evidence of early civilization among the natives in the New World pleased him, for it supported Barton's own theory. The American based his argument on the existence of "indian fortifications" that were "scatted in immense numbers through almost every part of the visited country beyond the great alleghaney-chain." Barton argued that these fortifications served as proof of Native Americans' "link to civilization." Furthermore Barton believed the western part of the United States was peopled before the eastern and that there were tribes in the West that "relinquished the form of society which we denominate <u>savage</u>." It was remarkable to Barton that "so few of these structures exist east of the alleghanies." He wrote that Banks's argument "concerning the antiquity of the <u>american-world</u> has afforded me much pleasure." Barton pledged that he "shall not forget to transmit to you a copy of my work when it shall have appeared." Benjamin Smith Barton to Joseph Banks, May 26, 1793, Benjamin Smith Barton Papers, page [folder] 12, Historical Society of Pennsylvania, Philadelphia, Pennsylvania.

101. Ibid.; my emphasis.

102. Dana Nelson, *National Manhood: Capitalist Citzenship and the Imagined Fraternity of White Men* (Durham, N.C.: Duke University Press, 1998) explores the circumstances under which men with competing identities, such as those of religion, class, and ethnicity, were brought together through a shared identity for white men based on professionalism and nationalism. White "national manhood" smoothed over class differences by its exclusion on the basis of race and gender. Nelson contributes to our understanding of the antidemocratic tendencies that developed in the postrevolutionary period. Her work highlights the anxiety and disappointment white American men experienced at this time and explains how this insecurity contributed to a widespread cultural logic that emphasized physical differences between white men and the "others" in their midst.

103. After the American Revolution, "a number of white Americans began to embark on serious studies of their own 'savages,'" as their way to enter into debates of moral phi-

losophers in Europe, who were accustomed to using fantastic "voyage literature" as their source of information on the New World. Ronald L. Meek, *Social Science and the Ignoble Savage* (Cambridge: Cambridge University Press, 1976), 218; Thomas Jefferson, *Notes on the State of Virginia*, ed. W. Peden (Chapel Hill: University of North Carolina Press, 1955), 62; R. H. Pearce, *The Savages of America*, rev. ed. (Baltimore: Johns Hopkins University Press, 1965), 91–96.

104. Meek, *Social Science and the Ignoble Savage*, 218–219; Jedidiah Morse, *The History of America*, 2nd ed. (Philadelphia, 1795), 31.

105. Jefferson, *Writings*, 190.

106. Anglo-Americans replicated the practice of symbolizing America by the "others" in their midst, and in fact often chose to represent themselves in the same way the British and Europeans had pictured them. Indeed, they found it valuable in certain situations to perform or portray knowledge of American Indians and enslaved Africans for European audiences. By the 1830s, as self-consciously national writers such as James Fenimore Cooper created a romantic American literature through works such as *The Last of the Mohicans*, the embrace of the "native" came to define American uniqueness. Americans of European descent would inherit the nobility of the "savage," thus countering their inability to ever be noble in the European sense (through an aristocracy of blood). The embrace of the "native," though rhetorically a claim of creating a unique American identity, was in part generated by European interest in the "savage." Jean-Jacques Rousseau's image of the "savage" as less corrupted by civilization and somehow naturally ennobled was one well-known example of European fascination with American Indians. On white Americans portraying Indians, see Philip J. Deloria, *Playing Indian* (New Haven, Conn.: Yale University Press, 1998). The necessary cost of embracing the nobility of the "native" was a vicious need to eradicate the actual existence of "savagery," thereby creating the mythic narrative of the disappearing "native." The phrase "last of the Mohicans" expressed a desire that Anglo-Americans would inherit the mantle of their noble Indian ancestors and at the same time the related fantasy that the actual Indians would just disappear. Though he does not discuss Cooper, Edward Watts, in *Writing Postcolonialism in the Early Republic* (Charlottesville: University Press of Virginia, 1998), analyzes early American literature using the perspectives of postcolonial theory. For Scottish Enlightenment thinkers and Rousseau on American Indians and stage theories of development, see Meek, *Social Science and the Ignoble Savage*.

107. There are countless instances of this phenomenon. A striking example is "The Oracle," a mezzotint published in London in March 1774. Created by British artist John Dixon, this image portrayed Father Time giving a magic lantern show to maidens meant as allegorical representations of Britannia (representing England), Scotland, Ireland, and America. The image for America is strikingly different from the rest of the group, most obviously because she is pictured as a dark-skinned "native" whereas the others are white. She is practically naked except for a feathered headdress, while the rest of the group is clothed in classical drapery and coifed hair. America crouches menacingly in the corner, bathed in shadows, while the rest of the figures are seated together in comfort and camaraderie. Colley discusses the significance of Dixon's image in *Britons*, 132–134. These images of America were also expressed in material objects of various kinds. For instance, the Chelsea-Derby Factory produced decorative sets that consisted of figurines representing Europe, Africa, and America (c. 1770–1775). The "European" figure was a white woman draped in fine printed clothing with a lamb at her feet. The "American" figure, in contrast, was a brown-skinned woman with bared chest and feathered headdress, carrying arrows, with an alligator (a long-standing icon for America) curled at her

feet. Jack P. Greene discusses representations of America and the New World in *The Intellectual Construction of America: Exceptionalism and Identity from 1492–1800* (Chapel Hill, N.C.: University of North Carolina Press, 1993).

108. For a discussion on the differences between Jefferson's and Samuel Smith's theories, see Jordan's discussion in *White over Black*, 442–444. For a study on the earlier colonial period, see Joyce Chaplin, *Subject Matter: Technology, the Body, and Science on the Anglo-American Frontier, 1500–1676* (Cambridge, Mass.: Harvard University Press, 2001).

109. As discussed in note 46 of the Introduction, like elite Anglo-Americans, the elite creole population in Latin America feared that they were being looked down upon by Europeans in the mother country. Benedict Anderson elaborates on this phenomenon in *Imagined Communities*.

110. As I noted, Hume had asserted: "There never was a civilized nation of any other complexion than white.... No ingenious manufactures amongst them, no arts, no sciences." David Hume, "Of National Characters," 1753–1754 ed. (first published in 1748), in *David Hume: Essays: Moral, Political, and Literary*, ed. T. H. Green and T. H. Grose, 2 vols. (London, 1875), 1:252 n., quoted in Jordan, *White over Black*, 253. Philadelphian and founding member of the American Philosophical Society Thomas Bond (1713–1784) made a similar statement in the Annual Oration of the American Philosophical Society for 1782. In his speech, Bond emphasized how important it was for the new nation to learn from European culture and to earn respect from the community of civilized European nations through cultural achievement in activities like science. He declared "Point out the Nation which has not Science, or that which has abandoned it and I will point out to you Savages or Slaves.... Science is the Nurse of universal Friendship. Bond, "Anniversary Oration" (Philadelphia: American Philosophical Society, [1782]), 8, 30–34; see Whitfield J. Bell, Jr., *Patriot-Improvers: Biographical Sketches of Members of the American Philosophical Society*, vol. 1 (Philadelphia: American Philosophical Society, 1997), 42.

111. See the insights presented by Benedict Anderson in *Imagined Communities* regarding the connections between Old World locations and their New World copies.

112. Writers in this period employed the terms "civilized" and "uncivilized" in publications about race. For instance, in *An Essay on the Causes of the Variety of Complexion and Figure in the Human Species* Samuel Stanhope Smith argued: "[U]ncivilized man is a lazy, improvident, and filthy animal." In his extended introduction to the reprint of Samuel Stanhope Smith's, *An Essay on the Causes of the Variety of Complexion and Figure in the Human Species*, Winthrop Jordan characterized the work as emblematic of the "prevailing thought" of the "intellectual currents of the late eighteenth and early nineteenth centuries." Smith, *An Essay on the Causes of the Variety of Complexion and Figure in the Human Species*, 2nd ed., enl. and improved (New-Brunswick, N.J.: J. Simpson; New York: Williams and Whiting, 1810 [New Brunswick]: J. Deare), 27. The commentary on the essay appears in Winthrop Jordan, "Introduction," Samuel Stanhope Smith, *Essay on the Causes of Variety of Complexion and Figure in the Human Species*, viii–ix. Samuel Stanhope Smith, *An Essay on the Causes of the Variety of Complexion and Figure in the Human Species* 2nd ed., enl. and improved (New-Brunswick, N.J.: J. Simpson; New York: Williams and Whiting, 1810 ([New Brunswick]: J. Deare), 27. For a study on the complexity of racial theory in the early national period, including the perspectives of African Americans, see Bruce Dain, *A Hideous Monster of the Mind: American Race Theory in the Early Republic* (Cambridge, Mass.: Harvard University Press, 2002). For a work on racial categorization in Britain, see Roxann Wheeler, *The*

Complexion of Race: Categories of Difference in Eighteenth-century British Culture (Philadelphia: University of Pennsylvania Press, 2000).

113. Smith's *Essay* went through many editions, two of which, the 1810 revised edition and the 1965 reprint of it, are listed in note 112 above. It was published in the United States and Great Britain. When citing direct quotes from Smith's book, I use the 1810 edition. See also Reverend Samuel Stanhope Smith, *An essay on the causes of the variety of complexion and figure in the human species: to which are added strictures on Lord Kaim's discourse, on the original diversity of mankind* (Philadelphia: Printed and sold by R. Aitken, 1787); *An essay on the causes of the variety of complexion and figure in the human species [electronic resource]. To which are added, Strictures on Lord Kames's discourse on the original diversity of mankind. By the Rev. Samuel Stanhope Smith, A new edition. With some additional notes, by a gentleman of the University of Edinburgh* (Philadelphia printed, and Edinburgh reprinted, for C. Elliot; and C. Elliot and T. Kay, London, 1788); Smith, *An essay on the causes of the variety of complexion and figure in the human species. To which are added, Strictures on Lord Kaims's [sic] discourse on the original diversity of mankind* (Philadelphia, Printed; London, Re-printed for John Stockdale, 1789).

114. For an example of Smith's utilization of these terms see, Smith, *Essay* (1810), 240–241.

115. Smith uses these terms frequently in this publication. For instance, "In the first place, then, climate produces its most deteriorating effects in a savage state of society; and, on the other hand, these effects are, in some degree, corrected by the arts and conveniences, of civilization." Smith, *Essay* (1810), 150.

116. Smith used the term "savages" throughout the work. For instance, "Nakedness, exposure to the weather, negligence of appearance, want of cleanliness, bad lodging, and poor diet, are always seen to impair the beauty of the human form, and the clearness of the skin. Hence, it results, that savages never can be perfectly fair. But when savage habits concur with the influence of an ardent sun, or an unwholesome atmosphere, the complexion of the people will partake of a tinge more or less dark in proportion to the predominance of one, or of both of these causes. There [sic] features will be more coarse and hard, and their persons less robust and athletic than those of men in civilized society who enjoy its advantages with temperance." Smith, *Essay* (1810), 155.

117. Jordan perceptively notes that Smith's *Essay* was a response to the disturbing question as to whether this "new man," the American "was a mulatto or a half-breed." His work was "eminently satisfying to Americans who were struggling to establish a viable national union. This struggle was intimately associated with the necessity of demonstrating to Europeans, particularly Englishmen, that the revolutionary republic was not going to fall apart at the seams and, indeed, that Americans were capable of polished accomplishments equal to those of the most cultivated nations of the Old World." Winthrop Jordan, "Introduction," Samuel Stanhope Smith, *Essay on the Causes of Variety of Complexion and Figure in the Human Species,* 2nd ed., ed. Winthrop Jordan (1810; reprint, Cambridge: Cambridge University Press, 1965), xvi.

118. The quote appears in an extended footnote, see Smith, *Essay* (1810), 71.

119. Smith, *Essay* (1810), 176.

120. Smith, *Essay* (1810), 177.

121. Smith, *Essay* (1810), 170–171.

122. The quote appears in an extended footnote, see Smith, *Essay* (1810), 71.

123. Dana Nelson, *National Manhood: Capitalist Citizenship and the Imagined Fraternity of White Men* (Durham, N.C.: Duke University Press, 1998), 7.

124. For influential studies on the complex history of the construction of whiteness, see the pioneering work of David Roediger, *Wages of Whiteness* (London: Verso, 2007),

Alexander Saxton, *The Rise and Fall of the White Republic: Class Politics and Mass Culture in Nineteenth-century America* (London: Verso, 1990). For later studies, see note 131 below.

125. Nelson, *White Manhood,* 70.

126. Winthrop Jordan notes that the "questions regarding the Negro's place in creation and of his color were played out upon an international stage." Though they were not only American problems, their formulations were based partly on information gathered from America. "To the extent that these questions were 'scientific,' they were necessarily international. Scientists belonged to an international fraternity, and trans-Atlantic communications, slow as they were in the eighteenth century, enabled natural philosophers in America to make claim to membership." Jordan, *White over Black,* 255.

127. Smith, *Essay* (1810), 57.

128. David Hosack wrote to Benjamin Rush informing him of the research that Manchester surgeon Charles White (1728–1813) had been doing on "Negro" subjects. Hosack told Rush that Dr. White had examined "a great number of them [the forearms of Africans]" and "found it very generally true that the fore arm is longer in proportion to the arm then in ye white subjects." White also cited two cases in which "Negro" subjects had two additional vertebra than "white subjects." While studying anatomy in London, Hosack attested to the fact that he witnessed a dissection with similar results. White, who earned his medical degree from the University of Edinburgh, posited the thesis that non-white races were inferior to whites because their darker pigmentation was proof that they were more primitive. He extended his thesis to women, citing that the dark areas of their bodies such as their areolas as evidence of their primitive nature. David Hosack to Benjamin Rush, May 7, 1800, Rush Letterbook, bound vol. 27, Benjamin Rush Papers, Library Company of Philadelphia In the letter cited above, Hosack mentions that he had "lately received from Dr. White surgeon of Manchester [*sic*] a very interesting work upon ye 'gradation observable in animated nature.'" This book contains White's theories on the relationship between the races. Charles White, *An Account of the Regular Gradation in Man, Animals and Vegetables* (London: C. Dilly, 1799). For biographical information on White, see J[ohn]. G[eorge]. Adami, "Charles White of Manchester, 1728–1813," *Medical Library and History Journal* 5 (1907): 1–18.

129. In contrast, Hindle notes in *Pursuit of Science* that in fields such as mathematics, "Americans felt nothing but disadvantage from their geographical removal from Europe" (93).

130. See Annette Gordon-Reed, *Thomas Jefferson and Sally Hemings: An American Controversy* (Charlottesville: University Press of Virginia, 1997); Kathleen Brown, *Good Wives, Nasty Wenches & Anxious Patriarchs: Gender, Race, and Power in Colonial Virginia* (Chapel Hill: University of North Carolina Press, 1996); Sharon Block, *Rape and Sexual Power in Early America* (Chapel Hill: University of North Carolina Press, 2006); Martha Hodes, ed., *Sex, Love, Race: Crossing Boundaries in North American History* (New York: New York University Press, 1999); Deborah Gray White, *Ar'n't I a Woman? Female Slaves in the Plantation South* (New York: Norton, 1985).

131. My discussion here is indebted to the innovative work of scholars of, for lack of a better term, "whiteness studies." See Cheryl I. Harris, "Whiteness as Property," *Harvard Law Review* 106 (1993): 1707–1791; Matthew Frye Jacobson, *Whiteness of a Different Color: European Immigrants and the Alchemy of Race* (Cambridge, Mass.: Harvard University Press, 1998), especially chap. 1, " 'Free White Persons' in the Republic, 1790–1840," 15–90; and Nelson, *Word in Black and White.* See also George Lipsitz, *Possessive Investment in Whiteness* (Philadelphia: Temple University Press, 1998). On the commod-

ification of race and its implications for American slavery, see Walter Johnson, *Soul by Soul: Life inside the Antebellum Slave Market* (Cambridge, Mass.: Harvard University Press, 1999). The classic study on slavery in America is Edmund S. Morgan, *American Slavery American Freedom: The Ordeal of Colonial Virginia* (New York: Norton, 1975).

CONCLUSION

1. The epigraph to this chapter is from Sidney Smith, review of *Statistical Annals of the United States (Philadelphia: T. Dobson & Sons, 1818),* by Adam Seybert, *Edinburgh Review* (January 1820): 69–80, quote appears on pages 79–80. Founded on October 10, 1802, the *Edinburgh Review* became the most influential magazine of its time. By 1818, it boasted a circulation of 13,500.

2. George Robert Gleig, *A History of the Campaigns of the British Army at Washington and New Orleans Under Generals Ross, Pakenham, and Lambert, in the Years 1814–1815; with Some Account of the Countries Visited,* 2nd ed. (London: John Murray, 1826). They reported that it was "in a state which indicated that they had been lately and precipitately abandoned" (Gleig, 130). Gleig (1753–1840) was a lieutenant at the time of the invasion of Washington. He also took part in the attack on Baltimore, and was present at the British failure at New Orleans. He later became a military chaplain and author. *Dictionary of National Biography,* s.v. "Gleig, George Robert."

3. Ibid.

4. Major General Robert Ross recorded the evening in his journal as well, and his account does not contradict Gleig's records. Ross noted that the party "found a table laid with forty covers. The fare, however, which was intended for *Jonathan* was voraciously devoured by *John Bull;* and the health of the Prince Regent and success to his Majesty's arms by sea and land, was drunk in the best wines." Quoted in Jon Latimer, *1812: War with America* (Cambridge, Mass.: Harvard University Press, 2007), 318.

5. See Latimer, *1812,* 316.

6. For firsthand accounts of this episode, see [George Robert Gleig], *A Narrative of the Campaigns of the British Army at Washington, Baltimore, and New Orleans* (Philadelphia, 1821), 134–135; [George Robert Gleig], *A Subaltern in America, Comprising His Narrative of the Campaigns of the British Arm…During the Late War* (Philadelphia, 1833); C. G. Moore-Smith, ed., *The Autobiography of Lieutenant-General Sir Harry Smith,* 2 vols. (London: J. Murray, 1902). Three editions of Gleig's work were published in London, 1821–1827. In 1821 an American edition was published in Philadelphia. The fourth edition was published in London in 1836, and a later one in 1847 was published under the title *The Campaigns of the British Army at Washington and New Orleans, in the Years 1814–1815.*

7. On entering the House of Lords, Rush felt as if he had entered onto "sacred ground." See Benjamin Rush to Ebenezer Hazard, London, October 22, 1768, in Scott Hammond, Kevin Hardwick, and Howard Lubert, eds., *Classics of American Political and Constitutional Thought, Origins through the Civil War,* vol. 1 (Indianapolis: Hackett, 2007), 199.

8. Ibid.

9. The details were as follows: at around 10:30 p.m., about 150 Royal British troops marched to the president's residence. They burned the official buildings in America's capital city in retaliation for the burning of York (modern-day Toronto). In an often-told story, George Washington's painting was saved under the direction of Dolley Madison. What is less well known is that a slave, Paul Jennings, was the one who carried it off. See Anthony Pitch, *The Burning of Washington: The British Invasion of 1814*

(Annapolis: U.S. Naval Institute Press, 2000), 117–122. See also James Pack, *The Man Who Burned the White House: Admiral Sir George Cockburn, 1772–1853* (Annapolis: U.S. Naval Institute Press, 1987), 13–20. For the War of 1812 more generally, see Steven Watts, *Republic Reborn: War and the Making of Liberal America, 1790–1820* (Baltimore: Johns Hopkins University Press, 1987), and Daniel Walker Howe, *What Hath God Wrought: The Transformation of America, 1815–1848* (New York: Oxford University Press, 2007). For a work on the War of 1812 from the British perspective, see Jon Latimer, *1812: War with America* (Cambridge, Mass.: Harvard University Press, 2007).

10. Richard Van Alstyne, *The American Empire: Its Historical Pattern and Evolution.* (London: Published for the Historical Association by Routledge and Paul, 1960). The main causes of the War of 1812 had to do with the lack of respect the British had for Americans. One particularly humiliating event was the Chesapeake Affair (also known as the Chesapeake-Leopard Affair), which occurred on June 22, 1807. The captain of a fourth-rate British warship, the *Leopard*, demanded to be allowed to board the *Chesapeake*, an American frigate. When the Americans refused, they were fired on and humiliated. This was a call to arms for the nation. See Norman K. Risjord, "1812: Conservatives, War Hawks, and the Nation's Honor," *William and Mary Quarterly* 18, no. 2 (1961) 196–210. See also J. C. A. Stagg, "James Madison and the 'Malcontents': The Political Origins of the War of 1812," *William and Mary Quarterly* 33, no. 4 (1976): 557–585, and "James Madison and the Coercion of Great Britain: Canada, the West Indies, and the War of 1812," *William and Mary Quarterly* 38, no. 1 (1981): 4–34.

11. Quoted in Latimer, *1812*, 13.

12. This point is made in ibid.

13. Britain's failure to send a representative caused great concern among Americans. Some felt it was discourteous; others felt it arrogant. After spending three years in London, John Adams returned home having been unable to accomplish much. He suspected malice on the part of the British. Beckles Willson, *Friendly Relations: A Narrative of Britain's Ministers and Ambassadors to America, 1791–1930* (Boston: Little, Brown, 1934), 3.

14. Willson, *Friendly Relations*, 3.

15. Francis Godolphin Osborne (1751–1799), the fifth Duke of Leeds, was the foreign secretary and served under William Pitt the Younger from 1783 to 1791. Willson, *Friendly Relations*, 3.

16. William Wyndham Grenville, first Baron Grenville (1759–1834), was a Whig politician who later became prime minister. When Hammond was writing to him, Grenville was the foreign secretary who succeeded the Duke of Leeds. Willson, *Friendly Relations*, 6.

17. George Hammond (1763–1853) served as the first British envoy to the United States between 1791 and 1795.

18. See T. H. Breen, *Marketplace of Revolution: How Consumer Politics Shaped American Independence* (New York: Oxford University Press, 2004).

19. Latimer, *1812*, 25. For work on impressment, see James Zimmerman, *Impressment of American Seamen* (New York: Columbia University Press, 1925).

20. Many British sailors deserted the British Royal Navy and signed up with the U.S. navy, which offered better treatment and better pay. Furthermore, the British insisted that any person born a British subject was still subject to impressment.

21. In a similar way, transatlantic objects eluded easy identification.

22. *Letters of Queen Victoria*, 2nd ser., 1:265, quoted in Paul Langford, "Manners and Character in Anglo-American Perceptions, 1750–1850," in *Anglo-American Attitudes:*

From Revolution to Partnership (Aldershot, England: Ashgate, 2000), 86. Charles Maurice de Talleyrand-Périgord (1754–1838) was the first Sovereign Prince of Beneventum.

23. Langford, "Manners and Character," 81.

24. Gaillard Hunt, ed., *The Writings of James Madison: Comprising His Public Papers and His Private Correspondence,* vol. 8 (New York: Putnam, 1908), 175; my emphasis.

25. Howe, *What Hath God Wrought,* 43–45. Even when domestic alternatives for goods entered the market, imports continued to play an important role in American life, as they brought the greatest amount of cultural cachet with them.

26. The British wanted to prevent the United States from trading with their French enemies despite America's official status as a neutral nation. The British exhibited a lingering proprietary attitude toward their former colonies in North America.

27. John K. Mahon, "British Strategy and Southern Indians: War of 1812," *Florida Historical Quarterly* 44, no. 4 (1966): 285–302.

28. See Howe, *What Hath God Wrought,* 43.

29. See *The Writings of Thomas Jefferson,* vol. 5, ed. H. A. Washington (Washington, D.C., 1854), 444.

30. Jedidiah Morse, *The American Geography; or, A View of the Present Situation of the United States of America* (Boston: Thomas & Andrews, 1789), 469, and *The American Geography,* 2nd ed. (London: John Stockdale, 1792), 469.

31. In *What Hath God Wrought,* Howe describes this period as that of the transportation and communication revolution.

32. *The Seventh Census, Report of the Superintendent of the Census for Dec. 1, 1852; To Which Is Appended the Report for Dec. 1, 1851. Printed by order of the House of Representatives of the United States,* 128.

33. Howe, *What Hath God Wrought,* 43–45.

34. Robert A. Gross, "Building a National Literature: The United States 1800–1890," in Simon Eliot and Jonathan Rose, eds., *A Companion to the History of the Book* (Malden, Mass.: Blackwell, 2007), 315. My argument here was greatly enriched by this essay.

35. Jacques Barzun, "America's Romance with Practicality," *Harper's,* February 1952, 70–78.

36. How else to explain the continuing flow of educated elites to Europe and Great Britain well into the early twentieth century, chasing the cachet of Oxford, Cambridge, and foreign degrees long after the American university system had achieved functional viability?

37. See Langford, "Manners and Character."

38. Lucy Larcom, *A New England Girlhood* (New York: Houghton Mifflin, 1889), 118.

39. See, for instance, the quotes by Larcom and Naipaul, 239.

40. Benjamin Waterhouse, *A Journal of a Young Man of Massachusetts* (originally published in Boston, 1816), reprinted in *Magazine of History* (1911), quoted in Langford, "Manners and Character," 77.

41. For example *The Mother's Remarks on a Set of Cuts for Children* (Philadelphia: Jacob Johnson, 1803) contained information that referred to English rather than American society. Although it was reprinted in the United States, the text and cuts were obviously taken directly from the English version. It included a discussion of the Royal Mail and an illustration containing the British flag. Oddly, although it was meant as a didactic tool for its young American readers, the book presented lessons that went against the political and ideological tenets on which the new nation was built. *The Mother's Remarks on a Set of Cuts for Children* included troublesome lessons for young

citizens of the new democratic American nation. The entry for "Queen" read: "The engraver has succeeded tolerably well here; but I know not whether he has done properly, in giving to her majesty a globe, as she is only queen consort, that is, the wife of a king." This snippet illustrates another common theme in British children's books: the global domination of the British Empire.

42. For studies on children's literature, see Gail S. Murray, "Rational Thought and Republican Virtues: Children's Literature, 1789–1820," *Journal of the Early Republic* 8, no. 2 (1988): 159–177; Anne Scott MacLeod, *A Moral Tale: Children's Fiction and American Culture, 1820–1860* (Hamden, Conn.: Archon Books, 1975); Geoffrey Summerfield, *Fantasy and Reason: Children's Literature in the Eighteenth Century* (Athens: University of Georgia Press, 1984); Monica Kiefer, *American Children through Their Books, 1700–1835* (Philadelphia: University of Pennsylvania Press, 1948); Jill P. May, *Children's Literature and Critical Theory: Reading and Writing for Understanding* (New York: Oxford University Press, 1995); Percy Muir, *English Children's Books, 1600–1900* (New York: Praeger, 1969). The classic study of childhood is Philippe Aries, *Centuries of Childhood: A Social History of Family Life* (New York: Knopf, 1962). He characterizes the eighteenth century as the period in which a new respect for children developed. For a material culture approach to childhood see Karin Calvert, *Children in the House: The Material Culture of Early Childhood, 1600–1900* (Boston: Northeastern University Press, 1992). For a discussion on colonialism in the British Empire and its relation to child-rearing and education see Ann Laura Stoler, *Race and the Education of Desire: Foucault's History of Sexuality and the Colonial Order of Things* (Durham, N.C.: Duke University Press, 1995), especially chap. 5, "Domestic Subversions and Children's Sexuality," 137–164. These books were reprinted repeatedly by American publishers across the country and frequently used as schoolbooks. The educational system in the United States was just starting to develop, and standardized texts were not yet available. Publication localities were dispersed regionally and popular with small publishers in states such as New Hampshire. If the location of publication is dispersed regionally, we can assume that they were popular, and therefore believed to be profitable, because small publishers were not able to take risks. Instead, they only published "bread and butter" publications whose sales made it well worth their purchasing the plates or taking the time to reset the book. In addition, we know that they were popular because they continued to be reissued even when the firms changed names.

43. Henry Adams, *The Education of Henry Adams: An Autobiography* (Boston: Houghton Mifflin, 2002), 45, quoted in Frank K. Prochaska, *The Eagle and the Crown: Americans and the British Monarchy* (New Haven, Conn.: Yale University Press, 2008), 36.

44. Henry Adams, *The Education of Henry Adams* (Teddington, England: Echo Library, 2006), 118.

45. Henry Adams, *The Education of Henry Adams* (Cambridge, Mass.: Massachusetts Historical Society, 1918), 180–181.

46. Scholars of the War of 1812 argue that the British thought of the American theater as peripheral to the real battle with the French. In some ways, this can be said of the American Revolution once other European nations became involved.

47. Adams, 1918, 181.

48. Alexis de Tocqueville's *Democracy in America* (New York: Harper Perennial, 2000), and Charles Dickens, *American Notes for General Circulation,* with an introduction by Patricia Ingham (London: Chapman and Hall, 1842; reprint, London: Penguin, 2000). Other authors of this genre include Frances Trollope, Basil Hall, Harriet Martineau, and Frederick Marryat.

49. The impulse to describe national character had its origins in the eighteenth century. As Langford describes it, "social conduct" and manners were seen to reflect the characteristics of the society that spawned them. There was a "growing fascination with national character and the ethnic imprints of peoples as opposed to the impact of governors and governments." Langford, "Manners and Character," 76. The vast genre of travel narratives written by English visitors to America provides primary documentation of American cultural insecurity. For collections of British travel narratives, see Jane Louise Mesick, *The English Traveller in America*, 1785–1835 (New York: Columbia University Press, 1922), Una Pope-Hennessy, *Three English Women in America* (London: Ernest Benn Limited, 1929), and Allan Nevins, comp., *American Social History as Recorded by British Travellers* (New York: Henry Holt and Company, 1923). Nevins's book, which contained a variety of British accounts of life in America, was later revised and reissued as Nevins, *America Through British Eyes* (New York: Oxford University Press, 1948). For examples of published British travelers' accounts about America, see Thomas Ashe, *Travels in America, performed in 1806* (London, Printed in Newburyport [Mass.], Reprinted for W. Sawyer & Co. by E. M. Blunt, 1808); Margaret Hall, *The Aristocratic Journey*, ed. Una Pope-Hennessy (New York: Putnam, 1931), and Frances Trollope, *Domestic Manners of the Americans,* ed. Donald Smalley (New York: Knopf, 1949). Americans also recorded these feelings in diaries and autobiographies; see H. M. Brackenridge, *Journal of a voyage up the River Missouri, performed in eighteen hundred and eleven,* 2nd ed. (Baltimore: Coale & Maxwell, 1815); Timothy Flint, *Recollections of the Last Ten Years,* ed. C. Hartley Grattan (New York: Knopf, 1932); Catharine M. Sedgwick, *The Power of Her Sympathy: The Autobiography and Journal of Catherine Maria Sedgwick*, ed. Mary Kelley (Boston: Massachusetts Historical Society, 1993).

50. Ralph Waldo Emerson, "The Young American," speech delivered to the Mercantile Library Association, Boston, February 7, 1844, in *Essays and Lectures* (New York: Literary Classics of America, 1983), 228.

51. Americans' childlike glee in the attentions Dickens lavished on them was evident in the details they published about him. People across the nation were eager spectators of his trip; they read about his movements in detailed newspaper accounts. One fawning report among the many that were published took notice of Dickens's "brown frock coat, a red figured vest, somewhat of the flash order, and a fancy scarf cravat, that concealed the collar and was fastened to the bosom in rather voluptuous folds by a double pin and chain." The author continued with a description of his body: "the whole region about the eyes was prominent with a noticeable development of nerves and vessels indicating, say the phrenologists, great vigour in the intellectual organs with which they are connected. The eyeballs completely filled their sockets." Worchester (Mass.) *Egis*, February 5, 1842; (New York) *Evening Post,* February 4, 1842; see *American Notes for General Circulation.*

52. For a critical analysis of Dickens's *Martin Chuzzlewit,* see John O. Jordan, *The Cambridge Companion to Charles Dickens* (New York: Cambridge University Press, 2001). See John Bowen, *Other Dickens: Pickwick to Chuzzlewit* (Oxford: Oxford University Press, 2003).

53. Jeremy Tambling writes: "The fate of being an American meeting Dickens is to be a postcolonial subject meeting someone from the center of English culture" and hence to provide fodder for his next social satire. Tambling, *Lost in the American City: Dickens, James and Kafka* (New York: Palgrave Macmillan, 2001), 26. It should be remembered that Dickens made a living mostly lampooning British characters. As avid readers of his books, American audiences should have been aware of this, yet their out-

rage points to the extreme sensitivity they had toward foreign criticism, which, as Emerson pointed out, was a sign of their vulnerability and weakness. My thanks to Alice Proschaska for her insightful reading of this chapter and her suggestions.

54. Attitudes about America's relationship to the former mother country changed in the years following the War of 1812, particularly among those individuals in the western settlements who had relocated outside of the established East Coast urban enclaves. What Dickens had observed was a population trying to shed the unbecoming humiliation and shame over their rusticity and provinciality for a more confident outlook toward the world. While the inequality between America and Great Britain had also existed during the colonial period, its meaning shifted with independence. As one scholar observed, "before 1783 an uncouth American was simply one kind of backward Englishman among many; after it he was specifically an American, condemned to backwardness by virtue of his origins." Langford, "Manners and Character," 80.

55. Dickens, *Martin Chuzzlewit*, with introduction by Ingham, vol. 2, chap. 4, 189, cited in Ingham, introduction to *Martin Chuzzlewit*, xxvi–xxvii.

56. Their itineraries tell us something about their goals for their trip. Those writing travel narratives tended to breeze through the more established New England urban centers, if they did not skip them all together, such was their haste to observe for themselves the outer extremes of rusticity or the horrors of southern slavery. Langford, "Manners and Character," 79.

57. It should be noted that the majority of the inhabitants of the new western settlements were originally from the East Coast.

58. Timothy Dwight, *Travels in New England and New York* (Cambridge, Mass.: Harvard University Press, 1969), 321.

59. Quoted in William Smith Bryan, *A History of the Pioneer Families of Missouri: with numerous sketches, anecdotes, adventures, etc., relating to early days in Missouri. Also the lives of Daniel Boone and the celebrated Indian chief, Black Hawk, with numerous biographies and histories of primitive institutions* (St. Louis: Bryan Brand, 1876), 68.

60. See Richard Bushman on the split in the nineteenth century between "city" and "country," which he argues were terms used to roughly divide the nation into regions of "refinement" and "coarseness." As he notes, and as I wish to note here, these terms are not accurate descriptions of any type of social reality but a "cultural and social polarity in a mental geography." Bushman, *Refinement of America: Persons, Houses, Cities* (New York: Knopf, 1992), 353.

61. Quotes from Robert Baird, *View of the Valley of the Mississippi* (Philadelphia: H. S. Tanner, 1834), 102. Bushman argues that the democratization of goods and the spread (class and geographic) of refinement signaled the change in American society after the Revolution. Bushman, *Refinement of America*. For other cultural histories of the development of middle-class culture in the nineteenth century see Karen Halttunen, *Confidence Men and Painted Women* (New Haven, Conn.: Yale University Press, 1982); Lawrence Levine, *Highbrow/Lowbrow: The Emergence of Cultural Hierarchy in America* (Cambridge, Mass.: Harvard University Press, 1988); John Kasson, *Rudeness and Civility: Manners in Nineteenth-century Urban America* (New York: Hill and Wang, 1990).

62. One could say that American cities in this period, while clearly less developed than London, could be considered equal to provincial cities in England. Michael Kammen argues that historians "have too often been misled by comparing colonial customs with those in London" when the "more sensible comparison is between the colonies and English provinces." I agree with him in terms of objective measures such as size and population, but my subjects defined London as the arbiter of taste and modeled

their cultural practices after what they imagined were the practices there. Provincial cities on the periphery of London were seen as rustic, but compared to U.S. cities it could always be said that *at least* they are still in England and in Europe. This speaks to my idea of the geography of *relative* location. See Michael Kammen, *People of Paradox: An Inquiry Concerning the Origins of American Civilization* (New York: Knopf, 1972), 28.

63. Benedict Anderson makes this point in *Imagined Communities.* The quotation from Timothy Dwight in the epigraph to this section is from Anonymous [Reverend Timothy Dwight], "Thoughts on American genius," *American Museum* (March 1787).

64. I wish to thank Karen Ordahl Kupperman for her helpful suggestions.

65. For a suggestive study of a similar dynamic in another context, see Daniel Hechter, *Internal Colonialism: The Celtic Fringe in British National Development* (New Brunswick, N.J.: Transaction, 1999).

66. Matthew Frye Jacobson has demonstrated that the definition of what European immigrant groups were considered white changed over time. See Jacobson, *Whiteness of a Different Color: European Immigrants and the Alchemy of Race* (Cambridge, Mass.: Harvard University Press, 1998). My thanks to Matt Jacobson for reading a draft of the manuscript of this book.

67. To unlock this connection, the notion of material culture needs to be expanded to challenge the prevailing definitions of objects as simply those things with height and heft and rounded or sharp corners. Analyzing imported and domestic material possessions such as porcelain, tea, and textiles, discussions of unbecoming require considering knowledge as an object, embodied in the maps and botanical prints that were exchanged across the Atlantic. These decorative items inhabited both the tangible and intangible worlds and were valued for their physical features as well as for the information they embodied. When placed in circulation within networks of exchange that ascribed worth to this knowledge, these items garnered an extremely high value. As such, they emerged as objectified forms of enlightened knowledge—itself a relatively scarce resource in the early national United States. Ultimately, these objects include information, knowledge, and even what people today would call identity—that can be exchanged and traded on the open market.

68. Joyce Chaplin points out that in early American history, it has been the scholars of the slave experience who have been the most deeply transnational in their focus. For instance, see the groundbreaking work of Ira Berlin and Phil Morgan, including Berlin, "From Creole to African: Atlantic Creoles and the Origins of African-American Society in Mainland North America," *William and Mary Quarterly* 53 (April 1996): 251–288, and Morgan, *Slave Counterpoint: Black Culture in the Eighteenth-century Chesapeake and Lowcountry* (Chapel Hill: University North Carolina Press, 1998). Chaplin, "Expansion and Exceptionalism in Early American History," *Journal of American History* 88, no. 4 (March 2003): 1449–1450.

69. Some scholars have examined the United States taking into account issues of postcoloniality. Most useful is Robert Blair St. George, editor's introduction to *Possible Pasts: Becoming Colonial in Early America* (Ithaca, N.Y.: Cornell University Press, 2000), and Michael Warner, "What's Colonial about Colonial America?" in *Possible Pasts: Becoming Colonial in Early America,* 49–70. See also Amy Kaplan and Donald Pease, eds., *Cultures of United States Imperialism* (Durham, N.C.: Duke University Press, 1993), and especially Amy Kaplan, "'Left Alone with America': The Absence of Empire in the Study of American Culture," in Kaplan and Pease, *Cultures of United States Imperialism,* 3–21; Amritjit Singh and Peter Schmidt, eds., *Postcolonial Theory and the United States: Race, Ethnicity, and Literature* (Jackson: University Press of Mississippi, 2000). See also

Malini Johar Schueller and Edward Watts, eds., *Messy Beginnings: Postcoloniality and Early American Studies* (New Brunswick, N.J.: Rutgers University Press, 2003). For studies that examine literature in the early republic taking postcolonial perspectives and issues into account, see Leonard Tennenhouse, *The Importance of Feeling English: American Literature and the British Diaspora, 1750–1850* (Princeton, N.J.: Princeton University Press, 2007); Edward Watts, *Writing and Post-colonialism in the Early Republic* (Charlottesville: University Press of Virginia, 1998); Lawrence Buell, "Melville and the Question of American Decolonization," *American Literature* 64, no. 2 (June 1992): 215–237; Leonard Tennenhouse, "The Americanization of Clarissa," *Yale Journal of Criticism* 11, no. 1 (1998): 177–196, and Richard Helgerson, "Language Lessons: Linguistic Colonialism, Linguistic Post-colonialism, and the Early Modern English Nation," *Yale Journal of Criticism* 11, no. 1 (1998): 289–300. As a whole, scholarship that has considered the United States from a postcolonial perspective has come out of the fields of literary theory and literature rather than history.

70. Joyce Chaplin makes this point in "Expansion and Exceptionalism in Early American History"; quote from 1454. As Chaplin notes in her review essay, other scholars have expressed skepticism regarding the use of the concept of the "postcolonial" in studying the United States; see, for instance, Peter Hulme, "Including America," *Ariel* 26 (January 1995): 117–123. For another view, see "Roundtable," *William and Mary Quarterly* 64 (2): 235–286, discussing Jack Greene's essay "Colonial History and National History: Reflections on a Continuing Problem," 235–250. Responses include my "Postcolonialism and Material Culture in the Early United States," 263–270, which elaborates on the ideas presented here.

71. Chaplin writes: "I think discussions of colonialism and postcolonialism may offer an important way for early Americans to avoid parochialism and to engage American history in a global debate." Chaplin, "Expansion and Exceptionalism in Early American History," 1454.

72. For historical studies that engage in the importance of empire in the development of the American nation, see Peter Onuf, *Jefferson's Empire: The Language of American Nationhood* (Charlottesville: University Press of Virginia, 2000), and Francis Jennings, *The Creation of America: Through Revolution to Empire* (New York: Cambridge University Press, 2000).

73. Here I am referencing the use of mimicry by V. S. Naipaul, *The Mimic Men* (London: Deutsch, 1967), and Homi Bhabha, "Of Mimicry and Man: The Ambivalence of Colonial Discourse," in Bhabha, ed., *The Location of Culture: Nation and Narration* (London: Routledge, 1990), 85–92.

74. Du Bois described "this sense of always looking at one's self through the eyes of others, of measuring one's soul by the tape of a world that looks on in amused contempt and pity." The quote originally appeared in Du Bois, "Strivings of the Negro People," *Atlantic Monthly,* August 1897, 194, and then in Du Bois, *The Souls of Black Folk* (Chicago: A. C. McClurg, 1903), chap. 1, "Of Our Spiritual Strivings," 3.

75. For a recent study of the movement, see Philip Gura, *American Transcendentalism: A History* (New York: Hill and Wang, 2007).

76. The New England elites who were a part of the movement looked to German Idealism and especially the work of Immanuel Kant for inspiration. By turning to the Continent, they hoped to escape the hold of English philosophers such as Locke. Yet, ironically, they learned about the German thinkers through English writers such as Samuel Taylor Coleridge and Thomas Carlyle.

77. Originally an address to the Phi Beta Kappa Society, August 31, 1837, entitled "An Oration, Delivered before the Phi Beta Kappa Society at Cambridge," this essay was

renamed "The American Scholar" when it was published in an essay collection in 1849. For more on the writer, see Lawrence Buell, *Emerson* (Cambridge, Mass.: Harvard University Press, 2003).

78. Quoted in Robert Weisbuch, "Post-colonial Emerson and the Erasure of Europe," in Joel Porte and Saundra Morris, eds., *The Cambridge Companion to Ralph Waldo Emerson* (Cambridge: Cambridge University Press, 1999), 194.

79. Emerson, *English Traits* (Boston: Phillips, Sampson, 1856), 9–10. The epigraph to this chapter is from this work.

80. Ibid., 274–275.

81. Emerson, *English Traits*, in *Essays and Lectures* (New York: Literary Classics of America, 1983), 916.

82. Ibid.

Index

Made in the USA
Middletown, DE
27 November 2020